Lauds and Vespers

Lauds and Vespers

Reverend Peter Stravinskas
GENERAL EDITOR

SCEPTER PUBLISHERS
PRINCETON, NEW JERSEY

IN COOPERATION WITH
NEWMAN HOUSE PRESS
MT. POCONO, PENNSYLVANIA

Published in 2001 by Scepter Publishers
20 Nassau Street, Princeton, NJ 08542

Textus Liturgiæ Horarum in Lingua Latina: Concordat cum originali. The facing English translation is not approved for liturgical use and is provided only as a guide to understanding the Latin text.

Reverend James P. Moroney
Executive Director
NCCB Secretariat for the Liturgy
3 November 2000

ISBN 1–889334–32–4

Composition by Shoreline Graphics, Rockland, Maine
Text set in Times New Roman

PRINTED IN THE UNITED STATES OF AMERICA

CONTENTS

ACKNOWLEDGMENTS

A project of this kind is a massive endeavor, demanding the involvement and commitment of many, whose assistance should be gratefully noted.

Project directors were Br. Michael Redmann and Br. Joshua Kibler, who spent countless hours ensuring a quality product. Typing of the Latin and English texts was the tedious responsibility of Marjorie Dicton, Suzanne Robbins, Mary Vacola, and Irene Weber, who completed their tasks with precision and good humor.

The English texts for the antiphons, orations, and intercessions were the work of the St. Gregory Foundation for Latin Liturgy. Special assistance for translation aspects was offered by the Reverend Samuel Weber, O.S.B., and Michael LaRue, whose insights were invaluable. The English texts for the hymns came from three sources: the Benedictine Nuns of St. Cecilia's Abbey on the Isle of Wight; the corpus of the Venerable John Henry Newman, graciously provided by the Oratory in Birmingham, England; and the *English Hymnal*.

PREFACE

This prayer book, the first of a series, contains the prayers from the Liturgy of the Hours for Lauds (Morning Prayer) and Vespers (Evening Prayer), for the Sundays and weekdays throughout the Church year (Ordinary Time). Subsequent volumes will contain the prayers used on saints' feast days, solemnities, and special seasons (such as Advent, Christmas, Lent, and Easter).

Complete editions in English of all the Hours, including the Office of Readings, the Middle Hours, and Compline (Night Prayer), can be found in the four-volume set *The Liturgy of the Hours*. The purpose of this present series is to promote use of the Latin prayers of the Liturgy of the Hours.

The two portions of the Liturgy of the Hours contained in this book, Lauds and Vespers, are arranged according to the complete structure of the liturgy; they are neither abridged nor modified. The text is presented both in English and in Latin so as to facilitate understanding of the Latin usage. The Latin texts are from the *Ordinarium Liturgiæ Horarum* and are therefore approved for liturgical use. The English texts are not official liturgical texts; they are from the Revised Standard Version (Catholic Edition) of the Bible and from translations arranged by the editor. These alternate English texts are included in order to help the faithful pray well and develop an appreciation for the magnificent liturgical heritage of the Latin Rite of the Catholic Church.

HOW TO PRAY LAUDS AND VESPERS

THE SECTIONS OF THIS BOOK

There are three sections of this book that contain the prayers for Lauds and Vespers: (I) the *Ordinarium Liturgiæ Horarum*; (II) the *Psalterium per Quattuor Hebdomadas Distributum*; and (III) the *Proprium de Tempore*. During the course of praying Lauds and Vespers, you will use prayers from each of these sections. It is helpful to keep each section marked at the proper page with a ribbon marker or a holy card.

The *Ordinarium* contains the prayers that are always the same and form the basic structure of the Hours. You will probably discover that you will learn some of these prayers by heart and then not need to turn to them to read the text. Other sections of the book make abbreviated references to these prayers to remind you when to say them.

The *Psalterium* contains the arrangement of the psalms and canticles, which are distributed throughout the Hours of the day over a four-week cycle. The cycle is set up so that the First Week *per annum* ("throughout the year," also called Ordinary Time) begins with Week I of the Psalter. Thus, the Fourth Week throughout the year uses Week IV, and then the Fifth Week throughout the year returns to Week I, and so on.

The *Proprium de Tempore* contains the prayers that change with the liturgical days and seasons, such as the prayers for a particular Sunday of the year.

THE STRUCTURE OF LAUDS AND VESPERS

Lauds and Vespers have the same basic structure. The detailed instructions on how to say them (called rubrics, because usually printed in red ink) are in the *Ordinarium*. Here is a simplified, step-by-step guide:

1. Introductory rite: The introductory prayers are always the same. Their full text is in the *Ordinarium*.

2. *Hymnus* (Hymn). A hymn for each Hour is given with each day in the *Psalterium*. It is sung or said after the Introductory Prayers.

3. *Psalmodia* (Psalmody). The psalms and canticles are said next. These are in the *Psalterium*, and will have three sections to be said. Lauds has a psalm, a canticle from the Old Testament, then another psalm; Vespers has two psalms, and then a canticle from the New Testament. Each psalm or canticle has an antiphon with it. You read the antiphon and the psalm, say the complete *Gloria Patri*, repeat the antiphon, and then move on to the next antiphon or section.

4. *Lectio Brevis* (Short Reading). A scriptural text a few verses long is read. It is in the *Psalterium*.

5. *Responsorium Breve* (Short Responsory). This is in the *Psalterium*. It is arranged on the presumption that the Hours are prayed in groups, with a leader reading one phrase of the prayer, and the rest of the congregation responding with another phrase. (When you are praying alone, it is not necessary to repeat phrases, except where the logical meaning of the prayer requires it.)

When the responsories are recited in a group, the structure is as follows (using the *Responsorium Breve* from Lauds of Sunday, Week I, as an example):

Leader: *Christe, Fili Dei vivi, * Miserére nobis.*
People: *Christe, Fili Dei vivi, * Miserére nobis.*

Leader: *Qui sedes ad déxteram Patris.*
People: *Miserére nobis.*
Leader: *Glória Patri, et Fílio, et Spirítui Sancto.*
People: *Christe, Fili Dei vivi, * Miserére nobis.*

N.b. Only the first half of the *Gloria Patri* is said here, and the verse is said in response.

6. *Canticum Evangelicum* (Gospel Canticle). The *Benedictus* (the Canticle of Zechariah) is said at Lauds, and the *Magnificat* (the Canticle of Mary) is said at Vespers. As with praying the psalms, you say the antiphon, read the canticle and the *Gloria Patri*, then repeat the antiphon. The text of each canticle is in the *Ordinarium*, the antiphons for Sundays are in the *Proprium de Tempore*, and the antiphons for weekdays are in the *Psalterium*.

7. *Preces* (Intercessions). Prayers for various intentions are said next. These are in the *Psalterium*.

8. *Pater Noster* (Our Father). The *Pater noster* is said without the final *Amen*, because it proceeds directly into the text of the Oration. The text of the Lord's Prayer is in the *Ordinarium*.

9. *Oratio* (Oration). This prayer provides a summary to the Hour. The *Oratio* for each Sunday throughout the year is in the *Proprium de Tempore*; on weekdays, the *Oratio* given in the *Psalterium* is used.

10. Concluding rite: After the *Oratio*, a priest or a deacon may give a blessing and dismissal similar to those at the end of Mass. These are in the *Ordinarium*. Without a priest or deacon presiding, the other concluding prayer found in the *Ordinarium* is said.

RUBRICS FOR SOLEMN LAUDS AND VESPERS

1. Introductory rite. STAND.
   Make the sign of the cross when the presider begins the prayer: *Deus, in adiutorium meum intende*. Bow while the Persons of the Trinity are mentioned during the *Gloria Patri*.

2. *Hymnus*. STAND.
   Bow during the Trinitarian doxology in the last verse of the hymn.

3. *Psalmodia*. SIT.
   Sit when the first verse of the first psalm begins.

   Bow during the *Gloria Patri* at the end of each psalm.

4. *Lectio Brevis*. SIT.

5. *Responsorium Breve*. SIT.
   Bow during the *Gloria Patri* in the responsory.

6. *Canticum Evangelicum*. STAND.
   All stand before the antiphon for the Gospel canticle.

   Make the sign of the cross when the first verse of the canticle begins. During solemn celebration, the altar is incensed; then the presiding priest or deacon and the people are incensed. Bow during the *Gloria Patri* at the end of the canticle.

7. *Preces*. STAND.
   The presiding priest or deacon introduces the petitions, then another minister may present the petitions.

8. *Pater Noster*. STAND.
   The presiding priest or deacon may give an invitation to prayer, or may start directly with the Lord's Prayer.

There is no *Amen* at the end, because the presider continues on to the Oration.

9. *Oratio*. STAND.
The presider says this prayer alone.

10. Concluding rite. STAND.
A presiding priest or deacon may give the blessing and dismissal similar to those at the end of Mass. Otherwise, the alternate concluding prayer is said.

I

Ordinarium / Ordinary

ORDINARIUM

AD LAUDES MATUTINAS

℣. Deus in adiutórium meum inténde.
℟. Dómine, ad adiuvándum me festína.

Glória Patri, et Fílio, *
  et Spirítui Sancto.
Sicut erat in princípio, et nunc et semper, *
  et in sǽcula sæculórum. Amen.

HYMNUS

PSALMODIA

LECTIO

RESPONSORIUM AD VERBUM DEI

ORDINARY OF LAUDS AND VESPERS

LAUDS

℣. O God, come to my assistance.
℟. O Lord, make haste to help me.

Glory be to the Father, and to the Son,
and to the Holy Spirit:
as it was in the beginning, is now, and ever shall be,
world without end. Amen.

Hymn

Then the appropriate hymn is said. For the Sunday and weekday offices, the hymn is given in the Psalter.

Psalmody

The psalmody follows the hymn and consists of one morning psalm, an Old Testament canticle, and another psalm of praise, together with the appropriate antiphons.

For the Sunday and weekday offices, the psalms, canticle, and antiphons are taken from the current week of the Psalter.

After the psalmody the reading follows.

Reading

For the Sunday and weekday offices, the reading is given in the Psalter.

A longer reading may be selected, especially in celebrations with the people, in accord with number 46 of the General Instruction; a short homily on the reading may also be added.

Response to the Word of God

A period of silence may be observed after the reading or homily.

Next a responsorial song or the responsory given after the reading follows.

Canticum Evangelicum

Lc 1:68–79

68 Benedíctus Dóminus Deus Ísrael, *
quia visitávit et fecit redemptiónem plebi suæ
69 et eréxit cornu salútis nobis *
in domo David púeri sui,
70 sicut locútus est per os sanctórum, *
qui a sǽculo sunt, prophetárum eius,
71 salútem ex inimícis nostris *
et de manu ómnium, qui odérunt nos;
72 ad faciéndam misericórdiam cum pátribus nostris *
et memorári testaménti sui sancti,
73 iusiurándum, quod iurávit ad Ábraham patrem nostrum, *
datúrum se nobis,
74 ut sine timóre, de manu inimicórum liberáti, *
serviámus illi
75 in sanctitáte et iustítia coram ipso *
ómnibus diébus nostris.
76 Et tu, puer, prophéta Altíssimi vocáberis: *
præíbis enim ante fáciem Dómini paráre vias eius,
77 ad dandam sciéntiam salútis plebi eius *
in remissiónem peccatórum eorum,
78 per víscera misericórdiæ Dei nostri, *
in quibus visitábit nos óriens ex alto,
79 illumináre his, qui in ténebris et in umbra mortis sedent *
ad dirigéndos pedes nostros in viam pacis.

Gospel Canticle

Luke 1:68–79

The following Gospel canticle with the appropriate antiphon is then said.

For the Sunday office, the antiphon is taken from the Proper of the Time; for the weekday office, from the Psalter.

68 Blessed be the Lord God of Israel,
for He has visited and redeemed His people,
69 and has raised up a horn of salvation for us
in the house of His servant David,
70 as He spoke by the mouth of His holy prophets
from of old,
71 that we should be saved from our enemies,
and from the hand of all who hate us;
72 to perform the mercy promised to our fathers,
and to remember His holy covenant,
73 the oath which He swore to our father Abraham,
74 to grant us that we, being delivered from the hand
of our enemies,
might serve Him without fear,
75 in holiness and righteousness before Him
all the days of our life.
76 And you, child, will be called the prophet of the
Most High;
for you will go before the Lord to prepare His
ways,
77 to give knowledge of salvation to His people
in the forgiveness of their sins,
78 through the tender mercy of our God,
when the day shall dawn upon us from on high
79 to give light to those who sit in darkness and in
the shadow of death,
to guide our feet into the way of peace.

Glória Patri, et Fílio, *
  et Spirítui Sancto.
Sicut erat in princípio, et nunc et semper, *
  et in sǽcula sæculórum. Amen.

PRECES

Præcéptis salutáribus móniti, et divína institutióne formáti, audémus dícere:

Pater noster, qui es in cælis:
sanctificétur nomen tuum;
advéniat regnum tuum;
fiat volúntas tua, sicut in cælo et in terra.
Panem nostrum cotidiánum da nobis hódie;
et dimítte nobis débita nostra
sicut et nos dimíttimus debitóribus nostris;
et ne nos indúcas in tentatiónem;
sed líbera nos a malo.

Per Dóminum nostrum Iesum Christum, Fílium tuum, qui tecum vivit et regnat in unitáte Spíritus Sancti, Deus, per ómnia sǽcula sæculórum.

Glory be to the Father, and to the Son,
and to the Holy Spirit:
as it was in the beginning, is now, and ever shall be,
world without end. Amen.

The antiphon is repeated as usual.

INTERCESSIONS

The intercessions follow the canticle.

For the Sunday and weekday offices, the intercessions are found in the Psalter.

All then say the Lord's Prayer. It may be preceded by a brief invitation, such as:

Taught by our Savior's command and formed by the word of God, we dare to say:

Our Father, Who art in heaven,
hallowed by Thy name;
Thy kingdom come;
Thy will be done, on earth as it is in heaven.
Give us this day our daily bread;
and forgive us our trespasses
as we forgive those who trespass against us;
and lead us not into temptation,
but deliver us from evil.

The concluding prayer, without the invitation **Let us pray**, is added immediately after the Lord's Prayer.

For the weekday offices, the concluding prayer is taken from the current week of the Psalter; in all other offices it is taken from the proper. The prayer is concluded as follows:

If the prayer is directed to the Father:

Through our Lord Jesus Christ, Your Son, Who lives and reigns with You in the unity of the Holy Spirit, God, for ever and ever.

Qui tecum vivit et regnat in unitáte Spíritus Sancti, Deus, per ómnia sǽcula sæculórum.

Qui vivis et regnas cum Deo Patre in unitáte Spíritus Sancti, Deus, per ómnia sǽcula sæculórum.

Dismissum

Dóminus vobíscum.
℟. Et cum spíritu tuo.

Benedícat vos omnípotens Deus, Pater, et Fílius, et Spíritus Sanctus.
℟. Amen.

Ite in pace.
℟. Deo grátias.

Dóminus nos benedícat, et ab omni malo deféndat, et ad vitam perdúcat ætérnam.
℟. Amen.

If it is directed to the Father after which a mention of the Son is made:

Who lives and reigns with You in the unity of the Holy Spirit, God, for ever and ever.

If it is directed to the Son:

Who live and reign with God the Father in the unity of the Holy Spirit, God, for ever and ever.

Response at the conclusion of the prayer:

Amen.

Dismissal

If a priest or deacon presides, he dismisses the people:

The Lord be with you.
℟. And with your spirit.

May almighty God, Father, Son, and Holy Spirit, bless you.
℟. Amen.

Another form of the blessing may be used, as at Mass.

Then he adds:

Go in peace.
℟. Thanks be to God.

In the absence of a priest or deacon and in individual recitation, Lauds concludes:

May the Lord bless us, defend us from all evil, and lead us to everlasting life.
℟. Amen.

AD VESPERAS

℟. Deus in adiutórium meum inténde.
℣. Dómine, ad adiuvándum me festína.

Glória Patri, et Fílio, *
et Spirítui Sancto.
Sicut erat in princípio, et nunc et semper, *
et in sǽcula sæculórum. Amen.

Hymnus

Psalmodia

Lectio

Responsorium ad Verbum Dei

VESPERS

℟. O God, come to my assistance.
℣. O Lord, make haste to help me.

Glory be to the Father, and to the Son,
and to the Holy Spirit:
as it was in the beginning, is now, and ever shall be,
world without end. Amen.

Hymn

Then the appropriate hymn is said.

For the Sunday and weekday offices, the hymn is given in the Psalter.

Psalmody

The psalmody follows the hymn and consists of two psalms or parts of psalms, and a New Testament canticle, together with the appropriate antiphons.

For the Sunday and weekday offices, the psalms, canticle, and antiphons are taken from the current week of the Psalter.

After the psalmody the reading follows.

Reading

For the Sunday and weekday offices, the reading is given in the Psalter.

A longer reading may be selected, especially in celebrations with the people, in accord with number 46 of the General Instruction; a short homily on the reading may also be added.

Response to the Word of God

A period of silence may be observed after the reading or homily.

Next a responsorial song or the responsory given after the reading follows.

CANTICUM EVANGELICUM

Lc 1:46–55

46 Magníficat *
ánima mea Dóminum,
47 et exsultávit spíritus meus *
in Deo salvatóre meo,
48 quia respéxit humilitátem ancíllæ suæ. *
Ecce enim ex hoc beátam me dicent omnes generatiónes,
49 quia fecit mihi magna, qui potens est, *
et sanctum nomen eius,
50 et misericórdia eius in progénies et progénies *
timéntibus eum.
51 Fecit poténtiam in bráchio suo, *
dispérsit supérbos mente cordis sui;
52 depósuit poténtes de sede *
et exaltávit húmiles;
53 esuriéntes implévit bonis *
et dívites dimísit inánes.
54 Suscépit Ísrael púerum suum, *
recordátus misericórdiæ,
55 sicut locútus est ad patres nostros, *
Ábraham et sémini eius in sæcula.

Glória Patri, et Fílio, *
et Spirítui Sancto.
Sicut erat in princípio, et nunc et semper, *
et in sæcula sæculórum. Amen.

Gospel Canticle

Luke 1:46–55

The following gospel canticle with the appropriate antiphon is then said.

For the Sunday office, the antiphon is taken from the Proper of the Time; for the weekday office, from the Psalter.

46 My soul magnifies the Lord,
47 and my spirit rejoices in God my Savior,
48 for He has regarded the low estate of His handmaiden.
For behold, henceforth all generations will call me blessed;
49 for He Who is mighty has done great things for me,
and holy is His name.
50 And His mercy is on those who fear Him
from generation to generation.
51 He has shown strength with His arm,
He has scattered the proud in the imagination of their hearts,
52 He has put down the mighty from their thrones,
and exalted those of low degree;
53 He has filled the hungry with good things,
and the rich He has sent empty away.
54 He has helped His servant Israel,
in remembrance of His mercy,
55 as He spoke to our fathers,
to Abraham and to his posterity for ever.

Glory be to the Father, and to the Son,
and to the Holy Spirit:
as it was in the beginning, is now, and ever shall be,
world without end. Amen.

Preces

Præcéptis salutáribus móniti, et divína institutióne formáti, audémus dícere:

Pater noster, qui es in cælis:
sanctificétur nomen tuum;
advéniat regnum tuum;
fiat volúntas tua, sicut in cælo et in terra.
Panem nostrum cotidiánum da nobis hódie;
et dimítte nobis débita nostra,
sicut et nos dimíttimus debitóribus nostris;
et ne nos indúcas in tentatiónem;
sed líbera nos a malo.

Per Dóminum nostrum Iesum Christum, Fílium tuum, qui tecum vivit et regnat in unitáte Spíritus Sancti, Deus, per ómnia sǽcula sæculórum.

Qui tecum vivit et regnat in unitáte Spíritus Sancti, Deus, per ómnia sǽcula sæculórum.

The antiphon is repeated as usual.

INTERCESSIONS

The intercessions follow the canticle.

For the Sunday and weekday offices, the intercessions are found in the Psalter.

All then say the Lord's Prayer. It may be preceded by a brief invitation, such as:

Taught by our Savior's command and formed by the word of God, we dare to say:

Our Father, Who art in heaven,
hallowed by Thy name;
Thy kingdom come;
Thy will be done, on earth as it is in heaven.
Give us this day our daily bread;
and forgive us our trespasses
as we forgive those who trespass against us;
and lead us not into temptation,
but deliver us from evil.

The concluding prayer, without the invitation Let us pray, is added immediately after the Lord's Prayer.

For the weekday offices, the concluding prayer is taken from the current week of the Psalter; in all other offices it is taken from the proper. The prayer is concluded as follows:

If the prayer is directed to the Father:
Through our Lord Jesus Christ, Your Son, Who lives and reigns with You in the unity of the Holy Spirit, God, for ever and ever.

If it is directed to the Father after which a mention of the Son is made:
Who lives and reigns with You in the unity of the Holy Spirit, God, for ever and ever.

Qui vivis et regnas cum Deo Patre in unitáte Spíritus Sancti, Deus, per ómnia sǽcula sæculórum.

Dismissum

Dóminus vobíscum.
℟. Et cum spíritu tuo.

Benedícat vos omnípotens Deus, Pater, et Fílius, et Spíritus Sanctus.
℟. Amen.

Ite in pace.
℟. Deo grátias.

Dóminus nos benedícat, et ab omni malo deféndat, et ad vitam perdúcat ætérnam.
℟. Amen.

If it is directed to the Son:

Who live and reign with God the Father in the unity of the Holy Spirit, God, for ever and ever.

Response at the conclusion of the prayer:

Amen.

Dismissal

If a priest or deacon presides, he dismisses the people:

The Lord be with you.
℟. And with your spirit.

May almighty God, Father, Son, and Holy Spirit, bless you.
℟. Amen.

Another form of the blessing may be used, as at Mass.

Then he adds:

Go in peace.
℟. Thanks be to God.

In the absence of a priest or deacon and in individual recitation, Vespers concludes:

May the Lord bless us, defend us from all evil, and lead us to everlasting life.
℟. Amen.

II

Psalterium / Psalter

Hebdomada I

Dominica, ad I Vesperas

Hymnus

Deus, Creátor ómnium
polìque rector, vestiéns
diem decóro, lúmine,
noctem sopóris grátia,

Artus solútos ut quies
reddat labóris úsui
mentésque fessas állevet
luctúsque solvat ánxios,

Grates perácto iam die
et noctis exórtu preces,
voti reos ut ádiuves,
hymnum canéntes sólvimus.

Te cordis ima cóncinant,
te vox canóra cóncrepet,
te díligat castus amor,
te mens adóret sóbria,

Ut cum profúnda cláuserit
diem calígo nóctium,
fides tenébras nésciat
et nox fide relúceat.

Christum rogámus et Patrem,
Christi Patrísque Spíritum;
unum potens per ómnia,
fove precántes, Trínitas. Amen.

Week I

Sunday, Vespers I

HYMN

Trans. *The English Hymnal*, 1933

Creator of the earth and sky,
Ruling the firmament on high,
Clothing the day with robes of light,
Blessing with gracious sleep the night,

That rest may comfort weary men,
And brace to useful toil again,
And soothe awhile the harassed mind,
And sorrow's heavy load unbind:

Day sinks; we thank Thee for Thy gift;
Night comes; and once again we lift
Our prayer and vows and hymns that we
Against all ills may shielded be,

Thee let the secret heart acclaim,
Thee let our tuneful voices name,
Round Thee our chaste affections cling,
Thee sober reason own as King.

That when black darkness closes day,
And shadows thicken round our way,
Faith may no darkness know, and night
From faith's clear beam may borrow light.

Pray we the Father and the Son,
And Holy Ghost: O Three in One,
Blest Trinity, whom all obey,
Guard Thou Thy sheep by night and day. Amen.

PSALMODIA

Ant. 1 Dirigátur, Dómine, orátio mea sicut incénsum in conspéctu tuo.

Psalmus 140 (141), 1–9

1 Dómine, clamávi ad te, ad me festína; *
intende voci meæ, cum clamo ad te.
2 Dirigátur orátio mea sicut incénsum in conspéctu tuo, *
elevátio mánuum meárum ut sacrifícium vespertínum.

3 Pone, Dómine, custódiam ori meo *
et vigíliam ad óstium labiórum meórum.
4 Non declínes cor meum in verbum malítiæ *
ad machinándas machinatiónes in impietáte
cum homínibus operántibus iniquitátem; *
et non cómedam ex delíciis eórum.
5 Percútiat me iustus in misericórdia et íncrepet me; †
óleum autem peccatóris non impínguet caput meum, *
quóniam adhuc et orátio mea in malítiis eórum

6 Deiécti in manus duras iúdicum eórum, *
áudient verba mea, quóniam suávia erant.
7 Sicut frusta dolántis et dirumpéntis in terra, *
dissipáta sunt ossa eórum ad fauces inférni.

PSALMODY

Ant. 1 Let my prayer be counted as incense before Thee, and the lifting up of my hands as an evening sacrifice!

Psalm 141:1–9

1 I call upon thee, O LORD; make haste to me!
Give ear to my voice, when I call to thee!
2 Let my prayer be counted as incense before thee,
and the lifting up of my hands as an evening sacrifice!

3 Set a guard over my mouth, O LORD,
keep watch over the door of my lips!
4 Incline not my heart to any evil,
to busy myself with wicked deeds
in company with men who work iniquity;
and let me not eat of their dainties!

5 Let a good man strike or rebuke me in kindness,
but let the oil of the wicked never anoint my head;
for my prayer is continually against their wicked deeds.
6 When they are given over to those who shall condemn them,
then they shall learn that the word of the LORD is true.
7 As a rock which one cleaves and shatters on the land,
so shall their bones be strewn at the mouth of Sheol.

8 Quia ad te, Dómine, Dómine, óculi mei; *
ad te confúgi, non effúndas ánimam meam.
9 Custódi me a láqueo, quem statuérunt mihi, *
et a scándalis operántium iniquitátem.

Glória Patri, et Fílio, *
et Spirítui Sancto.
Sicut erat in princípio, et nunc et semper, *
et in sǽcula sæculórum. Amen.

Ant. Dirigátur, Dómine, orátio mea sicut incénsum in conspéctu tuo.
Ant. 2 Tu es refúgium meum, Dómine, pórtio mea in terra vivéntium.

Psalmus 141 (142)

2 Voce mea ad Dóminum clamo, *
voce mea ad Dóminum déprecor;
3 effúndo in conspéctu eius lamentatiónem meam, *
et tribulatiónem meam ante ipsum pronúntio.

4 Cum déficit in me spíritus meus, *
tu nosti sémitas meas.
In via, qua ambulábam, *
abscondérunt láqueum mihi.
5 Considerábam ad déxteram et vidébam, *
et non erat qui cognósceret me.
Périit fuga a me, *
et non est qui requírat ánimam meam.

8 But my eyes are toward thee, O LORD God;
in thee I seek refuge; leave me not defenseless!
9 Keep me from the trap which they have laid for me,
and from the snares of evildoers!

Glory be to the Father, and to the Son,
and to the Holy Spirit.
As it was in the beginning, is now,
and ever shall be. Amen.

Ant. 1 Let my prayer be counted as incense before Thee, and the lifting up of my hands as an evening sacrifice!

Ant. 2 I cry to Thee, O Lord; I say, Thou art my refuge, my portion in the land of the living.

Psalm 142

1 I cry with my voice to the LORD,
with my voice I make supplication to the LORD.
2 I pour out my complaint before him,
I tell my trouble before him.
3 When my spirit is faint,
thou knowest my way!

In the path where I walk
they have hidden a trap for me.
4 I look to the right and watch,
but there is none who takes notice of me;
no refuge remains to me,
no man cares for me.

6 Clamávi ad te, Dómine; †
dixi: « Tu es refúgium meum *
pórtio mea in terra vivéntium.
7 Inténde ad deprecatiónem meam, *
quia humiliátus sum nimis.
Líbera me a persequéntibus me, *
quia confortáti sunt super me.
8 Educ de custódia ánimam meam *
ad confiténdum nómini tuo;
me circúmdabunt iusti, *
cum retribúeris mihi ».

Ant. Tu es refúgium meum, Dómine, pórtio mea in terra vivéntium.
Ant. 3 Humiliávit semetípsum Dóminus Iesus, propter quod et Deus exaltávit illum in sǽcula.

Canticum PHIL 2, 6–11

6 Christus Iesus, cum in forma Dei esset, *
non rapínam arbitrátus est esse se æquálem Deo,
7 sed semetípsum exinanívit formam servi accípiens, †
in similitúdinem hóminum factus; *
et hábitu invéntus ut homo,
8 humiliávit semetípsum †
factus obœ́diens usque ad mortem, *
mortem autem crucis.

9 Propter quod et Deus illum exaltávit †
et donávit illi nomen, *
quod est super omne nomen,
10 ut in nómine Iesu omne genu flectátur *
cæléstium et terréstrium et infernórum

5 I cry to thee, O Lord;
I say, Thou art my refuge,
my portion in the land of the living.
6 Give heed to my cry;
for I am brought very low!

Deliver me from my persecutors;
for they are too strong for me!
7 Bring me out of prison,
that I may give thanks to thy name!
The righteous will surround me;
for thou wilt deal bountifully with me.

Ant. 2 I cry to Thee, O Lord; I say, Thou art my refuge, my portion in the land of the living.
Ant. 3 The Lord Jesus humbled Himself, and so God exalted Him forever.

Canticle Philippians 2:6–11

6 Though he was in the form of God,
Jesus did not count equality with God a thing to be grasped,
7 but emptied himself, taking the form of a servant,
being born in the likeness of men.
8 And being found in human form
he humbled himself
and became obedient unto death,
even death on a cross.
9 Therefore God has highly exalted him
and bestowed on him the name
which is above every name,
10 that at the name of Jesus every knee should bow,
in heaven and on earth and under the earth,

11 et omnis lingua confiteátur: *
« Dóminus Iesus Christus! », in glóriam Dei Patris.

Ant. Humiliávit semetípsum Dóminus Iesus, propter quod et Deus exaltávit illum in sǽcula.

LECTIO BREVIS — ROM 11, 33-36

O altitúdo divitiárum et sapiéntiæ et sciéntiæ Dei! Quam incomprehensibília sunt iudícia eius et investigábiles viæ eius! Quis enim cognóvit sensum Dómini? Aut quis consiliárius eius fuit? Aut quis prior dedit illi, et retribuétur ei? Quóniam ex ipso et per ipsum et in ipsum ómnia. Ipsi glória in sǽcula. Amen.

RESPONSORIUM BREVE

℟. Quam magnificáta sunt * Opera tua, Dómine. Quam.
℣. Omnia in sapiéntia fecísti. * Opera tua, Dómine. Glória Patri. Quam.

PRECES

Uni Deo, Patri et Fílio et Spirítui Sancto, glóriam dicéntes, humíliter deprecémur: *Adésto pópulo tuo, Dómine.*

Dómine sancte, Pater omnípotens, fac ut in terra nostra oriátur iustítia,
—et sedébit pópulus tuus in pulchritúdine pacis.

Da plenitúdinem géntium in regnum tuum intráre,
—et sic omnes pópuli salvi fient.

11 and every tongue confess
that Jesus Christ is Lord,
in the glory of God the Father.

Ant. 3 The Lord Jesus humbled Himself, and God so exalted Him forever.

SHORT READING — Romans 11:25, 30–36

O the depth of the riches and wisdom and knowledge of God! How unsearchable are his judgments and how inscrutable his ways!

"For who has known the mind of the Lord,
or who has been his counselor?"
"Or who has given a gift to him
that he might be repaid?"

For from him and through him and to him are all things. To him be glory for ever. Amen.

SHORT RESPONSORY

℟. How wondrous are Your works, O Lord;
℣. in wisdom You have wrought them all.

Magnificat ant. as in Proper of the Time.

INTERCESSIONS

Giving glory to the one God, Father, Son, and Holy Spirit, let us humbly beg: *Be present to Your people, Lord.*

O Holy Lord, all-powerful Father, make justice arise in our land,
—and Your people will dwell in the beauty of peace.

Grant that the fulness of the nations enter into Your kingdom,
—so that all peoples may be saved.

Præsta ut in tua pace cóniuges máneant et voluntáte,
—atque in mútua semper caritáte vivant.
Remunerári dignáre, Dómine, omnes nobis bona faciéntes,
—et vitam ætérnam da eis.
Odio et bellis perémptos réspice miserátus,
—eos in cæléstem réquiem dignáre suscípere.

Pater noster.

ORATIO

Grant that spouses abide in Your peace and goodwill,
—and live always in mutual love.
Deign to reward, O Lord, all our benefactors,
—and grant them eternal life.
Look with mercy upon the victims of hatred and war,
—deign to receive them into heavenly rest.

Our Father.

Oration

As in Proper of the Time.

Hebdomada I

Dominica, ad Laudes matutinas

Hymnus

Ætérne rerum cónditor,
noctem diémque qui regis,
et témporum das témpora
ut álleves fastídium,

Præco diéi iam sonat,
noctis profúndæ pérvigil,
noctúrna lux viántibus
a nocte noctem ségregans.

Hoc excitátus lúcifer
solvit polum calígine;
hoc omnis errónum chorus
vias nocéndi déserit.

Hoc nauta vires cólligit
pontíque mitéscunt freta;
hoc, ipse Petr*a* Ecclésiæ,
canénte, culpam díluit.

Iesu, labántes réspice
et nos vidéndo córrige;
si réspicis, lapsus cadunt
fletúque culpa sólvitur.

Tu, lux, refúlge sénsibus
mentísque somnum díscute;
te nostra vox primum sonet
et vota solvámus tibi.

Week I

Sunday, Lauds

Hymn

Trans. J. H. Newman

Framer of the earth and sky,
  Ruler of the day and night,
With a glad variety,
  Tempering all and making light;

Gleams upon our dark path flinging,
  Cutting short each night begun,
Hark! for chanticleer is singing,
  Hark! he chides the lingering sun.

And the morning star replies,
  And lets loose the imprison'd day;
And the godless bandit flies
  From his haunt and from his prey.

Shrill it sounds, the storm relenting
  Soothes the weary seaman's ears;
Once it wrought a great repenting,
  In that flood of Peter's tears.

Rouse we; let the blithesome cry
  Of that bird our hearts awaken;
Chide the slumberers as they lie,
  And arrest the sin-o'ertaken.

Hope and health are in his strain,
  To the fearful and the ailing;
Murder sheathes his blade profane,
  Faith revives when faith was failing.

Sit, Christe, rex piíssime,
tibi Patríque glória
cum Spíritu Paráclito,
in sempitérna sǽcula. Amen.

PSALMODIA

Ant. 1 Ad te de luce, vígilo, Deus, ut vídeam virtútem tuam, allelúia.

Psalmus 62 (63), 2–9

2 Deus, Deus meus, es tu, *
ad te de luce vígilo.
Sitívit in te ánima mea, *
te desiderávit caro mea.
In terra desérta et árida et inaquósa, †
3 sic in sancto appárui tibi, *
ut vidérem virtútem tuam et glóriam tuam.
4 Quóniam melior est misericórdia tua super vitas, *
lábia mea laudábunt te.

5 Sic benedícam te in vita mea *
et in nómine tuo levábo manus meas.
6 Sicut ádipe et pinguédine repleátur ánima mea, *
et lábiis exsultatiónis laudábit os meum.

Jesu, Master! when we sin,
Turn on us Thy healing face;
It will melt the offence within
Into penitential grace:

Beam on our bewilder'd mind,
Till its dreamy shadows flee;
Stones cry out where Thou hast shined,
Jesu! musical with Thee.

To the Father and the Son,
And the Spirit, who in heaven
Ever witness, Three and One,
Praise on earth be ever given.

PSALMODY

Ant. 1 As morning breaks I look to Thee, O God, to be my strength this day, alleluia.

Psalm 63:1–8

1 O God, thou art my God, I seek thee,
my soul thirsts for thee;
my flesh faints for thee,
as in a dry and weary land where no water is.
2 So I have looked upon thee in the sanctuary,
beholding thy power and glory.
3 Because thy steadfast love is better than life,
my lips will praise thee.
4 So I will bless thee as long as I live;
I will lift up my hands and call on thy name.

5 My soul is feasted as with marrow and fat,
and my mouth praises thee with joyful lips,
6 when I think of thee upon my bed,
and meditate on thee in the watches of the night;

7 Cum memor ero tui super stratum meum, *
in matutínis meditábor de te,
8 quia fuísti adiútor meus, *
et in velaménto alárum tuárum exsultábo.

9 Adhǽsit ánima mea post te, *
me suscépit déxtera tua.

Ant. Ad te de luce vígilo, Deus, ut vídeam virtútem tuam, allelúia.

Ant. 2 Tres ex uno ore clamábant in camíno ignis et psallébant: Benedíctus Deus, allelúia.

Canticum DAN 3, 57–88, 56

57 Benedícite, ómnia ópera Dómini, Dómino, *
laudáte et superexaltáte eum in sǽcula.
58 Benedícite, cæli, Dómino, *
59 benedícite, ángeli Dómini, Dómino.

60 Benedícite, aquæ omnes, quæ super cælos sunt, Dómino, *
61 benedícat omnis virtus Dómino.
62 Benedícite, sol et luna, Dómino, *
63 benedícite, stellæ cæli, Dómino.

64 Benedícite, omnis imber et ros, Dómino, *
65 benedícite, omnes venti, Dómino.
66 Benedícite, ignis et æstus, Dómino, *
67 benedícite, frigus et æstus, Dómino.

68 Benedícite, rores et pruína, Dómino, *
69 benedícite, gelu et frigus, Dómino.
70 Benédicite, glácies et nives, Dómino, *
71 benedícite, noctes et dies, Dómino.

7 for thou hast been my help,
and in the shadow of thy wings I sing for joy.
8 My soul clings to thee;
thy right hand upholds me.

Ant. 1 As morning breaks I look to You, O God, to be my strength this day, alleluia.
Ant. 2 From the midst of the flames the three cried out with one voice and song: Blessed be God, alleluia.

Canticle Daniel 3:35–66a, 34

35 "Bless the Lord, all works of the Lord,
sing praise to him and highly exalt him for ever.
36 Bless the Lord, you heavens,
37 Bless the Lord, you angels of the Lord,
38 Bless the Lord, all waters above the heaven,
39 Bless the Lord, all powers,
40 Bless the Lord, sun and moon,
41 Bless the Lord, stars of heaven,
42 Bless the Lord, all rain and dew,
43 Bless the Lord, all winds,
44 Bless the Lord, fire and heat,
45 Bless the Lord, winter cold and summer heat,
46 Bless the Lord, dews and snows,
47 Bless the Lord, nights and days,
48 Bless the Lord, light and darkness,
49 Bless the Lord, ice and cold,
50 Bless the Lord, frosts and snows,
51 Bless the Lord, lightnings and clouds,

72 Benedícite, lux et ténebræ, Dómino, *
73 benedícite, fúlgura et nubes, Dómino.
74 Benedícat terra Dóminum, *
laudet et superexáltet eum in sǽcula.

75 Benedícite, montes et colles, Dómino, *
76 benedícite, univérsa germinántia in terra,
Dómino.
77 Benedícite, mária et flúmina, Dómino, *
78 benedícite, fontes, Dómino.

79 Benedícite, cete et ómnia quæ movéntur in aquis,
Dómino, *
80 benedícite, omnes vólucres cæli, Dómino.
81 Benedícite, omnes béstiæ et pécora, Dómino, *
82 benedícite, fílii hóminum, Dómino.

83 Bénedic, Israel, Dómino, *
laudáte et superexaltáte eum in sǽcula.
84 Benedícite, sacerdótes Dómini, Dómino, *
85 benedícite, servi Dómini, Dómino.

86 Benedícite, spíritus et ánimæ iustórum,
Dómino, *
87 benedícite, sancti et húmiles corde, Dómino.
88 Benedícite, Ananía, Azaría, Mísael, Dómino, *
laudáte et superexaltáte eum in sǽcula.

Benedicámus Patrem et Fílium cum Sancto
Spíritu; *
laudémus et superexaltémus eum in sǽcula.
56 Benedíctus es in firmaménto cæli *
et laudábilis et gloriósus in sǽcula.

Ant. Tres ex uno ore clamábant in camíno ignis et psallébant: Benedíctus Deus, allelúia.

52 Let the earth bless the Lord;
let it sing praise to him and highly exalt him for ever.
53 Bless the Lord, mountains and hills,
54 Bless the Lord, all things that grow on the earth,
55 Bless the Lord, you springs,
56 Bless the Lord, seas and rivers,
57 Bless the Lord, you whales and all creatures that move in the waters,
58 Bless the Lord, all birds of the air,
59 Bless the Lord, all beasts and cattle,
60 Bless the Lord, you sons of men,
61 Bless the Lord, O Israel,
62 Bless the Lord, you priests of the Lord,
63 Bless the Lord, you servants of the Lord,
64 Bless the Lord, spirits and souls of the righteous,
65 Bless the Lord, you who are holy and humble in heart,
66 Bless the Lord, Hananiah, Azariah, and Mishael,
sing praise to him and highly exalt him for ever.
Let us bless the Father and the Son with the Holy Spirit,
let us sing praise and highly exalt him for ever.
34 Blessed art thou in the firmament of heaven
and to be sung and glorified for ever.

After this canticle, the *Gloria Patri* is not said.

Ant. 2 From the midst of the flames the three cried out with one voice and song: Blessed be God, alleluia.

Ant 3. Fílii Sion exsúltent in rege suo, allelúia.

Psalmus 149

1 Cantáte Dómino cánticum novum; *
laus eius in ecclésia sanctórum.
2 Lætétur Israel in eo, qui fecit eum, *
et fílii Sion exsúltent in rege suo.
3 Laudent nomen eius in choro, *
in týmpano et cíthara psallant ei,
4 quia beneplácitum est Dómino in pópulo suo, *
et honorábit mansuétos in salúte.
5 Iúbilent sancti in glória, *
læténtur in cubílibus suis.
6 Exaltatiónes Dei in gútture eórum *
et gládii ancípites in mánibus eórum,
7 ad faciéndam vindíctam in natiónibus, *
castigatiónes in pópulis,
8 ad alligándos reges eórum in compédibus *
et nóbiles eórum in mánicis férreis,
9 ad faciéndum in eis iudícium conscríptum: *
glória hæc est ómnibus sanctis eius.

Ant. Fílii Sion exsúltent in rege suo, allelúia.

LECTIO BREVIS — AP 7, 10B. 12

Salus Deo nostro, qui sedet super thronum, et Agno. Benedíctio et glória et sapiéntia et gratiárum áctio et honor et virtus et fortitúdo Deo nostro in sǽcula sæculórum. Amen.

Ant. 3 Let the sons of Zion rejoice in their King, alleluia.

Psalm 149

1 Praise the LORD!
Sing to the LORD a new song,
His praise in the assembly of the faithful!
2 Let Israel be glad in his maker,
let the sons of Zion rejoice in their King!
3 Let them praise his name with dancing,
making melody to him with timbrel and lyre!
4 For the LORD takes pleasure in his people;
he adorns the humble with victory.
5 Let the faithful exult in glory;
let them sing for joy on their couches.
6 Let the high praises of God be in their throats
and two-edged swords in their hands,
7 to wreak vengeance on the nations
and chastisement on the peoples,
8 to bind their kings with chains
and their nobles with fetters of iron,
9 to execute on them the judgment written!
This is glory for all his faithful ones.
Praise the LORD!

Ant. 3 Let the sons of Zion rejoice in their King, alleluia.

SHORT READING Revelation 7:10b, 12

"Salvation belongs to our God who sits upon the throne, and to the Lamb!" "Amen! Blessing and glory and wisdom and thanksgiving and honor and power and might be to our God for ever and ever! Amen."

RESPONSORIUM BREVE

℟. Christe, Fili Dei vivi, * Miserére nobis. Christe.
℣. Qui sedes ad déxteram Patris. * Miserére nobis.
Glória Patri. Christe.

PRECES

Christum Dóminum, diem et solem nostrum, qui illúminat omnem hóminem, et qui nescit occásum, laudémus clamántes: *O Dómine, vita et salus nostra!*

Primítias huius diéi, síderum Creátor, a tua pietáte gratánter suscípimus.
—Resurrectiónem tuam commemorámus.

Spíritus tuus bonus hódie nos tuum fácere dóceat beneplácitum,
—et tua Sapiéntia dedúcat nos semper.

Magno cum gáudio cœ́tui dominicáli da nobis interésse,
—in circúitu mensæ verbi et córporis tui.

Grátias agunt tibi ánimæ nostræ,
—pro innúmeris benefíciis tuis.

Pater noster.

ORATIO

Short Responsory

℟. Christ, Son of the living God, have mercy on us.
℣. You that are seated at the right hand of the Father.

Benedictus ant. as in Proper of the Time.

Intercessions

Christ the Lord—our day and our sun, Who enlightens every man and knows no setting, let us praise Him, crying out: *O Lord, our life and salvation!*

Creator of the stars, by Your graciousness we gratefully offer the first-fruits of this day:
—as we commemorate Your Resurrection.

May Your good spirit teach us this day to do what is well-pleasing to You,
—and may Your Wisdom guide us always.

Grant that we, with great joy, may be among the company of the Lord,
—around the table of Your Word and Body.

Our spirits give thanks to You,
—for Your countless benefits.

Our Father.

Oration

As in Proper of the Time.

Hebdomada I

Dominica, ad II Vesperas

Hymnus

Lucís creátor óptime,
lucem diérum próferens,
primórdiis lucis novæ
mundi parans oríginem;

Qui mane iunctum vésperi
diem vocári præcipis:
tætrum chaos illábitur;
audi preces cum flétibus.

Ne mens graváta crímine
vitæ sit exsul múnere,
dum nil perénne cógitat
seséque culpis ílligat.

Cælórum pulset íntimum,
vitále tollat præmium;
vitémus omne nóxium,
purgémus omne péssimum.

Præsta, Pater piíssime,
Patríque compar Unice,
cum Spíritu Paráclito
regnans per omne sæculum. Amen.

Psalmodia

Ant. 1 Virgam poténtiæ suæ emíttet Dóminus ex Sion, et regnábit in ætérnum, allelúia.

Week I

Sunday, Vespers II

Hymn

Trans. J. H. Newman

Father of Lights, by whom each day
Is kindled out of night,
Who, when the heavens were made, didst lay
Their rudiments in light;

Thou, who didst bind and blend in one
The glistening morn and evening pale,
Hear Thou our plaint, when light is gone,
And lawlessness and strife prevail.

Hear, lest the whelming weight of crime
Wreck us with life in view;
Lest thoughts and schemes of sense and time
Earn us a sinner's due.

So may we knock at Heaven's door,
And strive the immortal prize to win,
Continually and evermore
Guarded without and pure within.

Grant this, O Father, Only Son,
And Spirit, God of grace,
To whom all worship shall be done
In every time and place.

Psalmody

Ant. 1 The Lord will send forth His mighty scepter from Zion, and He will reign for ever, alleluia.

Psalmus 109 (110), 1–5, 7

1 Dixit Dóminus Dómino meo: *
« Sede a dextris meis,
donec ponam inimícos tuos *
scabéllum pedum tuórum ».

2 Virgam ponténtiæ tuae emíttet Dóminus ex Sion: *
dumináre in médio inimicórum tuórum.
3 Tecum principátus in die virtútis tuæ, †
in splendóribus sanctis, *
ex útero ante lucíferum génui te.
4 Iurávit Dóminus et non pænitébit eum: *
« Tu es sacérdos in ætérnum secúndum órdinem Melchísedech ».
5 Dóminus a dextris tuis, *
conquassábit in die iræ suæ reges.

7 De torrénte in via bibet, *
proptérea exaltábit caput.

Ant. Virgam poténtiæ suæ emíttet Dóminus ex Sion, et regnábit in ætérnum, allelúia.
Ant. 2 A fácie Dómini mota est terra, allelúia.

Psalmus 113 A (114)

1 In éxitu Israel de Ægýpto, *
domus Iacob de pópulo bárbaro,
2 factus est Iuda sanctuárium eius, *
Israel potéstas eius.

Psalm 110:1–5, 7

1 The LORD says to my lord:
"Sit at my right hand,
till I make your enemies your footstool."

2 The LORD sends forth from Zion
your mighty scepter.
Rule in the midst of your foes!
3 Your people will offer themselves freely
on the day you lead your host
upon the holy mountains.
From the womb of the morning
like dew your youth will come to You.
4 The LORD has sworn
and will not change his mind,
"You are a priest for ever
after the order of Melchizedek."

5 The LORD is at your right hand;
he will shatter kings on the day of his wrath.

7 He will drink from the brook by the way;
therefore he will lift up his head.

Ant. The Lord will send forth His mighty scepter from Zion, and He will reign for ever, alleluia.
Ant. 2 The earth is shaken before the face of the Lord.

Psalm 114

1 When Israel went forth from Egypt,
the house of Jacob from a people of strange language,
2 Judah became his sanctuary,
Israel his dominion.

3 Mare vidit et fugit, *
Iordánis convérsus est retrórsum;
4 montes saltavérunt ut aríetes, *
et colles sicut agni óvium.

5 Quid est tibi, mare, quod fugísti? *
Et tu, Iordánis, quia convérsus es retrórsum?
6 Montes, quod saltástis sicut aríetes, *
et colles, sicut agni óvium?

7 A fácie Dómini contremísce, terra, *
a fácie Dei Iacob,
8 qui convértit petram in stagna aquárum *
et sílicem in fontes aquárum.

Ant. A fácie Dómini mota est terra, allelúia.
Ant. 3 Regnávit Dóminus Deus noster omnípotens, allelúia.

Canticum Cf. Ap 19, 1-2. 5-7

Allelúia.
1 Salus et glória et virtus Deo nostro, *
(℟. Allelúia.)
2 quia vera et iusta iudícia eius.
℟. Allelúia (allelúia).

Allelúia.
5 Laudem dícite Deo nostro, omnes servi eius *
(℟. Allelúia.)
et qui timétis eum, pusílli et magni!
℟. Allelúia (allelúia).

3 The sea looked and fled,
Jordan turned back,
4 The mountains skipped like rams,
the hills like lambs.

5 What ails you, O sea, that you flee?
O Jordan, that you turn back?
6 O mountains, that you skip like rams?
O hills, like lambs?

7 Tremble, O earth, at the presence of the LORD,
at the presence of the God of Jacob,
8 who turns the rock into a pool of water,
the flint into a spring of water.

Ant. 2 The earth is shaken before the face of the Lord.

Ant. 3 The Lord God, the Almighty, reigns, alleluia.

Canticle See Revelation 19:1–7

Alleluia.
Salvation and glory and power belong to our God;
(℟. Allelúia.)
for his judgments are true and just;
℟. Allelúia (alleluia).

Alleluia.
Praise our God, all you his servants,
(℟. Allelúia.)
you who fear him, small and great.
℟. Allelúia (alleluia).

Allelúia.
6 Quóniam regnávit Dóminus,
Deus noster omnípotens. *
(℟. Allelúia.)
7 Gaudeámus et exsultémus et demus glóriam ei.
℟. Allelúia (allelúia).

Allelúia.
Quia venérunt núptiæ Agni, *
(℟. Allelúia.)
et uxor eius præparávit se.
℟. Allelúia (allelúia).

Ant. Regnávit Dóminus Deus noster omnípotens, Allelúia

Lectio Brevis 2 Cor 1, 3–4

Benedíctus Deus et Pater Dómini nostri Iesu Christi, Pater misericordiárum et Deus totíus consolatiónis, qui consolátur nos in omni tribulatióne nostra, ut possímus et ipsi consolári eos, qui in omni pressúra sunt, per exhortatiónem, qua exhortámur et ipsi a Deo.

Responsorium Breve

℟. Benedíctus es, Dómine, * In firmaménto cæli. Benedíctus.
℣. Et laudábilis et glóriosus in sæcula. * In firmaménto cæli. Glória Patri. Benedíctus.

Preces

Christum Dóminum adorántes, qui est caput nostrum et cuius nos membra sumus cum exsultatióne clamémus: *Advéniat regnum tuum, Dómine.*

Alleluia.
For, the Lord our God the Almighty reigns;
(℟. Allelúia.)
let us rejoice and exult and give him the glory.
℟. Allelúia (alleluia).

Alleluia.
For the marriage of the Lamb has come,
(℟. Allelúia.)
and his Bride has made Herself ready.
℟. Allelúia (alleluia).

Ant. 3 The Lord God, the Almighty, reigns, alleluia.

SHORT READING 2 Corinthians 1:3–7

Blessed be the God and Father of our Lord Jesus Christ, the Father of mercies and God of all comfort, who comforts us in all our affliction, so that we may be able to comfort those who are in any affliction, with the comfort with which we ourselves are comforted by God.

SHORT RESPONSORY

℟. Blessed are you, O Lord, in the firmament of heaven.
℣. Praiseworthy and glorious forever.

Magnificat ant. as in Proper of the Time.

INTERCESSIONS

Adoring Christ the Lord, Who is our Head and of Whose Body we are members, let us cry out with exultation: *Thy kingdom come, O Lord.*

Ecclésiam tuam, Salvátor noster, unitátis géneris humáni vivídius constítue sacraméntum
—et efficácius cunctis géntibus salútis mystérium.
Episcopórum collégio cum Papa nostro semper adésto,
—iísque unitátis, caritátis pacísque dona largíre.
Fac ut árctius uniántur tibi divíno cápiti christiáni,
—et regnum tuum testimónio vitæ procláment.
Pacem mundo præstáre dignéris,
—ut secúritas et tranquíllitas ubíque floréscant.
Novíssimæ resurrectiónis glóriam concéde defúnctis,
—et illórum nos beatitúdinis fac esse consórtes.

Pater noster.

ORATIO

Our Savior, establish Your Church as a more lively sign of the unity of the human race,
—and a more effective sign of salvation for all the nations.

Always be present to the college of bishops united with our Pope,
—and bestow on them the gifts of unity, charity, and peace.

Make all Christians to be more closely united to You as their Divine Head,
—and may they proclaim Your kingdom by the witness of their life.

Deign to grant peace to the world,
—that in all places security and tranquillity may flourish.

Grant unto the dead the glory of resurrection at the last,
—and make us their companions in blessedness.

Our Father.

Oration

As in Proper of the Time.

Hebdomada I

Feria II, ad Laudes matutinas

Hymnus

Splendor patérnæ glóriæ,
de luce lucem próferens,
lux lucis et fons lúminis,
diem dies illúminans,

Verúsque sol, illábere
micans nitóre pérpeti,
iubárque Sancti Spíritus
infúnde nostris sénsibus.

Votis vocémus et Patrem,
Patrem perénnis glóriæ,
Patrem poténtis grátiæ,
culpam reléget lúbricam.

Infórmet actus strénuos,
dentem retúndat ínvidi,
casus secúndet ásperos,
donet geréndi grátiam.

Mentem gubérnat et regat
casto, fidéli córpore;
fides calóre férveat,
fraudis venéna nésciat.

Christúsque nobis sit cibus,
potúsque noster sit fides;
læti bibámus sóbriam
ebrietátem Spíritus.

Week I

Monday, Lauds

Hymn Trans. J. H. Newman

Of the Father Effluence bright,
Out of Light evolving light,
Light from Light, unfailing Ray,
Day creative of the day:

Truest Sun, upon us stream
With Thy calm perpetual beam,
In the Spirit's still sunshine
Making sense and thought divine.

Seek we too the Father's face
Father of almighty grace,
And of majesty excelling,
Who can purge our tainted dwelling;

Who can aid us, who can break
Teeth of envious foes, and make
Hours of loss and pain succeed,
Guiding safe each duteous deed,

And infusing self-control,
Fragrant chastity of soul,
Faith's keen flame to soar on high,
Incorrupt simplicity.

Christ Himself for food be given,
Faith become the cup of Heaven,
Out of which the joy is quaff'd
Of the Spirit's sobering draught.

Lætus dies hic tránseat;
pudor sit ut dilúculum,
fides velut merídies,
crepúsculum mens nésciat.

Auróra cursus próvehit;
Auróra totus pródeat,
in Patre totus Fílius
et totus in Verbo Pater. Amen.

PSALMODIA

Ant. 1 Ad te orábo, Dómine, mane exáudies vocem meam.

Psalmus 5, 2–10. 12–13

2 Verba mea áuribus pércipe, Dómine; *
intéllege gémitum meum.
3 Inténde voci clamóris mei, *
rex meus et Deus meus.

4 Quóniam ad te orábo, Dómine, †
mane exáudies vocem meam; *
mane astábo tibi et exspectábo.
5 Quóniam non Deus volens iniquitátem tu es; †
neque habitábit iuxta te malígnus, *
6 neque permanébunt iniústi ante óculos tuos.

7 Odísti omnes, qui operántur iniquitátem, †
perdes omnes, qui loquúntur mendácium; *
virum sánguinum et dolósum abominábitur
Dóminus.

With that joy replenishèd,
Morn shall glow with modest red,
Noon with beaming faith be bright,
Eve be soft without twilight.

It has dawn'd;—upon our way,
Father in Thy Word, this day,
In Thy Father Word Divine,
From Thy cloudy pillar shine.

To the Father, and the Son,
And the Spirit, Three and One,
As of old, and as in Heaven,
Now and here be glory given.

PSALMODY

Ant. 1 To Thee, O Lord, shall I pray, and Thou wilt hear me in the morning.

Psalm 5:2–10, 12

2 Hearken to the sound of my cry,
my King and my God,
for to thee do I pray.
3 O LORD, in the morning thou dost hear my voice;
in the morning I prepare a sacrifice for thee, and watch.

4 For thou art not a God who delights in wickedness;
evil may not sojourn with thee.
5 The boastful may not stand before thy eyes;
thou hatest all evildoers.
6 Thou destroyest those who speak lies;
the LORD abhors bloodthirsty and deceitful men.

8 Ego autem in multitúdine misericórdiæ tuæ †
introíbo in domum tuam;
adorábo ad templum sanctum tuum in timóre
tuo.

9 Dómine, deduc me in iustítia tua propter inimícos
meos, *
dírige in conspéctu meo viam tuam.
10 Quóniam non est in ore eórum véritas, *
cor eórum fóvea;
sepúlcrum patens est guttur eórum, *
mólliunt linguas suas.

12 Et omnes, qui sperant in te, læténtur, *
in ætérnum exsúltent.
Obumbrábis eis, et gloriabúntur in te, *
qui díligunt nomen tuum;
13 quóniam tu benedíces iusto, Dómine, *
quasi scuto, bona voluntáte coronábis eum.

Ant. Ad te orábo, Dómine, mane exáudies vocem meam.
Ant. 2 Laudámus nomen tuum ínclitum, Deus noster.

Canticum 1 Chr 29, 10–13

10 Benedíctus es, Dómine Deus Israel patris nostri, *
ab ætérno in ætérnum.
11 Tua est, Dómine, magnificéntia et poténtia, *
glória, splendor atque maiéstas.
Cuncta enim, quæ in cælo sunt et in terra, tua sunt, *
tuum, Dómine, regnum, et tu eleváris ut caput
super ómnia.

7 But I through the abundance of thy steadfast love
will enter thy house,
I will worship toward thy holy temple
in the fear of thee.
8 Lead me, O LORD, in thy righteousness because of
my enemies;
make thy way straight before me.

9 For there is no truth in their mouth;
their heart is destruction,
their throat is an open sepulchre,
they flatter with their tongue.
10 Make them bear their guilt, O God;
let them fall by their own counsels;
because of their many transgressions cast them
out,
for they have rebelled against thee.

12 For thou dost bless the righteous, O LORD;
thou dost cover him with favor as with a shield.

Ant. 1 To Thee, O Lord, shall I pray, and Thou wilt hear me in the morning.
Ant. 2 We praise Thy glorious name, O Lord, our God.

Canticle I Chronicles 29:10–13

10 "Blessed art thou, O Lord, the God of Israel our
father, for ever and ever.
11 Thine, O Lord, is the greatness, and the power,
and the glory, and the victory, and the majesty;
for all that is in the heavens and in the earth is
thine; thine is the kingdom, O Lord, and thou
art exalted as Head above all.

12 De te sunt divítiæ et glória, *
tu domináris ómnium.
In manu tua virtus et poténtia, *
in manu tua est magnificáre et firmáre ómnia.
13 Nunc ígitur, Deus noster, confitémur tibi *
et laudámus nomen tuum ínclitum.

Ant. Laudámus nomen tuum ínclitum, Deus noster.
Ant. 3 Adoráte Dóminum in aula sancta eius.

Psalmus 28 (29)

1 Afférte Dómino, fílii Dei, *
afférte Dómino glóriam et poténtiam,
2 afférte Dómino glóriam nóminis eius, *
adoráte Dóminum in splendóre sancto.

3 Vox Dómini super aquas; †
Deus maiestátis intónuit,
Dóminus super aquas multas.
4 Vox Dómini in virtúte,
vox Dómini in magnificéntia.

5 Vox Dómini confringéntis cedros; *
et confrínget Dóminus cedros Líbani.
6 Et saltáre fáciet, tamquam vítulum, Líbanum, *
et Sárion, quemádmodum fílium unicórnium.

7 Vox Dómini intercidéntis flammam ignis, †
8 vox Dómini concutiéntis desértum, *
et concútiet Dóminus desértum Cades.
9 Vox Dómini properántis partum cervárum, †
et denudábit condénsa;
et in templo eius omnes dicent glóriam.

12 Both riches and honor come from thee, and thou
rulest over all. In thy hand are power and
might; and in thy hand it is to make great and
to give strength to all.
13 And now we thank thee, our God, and praise thy
glorious name.

Ant. 2 We praise Thy glorious name, O Lord, our God.
Ant. 3 Adore the Lord in His holy court.

Psalm 29

1 Ascribe to the LORD, O heavenly beings,
ascribe to the LORD glory and strength.
2 Ascribe to the LORD the glory of his name;
worship the LORD in holy array.

3 The voice of the LORD is upon the waters;
the God of glory thunders,
the LORD, upon many waters.
4 The voice of the LORD is powerful,
the voice of the LORD is full of majesty.

5 The voice of the LORD breaks the cedars,
the LORD breaks the cedars of Lebanon.
6 He makes Lebanon to skip like a calf,
and Sirion like a young wild ox.

7 The voice of the LORD flashes forth flames of fire.
8 The voice of the LORD shakes the wilderness,
the LORD shakes the wilderness of Kadesh.

9 The voice of the LORD makes the oaks to whirl,
and strips the forests bare;
and in his temple all cry, "Glory!"

10 Dóminus super dilúvium hábitat, *
et sedébit Dóminus rex in ætérnum.
11 Dóminus virtútem pópulo suo dabit, *
Dóminus benedícet pópulo suo in pace.

Ant. Adoráte Dóminum in aula sancta eius.

LECTIO BREVIS 2 Th 3, 10b–13

Si quis non vult operári, nec mandúcet. Audímus enim inter vos quosdam ambuláre inordináte, nihil operántes sed curióse agéntes; his autem, qui eiúsmodi sunt, præcípimus et obsecrámus in Dómino Iesu Christo, ut cum quiéte operántes suum panem mandúcent. Vos autem, fratres, nolíte defícere benefaciéntes.

RESPONSORIUM BREVE

℟. Benedíctus Dóminus. * A sǽculo et usque in sǽculum. Benedíctus.
℣. Qui facit mirabília solus. * A sǽculo et usque in sǽculum. Glória Patri. Benedíctus.

Ad Benedíctus, ant. Benedíctus Dóminus Deus noster.

PRECES

Christum magnificémus, plenum grátia et Spíritu Sancto, et fidénter eum implorémus: *Spíritum tuum da nobis, Dómine.*

Concéde nobis diem istum iucúndum, pacíficum et sine mácula.
—ut, ad vésperam perdúcti, cum gáudio et mundo corde te collaudáre valeámus.

Sit hódie splendor tuus super nos,
—et opus mánuum nostrárum dírige.

10 The LORD sits enthroned over the flood;
the LORD sits enthroned as king for ever.
11 May the LORD give strength to his people!
May the LORD bless his people with peace!

Ant. 3 Adore the Lord in His holy court.

SHORT READING 2 Thessalonians 3:10b–13

If anyone will not work, let him not eat. For we hear that some of you are living in idleness, mere busybodies, not doing any work. Now such persons we command and exhort in the Lord Jesus Christ to do their work in quietness and to earn their own living. Brethren, do not be weary in well-doing.

SHORT RESPONSORY

℟. Blessed be the Lord, from age to age.
℣. Who alone has done marvelous deeds.

Benedictus ant. Blessed be the Lord our God.

INTERCESSIONS

Let us magnify Christ, full of grace and the Holy Spirit, and confidently let us implore Him:
O Lord, grant us Your Spirit.

Grant us that this day might be joyful, peaceful and without sin,
—so that brought to eventide we might praise You with a glad and a clean heart.

May Your glory shine on us this day,
—and direct the work of our hands.

Osténde fáciem tuam super nos ad bonum in pace,
—ut hódie manu tua válida contegámur.
Réspice propítius omnes, qui oratiónibus nostris confídunt,
—eos adímple bonis ánimae et córporis univérsis.

Pater noster.

ORATIO

Actiónes nostras, quæsumus, Dómine aspirándo præveni et adiuvándo proséquere, ut cuncta nostra operátio a te semper incípiat, et per te cœpta finiátur. Per Dóminum.

Reveal Your face to us to our good in peace,
—that today we might be shielded by Your powerful hand.
Look favorably on all who rely on our prayers,
—fill them with all the good things of soul and body.

Our Father.

ORATION

Direct, O Lord, our actions, we ask, that aspiring to come before You and helping us to follow You, all our work might always begin with You, and through You find completion. Through our Lord.

Hebdomada I

Feria II, ad Vesperas

Hymnus

Imménse cæli cónditor,
qui, mixta ne confúnderent,
aquæ fluénta dívidens,
cælum dedísti límitem,

Firmans locum cæléstibus
simúlque terræ rívulis,
ut unda flammas témperet,
terræ solum ne díssipet:

Infúnde nunc piíssime,
donum perénnis grátiæ,
fraudis novæ ne cásibus
nos error átterat vetus

Lucem fides invéniat,
sic lúminis iubar ferat;
hæc vana cuncta térreat,
hanc falsa nulla cómprimant.

Præsta, Pater piíssime,
Patríque compar Unice,
cum Spíritu Paráclito
regnans per omne sæculum. Amen.

Psalmodia

Ant. 1 Oculi Dómini in páuperem respíciunt.

Week I

Monday, Vespers

Hymn

Trans. J. H. Newman

Lord of unbounded space,
Who, lest the sky and main
Should mix, and heaven should lose its place,
Didst the rude waters chain;

Parting the moist and rare,
That rills on earth might flow
To soothe the angry flame, whene'er
It ravens from below;

Pour on us of Thy grace
The everlasting spring;
Lest our frail steps renew the trace
Of ancient wandering.

May faith in lustre grow,
And rear her star in heaven,
Paling all sparks of earth below,
Unquenched by damps of even.

Grant it, O Father, Son,
And Holy Spirit of grace,
To whom be glory, Three on One,
In every time and place.

Psalmody

Ant. 1 The eyes of the Lord look upon the poor man.

Psalmus 10 (11)

1 In Dómino confído, quómodo dícitis ánimæ
meæ: *
« Tránsmigra in montem sicut passer?

2 Quóniam ecce peccatóres intendérunt arcum, †
paravérunt sagíttas suas super nervum, *
ut sagíttent in obscúro rectos corde.
3 Quando fundaménta evertúntur, *
iustus quid fáciat? ».

4 Dóminus in templo sancto suo, *
Dóminus, in cælo sedes eius.
Oculi eius in páuperem respíciunt, *
pálpebræ eius intérrogant fílios hóminum.
5 Dóminus intérrogat iustum et ímpium; *
qui autem díligit iniquitátem, odit ánima eius.
6 Pluet super peccatóres carbónes; *
ignis et sulphur et spíritus procellárum pars
cálicis eórum.

7 Quóniam iustus Dóminus et iustítias diléxit, *
recti vidébunt vultum eius.

Ant. Oculi Dómini in páuperem respíciunt.
Ant. 2 Beáti mundo corde, quóniam ipsi Deum vidébunt.

Psalmus 14 (15)

1 Dómine, quis habitábit in tabernáculo tuo?
Quis requiéscet in monte sancto tuo?

2 Qui ingréditur sine mácula et operátur iustítiam, *
qui lóquitur veritátem in corde suo,

Psalm 11

1 In the LORD I take refuge;
how can you say to me,
"Flee like a bird to the mountains;
2 for lo, the wicked bend the bow,
they have fitted their arrow to the string,
to shoot in the dark at the upright in heart;
3 if the foundations are destroyed,
what can the righteous do?"

4 The LORD is in his holy temple,
the LORD's throne is in heaven;
his eyes behold, his eyelids test, the children of men.
5 The LORD tests the righteous and the wicked,
and his soul hates him that loves violence.
6 On the wicked he will rain coals of fire and brimstone;
a scorching wind shall be the portion of their cup.
7 For the LORD is righteous, he loves righteous deeds;
the upright shall behold his face.

Ant. 1 The eyes of the Lord look upon the poor man.
Ant. 2 Blessed are the pure of heart, for they shall see God.

Psalm 15

1 O LORD, who shall sojourn in thy tent?
Who shall dwell on thy holy hill?

2 He who walks blamelessly, and does what is right,
and speaks truth from his heart;

3 qui non egit dolum in lingua sua, †
nec fecit próximo suo malum *
et oppróbrium non íntulit próximo suo.

4 Ad níhilum reputátus est in conspéctu eius malígnus, *
timéntes autem Dóminum gloríficat.
Qui iurávit in detriméntum suum et non mutat, †
5 qui pecúniam suam non dedit ad usúram *
et múnera super innocéntem non accépit.

Qui facit hæc, *
non movébitur in ætérnum.

Ant. Beáti mundo corde, quóniam ipsi Deum vidébunt.

Ant. 3 In Fílio suo elégit nos Deus in adoptiónem filiórum.

Canticum — Eph 1, 3–10

3 Benedíctus Deus et Pater Dómini nostri Iesu Christi, *
qui benedíxit nos in omni benedictióne spirituáli in cæléstibus in Christo,

4 sicut elégit nos in ipso ante mundi constitutiónem, †
ut essémus sancti et immaculáti *
in conspéctu eius in caritáte,
5 qui prædestinávit nos in adoptiónem filiórum †
per Iesum Christum in ipsum, *
secúndum beneplácitum voluntátis suæ,

6 in laudem glóriæ grátiæ suæ, *
in qua gratificávit nos in Dilécto,

3 who does not slander with his tongue,
and does no evil to his friend,
nor takes up a reproach against his neighbor;
4 in whose eyes a reprobate is despised,
but who honors those who fear the LORD;
who swears to his own hurt and does not change;
5 who does not put out his money at interest,
and does not take a bribe against the innocent.
6 He who does these things shall never be moved.

Ant. 2 Blessed are the pure of heart, for they shall see God.

Ant. 3 God chose us in His Son to be His adopted sons.

Canticle

Ephesians 1:3–10

3 Blessed be the God and Father of our Lord Jesus Christ, who has blessed us in Christ with every spiritual blessing in the heavenly places,
4 even as he chose us in him before the foundation of the world, that we should be holy and blameless before him.
5 He destined us in love to be his sons through Jesus Christ, according to the purpose of his will,
6 to the praise of his glorious grace which he freely bestowed on us in the Beloved.

7 in quo habémus redemptiónem per sánguinem
eius, *
remissiónem peccatórum,

secúndum divítias grátiæ eius, †
8 qua superabundávit in nobis *
in omni sapiéntia et prudéntia

9 notum fáciens nobis mystérium voluntátis suæ, *
secúndum beneplácitum eius,

quod propósuit in eo, *
10 in dispensatiónem plenitúdinis témporum:
recapituláre ómnia in Christo, *
quæ in cælis et quæ in terra.

Ant. In Fílio suo elégit nos Deus in adoptiónem filiórum.

LECTIO BREVIS Col 1, 9b-11

Impleámini agnitióne voluntátis eius in omni sapiéntia et intelléctu spiritáli, ut ambulétis digne Dómino per ómnia placéntes, in omni ópere bono fructificántes et crescéntes in sciéntia Dei, in omni virtúte confortáti secúndum poténtiam claritátis eius in omnem patiéntiam et longanimitátem, cum gáudio.

RESPONSORIUM BREVE

℟. Sana ánimam meam, * Quia peccávi tibi. Sana.
℣. Ego dixi: Dómine, miserére mei, * Quia peccávi tibi. Glória Patri. Sana.

Ad Magnificat, ant. Magníficat ánima mea Dóminum, quia respéxit Deus humilitátem meam.

7 In him we have redemption through his blood, the forgiveness of our trespasses, according to the riches of his grace
8 which he lavished upon us.
9 For he has made known to us in all wisdom and insight the mystery of his will, according to his purpose which he set forth in Christ
10 as a plan for the fulness of time, to unite all things in him, things in heaven and things on earth.

Ant. 3 God chose us in His Son to be His adopted sons.

SHORT READING Colossians 1:9b–13

May be filled with the knowledge of his will in all spiritual wisdom and understanding, to lead a life worthy of the Lord, fully pleasing to him, bearing fruit in every good work and increasing in the knowledge of God. May you be strengthened with all power, according to his glorious might, for all endurance and patience with joy.

SHORT RESPONSORY

℟. Heal my soul, for I have sinned against You.
℣. I said: Lord, have mercy upon me.

Magnificat ant. My soul magnifies the Lord, for God has regarded the low estate of His handmaiden.

Preces

Deus cum pópulo suo pactum íniit sempitérnum, neque désinit illi benefácere. Ideo ei grátias agámus et fidénti ánimo nostram ad eum dirigámus oratiónem: *Bénefac pópulo tuo, Dómine.*

Salvum fac pópulum tuum, Dómine,
—et bénedic hereditáti tuæ.

Cóngrega in unum christiáno nómine decorátos,
—ut credat mundus in Christum, quem misísti.

Grátiam tuam ómnibus amícis nostris confer et notis,
—bonúmque Christi odórem fac ut ipsi diffúndant.

Amórem tuum agonizántibus manifésta,
—da ut salútem tuam eórum óculi vídeant.

Erga defúnctos misericórditer age.
—ággrega eos quiescéntibus in Christo.

Pater noster.

Oratio

Magníficet te, Dómine, hæc nostræ servitútis proféssio, ut qui propter nostram salútem humilitátem Maríæ Vírginis respexísti, ad plenitúdinem redemptiónis nos fácias exaltári. Per Dóminum.

INTERCESSIONS

God has entered into an eternal covenant with His people and never ceases to bless them. Therefore, let us give thanks to Him and with a confident spirit direct our prayer to Him: *Bless Your people, O Lord.*

Save Your people, O Lord,
—and bless Your inheritance.

Gather into one all those who bear the honor of the name Christian,
—that the world may believe in the Christ Whom You sent.

Bestow Your grace on all our friends and acquaintances,
—that they may spread the sweet fragrance of Christ.

Make manifest Your love to the dying,
—that their eyes may see Your salvation.

Deal mercifully with the deceased,
—and gather them into the number of those who sleep in Christ.

Our Father.

ORATION

May this offering of our service magnify You, O Lord, for, as You looked upon the humility of the Virgin Mary to save us, make us, then, to be exalted to the fulness of redemption. Through Christ our Lord.

Hebdomada I

Feria III, ad Laudes matutinas

Hymnus

Pergráta mundo núntiat
auróra solis spícula,
res et colóre véstiens
iam cuncta dat nitéscere.

Qui sol per ævum prænites,
o Christe, nobis vívidus,
ad te canéntes vértimur,
te gestiéntes pérfrui.

Tu Patris es sciéntia
Verbúmque per quod ómnia
miro refúlgent órdine
mentésque nostras áttrahunt.

Da lucis ut nos fílii
sic ambulémus ímpigri,
ut Patris usque grátiam
mores et actus éxprimant.

Sincéra præst*a* ut prófluant
ex ore nostro iúgiter,
et veritátis dúlcibus
ut excitémur gáudiis.

Sit, Christe, rex piíssime,
tibi Patríque glória
cum Spíritu Paráclito,
in sempitérna sǽcula. Amen.

Week I

Tuesday, Lauds

Hymn Trans. The Benedictine Nuns, St. Cecilia's Abbey

The beauty of the rising sun
Begins to tint the world with light,
Awakened nature glows with life
As form and colour disappear.

Lord Jesus Christ, You far surpass
The sun that shines since time began;
We turn to You with joyous song
That You may bless us with Your smile.

You are God's knowledge infinite,
His Word, through Whom all things were made;
Their wondrous order speaks to us
And draws our hearts and minds to You.

Give us Your light that like true sons
Intrepid we may tread life's path.
May all our ways and actions show
The gift of God the Father's grace.

Let every word our lips may say
Prove our sincerity and truth,
That our serenity of soul
May radiate our inward joy.

O Christ our King and tender Lord,
All glory ever be to You,
Who with the Holy Spirit reign
With God the Father's might supreme.
Amen.

PSALMODIA

Ant. 1 Innocens mánibus et mundo corde ascéndet in montem Dómini.

Psalmus 23 (24)

1 Dómini est terra et plenitúdo eius, *
orbis terrárum et qui hábitant in eo.
2 Quia ipse super mária fundávit eum *
et super flúmina firmávit eum.
3 Quis ascéndet in montem Dómini, *
aut quis stabit in loco sancto eius?
4 Innocens mánibus et mundo corde, †
qui non levávit ad vana ánimam suam, *
nec iurávit in dolum.
5 Hic accípiet benedictiónem a Dómino *
et iustificatiónem a Deo salutári suo.
6 Hæc est generátio quæréntium eum, *
quæréntium fáciem Dei Iacob.
7 Attóllite, portæ, cápita vestra, †
et elevámini, portæ æternáles, *
et introíbit rex glóriæ.
8 Quis est iste rex glóriæ? *
Dóminus fortis et potens,
Dóminus potens in prœlio.
9 Attóllite, portæ, cápita vestra, †
et elevámini, portæ æternáles, *
et introíbit rex glóriæ.
10 Quis est iste rex glóriæ.
Dóminus virtútum ipse est rex glóriæ.

PSALMODY

Ant. 1 He who has clean hands and a pure heart will ascend the mountain of the Lord.

Psalm 24

1 The earth is the LORD's and the fulness thereof,
the world and those who dwell therein;
2 for he has founded it upon the seas,
and established it upon the rivers.

3 Who shall ascend the hill of the LORD?
And who shall stand in his holy place?
4 He who has clean hands and a pure heart,
who does not lift up his soul to what is false,
and does not swear deceitfully.
5 He will receive blessing from the LORD,
and vindication from the God of his salvation.
6 Such is the generation of those who seek him,
who seek the face of the God of Jacob.

7 Lift up your heads, O gates!
and be lifted up, O ancient doors!
that the King of glory may come in.
8 Who is the King of Glory?
The LORD, strong and mighty,
the LORD, mighty in battle!
9 Lift up your heads, O gates!
and be lifted up, O ancient doors!
that the King of glory may come in.
10 Who is this King of glory?
The LORD of hosts,
he is the King of glory!

Ant. Innocens mánibus et mundo corde ascéndet in montem Dómini.

Ant. 2 Exaltáte Regem sæculórum in opéribus vestris.

Canticum Tob 13, 2–8

2 Benedíctus Deus vivens in ævum, †
et regnum illíus, *
quia ipse flagéllat et miserétur,
dedúcit usque ad ínferos deórsum †
et redúcit a perditióne maiestáte sua, *
et non est qui effúgiat manum eius.

3 Confitémini illi, fílii Israel, coram natiónibus, †
quia ipse dispérsit vos in illis *
4 et ibi osténdit maiestátem suam.
Et exaltáte illum coram omni vivénte, †
quóniam Dóminus noster, et ipse est pater
noster *
et ipse est Deus noster in ómnia sǽcula.

5 Flagellábit vos ob iniquitátes vestras *
et ómnium miserébitur vestrum
et cólliget vos ab ómnibus natiónibus, *
ubicúmque dispérsi fuéritis.

6 Cum convérsi fuéritis ad illum †
in toto corde vestro et in tota ánima vestra, *
ut faciátis coram illo veritátem,
tunc revertétur ad vos *
et non abscóndet a vobis fáciem suam ámplius.

Et nunc aspícite, quæ fecit vobíscum, *
et confitémini illi in toto ore vestro.
Benedícite Dóminum iustítiæ *
et exaltáte regem sæculórum.

Ant. 1 He who has clean hands and a pure heart will ascend the mountain of the Lord.
Ant. 2 Praise the King of the ages in your deeds.

Canticle Tobit 13:1–8

1 "Blessed is God who lives for ever,
and blessed is his kingdom.
2 For he afflicts, and he shows mercy;
he leads down to Hades, and brings up again,
and there is no one who can escape his hand.
3 Acknowledge him before the nations, O sons of Israel;
for he has scattered us among them.
4 Make his greatness known there,
and exalt him in the presence of all the living;
because he is our LORD and God,
he is our Father for ever.
5 He will afflict us for our iniquities;
and again he will show mercy,
and will gather us from all the nations
among whom you have been scattered.
6 If you turn to him with all your heart and with all your soul,
to do what is true before him,
then he will turn to you
and will not hide his face from you.
But see what he will do with you;
give thanks to him with your full voice.
Praise the LORD of righteousness,
and exalt the King of the ages.
I give him thanks in the land of my captivity,
and I show his power and majesty to a nation of sinners.

Ego in terra captivitátis meæ confíteor illi *
et osténdo virtútem et maiestátem eius genti
peccatórum.
Convertímini, peccatóres, †
et fácite iustítiam coram illo. *
Quis scit, si velit vos
et fáciat vobis misericórdiam?

7 Ego et ánima mea regi cæli lætatiónes dícimus, *
et ánima mea lætábitur ómnibus diébus vitæ suæ.
8 Benedícite Dóminum, omnes elécti, †
et omnes laudáte maiestátem illíus. *
Agite dies lætítiæ et confitémini illi.

Ant. Exaltáte Regem sæculórum in opéribus vestris.
Ant. 3 Rectos decet collaudátio.

Psalmus 32 (33)

1 Exsultáte, iusti, in Dómino; *
rectos decet collaudátio.
2 Confitémini Dómino in cíthara, *
in psaltério decem chordárum psállite illi.

3 Cantáte ei cánticum novum, *
bene psállite ei in vociferatióne,
4 quia rectum est verbum Dómini, *
et ómnia ópera eius in fide.
5 Díligit iustítiam et iudícium; *
misericórdia Dómini plena est terra.
6 Verbo Dómini cæli facti sunt, *
et spíritu oris eius omnis virtus eórum.

Turn back, you sinners, and do right before him;
who knows if he will accept you and have mercy on you?
7 I exalt my God;
my soul exalts the king of heaven,
and will rejoice in his majesty.
8 Let all men speak,
and give him thanks in Jerusalem.

Ant. 2 Praise the King of the ages in your deeds.
Ant. 3 Praise befits the upright.

Psalm 33

1 Rejoice in the LORD, O you righteous!
Praise befits the upright.
2 Praise the LORD with the lyre,
make melody to him with the harp of ten strings!
3 Sing to him a new song
play skilfully on the strings, with loud shouts.

4 For the word of the LORD is upright;
and all his work is done in faithfulness.
5 He loves righteousness and justice;
the earth is full of the steadfast love of the LORD.

6 By the word of the LORD the heavens were made,
and all their host by the breath of his mouth.

7 Cóngregans sicut in utre aquas maris, *
ponens in thesáuris abýssos.

8 Tímeat Dóminum omnis terra, *
a fácie autem eius formídent omnes
inhabitántes orbem.
9 Quóniam ipse dixit, et facta sunt, *
ipse mandávit, et creáta sunt.
10 Dóminus díssipat consília géntium, *
írritas facit cogitatiónes populórum.
11 Consílium autem Dómini in ætérnum manet, *
cogitatiónes cordis eius in generatióne et
generatiónem.

12 Beáta gens, cui Dóminus est Deus, *
pópulus, quem elégit in hereditátem sibi.
13 De cælo respéxit Dóminus, *
vidit omnes fílios hóminum.
14 De loco habitáculi sui respéxit *
super omnes, qui hábitant terram,
15 qui finxit singillátim corda eórum, *
qui intéllegit ómnia ópera eórum.

16 Non salvátur rex per multam virtútem, *
et gigas non liberábitur in multitúdine virtútis
suæ.
17 Fallax equus ad salútem, *
in abundántia autem virtútis suæ non salvábit.
18 Ecce óculi Dómini super metuéntes eum, *
in eos, qui sperant super misericórdia eius,
19 ut éruat a morte ánimas eórum *
et alat eos in fame.

20 Anima nostra sústinet Dóminum, *

7 He gathered the waters of the sea as in a bottle;
he puts the deeps in storehouses.

8 Let all the earth fear the LORD,
let all the inhabitants of the world stand in awe of him!
9 For he spoke, and it came to be;
he commanded, and it stood forth.

10 The Lord brings the counsel of the nations to nought;
he frustrates the plans of the peoples.
11 The counsel of the LORD stands for ever,
the thoughts of his heart to all generations.
12 Blessed is the nation whose God is the LORD,
the people whom he has chosen as his heritage!

13 The LORD looks down from heaven,
he sees all the sons of men;
14 from where he sits enthroned he looks forth
on all the inhabitants of the earth,
15 he who fashions the hearts of them all,
and observes all their deeds.
16 A king is not saved by his great army;
a warrior is not delivered by his great strength.
17 The war horse is a vain hope for victory,
and by its great might it cannot save.

18 Behold, the eye of the LORD is on those who fear him,
on those who hope in his steadfast love,
19 that he may deliver their soul from death,
and keep them alive in famine.

20 Our soul waits for the LORD;

quóniam adiútor et protéctor noster est;
21 quia in eo lætábitur cor nostrum, *
et in nómine sancto eius sperávimus.
22 Fiat misericórdia tua, Dómine, super nos, *
quemádmodum sperávimus in te.

Ant. Rectos decet collaudátio.

Lectio Brevis

Rom 13, 11b. 12–13a

Hora est iam vos de somno súrgere. Nox procéssit, dies autem appropiávit. Abiciámus ergo ópera tenebrárum et induámur arma lucis. Sicut in die honéste ambulémus.

Responsorium Breve

℟. Deus meus, adiútor meus, * Et sperábo in eum. Deus meus.
℣. Refúgium meum et liberátor meus. * Et sperábo in eum. Gloria Patri. Deus meus.

Ad Benedictus, ant. Eréxit nobis Dóminus cornu salútis, sicut locútus est per os prophetárum suórum.

Preces

Vocatiónis cæléstis partícipes facti, fratres caríssimi, Iesum, pontíficem confessiónis nostræ, benedicámus clamántes: *Dómine Deus noster et salvátor noster.*

O Rex omnípotens, qui, per baptísmum, regále nobis sacerdótium contulísti,
—fac ut laudis tibi semper sacrifícium offerámus.

Da nobis mandáta tua serváre,
—ut per Sanctum Spíritum in te maneámus et tu in nobis.

he is our help and shield.
21 Yea, our heart is glad in him,
because we trust in his holy name.
22 Let thy steadfast love, O LORD, be upon us,
even as we hope in thee.

Ant. 3 Praise befits the upright.

SHORT READING Romans 13:11b, 12–13a

It is full time now for you to wake from sleep. The night is far gone, the day is at hand. Let us then cast off the works of darkness and put on the armor of light; let us conduct ourselves becomingly as in the day.

SHORT RESPONSORY

℟. My God, my helper, in whom I shall hope.
℣. My refuge and my liberator.

Benedictus ant. The Lord has raised up a horn of salvation for us, as He spoke by the mouth of His prophets.

INTERCESSIONS

Most dear brethren, made participants of the heavenly calling, let us bless Jesus, High Priest of our confession, crying out: *O Lord, our God and our Savior.*

O omnipotent King Who, through baptism, have conferred on us a royal priesthood,
—make it so that we may offer You a sacrifice of praise.

Grant us to observe Your commandments,
—that through the Holy Spirit we might remain in You and You in us.

Sapiéntiam tuam da nobis ætérnam,
—ut nobíscum sit hódie et nobíscum operétur.
Concéde nobis hódie néminem umquam contristáre,
—omnes autem, qui nobíscum sunt, lætificáre.

Pater noster.

ORATIO

Matutína súpplicum vota, Dómine, propítius intuére, et occúlta cordis nostri remédio tuæ clarífica pietátis, ut desidéria tenebrósa non téneant, quos lux cæléstis grátiæ reparávit. Per Dóminum.

Grant us Your eternal wisdom,
—that it may be with us today and work within us.
Grant that today we may not cause sadness to anyone,
—rather, let all who are with us rejoice.

Our Father.

ORATION

O Lord, favorably attend to our morning prayers of supplication, and bring into the light the hidden things of our heart by the medicine of Your kindness, that dark desires might not bind those whom the heavenly light of grace has restored. Through our Lord.

Hebdomada I

Feria III, ad Vesperas

Hymnus

Tellúris ingens cónditor,
mundi solum qui éruens,
pulsis aquæ moléstiis,
terram dedísti immóbilem,

Ut germen aptum próferens,
fulvis decóra flóribus,
fecúnda fructu sísteret
pastúmque gratum rédderet:

Mentis perústæ vúlnera
munda viróre grátiæ
ut facta fletu díluat
motúsque pravos átterat,

Iussis tuis obtémperet,
nullis malis appróximet,
bonis repléri gáudeat
et mortis actum nésciat.

Præsta, Pater piíssime,
Patríque compar Unice,
cum Spíritu Paráclito
regnans per omne sæculum. Amen.

Psalmodia

Ant. 1 Tríbuit Dóminus victóriam Christo suo.

Week I

Tuesday, Vespers

HYMN — Trans. J. H. Newman

All-bountiful Creator, who,
  When Thou didst mould the world, didst drain
The waters from the mass, that so
  Earth might immovable remain;

That its dull clods it might transmute
  To golden flowers in vale or wood,
To juice of thirst-allaying fruit,
  And grateful herbage spread for food;

Wash Thou our smarting wounds and hot,
  In the cool freshness of Thy grace;
Till tears start forth the past to blot,
  And cleanse and calm Thy holy place;

Till we obey Thy full behest,
  Shun the world's tainted touch and breath,
Joy in what highest is and best,
  And gain a spell to baffle death.

Grant it, O Father, Only Son,
  And Holy Spirit, God of Grace;
To whom all glory, Three in One,
  Be given in every time and place.

PSALMODY

Ant. 1 The Lord has granted victory to His Christ.

Psalmus 19 (20)

2 Exáudiat te Dóminus in die tribulatiónis, *
prótegat te nomen Dei Iacob.
3 Mittat tibi auxílium de sancto *
et de Sion tueátur te.

4 Memor sit omnis sacrifícii tui *
et holocáustum tuum pingue hábeat.
5 Tríbuat tibi secúndum cor tuum *
et omne consílium tuum adímpleat.

6 Lætábimur in salutári tuo †
et in nómine Dei nostri levábimus signa; *
ímpleat Dóminus omnes petitiónes tuas.

7 Nunc cognóvi quóniam salvum fecit Dóminus
christum suum: †
exaudívit illum de cælo sancto suo, *
in virtútibus salútis déxteræ eius.

8 Hi in cúrribus et hi in equis, *
nos autem nomen Dómini Dei nostri
invocávimus.
9 Ipsi incurváti sunt et cecidérunt, *
nos autem surréximus et erécti sumus.

10 Dómine, salvum fac regem, *
et exáudi nos in die, qua invocavérimus te.

Ant. Tríbuit Dóminus victóriam Christo suo.
Ant. 2 Cantábimus et psallémus virtútes tuas.

Psalmus 20 (21), 2–8. 14

2 Dómine, in virtúte tua lætábitur rex, *
et super salutáre tuum exsultábit veheménter.

Psalm 20

1 The LORD answer you in the day of trouble!
The name of the God of Jacob protect you!
2 May he send you help from the sanctuary,
and give you support from Zion!
3 May he remember all your offerings,
and regard with favor your burnt sacrifices!

4 May he grant you your heart's desire,
and fulfill all your plans!
5 May we shout for joy over your victory,
and in the name of our God set up our banners!
May the LORD fulfil all your petitions!

6 Now I know that the LORD will help his anointed;
he will answer him from his holy heaven
with mighty victories by his right hand.
7 Some boast of chariots, and some of horses;
but we boast of the name of the Lord our God.
8 They will collapse and fall;
but we shall rise and stand upright.

9 Give victory to the king, O LORD;
answer us when we call.

Ant. 1 The Lord has granted victory to His Christ.
Ant. 2 We shall sing and praise your mighty works.

Psalm 21:2–7, 13

2 Thou hast given him his heart's desire,
and hast not withheld the request of his lips.

3 Desidérium cordis eius tribuísti ei *
et voluntátem labiórum eius non denegásti.
4 Quóniam prævenísti eum in benedictiónibus dulcédinis; *
posuísti in cápite eius corónam de auro puríssimo.
5 Vitam pétiit a te, et tribuísti ei, *
longitúdinem diérum in sæculum et in sæculum sæculi.

6 Magna est glória eius in salutári tuo, *
magnificéntiam et decórem impónes super eum;
7 quóniam pones eum benedictiónem in sæculum sæculi, *
lætificábis eum in gáudio ante vultum tuum.
8 Quóniam rex sperat in Dómino *
et in misericórdia Altíssimi non commovébitur.

14 Exaltáre, Dómine, in virtúte tua; *
cantábimus et psallémus virtútes tuas.

Ant. Cantábimus et psallémus virtútes tuas.
Ant. 3 Fecísti nos, Dómine, regnum et sacerdótes Deo nostro.

Canticum Ap 4, 11; 5, 9. 10. 12

4,11 Dignus es, Dómine et Deus noster, *
accípere glóriam et honórem et virtútem,
quia tu creásti ómnia, *
et propter voluntátem tuam erant et creáta sunt.

5,9 Dignus es, Dómine, accípere librum *
et aperíre signácula eius,
quóniam occísus es †
et redemísti Deo in sánguine tuo *

3 For thou dost meet him with goodly blessings;
thou dost set a crown of fine gold upon his head.
4 He asked life of thee; thou gavest it to him,
length of days for ever and ever.
5 His glory is great through thy help;
splendor and majesty thou dost bestow upon him.
6 Yea, thou dost make him most blessed for ever;
thou dost make him glad with the joy of thy presence.
7 For the king trusts in the LORD;
and through the steadfast love of the Most High he shall not be moved.

13 Be exalted, O LORD, in thy strength!
We will sing and praise thy power.

Ant. 2 We shall sing and praise your mighty works.
Ant. 3 Thou hast made us, O Lord, a kingdom and priests for our God.

Canticle Revelation 4:11; 5:9, 10, 12

11 "Worthy art thou, our Lord and God, to receive glory and honor and power, for thou didst create all things, and by thy will they existed and were created."

9 "Worthy art thou to take the scroll and to open its seals,
for thou wast slain and by thy blood didst ransom men for God

ex omni tribu et lingua et pópulo et natióne
10 et fecísti eos Deo nostro regnum et sacerdótes, *
et regnábunt super terram.

12 Dignus est Agnus, qui occísus est, †
accípere virtútem et divítias et sapiéntiam *
et fortitúdinem et honórem et glóriam et
benedictiónem.

Ant. Fecísti nos, Dómine, regnum et sacerdótes Deo nostro.

LECTIO BREVIS 1 Io 3, 1a. 2

Vidéte qualem caritátem dedit nobis Pater, ut fílii Dei nominémur, et sumus! Caríssimi, nunc fílii Dei sumus, et nondum manifestátum est quid érimus; scimus quóniam, cum ipse apparúerit, símiles ei érimus, quóniam vidébimus eum, sícuti est.

RESPONSORIUM BREVE

℟. In ætérnum, Dómine, * Pérmanet verbum tuum. In ætérnum.

℣. In sǽculum sǽculi véritas tua. * Pérmanet verbum tuum. Gloria Patri. In ætérnum.

Ad Magnificat, ant. Exsúltet spíritus meus in Dómino Deo, salutári meo.

PRECES

Christo Dómino, in médio nostri vivénti, nos, pópulus eius acquisitiónis, laudes persolvámus et supplicémus dicéntes: *Ad laudem tuam exáudi nos, Dómine.*

from every tribe and tongue and people and nation,
10 and hast made them a kingdom and priests to our God,
and they shall reign on earth."
12 "Worthy is the lamb who was slain, to receive power and wealth and wisdom and might and honor and glory and blessing!"

Ant. 3 Thou hast made us, O Lord, a kingdom and priests for our God.

Short Reading

1 John 3:1a, 2

See what love the Father has given us, that we should be called children of God; and so we are. Beloved, we are God's children now; it does not yet appear what we shall be, but we know that when he appears we shall be like him, for we shall see him as he is.

Short Responsory

℟. Through all eternity, O Lord, Your word endures,
℣. and Your faithfulness forever.

Magnificat ant. May my spirit rejoice in the Lord God, my Savior.

Intercessions

To Christ the Lord, living in our midst, let us, His adopted people, render Him praises and beseech Him saying: *To your praise, hear us, Lord.*

Dómine, rex et dominátor géntium, adésto pópulis et ómnibus potestátem habéntibus,
—ut commúne bonum iuxta legem tuam concórditer persequántur.
Tu, qui captívam duxísti nostram captivitátem,
—restítue ad filiórum libertátem fratres, qui córpore vel spíritu captivitátem patiúntur.
Semper irreprehensíbiles iúvenes nostri tibi sátagant inveníri,
—et tibi vocánti magnanímiter obsecúndent.
Fac ut exémplum tuum púeri imiténtur,
—atque sapiéntia et grátia semper profíciant.
Defúncti in regnum suscipiántur ætérnum,
—ubi nos tecum conregnatúros sperámus.

Pater noster.

ORATIO

Grátias tibi ágimus, Dómine Deus omnípotens, qui nos ad hanc horam vespertínam perveníre tribuísti, te supplíciter deprecántes, ut elevátio mánuum nostrárum sit in conspéctu tuo acceptábile sacrifícium. Per Dóminum.

Lord, King and Master of the nations, be present to Your people and to all who hold power,
—that they may pursue the common good according to Your law.

You, Who have rendered captive our captivity,
—restore to the freedom of sonship our brothers who suffer a captivity in body or in spirit.

May our youth be content to be found blameless always by You,
—and may they virtuously conform to Your calling.

Grant that our children may imitate Your example,
—and may advance always in wisdom and in grace.

May the deceased be accepted into Your reign,
—where we hope to reign with You.

Our Father.

ORATION

We give thanks to You, Lord God Almighty, Who have brought us to this evening hour, humbly beseeching You, that the raising of our hands in Your sight may be an acceptable sacrifice. Through our Lord.

Hebdomada I

Feria IV, ad Laudes matutinas

Hymnus

Nox et tenébr*æ* et núbila,
confúsa mund*i* et túrbida,
lux intrat, albéscit polus:
Christus venit; discédite.

Calígo terræ scínditur
percússa solis spículo,
rebúsque iam color redit
vultu niténtis síderis.

Sic nostra mox obscúritas
fraudísque pectus cónscium,
ruptis retéctum núbibus,
regnánte palléscet Deo.

Te, Christe, solum nóvimus,
te mente pur*a* et símplici
rogáre curváto genu
flend*o* et canéndo díscimus.

Inténde nostris sénsibus
vitámque totam díspice:
sunt multa fucis íllita
quæ luce purgéntur tua.

Sit, Christe, rex piíssime,
tibi Patríque glória
cum Spíritu Paráclito,
in sempitérna sǽcula. Amen.

Week I

Wednesday, Lauds

Hymn

Trans. J. H. Newman

Haunting gloom and flitting shades,
  Ghastly shapes, away!
Christ is rising, and pervades
  Highest Heaven with day.

He with His bright spear the night
  Dazzles and pursues:
Earth wakes up and glows with light
  Of a thousand hues.

Thee, O Christ, and Thee alone,
  With single mind,
We with chant and plaint would own:
  To Thy flock be kind.

Much it needs Thy light divine.
  Spot and stain to clean;
Light of Angels, on us shine
  With Thy face serene.

To the Father, and the Son,
  And the Holy Ghost,
Here be glory, as is done
  By the angelic host.

PSALMODIA

Ant. 1 Deus, in lúmine tuo vidébimus lumen.

Psalmus 35 (36)

2 Susúrrat iníquitas ad ímpium in médio cordis
eius; *
non est timor Dei ante óculos eius.

3 Quóniam blandítur ipsi in conspéctu eius, *
ut non invéniat iniquitátem suam et óderit.
4 Verba oris eius iníquitas et dolus, *
désiit intellégere, ut bene ágeret.
5 Iniquitátem meditátus est in cubíli suo, †
ástitit omni viæ non bonæ, *
malítiam autem non odívit.

6 Dómine, in cælo misericórdia tua *
et véritas tua usque ad nubes;
7 iustítia tua sicut montes Dei, †
iudícia tua abýssus multa: *
hómines et iuménta salvábis, Dómine.

8 Quam pretiósa misericórdia tua, Deus! *
Fílii autem hóminum in tégmine alárum tuárum
sperábunt;
9 inebriabúntur ab ubertáte domus tuæ, *
et torrénte voluptátis tuæ potábis eos.
10 Quóniam apud te est fons vitæ, *
et in lúmine tuo vidébimus lumen.

11 Prætende misericórdiam tuam sciéntibus te *
et iustítiam tuam his, qui recto sunt corde.

PSALMODY

Ant. 1 O God, in Thy light do we see light.

Psalm 36

1 Transgression speaks to the wicked deep in his heart;
there is no fear of God before his eyes.
2 For he flatters himself in his own eyes
that his iniquity cannot be found out and hated.
3 The words of his mouth are mischief and deceit;
he has ceased to act wisely and do good.
4 He plots mischief while on his bed;
he sets himself in a way that is not good;
he spurns not evil.

5 Thy steadfast love, O LORD, extends to the heavens,
thy faithfulness to the clouds.
6 Thy righteousness is like the mountains of God,
thy judgments are like the great deep;
man and beast thou savest, O LORD.

7 How precious is thy steadfast love, O God!
The children of men take refuge in the shadow of thy wings.
8 They feast on the abundance of thy house,
and thou givest them drink from the river of thy delights.
9 For with thee is the fountain of life;
in thy light do we see light.

10 O continue thy steadfast love to those who know thee,
and thy salvation to the upright of heart!

12 Non véniat mihi pes supérbiæ, *
et manus peccatóris non móveat me.
13 Ibi cecidérunt, qui operántur iniquitátem, *
expúlsi sunt, nec potuérunt stare.

Ant. Deus, in lúmine tuo vidébimus lumen.
Ant. 2 Dómine, magnus es tu, et præclárus in virtúte tua.

Canticum Iudt 16, 1–2. 13–15

1 Incípite Deo meo in týmpanis, *
cantáte Dómino meo in cýmbalis,
modulámini illi psalmum novum, *
exaltáte et invocáte nomen ipsíus.
2 Tu es Deus cónterens bella, †
qui ponis castra in médio pópuli tui, *
ut erípias me de manu persequéntium me.

13 Cantábo Deo meo hymnum novum: †
Dómine, magnus es tu et clarus, *
mirábilis in virtúte et insuperábilis.
14 Tibi sérviat omnis creatúra tua, *
quóniam dixísti, et facta sunt,
misísti spíritum tuum, et ædificáta sunt, *
et non est, qui resístat voci tuæ.

15 Montes enim a fundaméntis agitabúntur cum aquis, *
petræ autem a fácie tua tamquam cera liquéscent.
Illis autem qui timent te *
propítius adhuc eris.

11 Let not the foot of arrogance come upon me,
nor the hand of the wicked drive me away.
12 There the evildoers lie prostrate,
they are thrust down, unable to rise.

Ant. 1 O God, in Thy light do we see light.
Ant. 2 O Lord, Thou art great and glorious, wonderful in strength.

Canticle Judith 16:2–3A, 13–15

2 Begin a song to my God with tambourines,
sing to my Lord with cymbals.
Raise to him a new psalm;
exalt him, and call upon his name.
3 For God is the Lord who crushes wars;
for he has delivered me out of the hands of my pursuers,
and brought me into his camp, in the midst of the people.

13 I will sing to my God a new song:
O Lord, thou art great and glorious, wonderful in strength, invincible.
14 Let all thy creatures serve thee,
for thou didst speak, and they were made.
Thou didst send forth thy Spirit, and it formed them;
there is none that can resist thy voice.
15 For the mountains shall be shaken to their foundations with the waters;
at thy presence the rocks shall melt like wax,
but to those who fear thee
thou wilt continue to show mercy.

Ant. Dómine, magnus es tu, et præclárus in virtúte tua.

Ant. 3 Iubiláte Deo in voce exsultatiónis.

Psalmus 46 (47)

2 Omnes gentes, pláudite mánibus, *
iubiláte Deo in voce exsultatiónis,
3 quóniam Dóminus Altíssimus, terríbilis, *
rex magnus super omnem terram.
4 Subiécit pópulos nobis *
et gentes sub pédibus nostris.
5 Elégit nobis hereditátem nostram, *
glóriam Iacob, quem diléxit.
6 Ascéndit Deus in iúbilo, *
et Dóminus in voce tubæ.

7 Psállite Deo, psállite; *
psállite regi nostro, psállite.
8 Quóniam rex omnis terræ Deus, *
psállite sapiénter.

9 Regnávit Deus super gentes, *
Deus sedet super sedem sanctam suam.
10 Príncipes populórum congregáti sunt *
cum pópulo Dei Abraham,
quóniam Dei sunt scuta terræ: *
veheménter elevátus est.

Ant. Iubiláte Deo in voce exsultatiónis.

LECTIO BREVIS — TOB 4, 14–15A. 16AB. 19

Atténde tibi, fili, in ómnibus opéribus tuis et esto sápiens in ómnibus sermónibus tuis et, quod óderis,

Ant. 2 Lord, Thou art great and glorious, wonderful in strength.
Ant. 3 With hymns of praise shout to God with loud songs of joy!

Psalm 47

1 Clap your hands, all peoples!
Shout to God with loud songs of joy!
2 For the LORD, the Most High, is terrible,
a great king over all the earth.
3 He subdued peoples under us,
and nations under our feet.
4 He chose our heritage for us,
the pride of Jacob whom he loves.

5 God has gone up with a shout,
the LORD with the sound of a trumpet.
6 Sing praises to God, sing praises!
Sing praises to our King, sing praises!
7 For God is the king of all the earth;
sing praises with a psalm!

8 God reigns over the nations;
God sits on his holy throne.
9 The princes of the peoples gather as the people of
the God of Abraham.
For the shields of the earth belong to God;
he is highly exalted!

Ant. 3 With hymns of praise shout to God with loud songs of joy!

SHORT READING Tobit 4:14, 16a, 19a
"Watch yourself, my son, in everything you do, and be disciplined in all your conduct. And what you hate, do

némini féceris. De pane tuo commúnica esuriénti et de vestiméntis tuis nudis; ex ómnibus, quæcúmque tibi abundáverint, fac eleemósynam. Omni témpore bénedic Dóminum et póstula ab illo, ut dirigántur viæ tuæ et omnes sémitæ tuæ et consília bene disponántur.

RESPONSORIUM BREVE

℟. Inclína cor meum, Deus, * In testimónia tua. Inclína.

℣. In via tua vivífica me. * In testimónia tua. Glória Patri. Inclína.

Ad Benedictus, ant. Fac nobíscum misericórdiam, Dómine, et memoráre testaménti tui sancti.

PRECES

Grátias agámus Christo eúmque semper laudémus, quia non dedignátur fratres vocáre quos sanctíficat. Ideo ei supplicémus: *Sanctífica fratres tuos, Dómine.*

Fac ut huius diéi inítia in honórem resurrectiónis tuæ puris tibi córdibus consecrémus,
—et diem totum tibi gratum sanctificatiónis opéribus faciámus.

Qui diem amóris tui signum, ad salútem et lætítiam nobis renovásti,
—rénova nos cotídie ad glóriam tuam.

Doce nos hódie te in ómnibus præséntem agnóscere,
—teque in mæréntibus præsértim et paupéribus inveníre.

Da nos hódie cum ómnibus pacem habére,
—némini vero malum réddere pro malo.

Pater noster.

not do to anyone. Give of your bread to the hungry, and of your clothing to the naked. Give all your surplus to charity. Bless the Lord God on every occasion; ask him that your ways may be made straight and that all your paths and plans may prosper."

SHORT RESPONSORY

℟. Incline my heart according to Your will, O God.

℣. Give me life according to Your way.

Benedictus ant. Be merciful with us, O Lord, and remember Your holy covenant.

INTERCESSIONS

Let us give thanks to Christ and let us always praise Him, for He does not disdain to call brothers those whom He sanctifies. Therefore, let us beseech Him: *Sanctify Your brothers, Lord.*

Grant that the beginnings of this day be in honor of Your resurrection, that we may consecrate pure hearts to You,
—and by works of holiness, let us make the whole day pleasing to You.

You that have created anew the day as a sign of Your love for our salvation and joy,
—re-create us each day unto Your glory.

Teach us today to recognize You present in all things,
—and to discover You especially in those who mourn and the poor.

Grant us today to have peace with all,
—to return to no one evil for evil.

Our Father.

ORATIO

Exáudi nos, Deus, salutáris noster, et nos pérfice sectatóres lucis et operários veritátis, ut qui ex te nati sumus lucis fílii, tui testes coram homínibus esse valeámus. Per Dóminum.

ORATION

Hear us, O God, our Savior, and make us followers of light and workers of the truth, that we who through You have been born sons of light might be able to be Your witnesses before men. Through our Lord.

Hebdomada I

Feria IV, ad Vesperas

Hymnus

Cæli Deus sanctíssime,
qui lúcidum centrum poli
candóre pingis ígneo
augens decóri lúmina,

Quarto die qui flámmeam
solis rotam constítuens,
lunæ minístras órdini
vagos recúrsus síderum,

Ut nóctibus vel lúmini
diremptiónis términum,
primórdiis et ménsium
signum dares notíssimum:

Illúmina cor hóminum,
abstérge sordes méntium,
resólve culpæ vínculum,
evérte moles críminum.

Præsta, Pater piíssime,
Patríque compar Unice,
cum Spíritu Paráclito
regnans per omne sæculum. Amen.

Psalmodia

Ant. 1 Dóminus illuminátio mea et salus mea, quem timébo? †

Week I

Wednesday, Vespers

Hymn Trans. J. H. Newman

O Lord, who, thron'd in the holy height,
Through plains of ether didst diffuse
The dazzling beams of light,
In soft transparent hues;

Who didst, on the fourth day, in heaven
Light the fierce cresset of the sun,
And the meek moon at even,
And stars that wildly run;

That they might mark and arbitrate
'Twixt alternating night and day,
And tend the train sedate
Of months upon their way;

Clear, Lord, the brooding night within,
And clean these hearts for Thy abode,
Unlock the spell of sin,
Crumble its giant load.

Grant it, O Father, Only Son,
And Holy Spirit, God of Grace,
To whom all praise be done
In every time and place.

Psalmody

Ant. 1 The Lord is my light and my salvation; whom shall I fear? The Lord is the stronghold of my life; of whom shall I be afraid?

Psalmus 26 (27)

I

1 Dóminus illuminátio mea et salus mea, *
quem timébo?
† Dóminus protéctor vitæ meæ, *
a quo trepidábo?

2 Dum appropiant super me nocéntes, *
ut edant carnes meas;
qui tríbulant me et inimíci mei, *
ipsi infirmáti sunt et cecidérunt.

3 Si consístant advérsum me castra, *
non timébit cor meum;
si exsúrgat advérsum me prœlium, *
in hoc ego sperábo.

4 Unum pétii a Dómino, hoc requíram: *
ut inhábitem in domo Dómini ómnibus diébus
vitæ meæ,
ut vídeam voluptátem Dómini *
et vísitem templum eius.

5 Quóniam occultábit me in tentório suo, *
in die malórum.
Abscóndet me in abscóndito tabernáculi sui, *
in petra exaltábit me.
6 Et nunc exaltátur caput meum *
super inimícos meos in circúitu meo.
Immolábo in tabernáculo eius hóstias
vociferatiónis, *
cantábo et psalmum dicam Dómino.

Psalm 27

I

1 The LORD is my light and my salvation;
whom shall I fear?
The LORD is the stronghold of my life;
of whom shall I be afraid?

2 When evil doers assail me,
uttering slanders against me,
my adversaries and foes,
they shall stumble and fall.

3 Though a host encamp against me,
my heart shall not fear;
though war arise against me,
yet I will be confident.

4 One thing have I asked of the LORD,
that I will seek after;
that I may dwell in the house of the LORD
all the days of my life,
to behold the beauty of the LORD,
and to inquire in his temple.

5 For he will hide me in his shelter
in the day of trouble;
he will conceal me under the cover of his tent,
he will set me high upon a rock.

6 And now my head shall be lifted up
above my enemies round about me;
and I will offer in his tent
sacrifices with shouts of joy;
I will sing and make melody to the LORD.

Ant. Dóminus illuminátio mea et salus mea, quem timébo?
Ant. 2 Vultum tuum, Dómine, requíram: ne avértas fáciem tuam a me.

II

7 Exáudi, Dómine, vocem meam, qua clamávi, *
miserére mei et exáudi me.
8 De te dixit cor meum: †
« Exquírite fáciem meam! ». *
Fáciem tuam, Dómine, exquíram.

9 Ne avértas fáciem tuam a me, *
ne declínes in ira a servo tuo.
Adiútor meus es tu, ne me reícias, *
neque derelínquas me, Deus salútis meæ.
10 Quóniam pater meus et mater mea dereliquérunt me, *
Dóminus autem assúmpsit me.

11 Osténde mihi, Dómine, viam tuam *
et dírige me in sémitam rectam propter inimícos meos.

12 Ne tradíderis me in ánimam tribulántium me; †
quóniam insurrexérunt in me testes iníqui *
et qui violéntiam spirant.

13 Credo vidére bona Dómini *
in terra vivéntium.
14 Exspécta Dóminum, viríliter age, *
et confortétur cor tuum, et sústine Dóminum.

Ant. 1 The Lord is my light and my salvation; whom shall I fear? The Lord is the stronghold of my life; of whom shall I be afraid?
Ant. 2 Thy face, Lord, do I seek. Hide not Thy face from me.

II

7 Hear, O LORD, when I cry aloud,
be gracious to me and answer me!
8 Thou hast said, "Seek ye my face."
My heart says to thee,
"Thy face, LORD, do I seek."
9 Hide not thy face from me.

Turn not thy servant away in anger,
thou who hast been my help.
Cast me not off, forsake me not,
O God of my salvation!
10 For my father and my mother have forsaken me,
but the LORD will take me up.

11 Teach me thy way, O LORD;
and lead me on a level path
because of my enemies.
12 Give me not up to the will of my adversaries;
for false witnesses have risen against me,
and they breathe out violence.

13 I believe that I shall see the goodness of the LORD
in the land of the living!
14 Wait for the LORD;
be strong, and let your heart take courage;
yea, wait for the LORD!

Ant. Vultum tuum, Dómine, requíram: ne avértas fáciem tuam a me.

Ant. 3 Ipse primogénitus omnis creatúræ, in ómnibus primátum tenens.

Canticum CF. COL 1, 12–20

12 Grátias agámus Deo Patri, *
qui idóneos nos fecit in partem sortis sanctórum
in lúmine;
13 qui erípuit nos de potestáte tenebrárum *
et tránstulit in regnum Fílii dilectiónis suæ,
14 in quo habémus redemptiónem, *
remissiónem peccatórum;
15 qui est imágo Dei invisíbilis, *
primogénitus omnis creatúræ,
16 quia in ipso cóndita sunt univérsa †
in cælis et in terra, *
visibília et invisibília,
sive throni sive dominatiónes *
sive principátus sive potestátes.

Omnia per ipsum et in ipsum creáta sunt, †
17 et ipse est ante ómnia,
et ómnia in ipso constant.

18 Et ipse est caput córporis ecclésiæ; †
qui est princípium, primogénitus ex mórtuis, *
ut sit in ómnibus ipse primátum tenens,
19 quia in ipso complácuit
omnem plenitúdinem habitáre *
20 et per eum reconciliáre ómnia in ipsum,
pacíficans per sánguinem crucis eius, *
sive quæ in terris sive quæ in cælis sunt.

Ant. 2 Thy face, Lord, do I seek. Hide not Thy face from me.
Ant. 3 He is the first-born of all creation, that in everything He might be pre-eminent.

Canticle Colossians 1:12–20

12 Let us give thanks to the Father, who has qualified us to share in the inheritance of the saints in light.
13 He has delivered us from the dominion of darkness and transferred us to the kingdom of his beloved Son,
14 in whom we have redemption, the forgiveness of sins.
15 He is the image of the invisible God, of the first born of all creation;
16 for in him all things were created, in heaven and on earth, visible and invisible, whether thrones or dominions or principalities or authorities— all things were created through him and for him.
17 He is before all things, and in him all things hold together.
18 He is the head of the body, the church; he is the beginning, the firstborn from the dead, that in everything he might be pre-eminent.
19 For in him all the fulness of God was pleased to dwell.
20 and through him to reconcile to himself all things, whether on earth or in heaven, making peace by the blood of his cross.

Ant. Ipse primogénitus omnis creatúræ, in ómnibus primátum tenens.

LECTIO BREVIS — IAC 1, 22. 25

Estóte factóres verbi et non auditóres tantum falléntes vosmetípsos. Qui autem perspéxerit in lege perfécta libertátis et permánserit, non audítor obliviósus factus sed factor óperis, hic beátus in facto suo erit.

RESPONSORIUM BREVE

℟. Rédime me, Dómine, * Et miserére mei. Rédime.
℣. Ne perdas cum ímpiis ánimam meam. * Et miserére mei. Glória Patri. Rédime.

Ad Magnificat, ant. Fecit mihi magna qui potens est, et sanctum nomen eius.

PRECES

In ómnibus nomen Dómini glorificétur, qui pópulum electiónis suæ infiníto amóre proséquitur. Ad eum ergo hæc nostra orátio ascéndat: *Caritátem tuam, Dómine, demónstra.*

Recordáre, Dómine, Ecclésiæ tuæ,
—ut eam serves ab omni malo et in dilectióne tua perfícias.

Fac ut gentes agnóscant te solum esse Deum,
—et Iesum Christum Fílium tuum, quem misísti.

Próspera cuncta nostris concéde propínquis,
—tríbue illis benedictiónem et vitam usque in sǽculum.

Affer solácium ópere et labóre onerátis,
—dignitátem víndica despectórum.

Ant. 3 He is the first born of all creation, that in everything He might be pre-eminent.

SHORT READING James 1:22, 25

But be doers of the word, and not hearers only, deceiving yourselves. He who looks into the perfect law, the law of liberty, and perseveres, being no hearer that forgets but a doer that acts, he shall be blessed in his doing.

SHORT RESPONSORY

℟. Redeem me, O Lord, and have mercy on me.
℣. Do not abandon my soul to the wicked.

Magnificat ant. He Who is mighty has done great things for me, and holy is His name.

INTERCESSIONS

In all things let the name of the Lord be glorified, Who accompanies the people of His election in infinite love. To Him, then, let this our prayer ascend: *Your love, Lord, make manifest.*

Remember, Lord, Your Church,
—that You may save Her from all evil, and perfect Her in Your love.

Grant that the nations may recognize You as the one God,
—and Christ, Your Son, Whom You sent.

Grant prosperity to our neighbors,
—give them blessing and life eternal.

Bear consolation to those burdened with work and labor,
—protect the dignity of the lowly.

Exútis hódie córpore misericórdiæ tuæ portæ patéscant,
—eos in regnum tuum placátus admítte.

Pater noster.

ORATIO

Adésto, Dómine, précibus nostris, et die noctúque nos prótege, ut vícibus témporum tua gubernatióne subiécti, tua semper incommutabilitáte firmémur. Per Dóminum.

May Your gates of mercy open for those who have died today,
—be pleased to admit them into Your reign.

Our Father.

ORATION

Attend, O Lord, to our prayers, and day and night protect us, for as the changes of time are subject to Your direction, so may we be strengthened always by Your constancy. Through our Lord.

Hebdomada I

Feria V, ad Laudes matutinas

Hymnus

Sol ecce surgit ígneus:
piget, pudéscit, pǽnitet,
nec teste quisquam lúmine
peccáre constánter potest.

Tandem facéssat cǽcitas,
quae nosmet in praeceps diu
lapsos sinístris gréssibus
erróre traxit dévio.

Haec lux serénum cónferat
purósque nos præstet sibi;
nihil loquámur súbdolum,
volvámus obscúrum nihil.

Sic tota decúrrat dies,
ne lingua mendax, ne manus
oc*u*líve peccent lúbrici,
ne noxa corpus ínquinet.

Specu*l*átor astat désuper,
qui nos diébus ómnibus
actúsque nostros próspicit
a luce prim*a* in vésperum.

Deo Patri sit glória
eiúsque soli Fílio
cum Spíritu Paráclito,
in sempitérna sǽcula. Amen.

Week I

Thursday, Lauds

HYMN Trans. J. H. Newman

See, the fiery sun is glowing
While the paly shades are going,
Which have led us far and long,
In a labyrinth of wrong.

May it bring us peace serene;
May it cleanse, as it is clean;
Plain and clear our words be spoke,
And our thoughts without a cloak;

So the day's account shall stand.
Guileless tongue and holy hand,
Steadfast eyes and unbeguiled,
"Flesh as of a little child."

There is One who from above
Watches how the still hours move
Of our day of service done,
From the dawn to setting sun.

To the Father, and the Son,
And the Spirit, Three and One,
As of old, and as in Heaven,
Now and here be glory given.

PSALMODIA

Ant. 1 Exsúrge, psaltérium et cíthara: excitábo auróram.

Psalmus 56 (57)

2 Miserére mei, Deus, miserére mei, *
quóniam in te cónfugit ánima mea;
et in umbra alárum tuárum confúgiam, *
donec tránseant insídiæ.
3 Clamábo ad Deum Altíssimum, *
Deum, qui benefécit mihi.

4 Mittet de cælo et liberábit me; †
dabit in oppróbrium conculcántes me. *
Mittet Deus misericórdiam suam et veritátem suam.
5 Anima mea recúmbit in médio catulórum leónum *
devorántium fílios hóminum.
Dentes eórum arma et sagíttæ *
et lingua eórum gládius acútus.

6 Exaltáre super cælos, Deus, *
super omnem terram glória tua.

7 Láqueum paravérunt pédibus meis, *
et incurvávit se ánima mea;
fodérunt ante fáciem meam fóveam, *
et ipsi incidérunt in eam.

8 Parátum cor meum, Deus, †
parátum cor meum; *
9 cantábo et psalmum dicam.

PSALMODY

Ant. 1 Awake, O harp and lyre! I will awake the dawn!

Psalm 57

1 Be merciful to me, O God, be merciful to me,
for in thee my soul takes refuge;
in the shadow of thy wings I will take refuge,
till the storms of destruction pass by.
2 I cry to God Most High,
to God who fulfils his purpose for me.
3 He will send from heaven and save me,
he will put to shame those who trample upon me.
God will send forth his steadfast love and his faithfulness!

4 I lie in the midst of lions
that greedily devour the sons of men;
their teeth are spears and arrows,
their tongues sharp swords.

5 Be exalted, O God, above the heavens!
Let thy glory be over all the earth!

6 They set a net for my steps;
my soul was bowed down.
They dug a pit in my way,
but they have fallen into it themselves.

7 My heart is steadfast, O God,
my heart is steadfast!
I will sing and make melody!

Exsúrge, glória mea, †
exsúrge, psaltérium et cíthara, *
excitábo auróram.
10 Confitébor tibi in pópulis, Dómine, *
et psalmum dicam tibi in natiónibus,
11 quóniam magnificáta est usque ad cælos
misericórdia tua *
et usque ad nubes véritas tua.
12 Exaltáre super cælos, Deus, *
super omnem terram glória tua.

Ant. Exsúrge, psaltérium et cíthara: excitábo auróram.
Ant. 2 Pópulus meus, ait Dóminus, bonis meis adimplébitur.

Canticum Ier 31, 10–14

10 Audíte verbum Dómini, gentes, *
et annuntiáte in ínsulis, quæ procul sunt, et dícite:
Qui dispérsit Israel, congregábit eum *
et custódiet eum sicut pastor gregem suum.

11 Redémit enim Dóminus Iacob *
et liberávit eum de manu potentióris.
12 Et vénient et laudábunt in monte Sion *
et cónfluent ad bona Dómini,
super fruménto et vino et óleo *
et fetu pécorum et armentórum;
erítque ánima eórum quasi hortus irríguus, *
et ultra non esúrient.

8 Awake, my soul!
Awake, O harp and lyre!
I will awake the dawn!
9 I will give thanks to thee, O Lord, among the peoples;
I will sing praises to thee among the nations.
10 For thy steadfast love is great to the heavens,
thy faithfulness to the clouds.

11 Be exalted, O God, above the heavens!
Let thy glory be over all the earth!

Ant. 1 Awake, O harp and lyre! I will awake the dawn!
Ant. 2 My people, says the Lord, shall be satisfied with My goodness.

Canticle Jeremiah 31:10–14

10 "Hear the word of the LORD, O nations,
and declare it in the coastlands afar off;
say, 'He who scattered Israel will gather him,
and will keep him as a shepherd keeps his flock.'
11 For the LORD has ransomed Jacob,
and has redeemed him from hands too strong for him.
12 They shall come and sing aloud on the height of Zion,
and they shall be radiant over the goodness of the Lord,
over the grain, the wine, and the oil,
and over the young of the flock and the herd;
their life shall be like a watered garden,
and they shall languish no more.

13 Tunc lætábitur virgo in choro, *
iúvenes et senes simul.
Et convértam luctum eórum in gáudium *
et consolábor eos et lætificábo a dolóre suo.
14 Et inebriábo ánimam sacerdótum pinguédine, *
et pópulus meus bonis meis adimplébitur.

Ant. Pópulus meus, ait Dóminus, bonis meis adimplébitur.

Ant. 3 Magnus Dóminus et laudábilis nimis, in civitáte Dei nostri. †

Psalmus 47 (48)

2 Magnus Dóminus et laudábilis nimis *
in civitáte Dei nostri.
3 † Mons sanctus eius collis speciósus, *
exsultátio univérsæ terræ.
Mons Sion, extréma acquilónis, *
cívitas regis magni.
4 Deus in dómibus eius notus *
factus est ut refúgium.

5 Quóniam ecce reges congregáti sunt, *
convenérunt in unum.
6 Ipsi cum vidérunt, sic admiráti sunt, *
conturbáti sunt, diffugérunt;
7 illic tremor apprehéndit eos, *
dolóres ut parturiéntis.
8 In spíritu oriéntis *
cónteres naves Tharsis.

13 Then shall the maidens rejoice in the dance,
and the young men and the old shall be merry.
I will turn their mourning into joy,
I will comfort them, and give them gladness for sorrow.
14 I will feast the soul of the priests with abundance,
and my people shall be satisfied with my goodness, says the LORD."

Ant. 2 My people, says the Lord, shall be satisfied with My goodness.
Ant. 3 Great is the Lord and greatly to be praised in the city of our God!

Psalm 48

1 Great is the LORD and greatly to be praised
in the city of our God!
His holy mountain, 2 beautiful in elevation,
is the joy of all the earth,
Mount Zion, in the far north,
the city of the great King.
3 Within her citadels God
has shown himself a sure defense.

4 For lo, the kings assembled,
they came on together.
5 As soon as they saw it, they were astounded,
they were in panic, they took to flight;
6 trembling took hold of them there,
anguish as of a woman in travail.
7 By the east wind thou didst shatter the ships of Tarshish.

9 Sicut audívimus, sic vídimus in civitáte Dómini
virtútum, †
in civitáte Dei nostri; *
Deus fundávit eam in ætérnum.
10 Recogitámus, Deus, misericórdiam tuam *
in médio templi tui.
11 Secúndum nomen tuum, Deus, †
sic et laus tua in fines terræ; *
iustítia plena est déxtera tua.
12 Lætétur mons Sion, †
et exsúltent fíliæ Iudæ *
propter iudícia tua.

13 Circúmdate Sion et complectímini eam, *
numeráte turres eius.
14 Pónite corda vestra in virtúte eius †
et percúrrite domos eius, *
ut enarrétis in progénie áltera.
15 Quóniam hic est Deus, Deus noster †
in ætérnum et in sæculum sæculi; *
ipse ducet nos in sæcula.

Ant. Magnus Dóminus et laudábilis nimis, in civitáte Dei nostri.

LECTIO BREVIS Is 66, 1–2

Hæc dicit Dóminus: Cælum thronus meus, terra autem scabéllum pedum meórum. Quæ ista domus, quam ædificábitis mihi, et quis iste locus quiétis meae? Omnia haec manus mea fecit et mea sunt univérsa ista, dicit Dóminus. Ad hunc autem respíciam, ad paupérculum et contrítum spíritu et treméntem sermónes meos.

8 As we have heard, so have we seen in the city of
the Lord of hosts,
in the city of our God,
which God establishes for ever.

9 We have thought on thy steadfast love, O God,
in the midst of thy temple.
10 As thy name, O God,
so thy praise reaches to the end of the earth.
Thy right hand is filled with victory;
11 Let Mount Zion be glad!
Let the daughters of Judah rejoice
because of thy judgments!

12 Walk about Zion, go round about her,
number her towers,
13 consider well her ramparts,
go through her citadels;
that you may tell the next generation
14 that this is God,
our God for ever and ever.
He will be our guide for ever.

Ant. 3 Great is the Lord and greatly to be praised in the city of our God!

SHORT READING Isaiah 66:1–2

Thus says the Lord:

"Heaven is my throne and the earth is my footstool; what is the house which you would build for me, and what is the place of my rest? All these things my hand has made, and so all these things are mine, says the Lord. But this is the man to whom I will look, he that is humble and contrite in spirit, and trembles at my word."

RESPONSORIUM BREVE

℟. Clamávi in toto corde meo: * Exáudi me, Dómine. Clamávi.
℣. Iustificatiónes tuas servábo. * Exáudi me, Dómine. Glória Patri. Clamávi.

Ad Benedictus, ant. In sanctitáte serviámus Dómino, et liberábit nos ab inimícis nostris.

PRECES

Grátias agámus Christo, qui lumen huius diéi nobis concédit, et ad eum clamémus: *Bénedic et sanctífica nos, Dómine.*
Qui te pro peccátis nostris hóstiam obtulísti,
—incépta et propósita suscípias hodiérna.
Qui óculos nostros lucis dono lætíficas novæ,
—lúcifer oriáris in córdibus nostris.
Tríbue hódie nos esse ómnibus longánimes,
—ut imitatóres tui fíeri possímus.
Audítam, Dómine, fac nobis mane misericórdiam tuam.
—Sit hódie gáudium tuum fortitúdo nostra.

Pater noster.

ORATIO

Omnípotens sempitérne Deus, véspere, mane et merídie maiestátem tuam supplíciter deprecámur, ut, expúlsis de córdibus nostris peccatórum ténebris, ad veram lucem, quæ Christus est, nos fácias perveníre. Qui tecum vivit.

Short Responsory

℟. From the depths of my heart have I cried to you; hear me, O Lord.
℣. Your righteous decrees I shall keep.

Benedictus ant. May we serve the Lord in holiness, and He will deliver us from our enemies.

Intercessions

Let us give thanks to Christ, Who grants us the light of this day, and to Him let us call: *Bless and sanctify us, Lord.*
You have offered Yourself as a sacrifice for our sins,
—may You accept the beginnings and intentions of this day.
You delight our eyes with the gift of new light,
—may You rise as the morning star in our hearts.
Allow us today to be patient with everyone,
—that we may be able to imitate Your actions.
O Lord, at the beginning of this day, make known Your mercy to us.
—May Your joy be our strength this day.

Our Father.

Oration

All-powerful and ever-living God, at evening, at morning and at the middle of the day we humbly beseech Your majesty, that, once the darkness of our sins has been driven from our hearts, You might cause us to arrive at the true light, Who is Christ. Who lives.

Hebdomada I

Feria V, ad Vesperas

HYMNUS

Magnæ Deus poténtiæ,
qui ex aquis ortum genus
partim remíttis gúrgiti,
partim levas in áera,

Demérsa lymphis ímprimens,
subvécta cælis írrogans,
ut, stirpe una pródita,
divérsa répleant loca:

Largíre cunctis sérvulis,
quos mundat unda sánguinis,
nescíre lapsus críminum
nec ferre mortis tædium,

Ut culpa nullam déprimat,
nullum levet iactántia,
elisa mens ne cóncidat,
eláta mens ne córruat.

Præsta, Pater piísime,
Patríque compar Unice,
cum Spíritu Paráclito
regnans per omne sæculum. Amen.

PSALMODIA

Ant. 1 Clamávi ad te, et sanásti me, Dómine; in ætérnum confitébor tibi.

Week I

Thursday, Vespers

HYMN Trans. J. H. Newman

O God, who hast given
the sea and the sky,
To fish and to bird
for dwelling to keep,
Both sons of the waters,
one low and one high,
Ambitious of heaven,
yet sunk in the deep;

Save, Lord, Thy servants,
whom Thou hast new made
In a laver of blood,
lest they trespass and die;
Lest pride should elate,
or the flesh should degrade,
And they stumble on earth,
or be dizzied on high.

To the Father and the Son
And the Spirit be done,
Now and always,
Glory and praise.

PSALMODY

Ant. 1 O Lord, I cried to Thee for help, and Thou hast healed me; I will give thanks to Thee forever.

Psalmus 29 (30)

2 Exaltábo te, Dómine, quóniam extraxísti me, *
nec delectásti inimícos meos super me.
3 Dómine Deus meus, clamávi ad te, *
et sanásti me.
4 Dómine, eduxísti ab inférno ánimam meam, *
vivificásti me, ut non descénderem in lacum.

5 Psállite Dómino, sancti eius, *
et confitémini memóriæ sanctitátis eius,
6 quóniam ad moméntum indignátio eius *
et per vitam volúntas eius.
Ad vésperum demorátur fletus, *
ad matutínum lætítia.

7 Ego autem dixi in securitáte mea: *
« Non movébor in ætérnum ».
8 Dómine, in voluntáte tua *
præstitísti decóri meo virtútem;
avertísti fáciem tuam a me, *
et factus sum conturbátus.
9 Ad te Dómine, clamábam *
et ad Deum meum deprecábar.

10 Quæ utílitas in sánguine meo, *
dum descéndo in corruptiónem?
Numquid confitébitur tibi pulvis *
aut annuntiábit veritátem tuam?

11 Audívit Dóminus et misértus est mei, *
Dóminus factus est adiútor meus.

Psalm 30

1 I will extol thee, O LORD, for thou hast drawn me up,
and hast not let my foes rejoice over me.
2 O LORD my God, I cried to thee for help,
and thou hast healed me.
3 O LORD, thou hast brought up my soul from Sheol,
restored me to life from among those gone down to the Pit.

4 Sing praises to the LORD, O you his saints,
and give thanks to his holy name.
5 For his anger is but for a moment,
and his favor is for a lifetime.
Weeping may tarry for the night,
but joy comes with the morning.

6 As for me, I said in my prosperity,
"I shall never be moved."
7 By thy favor, O LORD,
thou hadst established me as a strong mountain;
thou didst hide thy face,
I was dismayed.

8 To thee, O LORD, I cried;
and to the Lord I made supplication:
9 "What profit is there in my death,
if I go down to the Pit?
Will the dust praise thee?
Will it tell of thy faithfulness?
10 Hear O LORD and be gracious to me!
O LORD, be thou my helper!"

12 Convertísti planctum meum in choros mihi, *
conscidísti saccum meum et accinxísti me
lætítia,
13 ut cantet tibi glória mea et non táceat. *
Dómine Deus meus, in ætérnum confitébor tibi.

Ant. Clamávi ad te, et sanásti me, Dómine; in ætérnum confitébor tibi.
Ant. 2 Beátus vir cui non imputávit Dóminus peccátum.

Psalmus 31 (32)

1 Beátus, cui remíssa est iníquitas *
et obtéctum est peccátum.
2 Beátus vir, cui non imputávit Dóminus
delíctum, *
nec est in spíritu eius dolus.

3 Quóniam tácui, inveteravérunt ossa mea, *
dum rugírem tota die.
4 Quóniam die ac nocte graváta est super me manus
tua, *
immutátus est vigor meus in ardóribus æstátis.

5 Peccátum meum cógnitum tibi feci *
et delíctum meum non abscóndi.
Dixi: « Confitébor advérsum me iniquitátem
meam Dómino ». *
Et tu remisísti impietátem peccáti mei.

11 Thou hast turned for me my mourning into
dancing;
thou hast loosed my sackcloth
and girded me with gladness,
12 that my soul may praise thee and not be silent.
O LORD my God, I will give thanks to thee for
ever.

Ant. 1 O Lord, I cried to Thee for help, and Thou hast healed me; I will give thanks to Thee forever.
Ant. 2 Blessed is the man to whom the LORD imputes no iniquity and in whose spirit there is no deceit.

Psalm 32

1 Blessed is he whose transgression is forgiven,
whose sin is covered.
2 Blessed is the man to whom the LORD imputes no
iniquity,
and in whose spirit there is no deceit.

3 When I declared not my sin, my body wasted
away
through my groaning all day long.
4 For day and night thy hand was heavy upon me;
my strength was dried up as by heat of the
summer.

5 I acknowledged my sin to thee,
and I did not hide my iniquity;
I said, "I will confess my transgressions to the
LORD";
then thou didst forgive the guilt of my sin.

6 Propter hoc orábit ad te omnis sanctus *
in témpore opportúno.
Et in dilúvio aquárum multárum *
ad eum non approximábunt.
7 Tu es refúgium meum, a tribulatióne conservábis me; *
exsultatiónibus salútis circúmdabit me.

8 Intelléctum tibi dabo et ínstruam te in via, qua gradiéris; *
firmábo super te óculos meos.
9 Nolíte fíeri sicut equus et mulus, *
quibus non est intelléctus;
in camo et freno si accédis ad constringéndum, *
non appróximant ad te.

10 Multi dolóres ímpii, *
sperántem autem in Dómino misericórdia circúmdabit.
11 Lætámini in Dómino et exsultáte, iusti, *
et gloriámini, omnes recti corde.

Ant. Beátus vir cui non imputávit Dóminus peccátum.
Ant. 3 Dedit ei Dóminus potestátem et honórem et regnum, et omnes pópuli ipsi sérvient.

Canticum Ap 11, 17–18; 12, 10b–12a

11,17 Grátias ágimus tibi, *
Dómine Deus omnípotens, qui es et qui eras, *
quia accepísti virtútem tuam magnam et regnásti.
18 Et irátæ sunt gentes, *
et advénit ira tua, et tempus mortuórum iudicári,

6 Therefore let every one who is godly offer prayer
to thee;
at a time of distress, in the rush of great waters,
they shall not reach him.
7 Thou art a hiding place for me, thou preservest
me from trouble;
thou dost encompass me with deliverance.

8 I will instruct you and teach you the way you
should go;
I will counsel you with my eye upon you.
9 Be not like a horse or a mule, without
understanding,
which must be curbed with bit and bridle,
else it will not keep with you.
10 Many are the pangs of the wicked;
but steadfast love surrounds him who trusts in
the LORD.
11 Be glad in the LORD, and rejoice, O righteous,
and shout for joy, all you upright in heart!

Ant. 2 Blessed is the man to whom the Lord imputes no iniquity, and in whose spirit there is no deceit.
Ant. 3 The Lord has given Him power, honor, and kingship; all people will serve Him.

Canticle

Revelation 11:17–18; 12:10b–12a

17 "We give thanks to thee, Lord God Almighty, who
art and who wast,
that thou hast taken thy great power and begun
to reign.
18 The nations raged, but thy wrath came,
and the time for the dead to be judged,

et réddere mercédem servis tuis prophétis et
sanctis *
et timéntibus nomen tuum, pusíllis et magnis.

12,10 Nunc facta est salus et virtus et regnum Dei
nostri *
et potéstas Christi eius,
quia proiéctus est accusátor fratrum nostrórum, *
qui accusábat illos ante conspéctum Dei nostri
die ac nocte.

11 Et ipsi vicérunt illum propter sánguinem Agni *
et propter verbum testimónii sui;
et non dilexérunt ánimam suam *
usque ad mortem.
12 Proptérea lætámini, cæli *
et qui habitátis in eis.

Ant. Dedit ei Dóminus potestátem et honórem et regnum, et omnes pópuli ipsi sérvient.

LECTIO BREVIS I PETR I, 6–9

Exsultátis, módicum nunc si opórtet contristáti in váriis tentatiónibus, ut probátio vestræ fídei pretiósior auro, quod perit, per ignem quidem probáto, inveniátur in laudem et glóriam et honórem in revelatióne Iesu Christi. Quem cum non vidéritis dilígitis, in quem nunc non vidéntes, credéntes autem, exsultátis lætítia inenarrábili et glorificáta, reportántes finem fídei vestræ salútem animárum.

for rewarding thy servants, the prophets and saints,
and those who fear thy name, both small and great,
and for destroying the destroyers of the earth."

10 "Now the salvation and the power and the kingdom of our God and the authority of his Christ have come,
for the accuser of our brethren has been thrown down, who accuses them day and night before our God.
11 And they have conquered him by the blood of the Lamb and by the word of their testimony, for they loved not their lives even unto death.
12 Rejoice then, O heaven and you that dwell therein!

Ant. 3 The Lord has given Him power, honor, and kingship; all people will serve Him.

SHORT READING

1 Peter 1:6–9

In this you rejoice, though now for a little while you may have to suffer various trials, so that the genuineness of your faith, more precious than gold which though perishable is tested by fire, may redound to praise and glory and honor at the revelation of Jesus Christ. Without having seen him you love him; though you do not now see him you believe in him and rejoice with unutterable and exalted joy. As the outcome of your faith you obtain the salvation of your souls.

RESPONSORIUM BREVE

℟. Cibávit nos Dóminus * Ex ádipe fruménti. Cibávit.

℣. Et de petra melle saturávit nos. * Ex ádipe fruménti. Glória Patri. Cibávit.

Ad Magnificat, ant. Depósuit Dóminus poténtes de sede, et exaltávit húmiles.

PRECES

Laudémus Deum auxílii nostri, in quo nostra spes tota résidet, eúmque invocémus devóte clamántes: *Réspice fílios tuos, Dómine.*

Dómine Deus noster, qui cum pópulo tuo fœdus ætérnum pepigísti,
—fac ut semper tua magnália recolámus.

Univérsum órdinem sacerdotálem in tua pérfice caritáte.
—et fidéles tuos in unitáte spíritus per vínculum pacis semper consérva.

Civitátem terrénam fac ut semper tecum exstruámus,
—ne forte in vanum labórent qui ædíficant eam.

Mitte operários in messem tuam,
—ut magnificétur nomen tuum in géntibus.

Propínquos et benefactóres defúnctos sanctis tuis accénse.
—et nos beátis aliquándo consócia.

Pater noster.

ORATIO

Deus, qui illúminas noctem et lumen facis post ténebras radiáre, concéde nobis, ut hanc noctem sine

Short Responsory

℟. The Lord has fed us with the finest wheat.
℣. And with honey from the rock has He filled us.

Magnificat ant. The Lord has put down the mighty from their thrones, and exalted those of low degree.

Intercessions

Let us praise the God of our help, in Whom all our hope resides, and let us invoke Him devoutly, crying out: *Look upon Your sons, Lord.*

Lord our God, Who made an eternal covenant with Your people,
—grant that we may always remember Your might.

Perfect in Your love the whole priestly order,
—and preserve always Your faithful in the unity of spirit through the bond of peace.

Grant that with You we may always build the earthly city;
—lest they work in vain who build it.

Send workers into Your vineyard,
—that Your name might be glorified among the nations.

Add to Your saints our deceased relatives and benefactors,
—and unite us, finally, to the blessed.

Our Father.

Oration

O God, Who illuminate the night and make light to radiate after the darkness, grant us that we may pass

impediménto Sátanæ transeámus, atque matutínis horis ante conspéctum tuum tibi grátias referámus. Per Dóminum.

this night without the hindrance of Satan, as well as to return to the morning hour praising You in Your sight. Through our Lord.

Hebdomada I

Feria VI, ad Laudes matutinas

HYMNUS

Ætérna cæli glória,
beáta spes mortálium,
celsi Paréntis Unice
castǽque proles Vírginis,

Da déxteram surgéntibus,
exsúrgat et mens sóbria
flagrans et in laudem Dei
grates repéndat débitas.

Ortus refúlget lúcifer
ipsámque lucem núntiat,
cadit calígo nóctium,
lux sancta nos illúminet,

Manésque nostris sénsibus
noctem repéllat sǽculi
omníque fine témporis
purgáta servet péctora.

Quæsíta iam primum fides
radícet altis sénsibus,
secúnda spes congáudeat;
tunc maior exstat cáritas.

Sit, Christe, rex piísime,
tibi Patríque glória
cum Spíritu Paráclito,
in sempitérna sǽcula. Amen.

Week I

Friday, Lauds

HYMN — Trans. J. H. Newman

Glory of the eternal Heaven,
Blessed hope to mortals given,
Of the Almighty Only Son,
And the Virgin's Holy One;
Raise us, Lord, and we shall rise
　　In a sober mood,
And a zeal, which glorifies
　　Thee from gratitude.

Now the day-star, keenly glancing,
Tells us of the Sun's advancing;
While the unhealthy shades decline,
Rise within us, Light Divine!
Rise, and, risen, go not hence,
　　Stay, and make us bright,
Streaming through each cleansèd sense,
　　On the outward night.

Then the foot of faith shall spread
In the heart new fashionèd;
Gladsome hope shall spring above,
And shall bear the fruit of love.
To the Father, and the Son.
　　And the Holy Ghost,
Here be glory, as is done
　　By the angelic host.

PSALMODIA

Ant. 1 Acceptábis sacrifícium iustítiæ super altáre tuum, Dómine.

Psalmus 50 (51)

3 Miserére mei, Deus, *
secúndum misericórdiam tuam;
et secúndum multitúdinem miseratiónum tuárum *
dele iniquitátem meam.
4 Amplius lava me ab iniquitáte mea *
et a peccáto meo munda me.

5 Quóniam iniquitátem meam ego cognósco, *
et peccátum meum contra me est semper.

6 Tibi, tibi soli peccávi *
et malum coram te feci,
ut iustus inveniáris in senténtia tua *
et æquus in iudício tuo.

7 Ecce enim in iniquitáte generátus sum, *
et in peccáto concépit me mater mea.
8 Ecce enim veritátem in corde dilexísti *
et in occúlto sapiéntiam manifestásti mihi.

9 Aspérges me hyssópo, et mundábor; *
lavábis me, et super nivem dealbábor.
10 Audíre me fácies gáudium et lætítiam, *
et exsultábunt ossa, quæ contrivísti.

11 Avérte fáciem tuam a peccátis meis *
et omnes iniquitátes meas dele.
12 Cor mundum crea in me, Deus, *
et spíritum firmum ínnova in viscéribus meis.

PSALMODY

Ant. 1 Thou wilt delight in right sacrifices on Thy altar, O Lord.

Psalm 51

1 Have mercy on me, O God,
according to thy steadfast love;
according to thy abundant mercy blot out my transgressions.
2 Wash me thoroughly from my iniquity,
and cleanse me from my sin!

3 For I know my transgressions,
and my sin is ever before me.
4 Against thee, thee only, have I sinned,
and done that which is evil in thy sight,
so that thou art justified in thy sentence
and blameless in thy judgment.
5 Behold, I was brought forth in iniquity,
and in sin did my mother conceive me.

6 Behold, thou desirest truth in the inward being;
therefore teach me wisdom in my secret heart.
7 Purge me with hyssop, and I shall be clean;
wash me, and I shall be whiter than snow.
8 Fill me with joy and gladness;
let the bones which thou hast broken rejoice.
9 Hide thy face from my sins,
and blot out all my iniquities.

10 Create in me a clean heart, O God,
and put a new and right spirit within me.

13 Ne proícias me a fácie tua *
et spíritum sanctum tuum ne áuferas a me.
14 Redde mihi lætítiam salutáris tui *
et spíritu promptíssimo confírma me.

15 Docébo iníquos vias tuas, *
et ímpii ad te convertént ur.
16 Líbera me de sanguínibus, Deus, Deus salútis meæ, *
et exsultábit lingua mea iustítiam tuam.

17 Dómine, lábia mea apéries, *
et os meum annuntiábit laudem tuam.
18 Non enim sacrifício delectáris, *
holocáustum, si ófferam, non placébit.
19 Sacrifícium Deo spíritus contribulátus, *
cor contrítum et humiliátum, Deus, non despícies.

20 Benígne fac, Dómine, in bona voluntáte tua Sion, *
ut ædificéntur muri Ierúsalem.
21 Tunc acceptábis sacrifícium iustítiæ, oblatiónes et holocáusta; *
tunc impónent super altáre tuum vítulos.

Ant. Acceptábis sacrifícium iustítiæ super altáre tuum, Dómine.

Ant. 2 In Dómino iustificábitur et laudábitur omne semen Israel.

11 Cast me not away from thy presence,
and take not thy holy Spirit from me.
12 Restore to me the joy of thy salvation,
and uphold me with a willing spirit.

13 Then I will teach transgressors thy ways.
And sinners will return to thee.
14 Deliver me from bloodguiltiness, O God,
thou God of my salvation,
and my tongue will sing aloud of thy
deliverance.

15 O Lord, open thou my lips,
and my mouth shall show forth thy praise.
16 For thou hast no delight in sacrifice;
were I to give a burnt offering, thou wouldst not
be pleased.
17 The sacrifice acceptable to God is a broken spirit;
a broken and contrite heart, O God, thou wilt
not despise.

18 Do good to Zion in thy good pleasure;
rebuild the walls of Jerusalem,
19 then wilt thou delight in right sacrifices,
in burnt offerings and whole burnt offerings;
then bulls will be offered on thy altar.

Ant. 1 Thou wilt delight in right sacrifices on Thy altar, O Lord.
Ant. 2 In the Lord all the offspring of Israel shall triumph and glory.

Canticum Is 45, 15–25

15 Vere tu es Deus abscónditus, *
Deus Israel salvátor.

16 Confúsi sunt et erubuérunt omnes, *
simul abiérunt in confusiónem fabricatóres idolórum.
17 Israel salvátus est in Dómino salúte ætérna; *
non confundémini et non erubescétis usque in sǽculum sǽculi.

18 Quia hæc dicit Dóminus, †
qui creávit cælos, ipse Deus, *
qui formávit terram et fecit eam, ipse fundávit eam;
non ut vácua esset, creávit eam, †
ut habitarétur, formávit eam: *
« Ego Dóminus, et non est álius.

19 Non in abscóndito locútus sum, *
in loco terræ tenebróso;
non dixi sémini Iacob: "Frustra quǽrite me". *
Ego Dóminus loquens iustítiam, annúntians recta.

20 Congregámini et veníte et accédite simul, *
qui salváti estis ex géntibus.
Nesciérunt, qui levant lignum sculptúræ suæ *
et rogant deum non salvántem.

Canticle Isaiah 45:15–25

15 Truly, thou art a God who hidest thyself,
O God of Israel, the Savior.
16 All of them are put to shame and confounded,
the makers of idols go in confusion together.
17 But Israel is saved by the LORD with everlasting
salvation;
you shall not be put to shame or confounded
to all eternity.

18 For thus says the LORD,
who created the heavens
(he is God!),
who formed the earth and made it
(he established it;
he did not create it a chaos,
he formed it to be inhabited!):
"I am the LORD, and there is no other.
19 I did not speak in secret,
in a land of darkness;
I did not say to the offspring of Jacob,
'Seek me in chaos.'
I the LORD speak the truth,
I declare what is right.

20 "Assemble yourselves and come,
draw near together,
you survivors of the nations!
They have no knowledge
who carry about their wooden idols,
and keep on praying to a god
that cannot save.

21 Annuntiáte et veníte et consiliámini simul. *
Quis audítum fecit hoc ab inítio, ex tunc prædixit illud?
Numquid non ego Dóminus, †
et non est ultra Deus absque me? *
Deus iustus et salvans non est præter me.

22 Convertímini ad me et salvi éritis, omnes fines terræ, *
quia ego Deus, et non est álius.

23 In memetípso iurávi: †
Egréssa est de ore meo iustítia, *
verbum, quod non revertétur;
quia mihi curvábitur omne genu, *
et iurábit omnis lingua ».
24 « Tantum in Dómino » dicent *
« sunt iustítiæ et robur! ».
Ad eum vénient et confundéntur †
omnes, qui repúgnant ei: *
25 in Dómino iustificábitur et laudábitur omne semen Israel.

Ant. In Dómino iustificábitur et laudábitur omne semen Israel.

Ant. 3 Introíte in conspéctu Dómini in exsultatióne.

Psalmus 99 (100)

2 Iubiláte Dómino, omnis terra, *
servíte Dómino in lætítia;
introíte in conspéctu eius *
in exsultatióne.

21 Declare and present your case;
let them take counsel together!
Who told this long ago?
Who declared it of old?
Was it not I, the LORD?
And there is no other god besides me,
a righteous God and a Savior;
there is none besides me.

22 "Turn to me and be saved,
all the ends of the earth!
For I am God and there is no other.
23 By myself I have sworn,
from my mouth has gone forth in righteousness
a word that shall not return:
'To me every knee shall bow,
every tongue shall swear.'

24 "Only in the LORD, it shall be said of me,
are righteousness and strength;
to him shall come and be ashamed,
all who were incensed against him.
25 In the LORD all the offspring of Israel
shall triumph and glory."

Ant. 2 In the Lord all the offspring of Israel shall triumph and glory.
Ant. 3 Come into His presence with singing.

Psalm 100

1 Make a joyful noise to the LORD, all you lands!
2 Serve the LORD with gladness!
Come into his presence with singing!

3 Scitóte quóniam Dóminus ipse est Deus; †
ipse fecit nos, et ipsíus sumus, *
pópulus eius et oves páscuæ eius.

4 Introíte portas eius in confessióne, †
átria eius in hymnis, *
confitémini illi, benedícite nómini eius.
5 Quóniam suávis est Dóminus; †
in ætérnum misericórdia eius, *
et usque in generatiónem et generatiónem
véritas eius.

Ant. Introíte in conspéctu Dómini in exsultatióne.

LECTIO BREVIS — EPH 4, 29–32

Omnis sermo malus ex ore vestro non procédat, sed si quis bonus ad ædificatiónem opportunitátis, ut det grátiam audiéntibus. Et nolíte contristáre Spíritum Sanctum Dei, in quo signáti estis in diem redemptiónis. Omnis amaritúdo et ira et indignátio et clamor et blasphémia tollátur a vobis cum omni malítia. Estóte autem invicem benígni, misericódes, donántes ínvicem, sicut et Deus in Christo donávit vobis.

RESPONSORIUM BREVE

℟. Audítam fac mihi mane * Misericórdiam tuam. Audítam.
℣. Notam fac mihi viam in qua ámbulem. * Misericórdiam tuam. Glória Patri. Audítam.

Ad Benedictus, ant. Vísitavit et fecit redemptiónem Dóminus plebis suæ.

3 Know that the LORD is God!
It is he that made us, and we are his;
we are his people, and the sheep of his pasture.

4 Enter his gates with thanksgiving,
and his courts with praise!
Give thanks to him, bless his name!

5 For the LORD is good;
his steadfast love endures for ever,
and his faithfulness to all generations.

Ant. 3 Come into His presence with singing.

SHORT READING Ephesians 4:29–32

Let no evil talk come out of your mouths, but only such as is good for edifying, as fits the occasion, that it may impart grace to those who hear. And do not grieve the Holy Spirit of God, in whom you were sealed for the day of redemption. Let all bitterness and wrath and anger and clamor and slander be put away from you, with all malice, and be kind to one another, tenderhearted, forgiving one another, as God in Christ forgave you.

SHORT RESPONSORY

℟. At daybreak, make me to hear of Your mercy.
℣. Make known to me the path in which I should walk.

Benedictus ant. The Lord has visited and redeemed His people.

PRECES

Christum, qui per crucem suam salútem géneri cóntulit humáno, adorémus, et pie clamémus:
Misericórdiam tuam nobis largíre, Dómine.

Christe, sol et dies noster, illúmina nos rádiis tuis.
—et omnes sensus malos iam mane compésce.

Custódi cogitatiónes, sermónes et ópera nostra,
—ut hódie in conspéctu tuo placére possímus.

Avérte fáciem tuam a peccátis nostris,
—et omnes iniquitátes nostras dele.

Per crucem et resurrectiónem tuam,
—reple nos consolatióne Spíritus Sancti.

Pater noster.

ORATIO

Deus, qui ténebras ignorántiæ Verbi tui luce depéllis, auge in córdibus nostris virtútem fídei quam dedísti, ut ignis, quem grátia tua fecit accéndi, nullis tentatiónibus exstinguátur. Per Dóminum.

INTERCESSIONS

Christ, Who through His cross has brought salvation to the human race, let us adore, and devoutly let us call out: *Bestow on us Your mercy, O Lord.*

Christ, our sun and day, enlighten us with Your rays,
—and now in the morning restrain all evil intentions.

Guard our thoughts, words and works,
—that today we might be pleasing in Your sight.

Turn away Your face from our sins.
—and blot out all our iniquities.

Through Your cross and resurrection,
—fill us with the consolation of the Holy Spirit.

Our Father.

ORATION

O God, Who dispel the darkness of ignorance with the light of Your Word, increase in our hearts the virtue of faith, which You have given, so that the fire, which Your grace has kindled, might not be extinguished by any temptations. Through our Lord.

Hebdomada I

Feria VI, ad Vesperas

Hymnus

Plasmátor hóminis, Deus,
qui, cuncta solus órdinans,
humum iubes prodúcere
reptántis et feræ genus;

Qui magna rerum córpora,
dictu iubéntis vívida,
ut sérviant per órdinem
subdens dedísti hómini:

Repélle a servis tuis
quicquid per immundítiam
aut móribus se súggerit,
aut áctibus s*e* intérserit.

Da gaudiórum prǽmia,
da gratiárum múnera;
dissólve litis víncula,
astrínge pacis fœdera.

Præsta, Pater piísime,
Patríque compar Unice,
cum Spíritu Paráclito
regnans per omne sǽculum. Amen.

Week I

Friday, Vespers

HYMN Trans. J. H. Newman

Whom all obey,
Maker of man! who from Thy height
Badest the dull earth bring to light
All creeping things, and the fierce might
Of beasts of prey;

And the huge make
Of wild or gentler animal,
Springing from nothing at Thy call,
To serve in their due time, and all
For sinners' sake;

Shield us from ill!
Come it by passion's sudden stress,
Lurk in our mind's habitual dress,
Or through our actions seek to press
Upon our will.

Vouchsafe the prize
Of sacred joy's perpetual mood,
And service-seeking gratitude,
And love to quell each strife or feud,
If it arise.

Grant it, O Lord!
To whom, the Father, Only Son,
And Holy Spirit, Three in One,
In heaven and earth all praise be done,
With one accord.

PSALMODIA

Ant. 1 Sana, Dómine, ánimam meam, quia peccávi tibi.

Psalmus 40 (41)

2 Beátus, qui intéllegit de egéno, *
in die mala liberábit eum Dóminus.
3 Dóminus servábit eum et vivificábit eum †
et beátum fáciet eum in terra *
et non tradet eum in ánimam inimicórum eius.
4 Dóminus opem feret illi super lectum dolóris eius; *
univérsum stratum eius versábis in infirmitáte eius.

5 Ego dixi: « Dómine, miserére mei; *
sana ánimam meam, quia peccávi tibi ».
6 Inimíci mei dixérunt mala mihi: *
« Quando moriétur, et períbit nomen eius? ».
7 Et si ingrediebátur, ut visitáret, vana loquebátur; †
cor eius congregábat iniquitátem sibi, *
egrediebátur foras et detrahébat.

8 Simul advérsum me susurrábant omnes inimíci mei; *
advérsum me cogitábant mala mihi:
9 « Malefícium effúsum est in eo; *
et, qui decúmbit, non adíciet ut resúrgat ».
10 Sed et homo pacis meæ, in quo sperávi, *
qui edébat panem meum, levávit contra me calcáneum.

11 Tu autem, Dómine, miserére mei *
et resúscita me, et retríbuam eis.

Psalmody

Ant. 1 Heal me, O Lord, for I have sinned against Thee.

Psalm 41

1 Blessed is he who considers the poor!
The Lord delivers him in the day of trouble;
2 the Lord protects him and keeps him alive;
he is called blessed in the land;
thou dost not give him up to the will of his enemies.
3 The Lord sustains him on his sick- bed;
in his illness thou healest all his infirmities.

4 As for me, I said, "O Lord, be gracious to me;
heal me, for I have sinned against thee!"
5 My enemies say of me in malice:
"When will he die, and his name perish?"
6 And when one comes to see me, he utters empty words,
while his heart gathers mischief;
when he goes out, he tells it abroad.
7 All who hate me whisper together about me;
they imagine the worst for me.

8 They say, "A deadly thing has fastened upon him;
he will not rise again from where he lies."
9 Even my bosom friend in whom I trusted,
who ate of my bread, has lifted his heel against me.
10 But do thou, O Lord, be gracious to me,
and raise me up, that I may requite them!

12 In hoc cognóvi quóniam voluísti me, *
quia non gaudébit inimícus meus super me;
13 me autem propter innocéntiam suscepísti *
et statuísti me in conspéctu tuo in ætérnum.

14 Benedíctus Dóminus Deus Israel *
a sǽculo et usque in sǽculum. Fiat, fiat.

Ant. Sana, Dómine, ánimam meam, quia peccávi tibi.

Ant. 2 Dóminus virtútum nobíscum, refúgium nobis Deus Iacob.

Psalmus 45 (46)

2 Deus est nobis refúgium, et virtus, *
adiutórium in tribulatiónibus invéntus est nimis.
3 Proptérea non timébimus, dum turbábitur terra, *
et transferéntur montes in cor maris.
4 Fremant et intuméscant aquæ eius, *
conturbéntur montes in elatióne eius.

5 Flúminis rivi lætíficant civitátem Dei, *
sancta tabernácula Altíssimi.
6 Deus in médio eius, non commovébitur; *
adiuvábit eam Deus mane dilúculo.
7 Fremuérunt gentes, commóta sunt regna; *
dedit vocem suam, liquefácta est terra.

8 Dóminus virtútum nobíscum. *
refúgium nobis Deus Iacob.

11 By this I know that thou art pleased with me,
in that my enemy has not triumphed over me.
12 But thou hast upheld me because of my integrity,
and set me in thy presence for ever.

13 Blessed be the Lord, the God of Israel,
from everlasting to everlasting!
Amen and Amen.

Ant. 1 Heal me, O Lord, for I have sinned against Thee.
Ant. 2 The Lord of hosts is with us; the God of Jacob is our refuge.

Psalm 46

1 God is our refuge and strength,
a very present help in trouble.
2 Therefore we will not fear though the earth
should change,
though the mountains shake in the heart of the
sea;
3 though its waters roar and foam,
though the mountains tremble with its tumult.

4 There is a river whose streams make glad the city
of God,
the holy habitation of the Most High.
5 God is in the midst of her, she shall not be moved;
God will help her right early.
6 The nations rage, the kingdoms totter;
he utters his voice, the earth melts.
7 The Lord of hosts is with us;
the God of Jacob is our refuge.

9 Veníte et vidéte ópera Dómini, *
quæ pósuit prodígia super terram.
Auferet bella usque ad finem terræ, †
10 arcum cónteret et confrínget arma *
et scuta combúret igne.
11 Vacáte et vidéte quóniam ego sum Deus: *
exaltábor in géntibus et exaltábor in terra.

12 Dóminus virtútum nobíscum, *
refúgium nobis Deus Iacob.

Ant. Dóminus virtútum nobíscum, refúgium nobis Deus Iacob.

Ant. 3 Omnes gentes vénient et adorábunt coram te, Dómine.

Canticum Ap 15, 3-4

3 Magna et mirabília ópera tua, *
Dómine Deus omnípotens;
iustæ et veræ viæ tuæ, *
Rex géntium!

4 Quis non timébit, Dómine, *
et glorificábit nomen tuum?
Quia solus Sanctus, †
quóniam omnes gentes vénient et adorábunt in conspéctu tuo, *
quóniam iudícia tua manifestáta sunt.

Ant. Omnes gentes vénient et adorábunt coram te, Dómine.

LECTIO BREVIS Rom 15, 1-3

Debémus nos firmióres imbecillitátes infirmórum sustinére, et non nobis placére. Unusquísque nostrum

8 Come, behold the works of the LORD,
how he has wrought desolations in the earth.
9 He makes wars cease to the end of the earth;
he breaks the bow, and shatters the spear,
he burns the chariots with fire!
10 "Be still, and know that I am God.
I am exalted among the nations,
I am exalted in the earth!"
11 The LORD of hosts is with us;
the God of Jacob is our refuge.

Ant. 2 The Lord of hosts is with us; the God of Jacob is our refuge.
Ant. 3 All nations shall come and worship Thee, O Lord.

Canticle Revelation 15:3–4

3 "Great and wonderful are thy deeds,
O Lord God the Almighty!
Just and true are thy ways,
O King of ages!
4 Who shall not fear and glorify thy name, O Lord?
For thou alone art holy.
All nations shall come and worship thee,
for thy judgments have been revealed."

Ant. 3 All nations shall come and worship Thee, O Lord.

SHORT READING Romans 15:1–3

We who are strong ought to bear with the failings of the weak, and not to please ourselves; let each of us

próximo pláceat in bonum ad ædificatiónem; étenim Christus non sibi plácuit, sed sicut scriptum est: Impropéria improperántium tibi cecidérunt super me.

RESPONSORIUM BREVE

℟. Christus diléxit nos et lavit nos * In sánguine suo. Christus.

℣. Et fecit nos Deo regnum et sacerdótium. * In sánguine suo. Glória Patri. Christus.

Ad Magnificat, ant. Suscépit nos Dóminus púeros suos, recordátus misericórdiæ suæ.

PRECES

Benedíctus Deus, qui propítius vota egéntium intuétur et esuriéntes replet bonis; fidénter ígitur ei supplicémus: *Osténde nobis, Dómine, misericórdiam tuam.*

Dómine, Pater noster clementíssime, te rogámus pro doléntibus membris Ecclésiæ tuæ,
—quorum caput, in ligno crucis suspénsum, sacrifícium vespertínum consummávit.

Solve compedítos, illúmina cæcos,
—pupíllos et víduas súscipe.

Tuam fidéles omnes índue armatúram,
—ut advérsus insídias diáboli consístere possint.

Nobis, Dómine, miséricors adésto in hora éxitus nostri,
—ut fidéles inveniámur et in tua pace ex hoc mundo transeámus.

Educ defúnctos in lucem, quam inhábitas,
—ut te conspíciant in ætérnum.

please his neighbor for his good, to edify him. For Christ did not please himself; but, as it is written. "The reproaches of those who reproached thee fell on me."

SHORT RESPONSORY

℟. Christ has loved us and washed us in his own blood.

℣. And has made us a kingdom and a priesthood for God.

Magnificat ant. The Lord has helped us, His children, in remembrance of His mercy.

INTERCESSIONS

Blessed be God, Who is mindful of the prayers of the needy and fills the hungry with good things; faithfully, then, let us beseech Him: *Show us Your mercy, O Lord.*

O Lord, our Father most merciful, we petition You on behalf of the suffering members of Your Church,

—the Head of whom, hanging on the wood of the Cross, consummated the evening sacrifice.

Release the captive, illumine the blind,

—accept widows and orphans.

Arm all Your faithful,

—that they may be able to stand against the deceptions of the devil.

To us, O Lord, be mercifully present at our hour of death,

—that we may be found faithful, and travel in Your peace from this world.

Lead the deceased into the light, which You inhabit,

—that they may behold You for all eternity.

Pater noster.

ORATIO

Concéde nobis, fámulis tuis, quǽsumus, Dómine, ut exémplis Fílii tui passiónis instrúcti ad iugum eius suáve portándum simus semper idónei. Qui tecum vivit.

Our Father.

ORATION

We ask, O Lord, that You pardon us, Your servants, that by the example of the Passion of Your Son, we may, by helping to carry His sweet burden, be always suitable to You. Who live and reign.

Hebdomada I

Sabbato, ad Laudes matutinas

Hymnus

Auróra iam spargit polum,
terris dies illábitur,
lucis resúltat spículum:
discédat omne lúbricum.

Iam vana noctis décidant,
mentis reátus súbruat,
quicquid tenébris hórridum
nox áttulit culpæ, cadet,

Ut mane illud último,
quod præstolámur cérnui,
in lucem nobis éffluat,
dum hoc canóre cóncrepat.

Deo Patri sit glória
eiúsque soli Fílio
cum Spíritu Paráclito,
in sempitérna sǽcula. Amen.

Psalmodia

Ant. 1 Prævenérunt óculi mei ad te dilúculo.

Week I

Saturday, Lauds

HYMN — Trans. J. H. Newman

The dawn is sprinkled o'er the sky,
  The day steals softly on;
Its darts are scatter'd far and nigh,
And all that fraudful is, shall fly
  Before the brightening sun;
Spectres of ill, that stalk at will,
  And forms of guilt that fright,
And hideous sin, that ventures in
  Under the cloak of night.

And of our crimes the tale complete,
  Which bows us in Thy sight,
Up to the latest, they shall fleet,
Out-told by our full members sweet,
  And melted by the light.
To Father, Son, and Spirit, One,
  Whom we adore and love,
Be given all praise now and always,
  Here as in Heaven above.

PSALMODY

Ant. 1 At dawn, my eyes have looked toward Thee.

Psalmus 118 (119), 145–152

145 Clamávi in toto corde, exáudi me, Dómine; *
iustificatiónes tuas servábo.
146 Clamávi ad te, salvum me fac, *
ut custódiam testimónia tua.

147 Prævéni dilúculo et clamávi, *
in verba tua supersperávi.
148 Prævenérunt óculi mei vigílias, *
ut meditárer elóquia tua.

149 Vocem meam audi secúndum misericórdiam
tuam, Dómine, *
secúndum iudícium tuum vivífica me.
150 Appropinquavérunt persequéntes me in malítia, *
a lege autem tua longe facti sunt.

151 Prope es tu, Dómine, *
et ómnia præcépta tua véritas.
152 Ab inítio cognóvi de testimóniis tuis, *
quia in ætérnum fundásti ea.

Ant. Prævenérunt óculi mei ad te dilúculo.

Ant. 2 Fortitúdo mea et laus mea Dóminus, et factus est mihi in salútem.

Canticum Ex 15, 1–4B, 8–13, 17–18

1 Cantémus Dómino: †
gloriόse enim magnificátus est, *
equum et ascensórem deiécit in mare.

2 Fortitúdo mea et robur meum Dóminus, *
et factus est mihi in salútem.

Psalm 119:145–152

145 With my whole heart I cry; answer me, O LORD!
I will keep thy statutes.
146 I cry to thee; save me,
that I may observe thy testimonies.
147 I rise before dawn and cry for help;
I hope in thy words.
148 My eyes are awake before the watches of the night,
that I may meditate upon thy promise.
149 Hear my voice in thy steadfast love;
O LORD, in thy justice preserve my life.
150 They draw near who persecute me with evil
purpose;
they are far from thy law.
151 But thou art near, O LORD,
and all thy commandments are true.
152 Long have I known from thy testimonies.
that thou hast founded them for ever.

Ant. 1 At dawn, my eyes have looked toward Thee.
Ant. 2 The Lord is my strength and my song, and He has become my salvation.

Canticle

Exodus 15:1–4a, 8–13, 17–18

1 "I will sing to the LORD, for he has triumphed
gloriously;
the horse and his rider he has thrown into the sea.
2 The LORD is my strength and my song,
and he has become my salvation;

Iste Deus meus, *
et glorificábo eum:
Deus patris mei, *
et exaltábo eum!

3 Dóminus quasi vir pugnátor; *
Iahveh nomen eius!
4 Currus pharaónis et exércitum eius *
proiécit in mare.

8 In spíritu furóris tui congregátæ sunt aquæ; †
stetit ut agger unda fluens, *
coagulátæ sunt abýssi in médio mari.

9 Dixit inimícus: « Pérsequar, comprehéndam; †
dívidam spólia, implébitur ánima mea: *
evaginábo gládium meum, interfíciet eos manus
mea! ».

10 Flavit spíritus tuus, et opéruit eos mare; *
submérsi sunt quasi plumbum in aquis
veheméntibus.

11 Quis símilis tui in diis, Dómine? †
Quis símilis tui, magníficus in sanctitáte, *
terríbilis atque laudábilis, fáciens mirabília?

12 Extendísti manum tuam, devorávit eos terra. *
13 Dux fuísti in misericórdia tua pópulo, quem
redemísti,
et portásti eum in fortitúdine tua *
ad habitáculum sanctum tuum.

17 Introdúces eos et plantábis *
in monte hereditátis tuæ,
firmíssimo habitáculo tuo, †

this is my God, and I will praise him,
my father's God, and I will exalt him.
3 The LORD is a man of war;
the LORD is his name.

4 "Pharaoh's chariots and his host he cast into the sea;
and his picked officers are sunk in the Red Sea.

8 At the blast of thy nostrils the waters piled up,
the floods stood up in a heap;
the deeps congealed in the heart of the sea.
9 The enemy said, 'I will pursue, I will overtake,
I will divide the spoil, my desire shall have its fill of them.
I will draw my sword, my hand shall destroy them.'
10 Thou didst blow with thy wind, the sea covered them;
they sank as lead in the mighty waters.

11 "Who is like thee, O LORD, among the gods?
Who is like thee, majestic in holiness,
terrible in glorious deeds, doing wonders?
12 Thou didst stretch out thy right hand,
the earth swallowed them.

13 "Thou hast led in thy steadfast love the people whom thou hast redeemed,
thou hast guided them by thy strength to thy holy abode.

17 Thou wilt bring them in, and plant them on thy own mountain,
the place, O LORD, which thou hast made for thy abode,

quod operátus es, Dómine, *
sanctuário, Dómine, quod firmavérunt manus tuæ.

18 Dóminus regnábit *
in ætérnum et ultra!

Ant. Fortitúdo mea et laus mea Dóminus, et factus est mihi in salútem.

Ant. 3 Laudáte Dóminum, omnes gentes. †

Psalmus 116 (117)

1 Laudáte Dóminum, omnes gentes, *
† collaudáte eum, omnes pópuli.

2 Quóniam confirmáta est super nos misericórdia eius, *
et véritas Dómini manet in ætérnum.

Ant. Laudáte Dóminum, omnes gentes.

LECTIO BREVIS 2 PETR 1, 10–11

Fratres, magis satágite, ut firmam vestram vocatiónem et electiónem faciátis. Hæc enim faciéntes non offendétis aliquándo; sic enim abundánter ministrábitur vobis intróitus in ætérnum regnum Dómini nostri et salvatóris Iesu Christi.

RESPONSORIUM BREVE

℟. Clamávi ad te, Dómine; * Tu es refúgium meum. Clamávi.

℣. Pórtio mea in terra vivéntium. * Tu es refúgium meum. Glória Patri. Clamávi.

Ad Benedictus, ant. Illúmina, Dómine, sedéntes in ténebris et umbra mortis.

the sanctuary, O LORD, which thy hands have
established.
18 The LORD will reign for ever and ever."

Ant. 2 The Lord is my strength and my song, and He has become my salvation.

Ant. 3 Praise the Lord, all nations!

Psalm 117

1 Praise the LORD, all nations!
Extol him, all peoples!
2 For great is his steadfast love toward us;
and the faithfulness of the LORD endures for
ever.
Praise the LORD!

Ant. 3 Praise the Lord, all nations!

SHORT READING 2 Peter 1:10–11

Therefore, brethren, be the more zealous to confirm your call and election, for if you do this you will never fall; so there will be richly provided for you an entrance in the eternal kingdom of our Lord and Savior Jesus Christ.

SHORT RESPONSORY

℟. I have cried to You, O Lord; You are my refuge.
℣. You are my portion in the land of the living.

Benedictus ant. Give light, O Lord, to those who sit in darkness and in the shadow of death.

Preces

Benedicámus Christum, qui vóluit per ómnia frátribus similári, ut misericors fíeret et fidélis póntifex ad Deum. Eum rogémus dicéntes:
Dilectiónis tuæ thesáuros nobis largíre, Dómine.

Sol iustítiæ, tibi dies noster consecrétur,
—qui in baptísmate nos illustrásti.

Per síngulas horas huius diéi benedicémus tibi,
—et laudábimus nomen tuum in ómnibus.

Qui Maríam matrem habuísti, verbo tuo dócilem,
—dírige hódie gressus nostros secúndum elóquium tuum.

Da nos, in rebus corruptibílibus peregrinántes, cæléstem incorruptiónem exspectáre,
—ut per fidem, spem et caritátem iam nunc beatitúdinis tuæ gáudia prægustémus.

Pater noster.

Oratio

Corda nostra, quæ´sumus, Dómine, resurrectiónis splendor illústret, quo mortis ténebris carére valeámus, et ad claritátem perveniámus ætérnam. Per Dóminum.

INTERCESSIONS

Let us bless Christ, Who wished to be like His brothers in all things, to become a merciful and faithful high priest to God. Let us ask Him, saying: *Lord, bestow on us the treasures of Your love.*

Sun of justice, let our day be consecrated to You,
—Who in baptism brought us to light.

At every hour of this day we shall bless You,
—and we shall praise Your name in all things.

You that had Mary as a mother, obedient to Your word,
—guide our steps today according to Your word.

Grant that we who wander amid passing things, may await that heaven which does not pass away,
—that through faith, hope and charity we might now have a foretaste of the joys of Your blessedness.

Our Father.

ORATION

Lord, we beseech You, may the splendor of the resurrection shine in our hearts, that we might escape the darkness of death and arrive at the brightness of eternal glory. Through our Lord.

Hebdomada II

Dominica, ad I Vesperas

Hymnus

Rerum, Deus, fons ómnium,
qui, rebus actis ómnibus,
totíus orbis ámbitum
censu replésti múnerum,

Ac, mole tanta cóndita,
tandem quiétem díceris
sumpsísse, dans labóribus
ut nos levémur grátius:

Concéde nunc mortálibus
deflére vitæ crímina,
instáre iam virtútibus
et muneári prósperis,

Ut cum treméndi iúdicis
horror suprémus cœ́perit,
lætémur omnes ínvicem
pacis repléti múnere.

Præsta, Pater piíssime,
Patríque compar Unice,
cum Spíritu Paráclito
regnans per omne sǽculum. Amen.

Psalmodia

Ant. 1 Lucérna pédibus meis verbum tuum, Dómine, allelúia.

Week II

Sunday, Vespers I

HYMN Trans. The Benedictine Nuns, St. Cecilia's Abbey

O God, the Source and Fount of life,
  Creating all things by Your will,
To give us joy You never cease
  The earth with wondrous gifts to fill.

And when creation was complete,
  Repose for man You also blessed
By resting on the seventh day,
  That he might toil again refreshed.

To fallen mortals grant the grace
  Of sorrow for each sin's offence,
And courage to begin anew
  And strive for virtue's recompense.

When Christ the Judge supreme appears
  To sift the present and the past,
May we His servants thrill with joy
  And peace to gaze on Him at last.

Most tender Father, hear our prayer,
  Whom we adore, with Christ the Lord,
And Holy Spirit of them both;
  Bless us who praise Your Trinity. Amen.

PSALMODY

Ant. 1 Thy word, O Lord, is a lamp to my feet, alleluia.

Psalmus 118 (119), 105–112

105 Lucérna pédibus meis verbus tuum *
et lumen sémitis meis.
106 Iurávi et státui *
custodíre iudícia iustítiæ tuæ.

107 Humiliátus sum usquequáque, Dómine; *
vivífica me secúndum verbum tuum.
108 Voluntária oris mei beneplácita sint, Dómine, *
et iudícia tua doce me.

109 Anima mea in mánibus meis semper, *
et legem tuam non sum oblítus.
110 Posuérunt peccatóres láqueum mihi, *
et mandátis tuis non errávi.

111 Heréditas mea testimónia tua in ætérnum, *
quia exsultátio cordis mei sunt.
112 Inclinávi cor meum ad faciéndas iustificatiónes tuas *
in ætérnum, in finem.

Ant. Lucérna pédibus meis verbus tuum, Dómine, allelúia.

Ant. 2 Adimplébis me lætítia cum vultu tuo, Dómine, allelúia.

Psalmus 15 (16)

1 Consérva me, Deus, *
quóniam sperávi in te.

2 Dixi Dómino: « Dóminus meus es tu, *
bonum mihi non est sine te ».
3 In sanctos, qui sunt in terra, ínclitos viros, *
omnis volúntas mea in eos.

Psalm 119:105–112

105 Thy word is a lamp to my feet
and a light to my path.
106 I have sworn an oath and confirmed it,
to observe thy righteous ordinances.
107 I am sorely afflicted;
give me life, O LORD, according to thy word!
108 Accept my offerings of praise, O LORD,
and teach me thy ordinances.
109 I hold my life in my hand continually,
but I do not forget thy law.
110 The wicked have laid a snare for me,
but I do not stray from thy precepts.
111 Thy testimonies are my heritage for ever;
yea, they are the joy of my heart.
112 I incline my heart to perform thy statutes
for ever, to the end.

Ant. 1 Thy word, O Lord, is a lamp to my feet, alleluia.

Ant. 2 Thou dost show me the path of life; in Thy presence there is fulness of joy, alleluia.

Psalm 16

1 Preserve me, O God, for in thee I take refuge.
2 I say to the Lord, "Thou art my Lord;
I have no good apart from thee."

3 As for the saints in the land, they are the noble,
in whom is all my delight.

4 Multiplicántur dolóres eórum, *
qui post deos aliénos acceleravérunt.
Non effúndam libatiónes eórum de sanguínibus, *
neque assúmam nómina eórum in lábiis meis.

5 Dóminus pars hereditátis meæ et cálicis mei: *
tu es qui détines sortem meam.
6 Funes cecidérunt mihi in præcláris; *
ínsuper et heréditas mea speciósa est mihi.
7 Benedícam Dóminum, qui tríbuit mihi intelléctum; *
ínsuper et in nóctibus erudiérunt me renes mei.
8 Proponébam Dóminum in conspéctu meo semper; *
quóniam a dextris est mihi non commovébor.
9 Propter hoc lætátum est cor meum, †
et exsultavérunt præcórdia mea; *
ínsuper et caro mea requiéscet in spe.

10 Quóniam non derelínques ánimam meam in inférno, *
nec dabis sanctum tuum vidére corruptiónem.
11 Notas mihi fácies vias vitæ, †
plenitúdinem lætítiæ cum vultu tuo, *
delectatiónes in déxtera tua usque in finem.

Ant. Adimplébis me lætítia cum vultu tuo, Dómine, allelúia.
Ant. 3 In nómine Iesu omne genu flectátur in cælo et in terra, allelúia.

4 Those who choose another god multiply their
sorrows;
their libations of blood I will not pour out
or take their names upon my lips.

5 The LORD is my chosen portion and my cup;
thou holdest my lot.
6 The lines have fallen for me in pleasant places;
yea, I have a goodly heritage.

7 I bless the LORD who gives me counsel;
in the night also my heart instructs me.
8 I keep the LORD always before me;
because he is at my right hand, I shall not be
moved.

9 Therefore my heart is glad, and my soul rejoices;
my body also dwells secure.
10 For thou dost not give me up to Sheol,
or let thy godly one see the Pit.

11 Thou dost show me the path of life;
in thy presence there is fulness of joy,
in thy right hand are pleasures for evermore.

Ant. 2 Thou dost show me the path of life; in Thy presence there is fulness of joy, alleluia.
Ant. 3 At the name of Jesus every knee should bend in heaven and on earth, alleluia.

Canticum

Phil 2, 6–11

6 Christus Iesus, cum in forma Dei esset, *
non rapínam arbitrátus est esse se æquálem Deo,
7 sed semetípsum exinanívit formam servi accípiens, †
in similitúdinem hóminum factus; *
et hábitu invéntus ut homo,
8 humiliávit semetípsum †
factus obœ́diens usque ad mortem, *
mortem autem crucis.
9 Propter quod et Deus illum exaltávit †
et donávit illi nomen, *
quod est super omne nomen,
10 ut in nómine Iesu omne genu flectátur *
cæléstium et terréstrium et infernórum
11 et omnis lingua confiteátur: *
« Dóminus Iesus Christus! » in glóriam Dei Patris.

Ant. In nómine Iesu omne genu flectátur in cælo et in terra, allelúia.

Lectio Brevis

Col 1, 2b–6a

Grátia vobis et pax a Deo Patre nostro. Grátias ágimus Deo Patri Dómini nostri Ieus Christi semper pro vobis orántes, audiéntes fidem vestram in Christo Iesu et dilectiónem, quam habétis in sanctos omnes, propter spem, quæ repósita est vobis in cælis, quam ante audístis in verbo veritátis evangélii, quod pervénit ad vos, sicut et in univérso mundo est fructíficans et crescens sicut et in vobis.

Canticle Philippians 2:6–11

6 Though he was in the form of God, Jesus did not
count equality with God a thing to be grasped,
7 but emptied himself, taking the form of a servant,
being born in the likeness of men.
8 And being found in human form he humbled
himself and became obedient unto death, even
death on a cross.
9 Therefore God has highly exalted him and
bestowed on him the name which is above
every name,
10 that at the name of Jesus every knee should bow,
in heaven and on earth and under the earth,
11 and every tongue confess that Jesus Christ is
Lord, to the glory of God the Father.

Ant. 3 At the name of Jesus every knee should bend in heaven and on earth, alleluia.

SHORT READING Colossians 1:2b–6a

Grace to you and peace from God our Father.

We always thank God, the Father of our Lord Jesus Christ, when we pray for you, because we have heard of your faith in Christ Jesus and of the love which you have for all the saints, because of the hope laid up for you in heaven. Of this you have heard before in the word of the truth, the gospel which has come to you, as indeed in the whole world it is bearing fruit and growing.

RESPONSORIUM BREVE

℟. A solis ortu usque ad occásum, * Laudábile nomen Dómini. A solis.

℣. Super cælos glória eius. * Laudábile nomen Dómini. Glória Patri. A solis.

PRECES

Deus plebem, quam elégit in hereditátem suam, ádiuvat et tuétur, ut sit beáta. Ei grátias agámus et pietátis eius mémores clamémus: *In te, Dómine, confídimus.*

Orámus te, Pater clementíssime, pro Papa nostro, N., et Epíscopo nostro, N.,
—prótege illos et tua virtúte sanctífica.

Infírmi se Christi sócios passiónum séntiant
—et consolatiónis eius semper partícipes.

Réspice in tua pietáte tecto caréntes,
—ut locum dignæ habitatiónis váleant inveníre.

Fructus terræ dare et conserváre dignéris,
—ut panem omnes cotidiánum repériant.

(vel:
Gentem nostram a malo defénde propítius,
—ut tua pace et prosperitáte fruátur.)

Tu, Dómine, magna defúnctos pietáte proséquere,
—mansiónem eis concéde cæléstem.

Pater noster.

ORATIO

Short Responsory

℟. From the rising of the sun to its setting, may the name of the Lord be praised.
℣. His glory is above the heavens.

Magnificat ant. as in Proper of the Time.

Intercessions

God helps and protects the people, whom He has chosen as His inheritance, that they may be blessed. Let us give thanks to Him and mindful of His loving-kindness, cry out: *In You, O Lord, we place our trust.*

We beseech You, most merciful Father, on behalf of our Pope, N., and our bishop, N.;
—by Your power, protect and sanctify them.

May the sick recognize themselves as fellow-sufferers with Christ,
—and always partakers of His consolation.

Regard, in Your generosity, the homeless,
—that they may find a worthy dwelling.

Deign to give and preserve the fruits of the earth,
—that all may continue to receive their daily bread.

(or:
Graciously defend our nation from evil,
—that it may enjoy Your peace and prosperity.)

O Lord, with great kindness, accompany the deceased,
—grant them a heavenly dwelling.

Our Father.

Oration

As in Proper of the Time.

Hebdomada II

Dominica, ad Laudes matutinas

HYMNUS

Ecce iam noctis tenuátur umbra,
lucis auróra rútilans corúscat;
nísibus totis rogitémus omnes cunctipoténtem,

Ut Deus, nostri miserátus, omnem
pellat angórem, tríbuat salútem,
donet et nobis pietáte patris regna polórum.

Præstet hoc nobis Déitas beáta
Patris ac Nati, paritérque Sancti
Spíritus, cuius résonat per omnem glória
mundum. Amen.

PSALMODIA

Ant. 1 Benedíctus qui venit in nómine Dómini, allelúia.

Week II

Sunday, Lauds

HYMN Trans. The Benedictine Nuns, St. Cecilia's Abbey

Out of the darkness
    in which night has held us;
See, dawn arises,
    shining now in splendour;
All our fresh ardour
    let us use in praising
God the Almighty.

That in His mercy
    He may always keep us,
Eager not slothful
    in His holy service
Then may He give us
    with a Father's bounty
Joy in His Kingdom.

May the assistance
    and the love protect us,
Of the great Godhead
    Father, Son, and Spirit,
Whose wondrous glory
    in the world around us
Ever finds echo. Amen.

PSALMODY

Ant. 1 Blessed be he who enters in the name of the Lord! alleluia.

Psalmus 117 (118)

1 Confitémini Dómino, quóniam bonus, *
quóniam in sæculum misericórdia eius.

2 Dicat nunc Israel, quóniam bonus, *
quóniam in sæculum misericórdia eius.
3 Dicat nunc domus Aaron, *
quóniam in sæculum misericórdia eius.
4 Dicant nunc, qui timent Dóminum, *
quóniam in sæculum misericórdia eius.

5 De tribulatióne invocávi Dóminum, *
et exaudívit me edúcens in latitúdinem
Dóminus.
6 Dóminus mecum, *
non timébo, quid fáciat mihi homo.
7 Dóminus mecum adiútor meus, *
et ego despíciam inimícos meos.

8 Bonum est confúgere ad Dóminum *
quam confídere in hómine.
9 Bonum est confúgere ad Dóminum *
quam confídere in princípibus.
10 Omnes gentes circuiérunt me, *
et in nómine Dómini excídi eos.
11 Circumdántes circumdedérunt me, *
et in nómine Dómini excídi eos.
12 Circumdedérunt me sicut apes †
et exarsérunt sicut ignis in spinis, *
et in nómine Dómini excídi eos.
13 Impelléntes impulérunt me, ut cáderem, *
et Dóminus adiúvit me.
14 Fortitúdo mea et laus mea Dóminus *
et factus est mihi in salútem.

Psalm 118

1 O give thanks to the LORD, for he is good;
his steadfast love endures for ever!

2 Let Israel say,
"His steadfast love endures for ever."
3 Let the house of Aaron say,
"His steadfast love endures for ever."
4 Let those who fear the LORD say,
"His steadfast love endures for ever."

5 Out of my distress I called on the LORD;
the LORD answered me and set me free.
6 With the LORD on my side I do not fear.
What can man do to me?
7 The LORD is on my side to help me;
I shall look in triumph on those who hate me.
8 It is better to take refuge in the LORD
than to put confidence in man.
9 It is better to take refuge in the LORD
than to put confidence in princes.

10 All nations surrounded me;
in the name of the LORD I cut them off!
11 They surrounded me, surrounded me on every side;
in the name of the LORD I cut them off!
12 They surround me like bees,
they blazed like a fire of thorns;
in the name of the LORD I cut them off!
13 I was pushed hard, so that I was falling,
but the LORD helped me.
14 The LORD is my strength and my song;
he has become my salvation.

15 Vox iubilatiónis et salútis *
in tabernáculis iustórum:
16 « Déxtera Dómini fecit virtútem! †
Déxtera Dómini exaltávit me; *
déxtera Dómini fecit virtútem! ».

17 Non móriar, sed vivam *
et narrábo ópera Dómini.
18 Castígans castigávit me Dóminus *
et morti non trádidit me.
19 Aperíte mihi portas iustítiæ; *
ingréssus in eas confitébor Dómino.

20 Hæc porta Dómini; *
iusti intrábunt in eam.

21 Confitébor tibi, quóniam exaudísti me *
et factus es mihi in salútem.

22 Lápidem, quem reprobavérunt ædificántes, *
hic factus est in caput ánguli;
23 a Dómino factum est istud *
et est mirábile in óculis nostris.
24 Hæc est dies, quam fecit Dóminus: *
exsultémus et lætémur in ea.

25 O Dómine, salvum me fac; *
O Dómine, da prosperitátem!

26 Benedíctus, qui venit in nómine Dómini. *
Benedícimus vobis de domo Dómini.
27 Deus Dóminus et illúxit nobis. *
Instrúite sollemnitátem in ramis condénsis
usque ad córnua altáris.

15 Hark, glad songs of victory
in the tents of the righteous:
"The right hand of the LORD does valiantly,
16 the right hand of the LORD is exalted,
the right hand of the LORD does valiantly!"
17 I shall not die, but I shall live,
and recount the deeds of the LORD.
18 The LORD has chastened me sorely,
but he has not given me over to death.

19 Open to me the gates of righteousness,
that I may enter through them
and give thanks to the LORD.

20 This is the gate of the LORD;
the righteous shall enter through it.

21 I thank thee that thou hast answered me
and hast become my salvation.
22 The stone which the builders rejected
has become the head of the corner.
23 This is the Lord's doing;
it is marvelous in our eyes.
24 This is the day which the LORD has made;
let us rejoice and be glad in it.
25 Save us, we beseech thee, O LORD!
O LORD, we beseech thee, give us success!

26 Blessed be he who enters in the name of the LORD!
We bless you from the house of the LORD.
27 The LORD is God, and he has given us light.
Bind the festal procession with branches,
up to the horns of the altar!

28 Deus meus es tu, et confitébor tibi, *
Deus meus, et exaltábo te.

29 Confitémini Dómino, quóniam bonus, *
quóniam in sæculum misericórdia eius.

Ant. Benedíctus qui venit in nómine Dómini, allelúia.

Ant. 2 Hymnum dicámus Deo nostro, allelúia.

Canticum DAN 3, 52–57

52 Benedíctus es, Dómine Deus patrum nostrórum, *
et laudábilis et superexaltátus in sæcula;
et benedíctum nomen glóriæ tuæ sanctum *
et superlaudábile et superexaltátum in sæcula.

53 Benedíctus es in templo sanctæ glóriæ tuæ *
et superlaudábilis et supergloriósus in sæcula.

54 Benedíctus es in throno regni tui *
et superlaudábilis et superexaltátus in sæcula.
55 Benedíctus es, qui intuéris abýssos †
sedens super chérubim, *
et laudábilis et superexaltátus in sæcula.
56 Benedíctus es in firmaménto cæli *
et laudábilis et gloriósus in sæcula.

57 Benedícite, ómnia ópera Dómini, Dómino, *
laudáte et superexaltáte eum in sæcula.

Ant. Hymnum dicámus Deo nostro, allelúia.

Ant. 3 Laudáte Dóminum secúndum multitúdinem magnitúdinis eius, allelúia.

28 Thou art my God, and I will give thanks to thee;
thou art my God, I will extol thee.

29 O give thanks to the Lord, for he is good;
for his steadfast love endures for ever!

Ant. 1 Blessed be he who enters in the name of the Lord! alleluia.

Ant. 2 Let us sing a hymn to our God, alleluia.

Canticle Daniel 3:29–35

29 Blessed art thou, O Lord, God of our fathers, and
to be praised and highly exalted for ever;
30 And blessed is thy glorious, holy name and to be
highly praised and highly exalted for ever;
31 Blessed art thou in the temple of thy holy glory
and to be extolled and highly glorified for
ever.
32 Blessed art thou, who sittest upon cherubim and
lookest upon the deeps, and to be praised and
highly exalted for ever.
33 Blessed art thou upon the throne of thy kingdom
and to be extolled and highly exalted for ever.
34 Blessed art thou in the firmament of heaven and
to be sung and glorified for ever.
35 "Bless the Lord, all works of the Lord, sing praise
to him and highly exalt him for ever."

Ant. 2 Let us sing a hymn to our God, alleluia.

Ant. 3 Praise the Lord according to His exceeding greatness, alleluia.

Psalmus 150

1 Laudáte Dóminum in sanctuário eius, *
laudáte eum in firmaménto virtútis eius.
2 Laudáte eum in magnálibus eius, *
laudáte eum secúndum multitúdinem
magnitúdinis eius.

3 Laudáte eum in sono tubæ, *
laudáte eum in psaltério et cíthara,
4 laudáte eum in týmpano et choro, *
laudáte eum in chordis et órgano,
5 laudáte eum in cýmbalis benesonántibus, †
laudáte eum in cýmbalis iubilatiónis:
omne quod spirat, laudet Dóminum.

Ant. Laudáte Dóminum secúndum multitúdinem magnitúdinis eius, allelúia.

LECTIO BREVIS Ez 36, 25-27

Effúndam super vos aquam mundam, et mundabímini ab ómnibus inquinaméntis vestris, et ab univérsis idólis vestris mundábo vos. Et dabo vobis cor novum et spíritum novum ponam in medio vestri et áuferam cor lapídeum de carne vestra et dabo vobis cor cárneum; et spíritum meum ponam in medio vestri et fáciam, ut in præcéptis meis ambulétis et iudícia mea custodiátis et operémini.

RESPONSORIUM BREVE

℟. Confitébimur tibi, Deus, * Et invocábimus nomen tuum. Confitébimur.
℣. Narrábimus mirabília tua. * Et invocábimus nomen tuum. Glória Patri. Confitébimur.

Psalm 150

1 Praise the LORD!
Praise God in his sanctuary;
praise him in his mighty firmament!
2 Praise him for his mighty deeds;
praise him according to his exceeding greatness!

3 Praise him with trumpet sound;
praise him with lute and harp!
4 Praise him with timbrel and dance;
praise him with strings and pipe!
5 Praise him with sounding cymbals;
praise him with loud clashing cymbals!
6 Let everything that breathes praise the LORD!
Praise the LORD!

Ant. 3 Praise the Lord according to His exceeding greatness, alleluia.

SHORT READING Ezekiel 36:25–28

I will sprinkle clean water upon you, and you shall be clean from all your uncleannesses, and from all your idols I will cleanse you. A new heart I will give you, and a new spirit I will put within you; and I will take out of your flesh the heart of stone and give you a heart of flesh. And I will put my spirit within you, and cause you to walk in my statutes and be careful to observe my ordinances.

SHORT RESPONSORY

℟. We shall confess You, O God, and call upon Your name.

℣. We shall proclaim Your marvelous deeds.

PRECES

Salvatóri nostro grátias agámus, qui in hunc mundum descéndit ut esset Deus nobíscum. Eum invocémus clamántes: *Christe, Rex glóriæ, sis lux et gáudium nostrum.*

Christe Dómine, lux óriens ex alto primítiæ resurrectiónis futúræ,
—da nos te sequi, ne in umbra mortis sedeámus, sed ut in lúmine vitæ ambulémus.

Bonitátem tuam in ómnibus creatúris diffúsam nobis osténde,
—ut tuam ubíque glóriam contemplémur.

Ne patiáris, Dómine, hódie malo nos vinci,
—sed fac ut in bono nos vincámus malum.

Qui in Iordáne baptizátus, a Sancto Spíritu es inúnctus,
—da nos hódie grátia agi Sancti Spíritus tui.

Pater noster.

ORATIO

Benedictus ant. as in Proper of the Time.

INTERCESSIONS

Let us give thanks to our Savior, Who descended into this world that He might be God with us. Let us invoke Him crying out: *Christ, King of glory, may You be our light and our joy.*

Christ the Lord, Light of the east from on high, the Firstfruits of the future resurrection,
—grant us to follow You, that we might not sit in the shadow of death, but walk in the light of life.

Show us Your goodness defused in every creature,
—that we might contemplate Your glory everywhere.

Do not permit us, Lord, to be conquered by evil today;
—but make us to overcome evil by good.

You, Who were baptized in the Jordan, were anointed by the Holy Spirit,
—grant us today to be moved by the grace of Your Holy Spirit.

Our Father.

ORATION

As in Proper of the Time.

Hebdomada II

Dominica, ad II Vesperas

Hymnus

O lux, beáta Trínitas
et principális Unitas,
iam sol recédit ígneus:
infúnde lumen córdibus.

Te mane laudem cármine,
te deprecémur véspere;
te nostra supplex glória
per cuncta laudet sǽcula.

Christum rogámus et Patrem,
Christi Patrísque Spíritum;
unum potens per ómnia,
fove precántes, Trínitas. Amen.

Psalmodia

Ant. 1 Sacérdos in ætérnum Christus Dóminus secúndum órdinem Melchísedech, allelúia.

Psalmus 109 (110), 1–5, 7

1 Dixit Dóminus Dómino meo: *
« Sede a dextris meis,
donec ponam inimícos tuos *
scabéllum pedum tuórum ».

2 Virgam poténtiæ tuæ emíttet Dóminus ex Sion: *
domináre in médio inimicórum tuórum.

Week II

Sunday, Vespers II

HYMN Trans. The Benedictine Nuns, St. Cecilia's Abbey

O Trinity of blessed light,
O Unity of princely might,
The fiery sun now goes his way;
Shed Thou within our hearts Thy ray.

To Thee our morning song of praise,
To Thee our evening prayer we raise;
Thy glory suppliant we adore
For ever and for evermore.

All laud to God the Father be;
All praise, eternal Son, to Thee;
All glory, as is ever meet,
To God the Holy Paraclete. Amen.

PSALMODY

Ant. 1 Christ the Lord is a priest for ever, after the order of Melchizedek, alleluia.

Psalm 110: 1–5, 7

1 The LORD says to my lord;
"Sit at my right hand,
till I make your enemies your footstool."

2 The LORD sends forth from Zion
your mighty scepter.
Rule in the midst of your foes!

3 Tecum principátus in die virtútis tuæ, †
in splendóribus sanctis, *
ex útero ante lucíferum génui te.

4 Iurávit Dóminus et non pænitébit eum: *
« Tu es sacérdos in ætérnum secúndum órdinem Melchísecech ».
5 Dóminus a dextris tuis, *
conquassábit in die iræ suæ reges.

7 De torrénte in via bibet, *
proptérea exaltábit caput.

Ant. Sacérdos in ætérnum Christus Dóminus secúndum órdinem Melchísedech, allelúia.
Ant. 2 Deus noster in cælo; ómnia quæcúmque vóluit, fecit, allelúia.

Psalmus 113b (115)

1 Non nobis, Dómine, non nobis, †
sed nómini tuo da glóriam *
super misericórdia tua et veritáte tua.
2 Quare dicent gentes: *
« Ubi est Deus eórum? »
3 Deus autem noster in cælo, *
ómnia, quæcúmque vóluit, fecit.

4 Simulácra géntium argéntum et aurum, *
ópera mánuum hóminum.
5 Os habent et non loquéntur, *
óculos habent et non vidébunt.

3 Your people will offer themselves freely
on the day you lead your host
upon the holy mountains.
From the womb of the morning
like dew your youth will come to you.
4 The LORD has sworn
and will not change his mind,
"You are a priest for ever
after the order of Melchizedek."

5 The Lord is at your right hand;
he will shatter kings on the day of his wrath.
7 He will drink from the brook by the way;
therefore he will lift up his head.

Ant. 1 Christ the Lord is a priest for ever, after the order of Melchizedek, alleluia.
Ant. 2 Our God is in the heavens; He does whatever He pleases, alleluia.

Psalm 115

1 Not to us, O LORD, not to us,
but to thy name give glory,
for the sake of thy steadfast love and thy faithfulness!
2 Why should the nations say,
"Where is their God?"

3 Our God is in the heavens;
he does whatever he pleases.
4 Their idols are silver and gold,
the work of men's hands.
5 They have mouths, but do not speak;
eyes, but do not see.

6 Aures habent et non áudient, *
nares habent et non odorábunt.
7 Manus habent et non palpábunt, †
pedes habent et non ambulábunt; *
non clamábunt in gútture suo.
8 Símiles illis erunt, qui fáciunt ea, *
et omnes, qui confídunt in eis.

9 Domus Israel sperávit in Dómino: *
adiutórium eórum et scutum eórum est.
10 Domus Aaron sperávit in Dómino: *
adiutórium eórum et scutum eórum est.
11 Qui timent Dóminum, speravérunt in Dómino: *
adiutórium eórum et scutum eórum est.

12 Dóminus memor fuit nostri *
et benedícet nobis:
benedícet dómui Israel, *
benedícet dómui Aaron,
13 benedícet ómnibus, qui timent Dóminum, *
pusíllis cum maióribus.

14 Adíciat Dóminus super vos, *
super vos et super fílios vestros.
15 Benedícti vos a Dómino, *
qui fecit cælum et terram.
16 Cæli, cæli sunt Dómino, *
terram autem dedit fíliis hóminum.
17 Non mórtui laudábunt te, Dómine, *
neque omnes, qui descéndunt in siléntium,
18 sed nos, qui vívimus, benedícimus Dómino *
ex hoc nunc et usque in sæculum.

6 They have ears, but do not hear;
noses, but do not smell.
7 They have hands, but do not feel;
feet, but do not walk;
and they do not make a sound in their throat.
8 Those who make them are like them;
so are all who trust in them.

9 O Israel, trust in the LORD!
He is their help and their shield.
10 O house of Aaron, put your trust in the LORD!
He is their help and their shield.
11 You who fear the LORD, trust in the LORD!
He is their help and their shield.
12 The LORD has been mindful of us; he will bless us;
he will bless the house of Israel;
he will bless the house of Aaron;
13 he will bless those who fear the LORD,
both small and great.

14 May the LORD give you increase,
you and your children!
15 May you be blessed by the LORD,
who made heaven and earth!

16 The heavens are the LORD's heavens,
but the earth he has given to the sons of men.
17 The dead do not praise the LORD,
nor do any that go down into silence.
18 But we will bless the LORD
from this time forth and for evermore.
Praise the LORD!

Ant. Deus noster in cælo; ómnia quæcúmque vóluit, fecit, allelúia.
Ant. 3 Laudem dícite Deo, omnes servi eius, pusílli et magni, allelúia.

Canticle Cf. Ap 19, 1–7

Allelúia.
1 Salus et glória et virtus Deo nostro, *
(℟. Allelúia.)
2 quia vera et iusta iudícia eius.
℟. Allelúia (allelúia).

Allelúia.
5 Laudem dícite Deo nostro, omnes servi eius *
(℟. Allelúia.)
et qui timétis eum, pusílli et magni!
℟. Allelúia (allelúia).

Allelúia
6 Quóniam regnávit Dóminus,
Deus noster omnípotens. *
(℟. Allelúia.)
7 Gaudeámus et exsultémus et demus glóriam ei.
℟. Allelúia (allelúia).

Allelúia.
Quia venérunt núptiæ Agni, *
(℟. Allelúia.)
et uxor eius præparávit se.
℟. Allelúia (allelúia).

Ant. Laudem dícite Deo, omnes servi eius, pusílli et magni, allelúia.

Ant. 2 Our God is in the heavens; He does whatever He pleases, alleluia.
Ant. 3 Praise our God, all you His servants small and great, alleluia.

Canticle See Revelation 19:1–7

Alleluia.
Salvation and glory and power belong to our God;
(℟. Alleluia.)
for his judgments are true and just;
℟. Alleluia (alleluia).

Alleluia.
Praise our God, all you his servants,
(℟. Alleluia.)
you that fear him, small and great.
℟. Alleluia (alleluia).

Alleluia.
For, the LORD our God the Almighty reigns;
(℟. Alleluia.)
let us rejoice and exult and give him glory.
℟. Alleluia (alleluia).

Alleluia.
For the marriage of the Lamb has come,
(℟. Alleluia.)
and his Bride has made Herself ready.
℟. Alleluia (alleluia).

Ant. 3 Praise our God, all you His servants small and great, alleluia.

Lectio Brevis — 2 Th 2, 13–14

Debémus grátias ágere Deo semper pro vobis, fratres, dilécti a Dómino, quod elégerit vos Deus primítias in salútem in sanctificatióne Spíritus et fide veritátis, ad quod et vocávit vos per evangélium nostrum in acquisitiónem glóriæ Dómini nostri Iesu Christi.

Responsorium Breve

℟. Magnus Dóminus noster, * Et magna virtus eius. Magnus.
℣. Et sapiéntiæ eius non est númerus. * Et magna virtus eius. Glória Patri. Magnus.

Preces

Laus et honor Christo, qui salváre in perpétuum potest accedéntes per semetípsum ad Deum, semper vivens ad interpellándum pro nobis. Qua fide suffúlti eum implorémus: *Meménto pópuli tui, Dómine.*

Iam declinánte die, Sol iustítiæ, te super cunctum genus humánum invocámus,
—ut luce tua, numquam decidénte, omnes sine fine fruántur.

Custódi testaméntum, quod sánguine divíno sanxísti,
—et sanctífica Ecclésiam tuam, ut sit immaculáta.

Meménto, Dómine congregatiónis tuæ,
—loci habitatiónis tuæ.

In viam pacis et prosperitátis dírige iter faciéntes,
—ut cum salúte et gáudio ad optáta loca pervéniant.

Short Reading 2 Thessalonians 2:13–14

But we are bound to give thanks to God always for you, brethren beloved by the Lord, because God chose you from the beginning to be saved through sanctification by the Spirit and belief in the truth. To this he called you through our gospel, so that you may obtain the glory of our Lord Jesus Christ.

Short Responsory

℣. Our Lord is great, mighty is His power.
℟. To His wisdom there is no limit.

Magnificat ant. as in Proper of the Time.

Intercessions

Praise and honor be to Christ, perpetually able to save those approaching the Father through Him and living always to intercede for us. Sustained in that faith, let us implore Him: *Remember Your people, O Lord.*

As day ends, O Sun of Justice, we invoke Your blessing upon the whole human race,
—that they may enjoy without end Your never-failing light.

Preserve the covenant which You have ratified in Your divine blood,
—and sanctify Your Church, that she may be immaculate.

Remember, O Lord, Your congregation,
—the place of Your dwelling.

Guide into the way of peace and prosperity, those making a journey
—that they may arrive at their destinations in safety and joy.

Animas, Dómine, súscipe defunctórum,
—véniam tuam eis concéde et glóriam sempitérnam.

Pater noster.

Oratio

Accept, O Lord, the souls of the departed,
—and grant them your eternal pardon and glory.

Our Father.

Oration
As in Proper of the Time

Hebdomada II

Feria II, ad Laudes matutinas

Hymnus

Lucis largítor spléndide,
cuius seréno lúmine
post lapsa noctis témpora
dies refúsus pánditur,

Tu verus mundi lúcifer,
non is qui parvi síderis
ventúræ lucis núntius
angústo fulget lúmine,

Sed toto sole clárior,
lux ipse totus et dies,
intérna nostri péctoris
illúminans præcórdia.

Evíncat mentis cástitas
quæ caro cupit árrogans,
sanctúmque puri córporis
delúbrum servet Spíritus.

Sit, Christe, rex piíssime,
tibi Patríque glória
cum Spíritu Paráclito
in sempitérna sǽcula. Amen.

Psalmodia

Ant. 1 Quando véniam et apparébo ante fáciem Dómini?

Week II

Monday, Lauds

HYMN
Trans. The Benedictine Nuns, St. Cecilia's Abbey

O lavish Giver of the light
That bathes the world in dawning glow;
The daylight cheers our hearts again
When sombre hours of night are past.

You are the world's true Morning Star,
Compared with whom the eager gleam
That heralds in the dawning light
Is but a timid, narrow ray.

True Light itself, Eternal Day,
You are far brighter than the sun,
Illuminating with your grace
The deep recesses of each heart.

And may our purity of mind
Suppress what lower nature claims,
So that our bodies too may be
The Holy Spirit's spotless shrine,

O Christ our King and tender Lord,
All glory ever be to you,
Who with the Holy Spirit reign
With God the Father's might supreme. Amen.

PSALMODY

Ant. 1 When shall I come and behold the face of God?

Psalmus 41 (42)

2 Quemádmodum desíderat cervus ad fontes
aquárum, *
ita desíderat ánima mea ad te, Deus.
3 Sitívit ánima mea ad Deum, Deum vivum; *
quando véniam et apparébo ante fáciem Dei?

4 Fuérunt mihi lácrimæ meæ panis die ac nocte, *
dum dícitur mihi quotídie:« Ubi est Deus
tuus? »
5 Hæc recordátus sum et effúdi in me ánimam
meam; †
quóniam transíbam in locum tabernáculi
admirábilis *
usque ad domum Dei,
in voce exsultatiónis et confessiónis, *
multitúdinis festa celebrántis.

6 Quare tristis es, ánima mea, *
et quare conturbáris in me?
Spera in Deo, quóniam adhuc confitébor illi, *
salutáre vultus mei et Deus meus.

7 In meípso ánima mea contristáta est; †
proptérea memor ero tui *
de terra Iordánis et Hermónim, de monte Misar.
8 Abýssus abýssum ínvocat in voce cataractárum
tuárum; *
omnes gúrgites tui et fluctus tui super me
transiérunt.

Psalm 42

1 As a hart longs
for flowing streams,
so longs my soul
for thee, O God.
2 My soul thirsts for God,
for the living God.
When shall I come and behold
the face of God?
3 My tears have been my food
day and night,
while men say to me continually,
"Where is your God?"

4 These things I remember,
as I pour out my soul:
how I went with the throng,
and led them in procession to the house of God,
with glad shouts and songs of thanksgiving,
a multitude keeping festival.
5 Why are you cast down, O my soul,
and why are you disquieted within me?
Hope in God; for I shall again praise him,
my help 6 and my God.

My soul is cast down within me,
therefore I remember thee
from the land of Jordan and of Hermon,
from Mount Mizar.
7 Deep calls to deep
at the thunder of thy cataracts;
all thy waves and thy billows
have gone over me.

9 In die mandávit Dóminus misericórdiam suam, †
et nocte cánticum eius apud me est: *
orátio ad Deum vitæ meæ.
10 Dicam Deo: *
« Suscéptor meus es.
Quare oblítus es mei, †
et quare contristátus incédo, *
dum afflígit me inimícus? ».
11 Dum confringúntur ossa mea, †
exprobravérunt mihi, qui tríbulant me, *
dum dicunt mihi quotídie: « Ubi est Deus tuus? ».

12 Quare tristis es ánima mea, *
et quare conturbáris in me?
Spera in Deo, quóniam adhuc confitébor illi, *
salutáre vultus mei et Deus meus.

Ant. Quando véniam et apparébo ante fáciem Dómini?

Ant. 2 Osténde nobis, Dómine, lucem miseratiónum tuárum.

Canticum Sir 36, 1-7. 13-16

1 Miserére nostri, Deus ómnium, et réspice nos *
et osténde nobis lucem miseratiónum tuárum;
2 et immítte timórem tuum super gentes, *
quæ non exquisiérunt te,
ut cognóscant quia non est Deus nisi tu, *
et enárrent magnália tua.

3 Alleva manum tuam super gentes aliénas, *
ut vídeant poténtiam tuam.

8 By day the LORD commands his steadfast love;
and at night his song is with me,
a prayer to the God of my life.

9 I say to God, my rock:
"Why hast thou forgotten me?
Why go I mourning
because of the oppression of the enemy?"
10 As with a deadly wound in my body,
my adversaries taunt me,
while they say to me continually,
"Where is your God?"

11 Why are you cast down, O my soul,
and why are you disquieted within me?
Hope in God; for I shall again praise him,
my help and my God.

Ant. 1 When shall I come and behold the face of God?
Ant. 2 Show us, O Lord, the light of Thy mercies.

Canticle Sirach 36:1–5, 10–13

1 Have mercy upon us, O Lord,
the God of all, and look upon us,
2 and cause the fear of thee to fall upon all the nations.
3 Lift up thy hand against foreign nations
and let them see thy might.

4 Sicut enim in conspéctu eórum sanctificátus es in nobis, *
sic in conspéctu nostro magnificáberis in eis,
5 ut cognóscant, sicut et nos cognóvimus, *
quóniam non est Deus præter te, Dómine.
6 Innova signa et ítera mirabília, *
7 glorífica manum et firma bráchium dextrum.

13 Cóngrega omnes tribus Iacob, *
et hereditábis eos sicut ab inítio.
14 Miserére plebi tuæ, super quam invocátum est nomen tuum, *
et Israel, quem coæquásti primogénito tuo.
15 Miserére civitáti sanctificatiónis tuæ, *
Ierúsalem, loco requiéi tuæ.
16 Reple Sion maiestáte tua *
et glória tua templum tuum.

Ant. Osténde nobis, Dómine, lucem miseratiónum tuárum.

Ant. 3 Benedíctus es, Dómine, in firmaménto cæli.

Psalmus 18 (19)A

2 Cæli enárrant glóriam Dei, *
et ópera mánuum eius annúntiat firmaméntum.
3 Dies diéi erúctat verbum, *
et nox nocti índicat sciéntiam.

4 Non sunt loquélæ neque sermónes, *
quorum non intellegántur voces:
5 in omnem terram exívit sonus eórum *
et in fines orbis terræ verba eórum.

4 As in us thou hast been sanctified before them,
so in them be thou magnified before us;
5 and let them know thee, as we have known
that there is no God but thee, O Lord.

10 Crush the heads of the rulers of the enemy,
who say, "There is no one but ourselves."
11 Gather all the tribes of Jacob,
and give them their inheritance, as at the beginning.
12 Have mercy, O Lord, upon the people called by thy name,
upon Israel, whom thou hast likened to a first-born son.
13 Have pity on the city of thy sanctuary,
Jerusalem, the place of thy rest.

Ant. 2 Show us, O Lord, the light of Thy mercies.
Ant. 3 Blessed art Thou, O Lord, in the firmament of heaven.

Psalm 19A

1 The heavens are telling the glory of God;
and the firmament proclaims his handiwork.
2 Day to day pours forth speech,
and night to night declares knowledge.
3 There is no speech, nor are there words;
their voice is not heard;
4 yet their voice goes out through all the earth,
and their words to the end of the world.

6 Soli pósuit tabernáculum in eis, †
et ipse tamquam sponsus procédens de thálamo suo, *
exsultávit ut gigas ad curréndam viam.
7 A fínibus cælórum egréssio eius †
et occúrsus eius usque ad fines eórum, *
nec est, quod se abscóndat a calóre eius.

Ant. Benedíctus es, Dómine, in firmaménto cæli.

LECTIO BREVIS — IER 15, 16

Invénti sunt sermónes tui, et comédi eos, et factum est mihi verbum tuum in gáudium et in lætítiam cordis mei, quóniam invocátum est nomen tuum super me, Dómine Deus exercítuum.

RESPONSORIUM BREVE

℟. Exsultáte, iusti, in Dómino; * Rectos decet collaudátio. Exsultáte.
℣. Cantáte ei cánticum novum. * Rectos decet collaudátio. Glória Patri. Exsultáte.

Ad Benedictus, ant. Benedíctus Dóminus, quia visitávit et liberávit nos.

PRECES

Salvátor noster fecit nos regnum et sacerdótium, ut hóstias Deo acceptábiles offerámus. Grati ígitur eum invocémus: *Serva nos in tuo ministério, Dómine.*

In them he has set a tent for the sun,
5 which comes forth like a bridegroom leaving his chamber,
and like a strong man runs its course with joy.
6 Its rising is from the end of the heavens,
and its circuit to the end of them;
and there is nothing hid from its heat.

Ant. 3 Blessed art Thou, O Lord, in the firmament of heaven.

Short Reading

Jeremiah 15:16

16 Thy words were found, and I ate them,
and thy words became to me a joy
and the delight of my heart;
for I am called by thy name,
O Lord, God of hosts.

Short Responsory

℟. Rejoice, you just, in the Lord; praise befits the upright.
℣. Sing to Him a new song.

Benedictus ant. Blessed be the Lord, for He has visited and freed us.

Intercessions

Our Savior has made of us a kingdom and a priesthood, that we might offer acceptable sacrifices to God. Thankfully, therefore, let us invoke Him:
Keep us in Your service, O Lord.

Christe, sacérdos ætérne, qui sanctum pópulo tuo sacerdótium concessísti,
—concéde, ut spiritáles hóstias Deo acceptábiles iúgiter offerámus.

Spíritus tui fructus nobis largíre propítius,
—patiéntiam, benignitátem et mansuetúdinem.

Da nobis te amáre, ut te, qui es cáritas, possideámus,
—et bene ágere, ut per vitam étiam nostram te laudémus.

Quæ frátribus nostris sunt utília, nos quærere concéde,
—ut salútem facílius consequántur.

Pater noster.

ORATIO

Dómine Deus omnípotens, qui ad princípium huius diéi nos perveníre fecísti, tua nos hódie salva virtúte, ut in hac die ad nullum declinémus peccátum, sed semper ad tuam iustítiam faciéndam, nostra procédant elóquia, dirigántur cogitatiónes et ópera. Per Dóminum.

Christ, eternal priest, Who have bestowed on Your people a holy priesthood,
—grant that we might perpetually offer acceptable spiritual sacrifices to God.
Mercifully endow us with the fruits of Your Spirit,
—patience, kindness and gentleness.
Grant us to love You, that we might possess You that are charity,
—and to do good that even by our life we might praise you.
Grant us to seek those things which are profitable to our brothers,
—that they might the more readily attain salvation.

Our Father.

ORATION

Lord God almighty, Who have brought us to the beginning of this day, save us today by Your strength, that in this day we may fall into no sin, but may our words always proceed, our thoughts and actions always be directed to doing Your justice. Through our Lord.

Hebdomada II

Feria II, ad Vesperas

Hymnus

Lúminis fons, lux et orígo lucis,
tu pius nostris précibus favéto,
luxque, peccáti ténebris fugátis,
  nos tu*a* adórnet.

Ecce transáctus labor est diéi,
teque nos tuti sumus adnuénte;
en tibi grates ágimus libéntes
  tempus in omne.

Solis abscéssus ténebras redúxit:
ille sol nobis rádiet corúscus
luce qui fulva fovet angelórum
  ágmina sancta.

Quas dies culpas hodiérna texit,
Christus deléto pius atque mitis,
pectus et puro rútilet nitóre
  témpore noctis.

Laus tibi Patri, decus atque Nato,
Flámini Sancto párilis potéstas,
cuncta qui sceptro régitis suprémo
  omne per ævum. Amen.

Psalmodia

Ant. 1 Speciósus forma præ fíliis hóminum, diffúsa est grátia in lábiis tuis.

Week II

Monday, Vespers

HYMN   Trans. The Benedictine Nuns, St. Cecilia's Abbey

O Fount of light, True Light itself,
  Smile down on us as here we pray.
May Your bright splendor shine on us,
  When shades of sin are cast away

We thank you for Your loving care
  While work and toil have been our lot,
And now that day its near its close,
  Dear Lord, we pray, forsake us not.

Though sun declines and shadows fall,
  Our souls draw light from those fair rays
The Sun of Justice ne'er withholds,
  On Whom the hosts of angels gaze.

May all the faults which we deplore,
  Be washed away by Christ our Light,
And may He purify our hearts
  Throughout the hours of coming night.

All glory, Father, be to You,
  Praise to the Spirit and the Son,
Who rule all things with pow'r supreme
  Till all created time is done. Amen.

PSALMODY

Ant. 1 You are the fairest of the sons of men; grace is poured upon your lips.

Psalmus 44 (45)

I

2 Eructávit cor meum verbum bonum, †
dico ego ópera mea regi. *
Lingua mea cálamus scribæ velóciter scribéntis.

3 Speciósus forma es præ fíliis hóminum, †
diffúsa est grátia in lábiis tuis, *
proptérea benedíxit te Deus in ætérnum.
4 Accíngere gládio tuo super femur tuum,
potentíssime, *
magnificéntia tua et ornátu tuo.
5 Et ornátu tuo procéde, currum ascénde *
propter veritátem et mansuetúdinem et
iustítiam.
Et dóceat te mirabília déxtera tua: †
6 sagíttæ tuæ acútæ—pópuli sub te cadent— *
in corda inimicórum regis.

7 Sedes tua, Deus in sæculum sæculi; *
sceptrum æquitátis sceptrum regni tui.
8 Dilexísti iustítiam et odísti iniquitátem, †
proptérea unxit te Deus, Deus tuus, *
óleo lætítiæ præ consórtibus tuis.

9 Myrrha et áloe et cásia ómnia vestiménta tua; *
e dómibus ebúrneis chordæ deléctant te.
10 Fíliæ regum in pretiósis tuis; *
ástitit regína a dextris tuis ornáta auro ex Ophir.

Psalm 45

I

1 My heart overflows with a goodly theme;
I address my verses to the king;
my tongue is like the pen of a ready scribe.

2 You are the fairest of the sons of men;
grace is poured upon your lips;
therefore God has blessed you for ever.
3 Gird your sword upon your thigh, O mighty one,
in your glory and majesty!

4 In your majesty ride forth victoriously
for the cause of truth and to defend the right;
let your right hand teach you dread deeds!
5 Your arrows are sharp
in the heart of the king's enemies;
the peoples fall under you.

6 Your divine throne endures for ever and ever.
Your royal scepter is a scepter of equity;
7 you love righteousness and hate wickedness.
Therefore God, your God, has anointed you
with the oil of gladness above your fellows;
8 your robes are all fragrant with myrrh and aloes
and cassia.
From ivory palaces stringed instruments make
you glad;
9 daughters of kings are among your ladies of
honor;
at your right hand stands the queen in gold of
Ophir.

Ant. Speciósus forma præ filiis hóminum, diffúsa est grátia in lábiis tuis.
Ant. 2 Ecce Sponsus venit: exíte óbviam ei.

II

11 Audi, fília, et vide †
et inclína aurem tuam *
et oblivíscere pópulum tuum et domum patris tui;
12 et concupíscet rex spéciem tuam. *
Quóniam ipse est dóminus tuus, et adóra eum.
13 Fília Tyri cum munéribus; *
vultum tuum deprecabúntur dívites plebis.

14 Gloriósa nimis fília regis intrínsecus, *
textúris áureis circumamícta.
15 In véstibus variegátis adducétur regi; *
vírgines post eam, próximæ eius, afferúntur tibi.
16 Afferúntur in lætítia et exsultatióne, *
adducúntur in domum regis.

17 Pro pátribus tuis erunt tibi fílii; *
constítues eos príncipes super omnem terram.
10 Memor ero nóminis tui *
in omni generatióne et generatióne;
proptérea pópuli confitebúntur tibi in ætérnum *
et in sǽculum sǽculi.

Ant. Ecce Sponsus venit: exíte óbviam ei.
Ant. 3 Propósuit Deus in plenitúdine témporum instauráre ómnia in Christo.

Ant. 1 You are the fairest of the sons of men; grace is poured upon your lips.
Ant. 2 Behold the Bridegroom is here; go out to meet Him.

II

10 Hear, O daughter, consider, and incline your ear;
forget your people and your father's house;
11 and the king will desire your beauty.
Since he is your lord, bow to him;
12 the people of Tyre will sue your favor with gifts,
the richest of the people 13 with all kinds of wealth.

The princess is decked in her chamber with gold-woven robes;
14 in many-colored robes she is led to the king,
with her virgin companions, her escort, in her train.
15 With joy and gladness they are led along
as they enter the palace of the king.

16 Instead of your fathers shall be your sons;
you will make them princes in all the earth.
17 I will cause your name to be celebrated in all generations;
therefore the peoples will praise you for ever and ever.

Ant. 2 Behold the Bridegroom is here; go out to meet Him.
Ant. 3 God planned to restore all things in Christ in the fulness of time.

Canticum Eph 1,3–10

3 Benedíctus Deus et Pater Dómini nostri Iesu
Christi, *
qui benedíxit nos in omni benedictióne spiritáli in
cæléstibus in Christo,
4 sicut elégit nos in ipso ante mundi
constitutiónem, †
ut essémus sancti et immaculáti *
in conspéctu eius in caritáte,
5 qui prædestinávit nos in adoptiónem filiórum †
per Iesum Christum in ipsum, *
secúndum beneplácitum voluntátis suæ,
6 in laudem glóriæ grátiæ suæ, *
in qua gratificávit nos in Dilécto,
7 in quo habémus redemptiónem per sánguinem
eius *
remissiónem peccatórum,
secúndum divítias grátiæ eius, †
8 qua superabundávit in nobis *
in omni sapiéntia et prudéntia
9 notum fáciens nobis mystérium voluntátis suæ, *
secúndum beneplácitum eius,
quod propósuit in eo, *
10 in dispensatiónem plenitúdinis témporum:
recapituláre ómnia in Christo, *
quæ in cælis et quæ in terra.

Ant. Propósuit Deus in plenitúdine témporum instauráre ómnia in Christo.

Canticle Ephesians 1:3–10

3 Blessed be the God and Father of our Lord Jesus Christ, who has blessed us in Christ with every spiritual blessing in the heavenly places,
4 even as he chose us in him before the foundation of the world, that we should be holy and blameless before him.
5 He destined us in love to be his sons through Jesus Christ, according to the purpose of his will,
6 to the praise of his glorious grace which he freely bestowed on us in the Beloved.
7 In him we have redemption through his blood, the forgiveness of our trespasses, according to the riches of his grace
8 which he lavished upon us.
9 For he has made known to us in all wisdom and insight the mystery of his will, according to his purpose which he set forth in Christ
10 as a plan for the fulness of time, to unite all things in him, things in heaven and things on earth.

Ant. 3 God planned to restore all things in Christ in the fulness of time.

Lectio Brevis

1 Th 2, 13

Grátias ágimus Deo sine intermissióne, quóniam cum accepissétis a nobis verbum audítus Dei, accepístis non ut verbum hóminum sed, sicut est vere, verbum Dei, quod et operátur in vobis, qui créditis.

Responsorium Breve

℟. Dirigátur, Dómine, * Ad te orátio mea. Dirigátur.
℣. Sicut incénsum in conspéctu tuo. * Ad te orátio mea. Glória Patri. Dirigátur.

Ad Magnificat, ant. Magníficet te semper ánima mea, Deus meus.

Preces

Laudémus Christum, qui díligit Ecclésiam eámque nutrit et fovet. Eum fidénter rogémus clamántes:
Adímple vota pópuli tui, Dómine.

Dómine Iesu, fac ut omnes hómines salvi fiant,
—et ad agnitiónem véniant veritátis.

Custódi Papam nostrum, N., et Epíscopum, N.,
—adiutórium illis tuæ virtútis impénde.

Cónsule iis, qui iustum sibi opus exóptant,
—ut vitam læti tránsigant et secúri.

Fias, Dómine, refúgium páuperi,
—sis ei adiútor in tribulatióne.

Tibi commendámus quos, dum víverent, sacro ministério decorásti;
—in cælésti sede te célebrent sine fine.

Pater noster

Short Reading
1 Thessalonians 2:13

We thank God constantly for this, that when you received the word of God which you heard from us, you accepted it not as the word of men but as what it really is, the word of God, which is at work in you believers.

Short Responsory

℣. May my prayer, O Lord, come before You.
℟. Like incense in your sight.

Magnificat ant. May my soul always magnify You, my God.

Intercessions

Let us praise Christ, Who loves His Church, nourishes and fosters her. Let us faithfully beseech Him, crying out: *Fulfill the supplications of Your people, O Lord.*

Lord Jesus, grant that all men may be saved,
—and come to a knowledge of the truth.

Keep our Pope, N., and our bishop, N.;
—provide them with the help of Your strength.

Assist those who are seeking just work for themselves,
—that they may lead their lives in happiness and security.

Be, O Lord, the refuge of the one who is poor,
—be to him a helper in tribulation.

We commend to You those whom, while they lived, You adorned with the sacred ministry;
—may they celebrate you without end at Your heavenly seat.

Our Father.

ORATIO

Deus omnípotens, qui hódie servos tuos inútiles in labóribus roborásti, hoc laudis súscipe, quod tibi offérimus, sacrifícium vespertínum, de suscéptis a te munéribus grátias referéntes. Per Dóminum.

ORATION

God Almighty, Who have strengthened today Your useless servants in their labors, accept this evening sacrifice of praise which we offer You, rendering thanks for the benefits received from You. Through our Lord.

Hebdomada II

Feria III, ad Laudes matutinas

HYMNUS

Ætérne lucis cónditor,
lux ipse totus et dies,
noctem nec ullam séntiens
natúra lucis pérpeti,

Iam cedit pallens próximo
diéi nox advéntui,
obtúndens lumen síderum
adest et clarus lúcifer.

Iam stratis læti súrgimus
grates canéntes et tuas,
quod cæcam noctem vícerit
revéctans rursus sol diem.

Te nunc, ne carnis gáudia
blandis subrépant æstibus,
dolis ne cedat sǽculi
mens nostra, sancte, quǽsumus.

Ira ne rixas próvocet,
gulam ne venter íncitet,
opum pervértat ne famis,
turpis ne luxus óccupet,

Sed firma mente sóbrii,
casto manéntes córpore
totum fidéli spíritu
Christo ducámus hunc diem.

Week II

Tuesday, Lauds

HYMN Trans. The Benedictine Nuns, St. Cecilia's Abbey

Eternal Maker of the light,
True Light itself, surpassing day,
No gloom or darkness can you know,
In your own light which has no end.

Pale shades of night are yielding fast,
Before the bold advance of day;
Resplendent shines the morning star
While other constellations fade.

We gladly rise to sing Your praise,
And thank You with renewed delight,
That rising sun brings back the day,
To conquer night's obscurity.

Most Holy One, we beg of You
Let not our souls be led astray,
By nature's pleasures and desires
Or by the world's deceiving glare.

Let no contention raise disputes,
Nor greed disgrace a Christian's name,
Nor greed for riches be a snare,
Nor evil thoughts corrupt our minds.

But let us show well-governed souls,
Within a body chaste and pure,
To spend this day in work and prayer,
For Christ our Leader and our Lord.

Præsta, Pater piíssime,
Patríque compar Unice,
cum Spíritu Paráclito
regnans per omne sæculum. Amen.

PSALMODIA

Ant. 1 Emítte lucem tuam et veritátem tuam, Dómine.

Psalmus 42 (43)

1 Iudica me, Deus †
et discérne causam meam de gente non sancta; *
ab hómine iníquo et dolóso érue me.
2 Quia tu es Deus refúgii mei; †
quare me reppulísti, *
et quare tristis incédo, dum afflígit me inimícus?

3 Emítte lucem tuam et veritátem tuam; *
ipsæ me dedúcant et addúcant in montem sanctum tuum et in tabernácula tua.
4 Et introíbo ad altáre Dei, †
ad Deum lætítiæ exsultatiónis meæ.
Confitébor tibi in cíthara, Deus, Deus meus.

5 Quare tristis es, ánima mea, *
et quare conturbáris in me?
Spera in Deo, quóniam adhuc confitébor illi, *
salutáre vultus mei et Deus meus.

Ant. Emítte lucem tuam et veritátem tuam, Dómine.

Ant. 2 Cunctis diébus vitæ nostræ, salvos nos fac, Dómine.

Most loving Father, hear our prayer
Through Jesus Christ Your only Son,
Who, with the Spirit, reigns with You,
Eternal Trinity in one. Amen.

PSALMODY

Ant. 1 Send out Thy light and Thy truth, O Lord.

Psalm 43

1 Vindicate me, O God, and defend my cause
against an ungodly people;
from deceitful and unjust men
deliver me!
2 For thou art the God in whom I take refuge;
why hast thou cast me off?
Why go I mourning
because of the oppression of the enemy?

3 Oh, send out thy light and thy truth;
let them lead me,
let them bring me to thy holy hill
and to thy dwelling!
4 Then I will go to the altar of God,
to God my exceeding joy;
and I will praise thee with the lyre,
O God, my God.

5 Why are you cast down, O my soul,
and why are you disquieted within me?
Hope in God; for I shall again praise him,
my help and my God.

Ant. 1 Send out Thy light and Thy truth, O Lord.
Ant. 2 All the days of our life, keep us safe, O Lord.

Canticum Is 38, 10–14. 17–20

10 Ego dixi: In dimídio diérum meórum †
vadam ad portas ínferi; *
quæsívi resíduum annórum meórum.

11 Dixi: Non vidébo Dóminum Deum in terra
vivéntium, †
non aspíciam hóminem ultra *
inter habitatóres orbis.

12 Habitáculum meum ablátum est et abdúctum
longe a me *
quasi tabernáculum pastórum;
convólvit sicut textor vitam meam; *
de stámine succídit me.

De mane usque ad vésperam *
confecísti me.
13 Prostrátus sum usque ad mane, *
quasi leo sic cónterit ómnia ossa mea;
de mane usque ad vésperam *
confecísti me.

14 Sicut pullus hirúndinis, sic mussitábo, *
meditábor ut colúmba;
attenuáti sunt óculi mei *
suspiciéntes in excélsum.

17 Tu autem eruísti ánimam meam *
a fóvea consumptiónis,
proiecísti enim post tergum tuum *
ómnia peccáta mea.

18 Quia non inférnus confitébitur tibi, *
neque mors laudábit te;

Canticle Isaiah 38:10–14, 17–20

10 I said, In the noontide of my days
I must depart;
I am consigned to the gates of Sheol
for the rest of my years.
11 I said, I shall not see the LORD
in the land of the living;
I shall look upon man no more
among the inhabitants of the world.
12 My dwelling is plucked up and removed from me
like a shepherd's tent;
like a weaver I have rolled up my life;
he cuts me off from the loom;
from day to night thou dost bring me to an end;
13 I cry for help until morning;
like a lion he breaks all my bones;
from day to night thou dost bring me to an end.

14 Like a swallow or a crane I clamor,
I moan like a dove.
My eyes are weary with looking upward.
O Lord, I am oppressed; be thou my security!

17 Lo, it was for my welfare
that I had great bitterness;
but thou hast held back my life
from the pit of destruction,
for thou hast cast all my sins behind thy back.
18 For Sheol cannot thank thee,
death cannot praise thee;
those who go down to the Pit cannot hope
for thy faithfulness.

non exspectábunt, qui descéndunt in lacum, *
veritátem tuam.

19 Vivens, vivens ipse confitébitur tibi, sicut et ego hódie; *
pater fíliis notam fáciet veritátem tuam.

20 Dómine, salvum me fac, †
et ad sonum cítharæ cantábimus cunctis diébus vitæ nostræ *
in domo Dómini.

Ant. Cunctis diébus vitæ nostræ, salvos nos fac, Dómine.
Ant. 3 Te decet hymnus, Deus, in Sion. †

Psalmus 64 (65)

2 Te decet hymnus, Deus, in Sion; *
† et tibi reddétur votum in Ierúsalem.

3 Qui audis oratiónem, *
ad te omnis caro véniet propter iniquitátem.
4 Etsi prævaluérunt super nos impietátes nostræ, *
tu propitiáberis eis.

5 Beátus, quem elegísti et assumpsísti; *
inhabitábit in átriis tuis.
Replébimur bonis domus tuæ, *
sanctitáte templi tui.
6 Mirabíliter in æquitáte exáudies nos, Deus salútis nostræ, *
spes ómnimum fínium terræ et maris longínqui.

19 The living, the living, he thanks thee,
as I do this day;
the father makes known to the children
thy faithfulness.

20 The LORD will save me
and we will sing to stringed instruments
all the days of our life,
at the house of the LORD.

Ant. 2 All the days of our life, keep us safe, O Lord.
Ant. 3 Praise is due to Thee, O God, in Zion.

Psalm 65

1 Praise is due to thee,
O God, in Zion;
and to thee shall vows be performed,
2 O thou who hearest prayer!
To thee shall all flesh come
3 on account of sins.
When our transgressions prevail over us,
thou dost forgive them.
4 Blessed is he whom thou dost choose and bring near,
to dwell in thy courts!
We shall be satisfied with the goodness of thy house,
thy holy temple!

5 By dread deeds thou dost answer us with deliverance,
O God of our salvation,
who art the hope of all the ends of the earth,
and of the farthest seas;

7 Firmans montes in virtúte tua, *
accínctus poténtia.
8 Compéscens sónitum maris, sónitum flúctuum eius *
et tumúltum populórum.
9 Et timébunt, qui hábitant términos terræ, a signis tuis; *
éxitus oriéntis et occidéntis delectábis.

10 Visitásti terram et inebriásti eam; *
multiplicásti locupletáre eam.
Flumen Dei replétum est aquis; †
parásti fruménta illórum, *
quóniam ita parásti eam.
11 Sulcos eius írrigans, glebas eius complánans; *
ímbribus emóllis eam, benedícis gérmini eius.

12 Coronásti annum benignitáte tua, *
et vestígia tua stillábunt pinguédinem.
13 Stillábunt páscua desérti, *
et exsultatióne colles accingéntur.
14 Indúta sunt óvibus prata, †
et valles abundábunt fruménto; *
clamábunt, étenim hymnum dicent.

Ant. Te decet hymnus, Deus, in Sion.

6 who by thy strength hast established the mountains,
being girded with might;
7 who dost still the roaring of the seas,
the roaring of their waves,
the tumult of the peoples;
8 so that those who dwell at earth's farthest bounds
are afraid at thy signs;
thou makest the outgoings of the morning and the evening
to shout for joy.

9 Thou visitest the earth and waterest it,
thou greatly enrichest it;
the river of God is full of water;
thou providest their grain,
for so thou hast prepared it.
10 Thou waterest its furrows abundantly,
settling its ridges,
softening it with showers,
and blessing its growth.
11 Thou crownest the year with thy bounty;
the tracks of thy chariot drip with fatness.
12 The pastures of the wilderness drip,
the hills gird themselves with joy,
13 the meadows clothe themselves with flocks,
the valleys deck themselves with grain,
they shout and sing together for joy.

Ant. 3 Praise is due to Thee, O God, in Zion.

LECTIO BREVIS 1 Tb 5, 4–5

Vos, fratres, non estis in ténebris, ut vos dies ille tamquam fur comprehéndat; omnes enim vos fílii lucis estis et fílii diéi. Non sumus noctis neque tenebrárum.

RESPONSORIUM BREVE

℟. Vocem meam audi, Dómine; * In verba tua supersperávi. Vocem.

℣. Prævéni dilúculo et clamávi. * In verba tua supersperávi. Glória Patri. Vocem.

Ad Benedictus, ant. De manu ómnium qui odérunt nos, salva nos, Dómine.

PRECES

Salvatóri nostro benedicámus, qui sua resurrectióne mundum clarificávit, et humíliter invocémus eum dicéntes: *Salva nos, Dómine, in sémita tua.*

Resurrectiónem tuam, Dómine Iesu, oratióne cólimus matutína,
—spes glóriæ tuæ diem nostrum illúminet.

Súscipe, Dómine, vota et propósita nostra,
—tamquam diéi nostri primítias.

Tríbue in dilectióne tua nos hódie profícere,
—ut ómnia in nostrum omniúmque bonum cooperéntur.

Da, Dómine, sic lucére lucem nostram coram homínibus,
—ut vídeant ópera nostra bona et Patrem gloríficent.

Pater noster.

Short Reading

1 Thessalonians 5:4–5

You are not in darkness, brethren, for that day to surprise you like a thief. For you are all sons of light and sons of the day; we are not of the night or of darkness.

Short Responsory

℟. Lord, hear my voice; I have trusted in Your words.
℣. At dawn I watched and cried out.

Benedictus ant. From the hand of all who hate us, save us, O Lord.

Intercessions

Let us bless our Savior, Who enlightened the world by His resurrection. Humbly, let us invoke Him saying: *Preserve us, O Lord, in Your way.*

Your resurrection, Lord Jesus, we venerate in our morning prayer,
—may the hope of Your glory enlighten our day.

Accept, O Lord, our prayers and supplications,
—as the first-fruits of our day.

Grant us to increase in Your love today,
—that all things might work together for our good and the good of all.

Grant, O Lord, that our light might shine before men,
—that they may see our good works and give glory to the Father.

Our Father.

Oratio

Dómine Iesu Christe, lux vera, qui omnes hómines illúminas ad salútem, nobis quǽsumus concéde virtútem, ut ante te vias pacis et iustítiæ præparémus. Qui vivis.

ORATION

Lord Jesus Christ, true Light, Who enlighten all men unto salvation, we ask You to grant us strength, that we might prepare the ways of peace and justice before You. Who live.

Hebdomada II

Feria III, ad Vesperas

Hymnus

Sator princépsque témporum,
clarum diem labóribus
Noctémque qui sopóribus
fixo distínguis órdine,

Mentem tu castam dírige,
obscúra ne siléntia
ad dira cordis vúlnera
telis patéscant ínvidi.

Vacent ardóre péctora,
faces nec ullas pérferant,
quæ nostr*o* hæréntes sénsui
mentis vigórem sáucient.

Præsta, Pater piíssime,
Patríque compar Unice,
Cum Spíritu Paráclito
regnans per omne sæculum. Amen.

Psalmodia

Ant. 1 Non potéstis Deo servíre et mammónæ.

Week II

Tuesday, Vespers

HYMN Trans. The Benedictine Nuns, St. Cecilia's Abbey

Great Ruler of all space and time,
You give us daylight to employ
In work for You, that with the night
Refreshing sleep we may enjoy.

While silence and the darkness reign
Preserve our souls from sin and harm,
Let nothing evil venture near
To cause us panic or alarm.

And while we thus renew our strength,
Quite free from taint of sinful fire
Let hearts and minds find rest in You,
Untroubled by ill-timed desire.

Most tender Father, hear our prayer,
Whom we adore with Christ the Lord,
And Holy Spirit of them both;
Bless us who praise Your Trinity.
Amen.

PSALMODY

Ant. 1 You cannot serve both God and mammon.

Psalmus 48(49)

I

2 Audíte hæc, omnes gentes, *
áuribus percípite, omnes, qui habitátis orbem:
3 quique húmiles et viri nóbiles, *
simul in unum dives et pauper!

4 Os meum loquétur sapiéntiam *
et meditátio cordis mei prudéntiam.
5 Inclinábo in parábolam aurem meam, *
apériam in psaltério ænígma meum.
6 Cur timébo in diébus malis, *
cum iníquitas supplantántium circúmdabit me?
7 Qui confídunt in virtúte sua *
et in multitúdine divitiárum suárum gloriántur.

8 Etenim seípsum non rédimet homo; *
non dabit Deo propitiatiónem suam.
9 Nímium est prétium redemptiónis ánimæ eius: †
ad últimum defíciet, *
10 ut vivat usque in finem, nec vídeat intéritum.
11 Et vidébit sapiéntes moriéntes; †
simul insípiens et stultus perîbunt *
et relínquent aliénis divítias suas.

12 Sepúlcra eórum domus illórum in ætérnum; †
tabernácula eórum in progéniem et
progéniem, *
etsi vocavérunt nomínibus suis terras suas.
13 Et homo, cum sit in honóre, non permanébit; †
comparátus est iuméntis, quæ péreunt, *
et símilis factus est illis.

Psalm 49

I

1 Hear this, all peoples!
Give ear, all inhabitants of the world,
2 both low and high,
rich and poor together!
3 My mouth shall speak wisdom;
the meditation of my heart shall be understanding.
4 I will incline my ear to a proverb;
I will solve my riddle to the music of the lyre.

5 Why should I fear in times of trouble,
when the iniquity of my persecutors surrounds me,
6 men who trust in their wealth
and boast of the abundance of their riches?
7 Truly no man can ransom himself,
or give to God the price of his life,
8 for the ransom of his life is costly,
and can never suffice,
9 that he should continue to live on for ever,
and never see the Pit.

10 Yea, he shall see that even the wise die,
the fool and the stupid alike must perish
and leave their wealth to others.
11 Their graves are their homes for ever,
their dwelling places to all generations,
though they named lands their own.
12 Man cannot abide in his pomp,
he is like the beasts that perish.

Ant. Non potéstis Deo servíre et mammónæ.
Ant. 2 Thesaurizáte vobis thesáuros in cælo, dicit Dóminus.

II

14 Hæc via illórum, quorum fidúcia in semetípsis, *
et finis eórum, qui cómplacent in ore suo.
15 Sicut oves in inférno pósiti sunt, *
mors depáscet eos;
descéndent præcípites ad sepúlcrum, †
et figúra eórum erit in consumptiónem: *
inférnus habitáculum eórum.

16 Verúmtamen Deus rédimet ánimam meam, *
de manu ínferi vere suscípiet me.
17 Ne timúeris, cum dives factus fúerit homo *
et cum multiplicáta fúerit glória domus eius,
18 quóniam, cum interíerit, non sumet ómnia, *
neque descéndet cum eo glória eius.

19 Cum ánimæ suæ in vita ipsíus benedíxerit: *
« Laudábunt te quod benefecísti tibi ».
20 tamen introíbit ad progéniem patrum suórum, *
qui in ætérnum non vidébunt lumen.

21 Homo, cum in honóre esset, non intelléxit; †
comparátus est iuméntis, quæ péreunt, *
et símilis factus est illis.

Ant. Thesaurizáte vobis thesáuros in cælo, dicit Dóminus.
Ant. 3 Dignus est Agnus qui occísus est accípere glóriam et honórem.

Ant. 1 You cannot serve both God and mammon.
Ant. 2 Store up for yourselves treasures in heaven, says the Lord.

II

13 This is the fate of those who have foolish confidence,
the end of those who are pleased with their portion.
14 Like sheep they are appointed for Sheol;
death shall be their shepherd;
straight to the grave they descend,
and their form shall waste away;
Sheol shall be their home.
15 But God will ransom my soul from the power of Sheol,
for he will receive me.

16 Be not afraid when one becomes rich,
when the glory of his house increases.
17 For when he dies he will carry nothing away;
his glory will not go down after him.
18 Though, while he lives, he counts himself happy,
and though a man gets praise when he does well for himself,
19 he will go to the generation of his fathers,
who will never more see the light.
20 Man cannot abide in his pomp,
he is like the beasts that perish.

Ant. 2 Store up for yourselves treasures in heaven, says the Lord.
Ant. 3 Worthy is the Lamb Who was slain to receive glory and blessing.

Canticum Ap 4, 11; 5, 9. 10. 12

4,11 Dignus es, Dómine et Deus noster, *
accípere glóriam et honórem et virtútem,
quia tu creásti ómnia, *
et propter voluntátem tuam erant et creáta sunt.

5,9 Dignus es, Dómine, accípere librum *
et aperíre signácula eius,
quóniam occísus es †
et redemísti Deo in sánguine tuo *
ex omni tribu et lingua et pópulo et natióne
10 et fecísti eos Deo nostro regnum et sacerdótes, *
et regnábunt super terram.

12 Dignus est Agnus, qui occísus est, †
accípere virtútem et divítias et sapiéntiam *
et fortitúdinem et honórem et glóriam et
benedictiónem.

Ant. Dignus est Agnus qui occísus est accípere glóriam et honórem.

Lectio Brevis Rom 3, 23–25a

Omnes peccavérunt et egent glória Dei, iustificáti gratis per grátiam ipsíus per redemptiónem, quæ est in Christo Iesu; quem propósuit Deus propitiatórium per fidem in sánguine ipsíus ad ostensiónem iustítiæ suæ.

Responsorium Breve

℟. Adimplébis me lætíia * Cum vultu tuo, Dómine. Adimplébis.

℣. Delectatiónes in déxtera tua usque in finem. * Cum vultu tuo, Dómine. Glória Patri. Adimplébis.

Canticle Revelation 4:11; 5:9, 10, 12

11 "Worthy art thou, our Lord and God,
to receive glory and honor and power,
for thou didst create all things,
and by thy will they existed and were created."

9 "Worthy art thou to take the scroll and open its seals,
for thou wast slain and by thy blood didst ransom men for God
from every tribe and tongue and people and nation,
10 and hast made them a kingdom and priests to our God,
and they shall reign on earth."

12 "Worthy is the Lamb who was slain, to receive power and wealth and wisdom and might and honor and glory and blessing!"

Ant. 3 Worthy is the Lamb Who was slain to receive glory and blessing.

SHORT READING Romans 3:23–25a

Since all have sinned and fall short of the glory of God, they are justified by his grace as a gift, through the redemption which is in Christ Jesus, whom God put forward as an expiation by his blood, to be received by faith.

SHORT RESPONSORY

℟. You shall fill me with joy in Your presence, O Lord.

℣. Delight at Your right hand forever.

Ad Magnificat, ant. Fac nobíscum, Dómine, magna, quia potens es, et sanctum nomen tuum.

PRECES

Christum, pastórem et epíscopum animárum nostrárum, laudémus, qui díligit et tuétur pópulum suum. In eo spem nostram ponéntes supplicémus: *Prótege pópulum tuum, Dómine.*

Prótege, Pastor ætérne, antístitem nostrum N.
—et cunctos Ecclésiæ tuæ pastóres.

Réspice propítius eos, qui persecutiónem patiúntur,
—eósque festína ab ómnibus tribulatiónibus liberáre.

Miserére, Dómine, ómnium egenórum,
—esuriéntibus escam largíre.

Illúmina cœtus légibus feréndis deputátos,
—ut in ómnibus sapiénti æquitáte decérnant.

Succúrre defúnctis, quos tuo sánguine redemísti,
—tecum ad núptias intráre mereántur.

Pater noster.

ORATIO

Dómine Deus, cuius est dies et cuius est nox, concéde solem iustítiæ in nostris córdibus permanére, ut ad lucem, quam inhábitas, perveníre possímus. Per Dóminum.

Magnificat ant. Do great things for us, O Lord, for You are mighty, and holy is Your name.

INTERCESSIONS

Let us praise Christ, the shepherd and overseer of our souls, Who loves and protects His people. Placing our hope in Him, let us beseech Him: *Protect Your people, O Lord.*

Protect, eternal Shepherd, our bishop, N.,
—and all the shepherds of Your Church.

Graciously look upon those who suffer persecution,
—and make haste to free them from every tribulation.

Have mercy, O Lord, on all the needy,
—provide food for the hungry.

Enlighten all legislative bodies,
—that in all things they may decide wisely and justly.

Be the help of the deceased, whom You redeemed by Your blood,
—may they merit to enter with You into the wedding feast.

Our Father.

ORATION

Lord God, Whose is the day and Whose is the night, grant that the Sun of Justice may rest in our hearts, that we might enter into that light where You dwell. Through our Lord.

Hebdomada II

Feria IV, ad Laudes matutinas

Hymnus

Fulgéntis auctor ætheris,
qui lunam lumen nóctibus,
solem diérum cúrsibus
certo fundásti trámite,

Nox atra iam depéllitur,
mundi nitor renáscitur,
novúsque iam mentis vigor
dulces in actus érigit.

Laudes sonáre iam tuas
dies relátus ádmonet,
vultúsque cæli blándior
nostra serénat péctora.

Vitémus omne lúbricum,
declínet prava spíritus,
vitam facta non ínquinent,
linguam culpa non ímplicet;

Sed, sol diem dum cónficit,
fides profúnda férveat,
spes ad promíssa próvocet,
Christo coniúngat cáritas.

Præsta, pater piíssime,
Patríque compar Unice,
cum Spíritu Paráclito
regnans per omne sæculum. Amen.

Week II

Wednesday, Lauds

HYMN Trans. The Benedictine Nuns, St. Cecilia's Abbey

Creator of the skies above,
The wisdom of Your plan decreed
That sun should give us light by day,
And moon should rule the hours of night.

The darkness is dispelled at last,
The world's great beauty is revealed;
Our strength of soul is fresh and keen
To spur us on to kindly deeds.

Returning day calls us to prayer,
And bids us sing Your praise anew;
The bright'ning aspect of the sky
Gives courage and serenity.

May we avoid all stain of sin,
No evil mar our thoughts this day,
No sinful action spoil our lives,
No wrong or idle words offend.

But while the sun draws on the day,
May our firm faith grow deeper yet
With hope that presses to the goal,
And love unites us all to Christ.

Most loving Father, hear our prayer
Through Jesus Christ, Your only Son,
Who, with the Spirit reigns with You,
Eternal Trinity in One. Amen.

PSALMODIA

Ant. 1 Deus, in sancto via tua: quis Deus magnus sicut Deus noster?

Psalmus 76 (77)

2 Voce mea ad Dóminum clamávi; *
voce mea ad Deum, et inténdit mihi.
3 In die tribulatiónis meæ Deum exquisívi, †
manus meæ nocte expánsæ sunt *
et non fatigántur.
Rénuit consolári ánima mea; †
4 memor sum Dei et ingemísco, *
exérceor, et déficit spíritus meus.

5 Vígiles tenuísti pálpebras óculi mei; *
turbátus sum et non sum locútus.
6 Cogitávi dies antíquos *
et annos ætérnos in mente hábui.
7 Meditátus sum nocte cum corde meo *
et exercitábar, et scopébam spíritum meum.

8 Numquid in ætérnum proíciet Deus, *
aut non appónet ut complacítior sit adhuc?
9 Aut defíciet in finem misericórdia sua, *
cessábit verbum a generatióne in generatiónem?
10 Aut obliviscétur miseréri Deus, *
aut continébit in ira sua misericórdias suas?

11 Et dixi: « Hoc vulnus meum, *
mutátio déxteræ Excélsi ».
12 Memor ero óperum Dómini, *
memor ero ab inítio mirabílium tuórum.
13 Et meditábor in ómnibus opéribus tuis *
et in adinventiónibus tuis exercébor.

PSALMODY

Ant. 1 Thy way, O God, is holy. What god is great like our God?

Psalm 77

1 I cry aloud to God,
aloud to God, that he may hear me.
2 In the day of my trouble I seek the LORD;
in the night my hand is stretched out without wearying;
my soul refuses to be comforted.

3 I think of God, and I moan;
I meditate, and my spirit faints.
4 Thou dost hold my eyelids from closing;
I am so troubled that I cannot speak.
5 I consider the days of old,
I remember the years long ago.
6 I commune with my heart in the night;
I meditate and search my spirit:
7 "Will the LORD spurn for ever,
and never again be favorable?
8 Has his steadfast love for ever ceased?
Are his promises at an end for all time?
9 Has God forgotten to be gracious?
Has he in anger shut up his compassion?"
10 And I say, "It is my grief
that the right hand of the Most High has changed."

11 I will call to mind the deeds of the LORD;
yea, I will remember thy wonders of old.
12 I will meditate on all thy works,
and muse on thy mighty deeds.

14 Deus in sancto via tua; *
quis deus magnus sicut Deus noster?
15 Tu es Deus, qui facis mirabília, *
notam fecísti in pópulis virtútem tuam.
16 Redemísti in bráchio tuo pópulum tuum, *
fílios Iacob et Ioseph.

17 Vidérunt te aquæ, Deus, †
vidérunt te aquæ et doluérunt; *
étenim commótæ sunt abýssi.
18 Effudérunt aquas núbila, †
vocem dedérunt nubes, *
étenim sagíttæ tuæ tránseunt.
19 Vox tonítrui tui in rota; †
illuxérunt coruscatiónes tuæ orbi terræ, *
commóta est et contrémuit terra.

20 In mari via tua et sémitæ tuæ in aquis multis; *
et vestígia tua non cognoscúntur.
21 Deduxísti sicut oves pópulum tuum *
in manu Móysi et Aaron.

Ant. Deus, in sancto via tua: quis Deus magnus sicut Deus noster?
Ant. 2 Exsultávit cor meum in Dómino, qui humíliat et súblevat.

Canticum I Sam 2, 1–10

1 Exsultávit cor meum in Dómino, *
exaltátum est cornu meum in Deo meo;
dilatátum est os meum super inimícos meos, *
quóniam lætáta sum in salutári tuo.

13 Thy way, O God, is holy.
What god is great like our God?
14 Thou art the God who workest wonders,
who hast manifested thy might among the peoples.
15 Thou didst with thy arm redeem thy people,
the sons of Jacob and Joseph.

16 When the waters saw thee, O God,
when the waters saw thee, they were afraid,
yea, the deep trembled.
17 The clouds poured out water;
the skies gave forth thunder;
thy arrows flashed on every side.
18 The crash of thy thunder was in the whirlwind;
thy lightnings lighted up the world;
the earth trembled and shook.
19 Thy way was through the sea,
thy path through the great waters;
yet thy footprints were unseen.
20 Thou didst lead thy people like a flock
by the hand of Moses and Aaron.

Ant. 1 Thy way, O God, is holy. What god is great like our God?

Ant. 2 My heart exults in the Lord, Who makes poor and makes rich.

Canticle I Samuel 2:1–10

1 "My heart exults in the Lord;
my strength is exalted in the Lord.
My mouth derides my enemies,
because I rejoice in thy salvation.

2 Non est sanctus ut est Dóminus; †
neque enim est álius extra te, *
et non est fortis sicut Deus noster.
3 Nolíte multiplicáre loqui sublímia gloriántes. *
Recédant supérba de ore vestro,
quia Deus scientiárum Dóminus est, *
et ab eo ponderántur actiónes.
4 Arcus fórtium confráctus est, *
et infírmi accíncti sunt róbore.
5 Saturáti prius pro pane se locavérunt, *
et famélici non eguérunt ámplius.
Stérilis péperit plúrimos, *
et, quæ multos habébat fílios, emárcuit.

6 Dóminus mortíficat et vivíficat, *
dedúcit ad inférnum et redúcit.
7 Dóminus páuperem facit et ditat, *
humíliat et súblevat;
8 súscitat de púlvere egénum *
et de stércore élevat páuperem,
ut sédeat cum princípibus *
et sólium glóriæ téneat.
Dómini enim sunt cárdines terræ, *
et pósuit super eos orbem.

9 Pedes sanctórum suórum servábit, †
et ímpii in ténebris conticéscent, *
quia non in fortitúdine sua roborábitur vir.
10 Dóminus cónteret adversários suos; *
super ipsos in cælis tonábit.

2 "There is none holy like the Lord,
there is none besides thee;
there is no rock like our God.
3 Talk no more so very proudly,
let not arrogance come from your mouth;
for the Lord is a God of knowledge,
and by him actions are weighed.
4 The bows of the mighty are broken,
but the feeble gird on strength.
5 Those who were full have hired themselves out
for bread,
but those who were hungry have ceased to
hunger.
The barren has borne seven,
but she who has many children is forlorn.
6 The Lord kills and brings to life;
he brings down to Sheol and raises up.
7 The Lord makes poor and makes rich;
he brings low, he also exalts.
8 He raises up the poor from the dust;
he lifts the needy from the ash heap,
to make them sit with princes
and inherit a seat of honor.
For the pillars of the earth are the Lord's,
and on them he has set the world.

9 "He will guard the feet of his faithful ones;
but the wicked shall be cut off in darkness;
for not by might shall a man prevail.
10 The adversaries of the Lord shall be broken to
pieces;
against them he will thunder in heaven.

Dóminus iudicábit fines terræ †
et dabit impérium regi suo *
et sublimábit cornu christi sui.

Ant. Exsultávit cor meum in Dómino, qui humíliat et súblevat.

Ant. 3 Dóminus regnávit, exsúltet terra. †

Psalmus 96 (97)

1 Dóminus regnávit! Exsúltet terra, *
† læténtur ínsulæ multæ.
2 Nubes et calígo in circúitu eius, *
iustítia et iudícium firmaméntum sedis eius.
3 Ignis ante ipsum præcédet *
et inflammábit in circúitu inimícos eius.
4 Illustrárunt fúlgura eius orbem terræ: *
vidit et contrémuit terra.
5 Montes sicut cera fluxérunt a fácie Dómini, *
a fácie Dómini omnis terra.
6 Annuntiavérunt cæli iustítiam eius, *
et vidérunt omnes pópuli glóriam eius.
7 Confundántur omnes, qui adórant sculptília †
et qui gloriántur in simulácris suis. *
Adoráte eum, omnes ángeli eius.
8 Audívit et lætáta est Sion, †
et exsultavérunt fíliæ Iudæ *
propter iudícia tua, Dómine.
9 Quóniam tu Dóminus, Altíssimus super omnem terram, *
nimis exaltátus es super omnes deos.

The Lord will judge the ends of the earth;
he will give strength to his king,
and exalt the power of his anointed."

Ant. 2 My heart exults in the Lord, Who makes poor and makes rich.
Ant. 3 The Lord reigns; let the earth rejoice.

Psalm 97

1 The LORD reigns; let the earth rejoice;
let the many coastlands be glad!

2 Clouds and thick darkness are round about him;
righteousness and justice are the foundation of his throne.
3 Fire goes before him,
and burns up his adversaries round about.
4 His lightnings lighten the world;
the earth sees and trembles.
5 The mountains melt like wax before the LORD,
before the LORD of all the earth.

6 The heavens proclaim his righteousness;
and all the peoples behold his glory.
7 All worshipers of images are put to shame,
who make their boast in worthless idols;
all gods bow down before him.
8 Zion hears and is glad,
and the daughters of Judah rejoice,
because of thy judgments, O God.
9 For thou, O LORD, art most high over all the earth;
thou art exalted far above all gods.

10 Qui dilígitis Dóminum, odíte malum; †
custódit ipse ánimas sanctórum suórum, *
de manu peccatóris liberábit eos.
11 Lux orta est iusto, *
et rectis corde lætítia.
12 Lætámini, iusti, in Dómino *
et confitémini memóriæ sanctitátis eius.

Ant. Dóminus regnávit, exsúltet terra.

LECTIO BREVIS Rom 8, 35. 37

Quis nos separábit a caritáte Christi? Tribulátio an angústia an persecútio an fames an núditas an perículum an gládius? Sed in his ómnibus supervíncimus per eum, qui diléxit nos.

RESPONSORIUM BREVE

℟. Benedícam Dóminum. * In omni témpore. Benedícam.
℣. Semper laus eius in ore meo. * In omni témpore. Glória Patri. Benedícam.

Ad Benedictus, ant. In sanctitáte serviámus Dómino ómnibus diébus nostris.

PRECES

Benedíctus Deus salvátor noster, qui usque ad consummatiónem sæculi se ómnibus diébus cum Ecclésia sua mansúrum promísit. Ideo ei grátias agéntes clamémus: *Mane nobíscum, Dómine.*

Mane nobíscum, Dómine, toto die,
—numquam declínet a nobis sol grátiæ tuæ.

Hunc diem tibi tamquam oblatiónem consecrámus,
—dum nos nihil pravi factúros aut probatúros pollicémur.

10 The LORD loves those who hate evil;
he preserves the lives of his saints;
he delivers them from the hand of the wicked.
11 Light dawns for the righteous,
and joy for the upright in heart.
12 Rejoice in the LORD, O you righteous,
and give thanks to his holy name!

Ant. 3 The Lord reigns; let the earth rejoice.

SHORT READING Romans 8:35, 37

Who shall separate us from the love of Christ? Shall tribulation, or distress, or persecution, or famine, or nakedness, or peril, or sword? No, in all these things we are more than conquerors through him who loved us.

SHORT RESPONSORY

℟. I shall bless the Lord at all times.
℣. His praise shall be ever on my lips.

Benedictus ant. In holiness, let us serve the Lord all the days of our life.

INTERCESSIONS

Blessed be God our Savior, Who promised to remain with His Church all days, even unto the consummation of the age. Therefore, giving Him thanks, let us cry out: *Stay with us, Lord.*

Stay with us, Lord, the whole day,
—may the sun of Your grace never set on us.

We consecrate this day to You as an oblation,
—as we promise neither to do nor to approve of any evil.

Fac, Dómine, ut donum lucis hic totus dies evádat,
—ut simus sal terræ et lux mundi.
Spíritus Sancti tui cáritas dírigat corda et lábia nostra,
—ut in tua iustítia semper et laude maneámus.

Pater noster.

Oratio

Emítte, quǽsumus, Dómine, in corda nostra tui lúminis claritátem, ut in via mandatórum tuórum iúgiter ambulántes, nihil umquam patiámur erróris. Per Dóminum.

Make, Lord, all this day to go forward as a gift of light,
—that we might be the salt of the earth and the light of the world.
May the charity of Your Holy Spirit direct our hearts and lips,
—that we might always remain in Your justice and praise.

Our Father.

ORATION
Send forth, we beseech You, O Lord, the brightness of Your light into our hearts, that walking perpetually in the way of Your commandments, we might never suffer any error. Through our Lord.

Hebdomada II

Feria IV, ad Vesperas

HYMNUS

Sol, ecce, lentus óccidens
montes et arv*a* et ǽquora
mæstus relínquit, ínnovat
sed lucis omen crástinæ,

Mirántibus mortálibus
sic te, Creátor próvide,
leges vicésque témporum
umbris dedíss*e* et lúmini.

Ac dum, tenébris ǽthera
siléntio preméntibus,
vigor labórum déficit,
quies cupíta quǽritur,

Spe nos fidéque dívites
tui beámur lúmine
Verbi, quod est a sǽculis
splendor patérnæ gloriæ.

Est ille sol qui nésciat
ortum vel umquam vésperum;
quo terra gestit cóntegi,
quo cæl*i* in ævum iúbilant.

Hac nos seréna pérpetim
da luce tandem pérfrui
cum Nat*o* et almo Spíritu
tibi novántes cántica. Amen.

Week II

Wednesday, Vespers

HYMN   Trans. The Benedictine Nuns, St. Cecilia's Abbey

As sun declines and shadows fall,
  The sea and hills will fade from sight;
Its fiery orb bids us farewell
  But promises tomorrow's light.

And thus, O God, Creator wise,
  You regulate in wondrous way
The laws of this great universe
  At which we marvel night and day.

While darkness rides across the sky,
  And stars their silent watches keep,
Your children leave their constant toil,
  Regaining strength by peaceful sleep.

Made rich in hope and solid faith,
  May we be blest throughout the night,
By Christ, the Word Who timeless reigns,
  True splendour of the Father's light.

He is the sun that never sets,
  No dusk can make His lustre die,
The kind Protector of the earth,
  The joy of all the saints on high.

O Father, Son, and Spirit too
  Grant us at last that light to see,
And full of joy Your praises sing,
  Bathed in Your love eternally. Amen.

PSALMODIA

Ant. 1 Exspectémus beátam spem et advéntum glóriæ Salvatóris nostri.

Psalmus 61 (62)

2 In Deo tantum quiésce, ánima mea, *
ab ipso enim salutáre meum.
3 Verúmtamen ipse refúgium meum et salutáre meum, *
præsídium meum, non movébor ámplius.
4 Quoúsque irrúitis in hóminem, †
contúnditis univérsi vos *
tamquam paríetem inclinátum et macériam depúlsam?
5 Verúmtamen de excélso suo cogitavérunt depéllere; †
delectabántur mendácio. *
Ore suo benedicébant et corde suo maledicébant.

6 In Deo tantum quiésce, ánima mea, *
quóniam ab ipso patiéntia mea.
7 Verúmtamen ipse Deus meus et salutáre meum, *
præsídium meum, non movébor.

8 In Deo salutáre meum et glória mea; *
Deus fortitúdinis meæ, et refúgium meum in Deo est.
9 Speráte in eo, omnis congregátio pópuli, †
effúndite coram illo corda vestra; *
Deus refúgium nobis.
10 Verúmtamen vánitas fílii Adam, *
mendácium fílii hóminum.

PSALMODY

Ant. 1 Let us await the blessed hope and glorious coming of our Savior.

Psalm 62

1 For God alone my soul awaits in silence;
from him comes my salvation.
2 He only is my rock and my salvation,
my fortress; I shall not be greatly moved.

3 How long will you set upon a man
to shatter him, all of you,
like a leaning wall, a tottering fence?
4 They only plan to thrust him down from his eminence.
They take pleasure in falsehood.
They bless with their mouths,
but inwardly they curse.

5 For God alone my soul waits in silence,
for my hope is from him.
6 He only is my rock and my salvation,
my fortress; I shall not be shaken.
7 On God rests my deliverance and my honor;
my mighty rock, my refuge is God.

8 Trust in him at all times, O people;
pour out your heart before him;
God is a refuge for us.

9 Men of low estate are but a breath,
men of high estate are a delusion;

In statéram si conscéndant, *
super fumum leves sunt omnes.

11 Nolíte speráre in violéntia †
et in rapína nolíte décipi; *
divítiæ si áffluant, nolíte cor appónere.
12 Semel locútus est Deus, *
duo hæc audívi:
quia potéstas Deo est, †
13 et tibi, Dómine, misericórdia; *
quia tu reddes unicuíque iuxta ópera sua.

Ant. Exspectémus beátam spem et advéntum glóriæ Salvatóris nostri.

Ant. 2 Illúminet vultum suum super nos Deus, et benedícat nobis.

Psalmus 66 (67)

2 Deus misereátur nostri et benedícat nobis; *
illúminet vultum suum super nos,
3 ut cognoscátur in terra via tua, *
in ómnibus géntibus salutáre tuum.

4 Confiteántur tibi pópuli, Deus; *
confiteántur tibi pópuli omnes.
5 Læténtur et exsúltent gentes, †
quóniam iúdicas pópulos in æquitáte *
et gentes in terra dírigis.

6 Confiteántur tibi pópuli, Deus, *
confiteántur tibi pópuli omnes.
7 Terra dedit fructum suum; *
benedícat nos Deus, Deus noster,

in the balances they go up;
they are together lighter than a breath.
10 Put no confidence in extortion,
set no vain hopes on robbery;
if riches increase, set not your heart on them.

11 Once God has spoken;
twice have I heard this:
that power belongs to God;
12 and that to thee, O LORD, belongs steadfast love.
For thou dost requite a man
according to his work.

Ant. 1 Let us await the blessed hope and glorious coming of our Savior.
Ant. 2 May God make His face to shine upon us, and may God bless us.

Psalm 67

1 May God be gracious to us and bless us
and make his face to shine upon us,

2 that thy way may be known upon earth,
thy saving power among all nations.
3 Let the peoples praise thee, O God;
let all the peoples praise thee!

4 Let the nations be glad and sing for joy,
for thou dost judge the peoples with equity
and guide the nations upon earth.
5 Let the peoples praise thee, O God;
let all the peoples praise thee!

6 The earth has yielded its increase;
God, our God, has blessed us.

8 benedícat nos Deus, *
et métuant eum omnes fines terræ.

Ant. Illúminet vultum suum super nos Deus, et benedícat nobis.

Ant. 3 In ipso cóndita sunt univérsa, et ómnia in ipso constant.

Canticum CF. COL 1, 12–20

12 Grátias agámus Deo Patri, *
qui idóneos nos fecit in partem sortis sanctórum in lúmine;
13 qui erípuit nos de potestáte tenebrárum *
et tránstulit in regnum Fílii dilectiónis suæ,
14 in quo habémus redemptiónem *
remissiónem peccatórum;
15 qui est imágo Dei invisíbilis, *
primogénitus omnis creatúræ,
16 quia in ipso cóndita sunt univérsa †
in cælis et in terra, *
visibília et invisibília,
sive throni sive dominatiónes *
sive principátus sive potestátes.

Omnia per ipsum et in ipsum creáta sunt, †
17 et ipse est ante ómnia, *
et ómnia in ipso constant.
18 Et ipse est caput córporis ecclésiæ; †
qui est princípium, primogénitus ex mórtuis, *
ut sit in ómnibus ipse primátum tenens,
19 quia in ipso complácuit omnem plenitúdinem habitáre *

7 God has blessed us;
let all the ends of the earth fear him!

Ant. 2 May God make His face to shine upon us, and may God bless us.

Ant. 3 In Him all things were created, and in Him all things hold together.

Canticle Colossians 1:12–20

12 Let us give thanks to the Father, who has qualified us to share in the inheritance of the saints in light.
13 He has delivered us from the dominion of darkness and transferred us to the kingdom of his beloved Son,
14 in whom we have redemption, the forgiveness of sins.
15 He is the image of the invisible God, the first-born of all creation;
16 for in him all things were created, in heaven and on earth, visible and invisible, whether thrones or dominions or principalities or authorities—all things were created through him and for him.
17 He is before all things, and in him all things hold together.
18 He is the head of the body, the church; he is the beginning, the first-born from the dead, that in everything he might be pre-eminent.
19 For in him all the fulness of God was pleased to dwell,

20 et per eum reconciliáre ómnia in ipsum,
pacíficans per sánguinem crucis eius, *
sive quæ in terris sive quæ in cælis sunt.

Ant. In ipso cóndita sunt univérsa, et ómnia in ipso constant.

Lectio Brevis

1 Petr 5, 5b–7

Omnes ínvicem humilitátem indúite, quia Deus supérbis resístit, humílibus autem dat grátiam. Humiliámini ígitur sub poténti manu Dei, ut vos exáltet in témpore, omnem sollicitúdinem vestram proiciéntes in eum, quóniam ipsi cura est de vobis.

Responsorium Breve

℟. Custódi nos, Domine, * Ut pupíllam óculi. Custódi.

℣. Sub umbra alárum tuárum prótege nos. * Ut pupíllam óculi. Glória Patri. Custódi.

Ad Magnificat, ant. Fac, Deus, poténtiam in brácchio tuo, dispérde supérbos et exálta húmiles.

Preces

Iubilémus Deo nostro, fratres caríssimi, qui máxime in benefíciis pópulo suo elargiéndis congáudet, et cum ánimi fervóre precémur: *Grátiam et pacem multíplica, Dómine.*

Ætérne Deus, cui mille anni sunt tamquam dies hestérna, quæ prætériit,
—esse vitam quasi florem mane germinántem, véspere autem arescéntem nos memoráre concéde.

Manna tuum pópulo largíre, ne esúriat,
—et aquam vivam, ne sítiat in ætérnum.

20 and through him to reconcile to himself all things
whether on earth or in heaven, making peace
by the blood of his cross.

Ant. 3 In Him all things were created, and in Him all things hold together.

SHORT READING 1 Peter 5:5b–7

Clothe yourselves, all of you, with humility toward one another, for "God opposes the proud, but gives grace to the humble."

Humble yourselves therefore under the mighty hand of God, that in due time he may exalt you. Cast all your anxieties on him, for he cares about you.

SHORT RESPONSORY

℟. Keep us, O Lord, as the apple of your eye.
℣. Protect us under the shadow of your wings

Magnificat ant. Show strength, O God, with Your arm; scatter the proud and exalt those of low degree.

INTERCESSIONS

Beloved brethren, let us rejoice in our God, Who greatly delights in bestowing benefits upon His people, and with fervor of spirit, let us pray:
Multiply Your grace and peace, O Lord.

Eternal God, for Whom a thousand years are like a single day which has passed,
—grant that we may remember that life is like a flower which blossoms in the morning, but in the evening withers.

Give Your manna to Your people, lest they hunger,
—and living water, lest they thirst forever.

Fac ut fidéles tui quæ sursum sunt quærant et sápiant,
—étiam témpora óperis et ótii in tuam glóriam vertant.
Aerem nobis, Dómine, largíre propítium,
—quo uberióres percipiámus fructus terræ.
(vel:
Ab ómnibus noxis líbera nos, Dómine,
—et copiósam benedictiónem super domus nostras effúnde.)
Visiónem vultus tui largíre defúnctis,
—et eius contemplatióne nos redde beátos.

Pater noster.

ORATIO

Deus, cuius sanctum est nomen et misericórdia a progénie in progénies celebrátur, pópulum tuum súscipe supplicántem, eíque tríbue perpétuo te magnificáre præcónio. Per Dóminum.

Grant that Your faithful might seek and know those things which are above,
—and may they turn their times of work and leisure to Your glory.

In Your kindness give us favorable weather, O Lord,
—that we might reap abundantly the fruits of the earth.

(or:

Free us from all harmful things, O Lord,
—and pour forth upon our homes Your bountiful blessing.)

Grant to the deceased the sight of Your face,
—and render us blessed in contemplation of it.

Our Father.

ORATION

O God, Whose name is holy and Whose mercy is celebrated from generation to generation, accept Your suppliant people, and grant that they may magnify You with a perpetual hymn of praise. Through our Lord.

Hebdomada II

Feria V, ad Laudes matutinas

Hymnus

Iam lucis orto sídere
Deum precémur súpplices,
ut in diúrnis áctibus
nos servet a nocéntibus.

Linguam refrénans témperet,
ne litis horror ínsonet;
visum fovéndo cóntegat,
ne vanitátes háuriat.

Sint pura cordis íntima,
absístat et vecórdia;
carnis terat supérbiam
potus cibíque párcitas;

Ut, cum dies abscésserit
noctémque sors redúxerit,
mundi per abstinéntiam
ipsi canámus glóriam.

Deo Patri sit glória
eiúsque soli Fílio
cum Spíritu Paráclito,
in sempitérna sǽcula. Amen.

Psalmodia

Ant. 1 Excita, Dómine, poténtiam tuam, ut salvos fácias nos.

Week II

Thursday, Lauds

HYMN Trans. The Benedictine Nuns, St. Cecilia's Abbey

Now that the daylight fills the sky,
We lift our hearts to God on high,
That He, in all we do or say,
Would keep us free from harm today:

Would guard our hearts and tongues from strife;
From anger's din would hide our life;
From all ill sights would turn our eyes;
Would close our ears from vanities:

Would keep our inmost conscience pure;
Our souls from folly would secure;
Would bid us check the pride of sense
With due and holy abstinence.

So we, when this new day is gone,
And night in turn is drawing on,
With conscience by the world unstained
Shall praise His name for victory gained.

All laud to God the Father be;
All praise, eternal Son, to Thee;
All glory as is ever meet,
To God the holy Paraclete. Amen.

PSALMODY

Ant. 1 Stir up Thy might, O Lord; and come to save us.

Psalmus 79 (80)

2 Qui pascis Israel, inténde, *
qui dedúcis velut, ovem Ioseph.
Qui sedes super chérubim, effúlge *
3 coram Ephraim, Béniamin et Manásse.
Excita poténtiam tuam et veni, *
ut salvos fácias nos.

4 Deus, convérte nos, *
illústra fáciem tuam, et salvi érimus.
5 Dómine Deus virtútum, *
quoúsque irascéris super oratiónem pópuli tui?
6 Cibásti nos pane lacrimárum *
et potum dedísti nobis in lácrimis copióse.
7 Posuísti nos in contradictiónem vicínis nostris, *
et inimíci nostri subsannavérunt nos.
8 Deus virtútum, convérte nos, *
illústra fáciem tuam, et salvi érimus.

9 Víneam de Ægýpto transtulísti, *
eiecísti gentes et plantásti eam.
10 Purgásti locum in conspéctu eius, *
plantásti radíces eius, et implévit terram.
11 Opérti sunt montes umbra eius *
et ramis eius cedri Dei;
12 exténdit pálmites suos usque ad mare *
et usque ad Flumen propágines suas.

13 Ut quid destruxísti macériam eius, *
et vindémiant eam omnes, qui prætergrediúntur viam?

Psalm 80

1 Give ear, O Shepherd of Israel,
thou who leadest Joseph like a flock!
Thou who art enthroned upon the cherubim, shine forth
2 before Ephraim and Benjamin and Manasseh!
Stir up thy might,
and come to save us!

3 Restore us, O God;
let thy face shine, that we may be saved!

4 O LORD God of hosts,
how long wilt thou be angry with thy people's prayers?
5 Thou hast fed them with the bread of tears,
and given them tears to drink in full measure.
6 Thou dost make us the scorn of our neighbors;
and our enemies laugh among themselves.

7 Restore us, O God of hosts;
let thy face shine, that we may be saved!

8 Thou didst bring a vine out of Egypt;
thou didst drive out the nations and plant it.
9 Thou didst clear the ground for it;
it took deep root and filled the land.
10 The mountains were covered with its shade,
the mighty cedars with its branches;
11 it sent out its branches to the sea,
and its shoots to the River.
12 Why then hast thou broken down its walls,
so that all who pass along the way pluck its fruit?

14 Exterminávit eam aper de silva, *
et singuláris ferus depástus est eam.

15 Deus virtútum, convértere, *
réspice de cælo et vide et vísita víneam istam.

16 Et prótege eam, quam plantávit déxtera tua, *
et super fílium hóminis, quem confirmásti tibi.
17 Incénsa est igni et suffóssa; *
ab increpatióne vultus tui períbunt.
18 Fiat manus tua super virum déxteræ tuæ, *
super fílium hóminis, quem confirmásti tibi.
19 Et non discedémus a te, vivificábis nos, *
et nomen tuum invocábimus.

20 Dómine Deus virtútum, convérte nos *
et illústra fáciem tuam, et salvi érimus.

Ant. Excita, Dómine, poténtiam tuam, ut salvos fácias nos.
Ant. 2 Magnífice fecit Dóminus, annuntiáte hoc in univérsa terra.

Canticum Is 12, 1-6

1 Confitébor tibi, Dómine, quóniam cum irátus eras mihi, *
convérsus est furor tuus, et consolátus es me.
2 Ecce Deus salútis meæ; *
fiduciáliter agam et non timébo,
quia fortitúdo mea et laus mea Dóminus, *
et factus est mihi in salútem.

13 The boar from the forest ravages it,
and all that move in the field feed on it.

14 Turn again, O God of hosts!
Look down from heaven, and see;
have regard for this vine,
15 the stock which thy right hand planted.
16 They have burned it with fire, they have cut it down;
may they perish at the rebuke of thy countenance!
17 But let thy hand be upon the man of thy right hand,
the son of man whom thou hast made strong for thyself!
18 Then we will never turn back from thee;
give us life, and we will call on thy name!

19 Restore us, O Lord God of hosts!
let thy face shine, that we may be saved!

Ant. 1 Stir up Thy might, O Lord; and come to save us.

Ant. 2 The Lord has done gloriously; let this be known in all the earth.

Canticle Isaiah 12:1–6

1 You will say in that day:
"I will give thanks to thee, O Lord,
for though thou wast angry with me,
thy anger turned away,
and thou didst comfort me.

2 "Behold, God is my salvation;
I will trust, and will not be afraid.

3 Et hauriétis aquas in gáudio *
de fóntibus salútis.
4 Et dicétis in die illa: *
« Confitémini Dómino et invocáte nomen eius,
notas fácite in pópulis adinventiónes eius; *
mementóte quóniam excélsum est nomen eius.
5 Cantáte Dómino, quóniam magnífice fecit; *
notum sit hoc in univérsa terra.
6 Exsúlta et lauda, quæ hábitas in Sion, *
quia magnus in médio tui Sanctus Israel ».

Ant. Magnífice fecit Dóminus, annuntiáte hoc in univérsa terra.

Ant. 3 Exsultáte Deo, adiutóri nostro. †

Psalmus 80 (81)

2 Exsultáte Deo adiutóri nostro, *
† iubiláte Deo Iacob.
3 Súmite psalmum et date týmpanum, *
psaltérium iucúndum cum cíthara.
4 Bucináte in neoménia tuba, *
in die plenæ lunæ, in sollemnitáte nostra.
5 Quia præcéptum in Israel est, *
et iudícium Deo Iacob.
6 Testimónium in Ioseph pósuit illud, †
cum exíret de terra Ægýpti; *
sermónem, quem non nóveram, audívi:

for the LORD God is my strength and my song,
and he has become my salvation."

3 With joy you will draw water from the wells of
salvation. 4And you will say in that day:
"Give thanks to the LORD,
call upon his name;
make known his deeds among the nations,
proclaim that his name is exalted.

5 "Sing praises to the LORD, for he has done
gloriously;
let this be known in all the earth.
6 Shout, and sing for joy, O inhabitant of Zion,
for great in your midst is the Holy One of
Israel."

Ant. 2 The Lord has done gloriously; let this be known in all the earth.
Ant. 3 Sing aloud to God our strength.

Psalm 81

1 Sing aloud to God our strength;
shout for joy to the God of Jacob!
2 Raise a song, sound the timbrel,
the sweet lyre with the harp.
3 Blow the trumpet at the new moon,
at the full moon, on our feast day.
4 For it is a statute for Israel,
an ordinance of the God of Jacob.
5 He made it a decree in Joseph,
when he went out over the land of Egypt.

I hear a voice I had not known:

7 « Divérti ab onéribus dorsum eius; *
manus eius a cóphino recessérunt.
8 In tribulatióne invocásti me et liberávi te, †
exaudívi te in abscóndito tempestátis, *
probávi te apud aquam Meríba.

9 Audi, pópulus meus, et contestábor te; *
Israel, útinam áudias me!
10 Non erit in te deus aliénus, *
neque adorábis deum extráneum.

11 Ego enim sum Dóminus Deus tuus. †
qui edúxi te de terra Ægýpti; *
dilàta os tuum, et implébo illud.

12 Et non audívit pópulus meus vocem meam, *
et Israel non inténdit mihi.
13 Et dimísi eos secúndum durítiam cordis eórum, *
ibunt in adinventiónibus suis.

14 Si pópulus meus audísset me, *
Israel si in viis meis ambulásset!
15 In brevi inimícos eórum humiliássem *
et super tribulántes eos misíssem manum
meam.

16 Inimíci Dómini blandiréntur ei, *
et esset sors eórum in sæcula;
17 et cibárem eos ex ádipe fruménti *
et de petra melle saturárem eos ».

Ant. Exsultáte Deo, adiutóri nostro.

6 "I relieved your shoulder of the burden;
your hands were freed from the basket.
7 In distress you called, and I delivered you;
I answered you in the secret place of thunder;
I tested you at the waters of Meribah.
8 Hear, O my people, while I admonish you!
O Israel, if you would but listen to me!
9 There shall be no strange god among you;
you shall not bow down to a foreign god.
10 I am the LORD your God,
who brought you up out of the land of Egypt.
Open your mouth wide, and I will fill it.

11 "But my people did not listen to my voice;
Israel would have none of me.
12 So I gave them over to their stubborn hearts,
to follow their own counsels.
13 O that my people would listen to me,
that Israel would walk in my ways!
14 I would soon subdue their enemies,
and turn my hand against their foes.
15 Those who hate the LORD would cringe toward him,
and their fate would last for ever.
16 I would feed you with the finest of the wheat,
and with honey from the rock I would satisfy you."

Ant. 3 Sing aloud to God our strength.

LECTIO BREVIS ROM 14, 17–19

Non est regnum Dei esca et potus, sed iustítia et pax et gáudium in Spíritu Sancto; qui enim in hoc servit Christo, placet Deo et probátus est homínibus. Itaque, quæ pacis sunt, sectémur et quæ ædificatiónis sunt in ínvicem.

RESPONSORIUM BREVE

℟. In matutínis, Dómine, * Meditábor de te. In matutínis.
℣. Quia factus es adiútor meus. * Meditábor de te. * Glória Patri. In matutínis.

Ad Benedictus, ant. Da sciéntiam salútis plebi tuæ, Dómine, et dimítte nobis peccáta nostra.

PRECES

Benedíctus Deus, Pater noster, qui fílios suos prótegit neque preces spernit eórum. Omnes humíliter eum implorémus orántes: *Illúmina óculos nostros, Dómine.*

Grátias tibi, Dómine, quia per Fílium tuum nos illumináasti,
—eius luce per longitúdinem diéi nos satiári concéde.

Sapiéntia tua, Dómine, dedúcat nos hódie,
—ut in novitáte vitæ ambulémus.

Præsta nobis advérsa pro te fórtiter sustinére,
—ut corde magno tibi iúgiter serviámus.

Dírige in nobis hódie cogitatiónes, sensus et ópera,
—ut tibi providénti dóciles obsequámur.

Short Reading
Romans 14:17–19

For the kingdom of God does not mean food and drink but righteousness and peace and joy in the Holy Spirit; he who thus serves Christ is acceptable to God and approved by men. Let us then pursue what makes for peace and for mutual upbuilding.

Short Responsory
℟. In the morning hours, I shall meditate on You, O Lord.
℣. For You have become my Helper.

Benedictus ant. Give knowledge of salvation to Your people, O Lord, and the forgiveness of our sins.

Intercessions
Blessed be God, our Father, Who protects His sons and does not spurn their prayers. Let us all humbly implore Him, praying: *Enlighten our eyes, O Lord.*

Thanks be to you, O Lord, for through your Son you have
enlightened us,
—grant us to be filled with His light all the day long.

Lord, may Your wisdom lead us today,
—that we may walk in the newness of life.

Grant that we may bravely endure adversity for You,
—so that we might continually serve You with a generous heart.

Direct in us today our thoughts, feelings and actions,
—that we might willingly follow You as our Provider.

Pater noster.

ORATIO

Te lucem veram et lucis auctórem, Dómine, deprecámur, ut, quæ sancta sunt, fidéliter meditántes, in tua iúgiter claritáte vivámus. Per Dóminum.

Our Father.

ORATION

To You true light and Author of light, O Lord, we pray, that faithfully meditating on things which are holy, we might live constantly in Your light. Through our Lord.

Feria V, ad Vesperas

Hymnus

Deus, qui claro lúmine
diem fecísti, Dómine,
tuam rogámus glóriam
dum pronus dies vólvitur.

Iam sol urgénte véspero
occásum suum gráditur,
mundum conclúdens ténebris,
suum obsérvans órdinem.

Tu ver*o*, excélse Dómine,
precántes tuos fámulos
diúrno lassos ópere
ne sinas umbris ópprimi,

Ut non fuscátis méntibus
dies abscédat sǽculi,
sed tua tecti grátia
cernámus lucem prósperam.

Præsta, Pater piíssme,
Patrique compar Unice,
cum Spíritu Paráclito
regnans per omne sǽculum. Amen.

Psalmodia

Ant. 1 Pósui te in lucem géntium, ut sis salus mea usque ad extrémum terræ.

Week II

Thursday, Vespers

HYMN — Trans. The Benedictine Nuns, St. Cecilia's Abbey

O Lord our God, Who made the day
  To gladden us with its fair light,
We praise Your name, imploring aid,
  For day will soon give place to night.

The evening shadows grow apace,
  Advancing, they will hide the sun,
As darkness creeps upon the earth
  When daylight hours their course have run.

We beg You, Lord and God Most High,
  Protect us with Your presence blessed,
Though weary, keep our souls in peace
  And not by gloom of night oppressed.

Let not Your lovely sun go down
  On hearts distressed with sin, and sore,
But sheltered by Your gentle grace,
  May we perceive the day once more.

Most tender Father, hear our prayer,
  Whom we adore, with Christ the Lord,
And Holy Spirit of them both;
  Bless us who praise Your Trinity. Amen.

PSALMODY

Ant. 1 I have made you a light to the nations, that you might be my salvation to the ends of the earth.

Psalmus 71 (72)

I

1 Deus, iudícium tuum regi da *
et iustítiam tuam fílio regis;
2 iúdicet pópulum tuum in iustítia *
et páuperes tuos in iudício.

3 Afferant montes pacem pópulo, *
et colles iustítiam.
4 Iudicábit páuperes pópuli †
et salvos fáciet fílios ínopis *
et humiliábit calumniatórem.
5 Et permanébit cum sole et ante lunam, *
in generatióne et generatiónem.

6 Descéndet sicut plúvia in gramen *
et sicut imber írrigans terram.
7 Florébit in diébus eius iustítia et abundántia pacis, *
donec auferátur luna.
8 Et dominábitur a mari usque ad mare *
et a Flúmine usque ad términos orbis terrárum.

9 Coram illo prócident íncolæ desérti, *
et inimíci eius terram lingent.
10 Reges Tharsis et ínsulæ múnera ófferent, *
reges Arabum et Saba dona addúcent.
11 Et adorábunt eum omnes reges, *
omnes gentes sérvient ei.

Psalm 72

I

1 Give the king thy justice, O God,
and thy righteousness to the royal son!
2 May he judge thy people with righteousness,
and thy poor with justice!
3 Let the mountains bear prosperity for the people,
and the hills, in righteousness!
4 May he defend the cause of the poor of the people,
give deliverance to the needy,
and crush the oppressor!

5 May he live while the sun endures,
and as long as the moon, throughout all generations!
6 May he be like rain that falls on the mown grass,
like showers that water the earth!
7 In his days may righteousness flourish,
and peace abound, till the moon be no more!

8 May he have dominion from sea to sea,
and from the River to the ends of the earth!
9 May his foes bow down before him,
and his enemies lick the dust!
10 May the kings of Tarshish and of the isles render him tribute,
may the kings of Sheba and Seba bring gifts!
11 May all kings fall down before him,
all nations serve him!

12 For he delivers the needy when he calls,
the poor and him who has no helper.

Ant. Pósui te in lucem géntium, ut sis salus mea usque ad extrémum terræ.

Ant. 2 Salvos fáciet Dóminus fílios páuperum; ex oppressióne rédimet ánimas eórum.

II

12 Quia liberábit ínopem clamántem *
et páuperem, cui non erat adiútor.
13 Parcet páuperi et ínopi *
et ánimas páuperum salvas fáciet.
14 Ex oppressióne et violéntia rédimet ánimas
eórum, *
et pretiósus erit sanguis eórum coram illo.

15 Et vivet, et dábitur ei de auro Arábiæ, †
et orábunt pro ipso semper; *
tota die benedícent ei.
16 Et erit ubértas fruménti in terra, *
in summis móntium fluctuábit;
sicut Líbanus fructus eius *
et florébit de civitáte sicut fenum terræ.

17 Sit nomen eius benedíctum in sæcula, *
ante solem permanébit nomen eius.
Et benedicéntur in ipso omnes tribus terræ, *
omnes gentes magnificábunt eum.

18 Benedíctus Dóminus Deus, Deus Israel, *
qui facit mirabília solus.
19 Et benedíctum nomen maiestátis eius in
ætérnum; *
et replébitur maiestáte eius omnis terra. Fiat, fiat.

Ant. 1 I have made you a light to the nations, that you might be my salvation to the ends of the earth.
Ant. 2 The Lord will save the sons of the poor; from oppression and violence He redeems their life.

II

13 He has pity on the weak and the needy,
and saves the lives of the needy.
14 From oppression and violence he redeems their life;
and precious is their blood in his sight.

15 Long may he live,
may gold of Sheba be given to him!
May prayer be made for him continually,
and blessings invoked for him all the day!
16 May there be abundance of grain in the land;
on the tops of the mountains may it wave;
may its fruit be like Lebanon;
and may men blossom forth from the cities
like the grass of the field!
17 May his name endure for ever,
his fame continue as long as the sun!
May men bless themselves by him,
all nations call him blessed!

18 Blessed be the Lord, the God of Israel,
who alone does wondrous things.
19 Blessed be his glorious name for ever;
may his glory fill the whole earth! Amen and Amen.

Ant. Salvos fáciet Dóminus filios páuperum; ex oppressióne rédimet ánimas eórum.
Ant. 3 Nunc facta est salus et regnum Dei nostri.

Canticum Ap 11, 17–18; 12, 10b–12a

11,17 Grátias ágimus tibi, *
Dómine Deus omnípotens,
qui es et qui eras, *
quia accepísti virtútem tuam magnam et regnásti.

18 Et irátæ sunt gentes, *
et advénit ira tua, et tempus mortuórum iudicári,
et réddere mercédem servis tuis prophétis et sanctis *
et timéntibus nomen tuum, pusíllis et magnis.

12,10 Nunc facta est salus et virtus et regnum Dei nostri *
et potéstas Christi eius,
quia proiéctus est accusátor fratrum nostrórum. *
qui accusábat illos ante conspéctum Dei nostri die ac nocte.
11 Et ipsi vicérunt illum propter sánguinem Agni *
et propter verbum testimónii sui;
et non dilexérunt ánimam suam *
usque ad mortem.
12 Proptérea lætámini, cæli *
et qui habitátis in eis.

Ant. 2 The Lord will save the sons of the poor; from oppression and violence He redeems their life.
Ant. 3 Now the salvation and kingdom of our God has begun.

Canticle

Revelation 11:17–18; 12:10b–12a

17 "We give thanks to thee, Lord God Almighty, who art and who wast, that thou hast taken thy great power and begun to reign.
18 The nations raged, but thy wrath came, and the time for the dead to be judged, for rewarding thy servants, the prophets and saints, and those who fear thy name, both small and great, and for destroying the destroyers of the earth."
10 "Now the salvation and the power and the kingdom of our God and the authority of his Christ have come, for the accuser of our brethren has been thrown down, who accuses them day and night before our God.
11 And they have conquered him by the blood of the Lamb and by the word of their testimony, for they loved not their lives even unto death.
12 Rejoice then, O heaven and you that dwell therein!

Ant. Nunc facta est salus et regnum Dei nostri.

LECTIO BREVIS 1 PETR 1, 22–23

Animas vestras castificántes in obœdiéntia veritátis ad fraternitátis amórem non fictum, ex corde ínvicem dilígite atténtius, renáti non ex sémine corruptíbili sed incorruptíbili per verbum Dei vivum et pérmanens.

RESPONSORIUM BREVE

℟. Dóminus pascit me, * Et nihil mihi déerit. Dóminus.

℣. In páscuis viréntibus me collocávit. * Et nihil mihi déerit. Glória Patri. Dóminus.

Ad Magnificat, ant. Esuriéntes iustítiam Dóminus saturávit et implévit bonis.

PRECES

Animas nostras ad Dóminum et Salvatórem nostrum pergráti levémus, qui benedícit pópulum suum in omni benedictióne spirituáli, et cum devotióne rogémus: *Bénedic pópulum tuum, Dómine.*

Miséricors Deus, consérva Papam nostrum, N., et Epíscopum nostrum, N.,
—incólumes custódi eos Ecclésiæ tuæ.

Regiónem nostram, Dómine, tuére benígnus,
—a malis nos líbera univérsis.

Voca fílios in circúitum mensæ tuæ,
—qui préssius te vírginem, páuperem et obœdiéntem sequántur.

Ancíllas tuas custódi, propósitum virginitátis proféssas,
—ut te, Agnum divínum, quocúmque íeris, sequántur.

Ant. 3 Now the salvation and kingdom of our God has begun.

SHORT READING I Peter 1:22–23

Having purified your souls by your obedience to the truth for a sincere love of the brethren, love one another earnestly from the heart. You have been born anew, not of perishable seed but of imperishable, through the living and abiding word of God.

SHORT RESPONSORY

℟. The Lord is my shepherd, there is nothing I shall want.

℣. He has made me to lie down in green pastures.

Magnificat ant. The Lord has satisfied those who hunger for justice and has filled them with good things.

INTERCESSIONS

Let us gratefully raise our spirits to our Lord and Savior, Who blesses His people with every spiritual blessing, and with devotion let us ask Him: *Bless Your people, O Lord.*

Merciful God, preserve our Pope, N., and our Bishop, N.,
—keep Your Church free from harm.

Look kindly, O Lord, on our land,
—free us from all evil.

Call around Your table Your children,
—that they may follow You more closely in chastity, poverty, and obedience.

Keep in Your care those who have professed virginity,
—that they might follow You, the Divine Lamb, wherever You lead.

Defúncti in tua pace requiéscant ætérna,
—et eórum nobíscum coniúnctio, spiritálium bonórum communicatióne, roborétur.

Pater noster.

Oratio

Vespertínæ laudis offícia persolvéntes, cleméntiam tuam, Dómine, deprecámur, ut a meditatióne legis tuæ cor nostrum recédere non permíttas, et nobis lumen ætérnæ vitæ dones et prǽmium. Per Dóminum.

May the deceased rest eternally in Your peace,
—and may their union with us be strengthened through the sharing of spiritual goods.

Our Father.

ORATION

As we conclude this hour of evening praise, we beseech Your mercy, O Lord, that You not allow our heart to rest from meditation on Your law and that You grant us the light and the reward of eternal life. Through our Lord.

Hebdomada II

Feria VI, ad Laudes matutinas

HYMNUS

Deus, qui cæli lumen es
satórque lucis, qui polum
patérno fultum brácchio
præclára pandis déxtera,

Auróra stellas iam tegit
rubrum sustóllens gúrgitem,
uméctis atque flátibus
terram baptízans róribus.

Iam noctis umbra línquitur,
polum calígo déserit,
typúsque Christi, lúcifer
diem sopítum súscitat.

Dies diérum tu, Deus,
lucísque lumen ipse es,
Unum potens per ómnia,
potens in unum Trínitas.

Te nunc, Salvátor, quæsumus
tibíque genu fléctimus,
Patrem cum Sancto Spíritu
totis laudántes vócibus. Amen

PSALMODIA

Ant. 1 Cor contrítum et humiliátum, Deus, non despícies.

Week II

Friday, Lauds

HYMN Trans. The Benedictine Nuns, St. Cecilia's Abbey

O God, the Light of Heaven's home,
You scatter light like golden grain;
Your fatherly right hand protects
The earth depending on Your pow'r.

The stars are hidden by the dawn,
That casts a red glow on the sky,
And with its moist, refreshing breeze
Bathes soil and plants in sparkling dew.

The shadows of the night are gone,
While fogs and mist disperse and flee;
The type of Christ, the morning star
Bestirs to life the drowsy day.

O God, You are the Day of days,
And very Light of light itself,
One and Almighty in Your works,
And mighty Trinity in One.

Our Saviour kind, we call to You
At daybreak, as we bow in prayer;
With newborn strength we sing our praise
To Father and Spirit too. Amen.

PSALMODY

Ant. 1 A broken and contrite heart, O God, Thou wilt not despise.

Psalmus 50 (51)

3 Miserére mei, Deus, *
secúndum misericórdiam tuam;
et secúndum multitúdinem miseratiónum
tuárum *
dele iniquitátem meam.
4 Amplius lava me ab iniquitáte mea *
et a peccáto meo munda me.

5 Quóniam iniquitátem meam ego cognósco, *
et peccátum meum contra me est semper.
6 Tibi, tibi soli peccávi *
et malum coram te feci,
ut iustus inveniáris in senténtia tua *
et æquus in iudício tuo.

7 Ecce enim in iniquitáte generátus sum, *
et in peccáto concépit me mater mea.
8 Ecce enim veritátem in corde dilexísti *
et in occúlto sapiéntiam manifestásti mihi.

9 Aspérges me hyssópo, et mundábor; *
lavábis me, et super nivem dealbábor.
10 Audíre me fácies gáudium et lætítiam, *
et exsultábunt ossa, quæ contrivísti.

11 Avérte fáciem tuam a peccátis meis *
et omnes iniquitátes meas dele.
12 Cor mundum crea in me, Deus, *
et spíritum firmum ínnova in viscéribus meis.

13 Ne proícias me a fácie tua *
et spíritum sanctum tuum ne áuferas a me.
14 Redde mihi lætítiam salutáris tui *
et spíritu promptíssimo confírma me.

Psalm 51

1 Have mercy on me, O God,
according to thy steadfast love;
according to thy abundant mercy blot out my transgressions.
2 Wash me thoroughly from my iniquity,
and cleanse me from my sin!
3 For I know my transgressions,
and my sin is ever before me.
4 Against thee, thee only, have I sinned,
and done that which is evil in thy sight,
so that thou art justified in thy sentence
and blameless in thy judgment.
5 Behold, I was brought forth in iniquity,
and in sin did my mother conceive me.

6 Behold, thou desirest truth in the inward being;
therefore teach me wisdom in my secret heart.
7 Purge me with hyssop, and I shall be clean;
wash me, and I shall be whiter than snow.
8 Fill me with joy and gladness;
let the bones which thou hast broken rejoice.
9 Hide thy face from my sins,
and blot out all my iniquities.

10 Create in me a clean heart, O God,
and put a new and right spirit within me.
11 Cast me not away from thy presence,
and take not thy holy Spirit from me.
12 Restore to me the joy of thy salvation,
and uphold me with a willing spirit.

15 Docébo iníquos vias tuas, *
et ímpii ad te converténtur.
16 Líbera me de sanguínibus, Deus, Deus salútis meæ, *
et exsultábit lingua mea iustítiam tuam.

17 Dómine, lábia mea apéries, *
et os meum annuntiábit laudem tuam.
18 Non enim sacrifício delectáris, *
holocáustum, si ófferam, non placébit.
19 Sacrifícium Deo spíritus contribulátus, *
cor contrítum et humiliátum, Deus, non despícies.
20 Benígne fac, Dómine, in bona voluntáte tua Sion, *
ut ædificéntur muri Ierúsalem.
21 Tunc acceptábis sacrifícium iustítiæ, oblatiónes et holocáusta; *
tunc impónent super altáre tuum vítulos.

Ant. Cor contrítum et humiliátum, Deus, non despícies.
Ant. 2 Cum irátus fúeris, Dómine, misericórdiæ recordáberis.

Canticum HAB 3, 2-4. 13A. 15-19

2 Dómine, audívi auditiónem tuam, *
et tímui, Dómine, opus tuum.
In médio annórum vivífica illud, *
in médio annórum notum fácies.
Cum irátus fúeris, *
misericórdiæ recordáberis.

13 Then I will teach transgressors thy ways,
and sinners will return to thee.
14 Deliver me from blood-guiltiness, O God,
thou God of my salvation,
and my tongue will sing aloud of thy
deliverance.

15 O Lord, open thou my lips,
and my mouth shall show forth thy praise.
16 For thou hast no delight in sacrifice;
were I to give a burnt offering, thou wouldst not
be pleased.
17 The sacrifice acceptable to God is a broken spirit;
a broken and contrite heart, O God, thou wilt
not despise.

18 Do good to Zion in thy good pleasure;
rebuild the walls of Jerusalem,
19 then wilt thou delight in right sacrifices,
in burnt offerings and whole burnt offerings;
then bulls will be offered on thy altar.

Ant. 1 A broken and contrite heart, O God, Thou wilt not despise.
Ant. 2 In wrath remember mercy.

Canticle Habakkuk 3:2–4, 13a, 15–19

2 O LORD, I have heard the report of thee,
and thy work, O LORD, do I fear.
In the midst of the years renew it;
in the midst of the years make it known;
in wrath remember mercy.

3 Deus a Theman véniet, *
et Sanctus de monte Pharan.
Operit cælos glóriæ eius, *
et laudis eius plena est terra.
4 Splendor eius ut lux erit, †
rádii ex mánibus eius: *
ibi abscóndita est fortitúdo eius.

13 Egréssus es in salútem pópuli tui, *
in salútem cum christo tuo.

15 Viam fecísti in mari equis tuis, *
in luto aquárum multárum.

16 Audívi, et conturbátus est venter meus, *
ad vocem contremuérunt lábia mea.
Ingréditur putrédo in óssibus meis, *
et subter me vacíllant gressus mei.
Conquiéscam in die tribulatiónis, *
ut ascéndat super pópulum, qui invádit nos.

17 Ficus enim non florébit, *
et non erit fructus in víneis;
mentiétur opus olívæ, *
et arva non ásferent cibum;
abscíssum est de ovíli pecus, *
et non est arméntum in præsépibus.

18 Ego autem in Dómino gaudébo *
et exsultábo in Deo salvatóre meo.
19 Dóminus Deus fortitúdo mea, †
et ponet pedes meos quasi cervórum *
et super excélsa mea dedúcet me.

3 God came from Teman,
and the Holy One from Mount Paran.
His glory covered the heavens,
and the earth was full of his praise.
4 His brightness was like the light,
rays flashed from his hand;
and there he veiled his power.

13 Thou wentest forth for the salvation of thy people,
for the salvation of thy anointed.
Thou didst crush the head of the wicked,
laying him bare from thigh to neck.

15 Thou didst trample the sea with thy horses,
the surging of mighty waters.
16 I hear, and my body trembles,
my lips quiver at the sound;
rottenness enters into my bones,
my steps totter beneath me.
I will quietly wait for the day of trouble
to come upon people who invade us.

Ant. Cum irátus fúeris, Dómine, misericórdiæ recordáberis.

Ant. 3 Lauda, Ierúsalem, Dóminum. †

Psalmus 147 (147 B)

12 Lauda, Ierúsalem, Dóminum; *
† colláuda Deum tuum, Sion.

13 Quóniam confortávit seras portárum tuárum, *
benedíxit fíliis tuis in te.
14 Qui ponit fines tuos pacem *
et ádipe fruménti sátiat te.
15 Qui emíttit elóquium suum terræ, *
velóciter currit verbum eius.
16 Qui dat nivem sicut lanam, *
pruínam sicut cínerem spargit.
17 Mittit crystállum suam sicut buccéllas; *
ante fáciem frígoris eius quis sustinébit?
18 Emíttet verbum suum et liquefáciet ea, *
flabit spíritus eius, et fluent aquæ.
19 Qui annúntiat verbum suum Iacob, *
iustítias et iudícia sua Israel.
20 Non fecit táliter omni natióni, *
et iudícia sua non manifestávit eis.

Ant. Lauda, Ierúsalem, Dóminum.

LECTIO BREVIS — EPH 2, 13-16

Nunc in Christo Iesu vos, qui aliquándo erátis longe, facti estis prope in sánguine Christi. Ipse est enim pax nostra, qui fecit utráque unum et médium paríetem macériæ solvit, inimicítiam, in carne sua, legem mandatórum in decrétis evácuans, ut duos condat in semetípso in unum novum hóminem, fáciens pacem,

Ant. 2 In wrath remember mercy.
Ant. 3 Praise the Lord, O Jerusalem!

Psalm 147:12–20

12 Praise the LORD, O Jerusalem!
praise your God, O Zion!
13 For he strengthens the bars of your gates;
he blesses your sons within you.
14 He makes peace in your borders;
he fills you with the finest of the wheat.
15 He sends forth his command to the earth;
his word runs swiftly.
16 He gives snow like wool;
he scatters hoarfrost like ashes.
17 He casts forth his ice like morsels;
who can stand before his cold?
18 He sends forth his word, and melts them;
he makes his wind blow, and the waters flow.
19 He declares his word to Jacob,
his statutes and ordinances to Israel.
20 He has not dealt thus with any other nation;
they do not know his ordinances.
Praise the LORD!

Ant. 3 Praise the Lord, O Jerusalem!

SHORT READING Ephesians 2:13–16

But now in Christ Jesus you who once were far off have been brought near in the blood of Christ. For he is our peace, who has made us both one, and has broken down the dividing wall of hostility, by abolishing in his flesh the law of commandments and ordinances, that he might create in himself one new man in place

et reconcíliet ambos in uno córpore Deo per crucem interfíciens inimicítiam in semetípso.

RESPONSORIUM BREVE

℟. Clamábo ad Dóminum altíssimum, * Qui benefécit mihi. Clamábo.
℣. Mittet de cælo et liberábit me. * Qui benefécit mihi. Glória Patri. Clamábo.

Ad Benedictus, ant. Per víscera misericórdiæ Dei nostri, visitávit nos Oriens ex alto.

PRECES

Christum, qui sánguine suo per Spíritum Sanctum semetípsum óbtulit Patri ad emundándam consciéntiam nostram ab opéribus mórtuis, adorémus et sincéro corde profiteámur: *In tua voluntáte pax nostra, Dómine.*

Diéi exórdium a tua benignitáte suscépimus,
—nobis páriter vitæ novæ concéde inítium.

Qui ómnia creásti providúsque consérvas,
—fac ut inspiciámus perénne tui vestígium in creátis.

Qui sánguine tuo novum et ætérnum testaméntum sanxísti,
—da ut, quæ præcipis faciéntes, tuo fidéles fœderi maneámus.

Qui, in cruce pendens, una cum sánguine aquam de látere effudísti,
—hoc salutári flúmine áblue peccáta nostra et civitátem Dei lætífica.

of the two, so making peace, and might reconcile us both to God in one body through the cross, thereby bringing the hostility to an end.

SHORT RESPONSORY

℟. I shall cry out to the Lord Most High, Who has done good to me.
℣. He shall send from heaven and save me.

Benedictus ant. Through the tender mercy of our God, the Dawn from on high has visited us.

INTERCESSIONS

Let us adore Christ, Who through the Holy Spirit offered Himself to the Father with His blood to cleanse our consciences from dead works, and with a sincere heart profess: *In Your will is our peace, O Lord.*

Through Your generosity we have received the beginning of the day,
—in like manner, grant us the beginning of a new life.

You that have created all things and preserve them in Your providence,
—grant that we might see the lasting impression of Yourself in creation.

You that with Your blood have ratified a new and eternal testament,
—grant that we might remain faithful to Your covenant.

You that, while hanging on the cross, poured forth blood and water from Your side,
—by this saving river wash away our sins and gladden the city of God.

Pater noster.

ORATIO

Præsta, quǽsumus, omnípotens Deus, ut laudes quas nunc tibi persólvimus, in ætérnum cum sanctis tuis ubérius decantáre valeámus. Per Dóminum.

Our Father.

ORATION

Grant, we beseech You, Almighty God, that Your praises which we have now completed we might sing more fervently with Your saints forever. Through our Lord.

Hebdomada II

Feria VI, ad Vesperas

Hymnus

Horis peráctis úndecim
ruit dies in vésperum;
solvámus omnes débitum
mentis libénter cánticum.

Labor diúrnus tránsiit
quo, Christe, nos condúxeras;
da iam colónis víneæ
promíssa dona glóriæ.

Mercéde quos nunc ádvocas,
quos ad futúrum múneras,
nos in labóre ádiuva
et post labórem récrea.

Sit, Christe, rex piíssime,
tibi Patríque glória
cum Spíritu Paráclito,
in sempitérna sæcula. Amen.

Psalmodia

Ant. 1 Dómine, líbera ánimam meam de morte, pedes meos a lapsu.

Week II

Friday, Vespers

HYMN Trans. The Benedictine Nuns, St. Cecilia's Abbey

The hours are passing swiftly by,
And into night the shades will flow,
So let us sing to God with joy
The grateful hymn of praise we owe.

The burden and the heat of day
Have passed in working for our Lord,
So may His vineyard workers all
Receive from Him the great reward.

Lord Jesus Christ, You call us now
To labor for our recompense,
Assist our work, then grant us rest,
Until Your love shall call us hence.

O Christ our King and tender Lord,
All glory ever be to You,
Who with the Holy Spirit reign
With God the Father's might supreme.
Amen.

PSALMODY

Ant. 1 Deliver my soul from death, O Lord, my feet from stumbling.

Psalmus 114 (116 A)

1 Diléxi, quóniam exáudit Dóminus *
vocem deprecatiónis meæ.
2 Quia inclinávit aurem suam mihi, *
cum in diébus meis invocábam.

3 Circumdedérunt me funes mortis, *
et angústiæ inférni invenérunt me.
Tribulatiónem et dolórem invéni †
4 et nomen Dómini invocábam: *
« O Dómine, líbera ánimam meam ».
5 Miséricors Dóminus et iustus, *
et Deus noster miserétur.
6 Custódiens párvulos Dóminus; *
humiliátus sum, et salvum me fáciet.

7 Convértere, ánima mea, in réquiem tuam, *
quia Dóminus benefécit tibi;
8 quia erípuit ánimam meam de morte, †
óculos meos a lácrimis, *
pedes meos a lapsu.
9 Ambulábo coram Dómino *
in regióne vivórum.

Ant. Dómine, líbera ánimam meam de morte, pedes meos a lapsu.

Ant. 2 Auxílium meum a Dómino, qui fecit cælum et terram.

Psalmus 120 (121)

1 Levábo óculos meos in montes: *
unde véniet auxílium mihi?
2 Auxílium meum a Dómino, *
qui fecit cælum, et terram.

Psalm 116:1–9

1 I love the LORD, because he has heard
my voice and my supplications.
2 Because he inclined his ear to me,
therefore I will call on him as long as I live.
3 The snares of death encompassed me;
the pangs of Sheol laid hold on me;
I suffered distress and anguish.
4 Then I called on the name of the LORD;
"O LORD, I beseech thee, save my life!"

5 Gracious is the LORD, and righteous;
our God is merciful.
6 The LORD preserves the simple;
when I was brought low, he saved me.
7 Return, O my soul, to your rest;
for the LORD has dealt bountifully with you.

8 For thou hast delivered my soul from death,
my eyes from tears,
my feet from stumbling;
9 I walk before the LORD
in the land of the living.

Ant. 1 Deliver my soul from death, O Lord, my feet from stumbling.
Ant. 2 My help comes from the Lord, Who made heaven and earth.

Psalm 121

1 I lift up my eyes to the hills.
From whence does my help come?
2 My help comes from the LORD,
who made heaven and earth.

3 Non dabit in commotiónem pedem tuum, *
neque dormitábit, qui custódit te.
4 Ecce non dormitábit neque dórmiet, *
qui custódit Israel.

5 Dóminus custódit te, †
Dóminus umbráculum tuum, *
ad manum déxteram tuam.
6 Per diem sol non percútiet te, *
neque luna per noctem.

7 Dóminus custódiet te ab omni malo; *
custódiet ánimam tuam Dóminus.
8 Dóminus custódiet intróitum tuum et éxitum tuum *
ex hoc nunc et usque in sæculum.

Ant. Auxílium meum a Dómino, qui fecit cælum et terram.

Ant 3. Iustæ et veræ sunt viæ tuæ, Rex sæculórum.

Canticum Ap 15, 3-4

3 Magna et mirabília ópera tua, *
Dómine Deus omnípotens;
iustæ et veræ viæ tuæ, *
Rex géntium!

4 Quis non timébit, Dómine, *
et glorificábit nomen tuum?
Quia solus Sanctus, †
quóniam omnes gentes vénient et adorábunt in conspéctu tuo, *
quóniam iudícia tua manifestáta sunt.

Ant. Iustæ et veræ sunt viæ tuæ, Rex sæculórum.

3 He will not let your foot be moved,
he who keeps you will not slumber.
4 Behold, he who keeps Israel
will neither slumber nor sleep.

5 The LORD is your keeper;
the LORD is your shade
on your right hand.
6 The sun shall not smite you by day,
nor the moon by night.

7 The LORD will keep you from all evil;
he will keep your life.
8 The LORD will keep
your going out and your coming in
from this time forth and for evermore.

Ant. 2 My help comes from the Lord, Who made heaven and earth.

Ant. 3 Just and true are Thy ways, O King of the ages.

Canticle Revelation 15:3–4

3 "Great and wonderful are thy deeds,
O Lord God the Almighty!
Just and true are thy ways,
O King of the ages!
4 Who shall not fear and glorify thy name, O Lord?
For thou alone art holy.
All nations shall come and worship thee,
for thy judgments have been revealed."

Ant. 3 Just and true are Thy ways, O King of the ages.

Lectio Brevis 1 Cor 2, 7-10a

Lóquimur Dei sapiéntiam in mystério, quæ abscóndita est, quam prædestinávit Deus ante sæcula in glóriam nostram, quam nemo príncipum huius sæculi cognóvit; si enim cognovíssent, numquam Dóminum glóriæ crucifixíssent. Sed sicut scriptum est: Quod óculus non vidit, nec auris audívit, nec in cor hóminis ascéndit, quæ præparávit Deus his, qui díligunt illum. Nobis autem revelávit Deus per Spíritum.

Responsorium Breve

℟. Christus mórtuus est pro peccátis nostris, * Ut nos offéret Deo. Christus.
℣. Mortificátus quidem carne, vivificátus autem Spíritu. * Ut nos offéret Deo. Glória Patri. Christus.

Ad Magnificat, ant. Recordáre, Dómine, misericórdiæ tuæ, sicut locútus es ad patres nostros.

Preces

Christum Dóminum benedicámus, qui lácrimas fléntium pius et miséricors abstérsit, eúmque amánter ac supplíciter invocémus: *Miserére pópuli tui, Dómine.*

Christe Dómine, qui húmiles consoláris,
—pone lácrimas páuperum in conspéctu tuo.

Audi, miséricors Deus, gémitus moriéntium,
—vísitet eos ángelus tuus atque confórtet.

Cognóscant éxsules cuncti providéntiam tuam,
—terréstri reddántur pátriæ et in cæléstem tandem intróeant.

Qui mísere in peccáto versántur, tuo cedant amóri,
—et tibi ac tuæ reconciliéntur Ecclésiæ.

SHORT READING   1 Corinthians 2:7–10a

But we impart a secret and hidden wisdom of God, which God decreed before the ages for our glorification. None of the rulers of this age understood this; for if they had, they would not have crucified the Lord of glory. But, as it is written, "What no eye has seen, nor ear heard, nor the heart of man conceived, what God has prepared for those who love him," God has revealed to us through the Spirit.

SHORT RESPONSORY

℟. Christ died for our sins to offer us to God.
℣. He died to this world of sin, and rose in the power of the Spirit.

Magnificat ant. Remember, O Lord, Your mercy, as You spoke to our fathers.

INTERCESSIONS

Let us bless Christ the Lord, Who, in His mercy and compassion, has wiped away the tears of those who weep, and in love and supplication let us call upon Him: *Have mercy on Your people, O Lord.*

O Lord Christ, Who console the humble,
—bring into Your sight the tears of the poor.

Hear, O merciful God, the cries of the dying,
—may Your angel visit and comfort them.

May all exiles come to know Your providence,
—may they be restored to their earthly country and enter as well into their heavenly abode.

May those who wander in the misery of sin yield to Your love,
—and may they be reconciled to You and to Your Church.

Defúnctos fratres salva propítius,
—ut plenam sortiántur redemptiónem tuam.

Pater noster.

Oratio

Deus, cuius ineffábilis sapiéntia in scándalo crucis mirabíliter declarátur, concéde nobis ita passiónis Fílii tui glóriam contuéri, ut in cruce ipsíus numquam cessémus fiduciáliter gloriári. Qui tecum.

Graciously save our deceased brethren,
—that they may share the fulness of Your redemption.

Our Father.

ORATION

O God, Whose ineffable wisdom is wondrously declared in the scandal of the cross, grant us so to contemplate the glory of Your Son's passion, that we may never cease to glory in His cross with confidence. Through our Lord.

Hebdomada II

Sabbato, ad Laudes matutinas

Hymnus

Diéi luce réddita,
lætis gratísque vócibus
Dei canámus glóriam,
Christi faténtes grátiam,

Per quem creátor ómnium
diem noctémque cóndidit,
ætérna lege sánciens
ut semper succédant sibi.

Tu vera lux fidélium,
quem lex vetérna non tenet,
noctis nec ortu súccidens,
ætérno fulgens lúmine.

Præsta, Pater ingénite,
totum ducámus iúgiter
Christo placéntes hunc diem
Sancto repléti Spíritu. Amen.

Psalmodia

Ant. 1 Annuntiámus mane misericórdiam tuam, Dómine, et veritátem tuam per noctem.

Week II

Saturday, Lauds

HYMN Trans. The Benedictine Nuns, St. Cecilia's Abbey

As light of day returns once more,
With joyful voices let us sing
To God of glory infinite,
To Christ our Lord for all His grace.

Through Whom the great Creator's will
Called day and night from nothingness,
Appointing them successive law,
Till time itself shall pass away.

True Light of every faithful soul
Unfettered by the claims of law;
No shades of night can fall that dim
Your dazzling and undying light.

O Father, uncreated Light,
Be with us as the hours go by,
That we may please Your Son our Lord,
Filled with the Spirit of Your love. Amen.

PSALMODY

Ant. 1 We declare Thy steadfast love in the morning, O Lord, and Thy faithfulness by night.

Psalmus 92

2 Bonum est confitéri Dómino *
et psállere nómini tuo, Altíssime,
3 annuntiáre mane misericórdiam tuam *
et veritátem tuam per noctem,
4 in decachórdo et psaltério, *
cum cántico in cíthara.

5 Quia delectásti me, Dómine, in factúra tua, *
et in opéribus mánuum tuárum exsultábo.

6 Quam magnificáta sunt ópera tua, Dómine: *
nimis profúndæ factæ sunt cogitatiónes tuæ.
7 Vir insípiens non cognóscet, *
et stultus non intélleget hæc.
8 Cum germináverint peccatóres sicut fenum, *
et florúerint omnes, qui operántur iniquitátem,
hoc tamen erit ad intéritum in sæculum sæculi; *
9 tu autem altíssimus in ætérnum, Dómine.

10 Quóniam ecce inimíci tui, Dómine, †
quóniam ecce inimíci tui períbunt, *
et dispergéntur omnes, qui operántur
iniquitátem.
11 Exaltábis sicut unicórnis cornu meum, *
perfúsus sum óleo úberi.
12 Et despíciet óculus meus inimícos meos, *
et in insurgéntibus in me malignántibus áudiet
auris mea.

13 Iustus ut palma florébit, *
sicut cedrus Líbani succréscet.
14 Plantáti in domo Dómini, *
in átriis Dei nostri florébunt.

Psalm 92

1 It is good to give thanks to the LORD,
to sing praises to thy name, O Most High;
2 to declare thy steadfast love in the morning,
and thy faithfulness by night,
3 to the music of the lute and the harp,
to the melody of the lyre.
4 For thou, O LORD, hast made me glad by thy work;
at the works of thy hands I sing for joy.

5 How great are thy works, O LORD!
Thy thoughts are very deep!
6 The dull man cannot know,
the stupid cannot understand this:
7 that, though the wicked sprout like grass
and all evildoers flourish,
they are doomed to destruction for ever,
8 but thou, O LORD, art on high for ever.
9 For lo, thy enemies, O LORD,
for lo, thy enemies shall perish;
all evildoers shall be scattered.

10 But thou hast exalted my horn like that of the wild ox;
thou hast poured over me fresh oil.
11 My eyes have seen the downfall of my enemies,
my ears have heard the doom of my evil assailants.

12 The righteous flourish like the palm tree,
and grow like a cedar in Lebanon.
13 They are planted in the house of the LORD,
they flourish in the courts of our God.

15 Adhuc fructus dabunt in senécta, *
úberes et bene viréntes erunt,
16 ut annúntient quóniam rectus Dóminus, refúgium meum, *
et non est iníquitas in eo.

Ant. Annuntiámus mane misericórdiam tuam, Dómine, et veritátem tuam per noctem.

Ant. 2 Date magnificéntiam Deo nostro.

Canticum DEUT 32, 1–12

1 Audíte, cæli, quæ loquor, *
áudiat terra verba oris mei!
2 Stillet ut plúvia doctrína mea, *
fluat ut ros elóquium meum
quasi imber super herbam *
et quasi stillæ super grámina.

3 Quia nomen Dómini invocábo: *
date magnificéntiam Deo nostro!
4 Petra, perfécta sunt ópera eius, *
quia omnes viæ eius iustítia.
Deus fidélis et absque ulla iniquitáte, *
iustus et rectus.

5 Peccavérunt ei, non fílii eius in sórdibus suis, *
generátio prava atque pervérsa.
6 Hæccine rédditis Dómino, *
pópule stulte et insípiens?
Numquid non ipse est pater tuus, *
qui possédit te, ipse fecit et stabilívit te?

7 Meménto diérum antiquórum, *
cógita generatiónes síngulas;

14 They still bring forth fruit in old age,
they are ever full of sap and green,
15 to show that the LORD is upright;
he is my rock, and there is no unrighteousness in him.

Ant. 1 We declare Thy steadfast love in the morning, O Lord, and Thy faithfulness by night.
Ant. 2 Ascribe greatness to our God.

Canticle Deuteronomy 32:1–12

1 "Give ear, O Heavens, and I will speak;
and let the earth hear the words of my mouth.
2 May my teaching drop as the rain,
my speech distil as the dew,
as the gentle rain upon the tender grass,
and as the showers upon the herb.
3 For I will proclaim the name of the LORD.
Ascribe greatness to our God!

4 "The Rock, his work is perfect;
for all his ways are justice.
A God of faithfulness and without iniquity,
just and right is he.
5 They have dealt corruptly with him,
they are no longer his children because of their blemish;
they are a perverse and crooked generation.
6 Do you thus requite the LORD,
you foolish and senseless people?
Is not he your father, who created you,
who made you and established you?
7 Remember the days of old,
consider the years of many genations;

intérroga patrem tuum, et annuntiábit tibi *
maióres tuos, et dicent tibi.
8 Quando dividébat Altíssimus gentes, *
quando separábat fílios Adam,
constítuit términos populórum *
iuxta númerum filiórum Israel;
9 pars autem Dómini pópulus eius, *
Iacob funículus hereditátis eius.

10 Invénit eum in terra desérta, *
in loco horróris et ululátu solitúdinis;
circúmdedit eum et atténdit *
et custodívit quasi pupíllam óculi sui.
11 Sicut áquila próvocans ad volándum pullos suos *
et super eos vólitans
expándit alas suas et assúmpsit eum *
atque portávit super pennas suas.
12 Dóminus solus dux eius fuit, *
et non erat cum eo deus aliénus.

Ant. Date magnificéntiam Deo nostro.
Ant. 3 Quam admirábile est nomen tuum, Dómine, in univérsa terra.

Psalmus 8

2 Dómine, Dóminus noster, *
quam admirábile est nomen tuum in univérsa terra,
quóniam eleváta est magnificéntia tua *
super cælos.

3 Ex ore infántium et lactántium †
perfecísti laudem propter inimícos tuos, *
ut déstruas inimícum et ultórem.

ask your father, and he will show you;
your elders, and they will tell you.
8 When the Most High gave to the nations their inheritance,
when he separated the sons of men,
he fixed the bounds of the peoples
according to the number of the sons of God.
9 For the LORD's portion is his people,
Jacob his allotted heritage.
10 "He found him in a desert land,
and in the howling waste of the wilderness;
he encircled him, he cared for him,
he kept him as the apple of his eye.
11 Like an eagle that stirs up its nest,
that flutters over its young,
spreading out its wings, catching them,
bearing them on its pinions,
12 the LORD alone did lead him,
and there was no foreign god with him.

Ant. 2 Ascribe greatness to our God.
Ant. 3 How majestic is Thy name in all the earth, O Lord!

Psalm 8

1 O LORD, our Lord,
how majestic is thy name in all the earth!

Thou whose glory above the heavens is chanted
2 by the mouth of babes and infants,
thou hast founded a bulwark because of thy foes,
to still the enemy and the avenger.

4 Quando vídeo cælos tuos, ópera digitórum
tuórum, *
lunam et stellas, quæ tu fundásti,
5 quid est homo, quod memor es eius, *
aut fílius hóminis quóniam vísitas eum?

6 Minuísti eum paulo minus ab ángelis, †
glória et honóre coronásti eum *
7 et constituísti eum super ópera mánuum tuárum.

Omnia subiecísti sub pédibus eius, †
8 oves et boves univérsas, *
ínsuper et pécora campi,
9 vólucres cæli et pisces maris, *
quæcúmque perámbulant sémitas maris.
10 Dómine, Dóminus noster, *
quam admirábile est nomen tuum in univérsa
terra!

Ant. Quam admirábile est nomen tuum, Dómine, in univérsa terra.

LECTIO BREVIS — ROM 12, 14–16A

Benedícite persequéntibus; benedícite et nolíte maledícere! Gaudére cum gaudéntibus, flere cum fléntibus. Idípsum ínvicem sentiéntes, non alta sapiéntes, sed humílibus consentiéntes.

RESPONSORIUM BREVE

℟. Exsultábunt lábia mea, * Cum cantávero tibi. Exsultábunt.

℣. Lingua mea meditábitur iustítiam tuam. * Cum cantávero tibi. Glória Patri. Exsultábunt.

3 When I look at thy heavens, the work of thy fingers,
the moon and the stars which thou hast established;
4 what is man that thou art mindful of him,
and the son of man that thou dost care for him?

5 Yet thou hast made him little less than God,
and dost crown him with glory and honor.
6 Thou hast given him dominion over the works of thy hands;
thou hast put all things under his feet,
7 all sheep and oxen,
and also the beasts of the field,
8 the birds of the air, and the fish of sea,
whatever passes along the paths of the sea.
9 O LORD, our Lord,
how majestic is thy name in all the earth!

Ant. 3 How majestic is Thy name in all the earth, O Lord!

SHORT READING Romans 12:14–16a

Bless those who persecute you; bless and do not curse them. Rejoice with those who rejoice, weep with those who weep. Live in harmony with one another; do not be haughty, but associate with the lowly.

SHORT RESPONSORY

℟. My lips will rejoice when I sing to You.
℣. My tongue will meditate on Your justice.

Ad Benedictus, ant. Dírige, Dómine, pedes nostros in viam pacis.

PRECES

Christi benignitátem et sapiéntiam celebrémus, qui in ómnibus frátribus nostris, præsértim mala patiéntibus, conspiciéndum et diligéndum se trádidit. Eum instánter orémus: *Pérfice nos in caritáte, Dómine.*

Resurrectiónem tuam iam mane recólimus,
—et benefícia redemptiónis tuæ cunctis optámus.

Præsta, Dómine, ut hódie testimónium de te perhibeámus,
—et hóstiam sanctam offerámus per te Patri placéntem.

Fac ut in ómnibus tuam agnoscámus imáginem,
—et tibi in eis ministrémus.

Christe, vitis vera, cuius nos pálmites sumus,
—da nos in te manére, ut fructum multum afferámus et Deum Patrem glorificémus.

Pater noster.

ORATIO

Laudent te, Dómine, ora nostra, laudet ánima, laudet et vita, et quia tui múneris est quod sumus, tuum sit omne quod vívimus. Per Dóminum.

Benedictus ant. Guide our feet, O Lord, into the way of peace.

INTERCESSIONS

Let us celebrate the kindness and wisdom of Christ, Who in all our brethren, especially in those suffering evil, handed Himself over to be seen and to be loved. Let us eagerly pray to Him: *Perfect us in charity, O Lord.*

We venerate Your resurrection this morning,
—and we desire the benefits of Your redemption for all.

Grant, O Lord, that we might bear witness to You today,
—and that through You we might offer a sacrifice pleasing to the Father.

Make us to acknowledge Your image in all people,
—and serve You in them.

Christ, true vine, Whose branches we are,
—grant us to remain in You, that we might bear much fruit and glorify God the Father.

Our Father.

ORATION

May our mouth, our soul and our life praise You, O Lord, and because all that we are is of Your gift, may we live entirely for You. Through our Lord.

Hebdomada III

Dominica, ad I Vesperas

Hymnus

Deus, Creátor ómnium
políque rector, vestiéns
diem decóro, lúmine,
noctem sopóris grátia,

Artus solútos ut quies
reddat labóris úsui
mentésque fessas állevet
luctúsque solvat ánxios,

Grates perácto iam die
et noctis exórtu preces,
voti reos ut ádjuves,
hymnum canéntes sólvimus.

Te cordis ima cóncinant,
te vox canóra cóncrepet,
te díligat castus amor,
te mens adóret sóbria,

Ut cum profúnda cláuserit
diem calígo nóctium,
fides tenébras nésciat
et nox fide relúceat.

Christum rogámus et Patrem,
Christi Patrísque Spíritum;
unum potens per ómnia,
fove precántes, Trínitas. Amen.

Week III

Sunday, Vespers I

HYMN

Trans. *The English Hymnal*, 1933

Creator of the earth and sky,
Ruling the firmament on high,
Clothing the day with robes of light,
Blessing with gracious sleep the night,

That rest may comfort weary men,
And brace to useful toil again,
And soothe awhile the harassed mind,
And sorrow's heavy load unbind:

Day sinks; we thank Thee for Thy gift;
Night comes; and once again we lift
Our prayer and vows and hymns that we
Against all ills may shielded be

Thee let the secret heart acclaim,
Thee let our tuneful voices name,
Round Thee our chaste affections cling,
Thee sober reason own as King.

That when black darkness closes day,
And shadows thicken round our way,
Faith may no darkness know, and night
From faith's clear beam may borrow light.

Pray we the Father and the Son,
And Holy Ghost: O Three in One,
Blest Trinity, whom all obey,
Guard Thou Thy sheep by night and day. Amen.

PSALMODIA

Ant. 1 A solis ortu usque ad occásum, laudábile nomen Dómini.

Psalmus 112 (113)

1 Laudáte, púeri Dómini, *
laudáte nomen Dómini.
2 Sit nomen Dómini benedíctum *
ex hoc nunc et usque in sæculum.
3 A solis ortu usque ad occásum *
laudábile nomen Dómini.

4 Excélsus super omnes gentes Dóminus, *
super cælos glória eius.
5 Quis sicut Dóminus Deus noster,
qui in altis hábitat *
6 et se inclínat, ut respíciat
in cælum et in terram?

7 Súscitans de terra ínopem, *
de stércore érigens páuperem,
8 ut cóllocet eum cum princípibus, *
cum princípibus pópuli sui.

9 Qui habitáre facit stérilem in domo, *
matrem filiórum lætántem.

Ant. A solis ortu usque ad occásum, laudábile nomen Dómini.

Ant. 2 Cálicem salutáris accípiam, et nomen Dómini invocábo.

PSALMODY

Ant. 1 From the rising of the sun to its setting, the name of the Lord is to be praised!

Psalm 113

1 Praise the Lord!
Praise, O servants of the Lord,
praise the name of the Lord!

2 Blessed be the name of the Lord
from this time forth and for ever more!
3 From the rising of the sun to its setting
the name of the Lord is to be praised!
4 The Lord is high above all nations,
and his glory above the heavens!

5 Who is like the Lord our God,
who is seated on high,
6 who looks far down
upon the heavens and the earth?
7 He raises the poor from the dust,
and lifts the needy from the ash heap,
8 to make them sit with princes,
with the princes of his people.
9 He gives the barren woman a home,
making her the joyous mother of children.
Praise the Lord!

Ant. 1 From the rising of the sun to its setting, the name of the Lord is to be praised!

Ant. 2 I will lift up the cup of salvation and call on the name of the Lord.

Psalmus 115 (116 B)

10 Crédidi, étiam cum locútus sum: *
« Ego humiliátus sum nimis ».
11 Ego dixi in trepidatióne mea: *
« Omnis homo mendax ».

12 Quid retríbuam Dómino *
pro ómnibus, quæ retríbuit mihi?
13 Cálicem salutáris accípiam *
et nomen Dómini invocábo.

14 Vota mea Dómino reddam *
coram omni pópulo eius.
15 Pretiósa in conspéctu Dómini *
mors sanctórum eius.

16 O Dómine, ego servus tuus, *
ego servus tuus et fílius ancíllæ tuæ.
Dirupísti víncula mea: †
17 tibi sacrificábo hostiam laudis *
et nomen Dómini invocábo.

18 Vota mea Dómino reddam *
coram omni pópulo eius,
19 in átriis domus Dómini, *
in médio tui, Ierúsalem.

Ant. Cálicem salutáris accípiam, et nomen Dómini invocábo.

Ant. 3 Humiliávit semetípsum Dóminus Iesus, propter quod et Deus exaltávit illum in sǽcula.

Psalm 116:10–19

10 I kept my faith, even when I said,
"I am greatly afflicted";
11 I said in my consternation,
"Men are all a vain hope."

12 What shall I render to the Lord
for all his bounty to me?
13 I will lift up the cup of salvation
and call on the name of the Lord,
14 I will pay my vows to the Lord
in the presence of all his people.

15 Precious in the sight of the Lord
is the death of his saints.
16 O Lord, I am thy servant;
I am thy servant, the son of thy handmaid.
Thou hast loosed my bonds.
17 I will offer to thee the sacrifice of thanksgiving
and call on the name of the Lord.
18 I will pay my vows to the Lord
in the presence of all his people,
19 in the courts of the house of the Lord,
in your midst, O Jerusalem.
Praise the Lord!

Ant. 2 I will lift up the cup of salvation and call on the name of the Lord.
Ant. 3 The Lord Jesus humbled Himself; therefore God has highly exalted Him for ever.

Canticum

PHIL 2, 6–11

6 Christus Iesus, cum in forma Dei esset, *
non rapínam arbitrátus est esse se æquálem Deo,
7 sed semetípsum exinanívit formam servi accípiens, †
in similitúdinem hóminum factus; *
et hábitu invéntus ut homo,
8 humiliávit semetípsum †
factus obœ́diens usque ad mortem, *
mortem autem crucis.

9 Propter quod et Deus illum exaltávit †
et donávit illi nomen, *
quod est super omne nomen,
10 ut in nómine Iesu omne genu flectátur *
cæléstium et terréstrium et infernórum
11 et omnis lingua confiteátur: *
« Dóminus Iesus Christus! » in glóriam Dei Patris.

Ant. Humiliávit semetípsum Dóminus Iesus, propter quod et Deus exaltávit illum in sǽcula.

LECTIO BREVIS HEBR 13, 20–21

Deus pacis, qui edúxit de mórtuis pastórem magnum óvium in sánguine testaménti ætérni, Dóminum nostrum Iesum, aptet vos in omni bono, ut faciátis voluntátem eius, fáciens in nobis, quod pláceat coram se per Iesum Christum, cui glória in sǽcula sæculórum. Amen.

Canticle Philippians 2:6–11

6 Christ Jesus, who, though he was in the form of
God, did not count equality with God a thing
to be grasped,
7 but emptied himself, taking the form of a servant,
being born in the likeness of men.
8 And being found in human form he humbled
himself and became obedient unto death, even
death on a cross.
9 Therefore God has highly exalted him and
bestowed on him the name which is above
every name,
10 that at the name of Jesus every knee should bow,
in heaven and on earth and under the earth,
11 and every tongue confess that Jesus Christ is
Lord, to the glory of God the Father.

Ant. 3 The Lord Jesus humbled Himself; therefore God has highly exalted Him for ever.

SHORT READING Hebrews 13:20–21

Now may the God of peace who brought again from the dead our Lord Jesus, the great shepherd of the sheep, by the blood of the eternal covenant, equip you with everything good that you may do his will, working in you that which is pleasing in his sight, through Jesus Christ; to whom be glory for ever and ever. Amen.

Responsorium Breve

℟. Quam magnificáta sunt * Opera tua, Dómine. Quam.

℣. Omnia in sapiéntia fecísti. * Opera tua, Dómine. Glória Patri. Quam.

Preces

Christus pópuli esuriéntis misértus est et prodígia pro illo sui operátus est amóris. Quorum mémores pia devotióne eum precémur: *Amórem tuum osténde nobis, Dómine.*

Confitémur, Dómine, ómnia benefícia nobis hódie de tua bonitáte processísse:
—ne revertántur ad te vácua, sed fructum ásserant in corde bono.

Lux et salus ómnium géntium, custódi testes quos in univérsum orbem misísti,
—Spíritus in eis ignem accénde.

Fac ut mundum ad præcelléntem dignitátem ipsíus omnes magis confórment,
—quátenus, te regénte, urgentióribus ætátis nostræ postulatiónibus generóse respóndeant.

Animárum médice et córporum, ægrótos álleva, moriéntibus adésto.
—et in tuis miseratiónibus nos vísita et réfove.

Defúnctos inter beátos annumeráre dignéris,
—quorum nómina sunt in libro vitæ.

Pater noster.

Oratio

Short Responsory

℣. How wondrous are Your works, O Lord;
℟. in wisdom You have wrought them all.

Magnificat ant. as in Proper of the Time.

Intercessions

Christ has been merciful to His hungry people and has worked wonders out of His love for them. Mindful of these things and with loving devotion, let us make our prayer to Him: *Show us Your love, O Lord.*

We profess, O Lord, that every benefit has come to us today out of Your goodness,
—may it not return to You void, but bear fruit within a good heart.

Light and salvation of all nations, protect the witnesses whom You have sent into the whole world,
—enkindle in them the fire of the Spirit.

Grant that all might bring the world closer to its surpassing dignity,
—so that, with You as their Ruler, they might respond generously to the more urgent demands of our age.

Physician of bodies and souls, relieve the sick, attend to the dying,
—and in Your mercy, visit and refresh us.

Deign to number the deceased among the blessed,
—whose names are in the book of life.

Our Father.

Oration

As in Proper of the Time.

Hebdomada III

Dominica, ad Laudes matutinas

HYMNUS

Ætérne rerum cónditor,
noctem diémque qui regis,
et témporum das témpora
ut álleves fastídium,

Præco diéi iam sonat,
noctis profúndæ pérvigil,
noctúrna lux viántibus
a nocte noctem ségregans.

Hoc excitátus lúcifer
solvit polum calígine;
hoc omnis errónum chorus
vias nocéndi déserit.

Hoc nauta vires cólligit
pontíque mitéscunt freta;
hoc, ipse Petr*a* Ecclésiæ,
canénte, culpam díluit.

Iesu, labántes réspice
et nos vidéndo córrige;
si réspicis, lapsus cadunt
fletúque culpa sólvitur.

Tu, lux, refúlge sénsibus
mentísque somnum díscute;
te nostra vox primum sonet
et vota solvámus tibi.

Week III

Sunday, Lauds

HYMN

Trans. J. H. Newman

Framer of the earth and sky,
  Ruler of the day and night,
With a glad variety,
  Tempering all and making light;

Gleams upon our dark path flinging,
  Cutting short each night begun,
Hark! for chanticleer is singing,
  Hark! he chides the lingering sun.

And the morning star replies,
  And lets loose the imprison'd day;
And the godless bandit flies
  From his haunt and from his prey.

Shrill it sounds, the storm relenting
  Soothes the weary seaman's ears;
Once it wrought a great repenting,
  In that flood of Peter's tears.

Rouse we; let the blithesome cry
  Of that bird our hearts awaken;
Chide the slumberers as they lie,
  And arrest the sin-o'ertaken.

Hope and health are in his strain,
  To the fearful and the ailing;
Murder sheathes his blade profane,
  Faith revives when faith was failing.

Sit, Christe, rex piíssime,
tibi Patríque glória
cum Spíritu Paráclito,
in sempitérna sǽcula. Amen.

PSALMODIA

Ant. 1 Mirábilis in altis Dóminus, allelúia.

Psalmus 92 (93)

1 Dóminus regnávit! Decórem indútus est; *
indútus est Dóminus, fortitúdine præcínxit se.
Etenim firmávit orbem terræ, *
qui non commovébitur.
2 Firmáta sedes tua ex tunc, *
a sǽculo tu es.

3 Elevavérunt flúmina, Dómine, †
elevavérunt flúmina vocem suam, *
elevavérunt flúmina fragórem suum.

4 Super voces aquárum multárum, †
super poténtes elatiónes maris, *
potens in altis Dóminus.

Jesu, Master! when we sin,
 Turn on us Thy healing face;
It will melt the offence within
 Into penitential grace:

Beam on our bewilder'd mind,
 Till its dreamy shadows flee;
Stones cry out where Thou hast shined,
 Jesu! musical with Thee.

To the Father and the Son,
 And the Spirit, who in heaven
Ever witness, Three and One,
 Praise on earth be ever given.

PSALMODY

Ant. 1 Glorious is the Lord on high, alleluia.

Psalm 93

1 The Lord reigns; he is robed in majesty;
 the Lord is robed, he is girded with strength.
Yea, the world is established; it shall never be moved;
2 Thy throne is established from of old;
 thou art from everlasting.

3 The floods have lifted up, O Lord,
 the floods have lifted up their voice,
 the floods lift up their roaring.
4 Mightier than the thunders of many waters,
 mightier than the waves of the sea,
 the Lord on high is mighty!

5 Testimónia tua credibília facta sunt nimis; *
domum tuam decet sanctitúdo, Dómine, in longitúdinem diérum.

Ant. Mirábilis in altis Dóminus, allelúia.

Ant. 2 Laudábilis es, Dómine, et superexaltátus in sǽcula, allelúia.

Canticum Dan 3, 57–88. 56

57 Benedícite, ómnia ópera Dómini, Dómino, *
laudáte et superexaltáte eum in sǽcula.
58 Benedícite, cæli, Dómino, *
59 benedícite, ángeli Dómini, Dómino.

60 Benedícite, aquæ omnes, quæ super cælos sunt, Dómino, *
61 benedícat omnis virtus Dómino.
62 Benedícite, sol et luna, Dómino, *
63 benedícite, stellæ cæli, Dómino.

64 Benedícite, omnis imber et ros, Dómino, *
65 benedícite, omnes venti, Dómino.
66 Benedícite, ignis et æstus, Dómino, *
67 benedícite, frigus et æstus, Dómino.

68 Benedícite, rores et pruína, Dómino, *
69 benedícite, gelu et frigus, Dómino.
70 Benedícite, glácies et nives, Dómino, *
71 benedícite, noctes et dies, Dómino.

72 Benedícite, lux et ténebræ, Dómino, *
73 benedícite, fúlgura et nubes, Dómino.
74 Benedícat terra Dóminum, *
laudet et superexáltet eum in sǽcula.

5 Thy decrees are very sure;
holiness befits thy house,
O Lord, for evermore.

Ant. 1 Glorious is the Lord on high, alleluia.
Ant. 2 Praiseworthy art Thou, O Lord, and highly exalted. To Thee, Lord, be highest glory and praise for ever, alleluia.

Canticle Cf. Daniel 3:35–66, 34

35 "Bless the Lord, all works of the Lord,
sing praise to him and highly exalt him for ever.
36 Bless the Lord, you heavens,
37 Bless the Lord, you angels of the Lord,
38 Bless the Lord, all waters above the heaven,
39 Bless the Lord, all powers,
40 Bless the Lord, sun and moon,
41 Bless the Lord, stars of heaven,
42 Bless the Lord, all rain and dew,
43 Bless the Lord, all winds,
44 Bless the Lord, fire and heat,
45 Bless the Lord, winter cold and summer heat,
46 Bless the Lord, dews and snows,
47 Bless the Lord, nights and days,
48 Bless the Lord light and darkness,
51 Bless the Lord, lightnings and clouds,
52 Let the earth bless the Lord;
let it sing praise to him and highly exalt him for ever.
53 Bless the Lord, mountains and hills,
54 Bless the Lord, all things that grow on the earth,
55 Bless the Lord, you springs,
56 Bless the Lord, seas and rivers,

75 Benedícite, montes et colles, Dómino, *
76 benedícite, univérsa germinántia in terra, Dómino.
77 Benedícite, mária et flúmina, Dómino, *
78 benedícite, fontes, Dómino.

79 Benedícite, cete et ómnia quæ movéntur in aquis, Dómino, *
80 benedícite, omnes vólucres cæli, Dómino.
81 Benedícite, omnes béstiæ et pécora, Dómino, *
82 benedícite, fílii hóminum, Dómino.

83 Bénedic, Israel, Dómino, *
laudáte et superexaltáte eum in sæcula.
84 Benedícite, sacerdótes Dómini, Dómino, *
85 benedícite, servi Dómini, Dómino.

86 Benedícite, spíritus et ánimæ iustórum, Dómino, *
87 benedícite, sancti et húmiles corde, Dómino.
88 Benedícite, Ananía, Azaría, Mísael, Dómino, *
laudáte et superexaltáte eum in sæcula.

Benedicámus Patrem et Fílium cum Sancto Spíritu; *
laudémus et superexaltémus eum in sæcula.
56 Benedíctus es in firmaménto cæli *
et laudábilis et gloriósus in sæcula.

Ant. Laudábilis es, Dómine, et superexaltátus in sæcula, allelúia.
Ant. 3 Laudáte Dóminum de cælis, allelúia. †

57 Bless the Lord, you whales and all creatures that
move in the waters,
58 Bless the Lord, all birds of the air,
59 Bless the Lord, all beasts and cattle,
60 Bless the Lord, you sons of men,
61 Bless the Lord, O Israel,
sing praise to him and highly exalt him for ever.
62 Bless the Lord, you priests of the Lord,
63 Bless the Lord, you servants of the Lord,
64 Bless the Lord, spirits and souls of the righteous,
65 Bless the Lord, you who are holy and humble in
heart,
66 Bless the Lord, Hananiah, Azariah, and Mishael,
sing praise to him and highly exalt him for ever;
Let us bless the Father and the Son with the Holy
Spirit;
Let us sing praise to him and highly exalt him for
ever.

34 Blessed art thou in the firmament of heaven
and to be sung and highly glorified for ever.

After this canticle, the *Gloria Patri* is not said.

Ant. 2 Praiseworthy art Thou, O Lord, and highly exalted. To Thee, Lord, be highest glory and praise for ever, alleluia.

Ant. 3 Praise the Lord from the heavens, alleluia.

Psalmus 148

1 Laudáte Dóminum de cælis, *
† laudáte eum in excélsis.
2 Laudáte eum, omnes ángeli eius, *
laudáte eum, omnes virtútes eius.

3 Laudáte eum, sol et luna, *
laudáte eum, omnes stellæ lucéntes.
4 Laudáte eum, cæli cælórum, *
et aquæ omnes, quæ super cælos sunt.

5 Laudent nomen Dómini, *
quia ipse mandávit, et creáta sunt;
6 státuit ea in ætérnum et in sæculum sæculi; *
præcéptum pósuit, et non præteríbit.

7 Laudáte Dóminum de terra, *
dracónes et omnes abyssi,
8 ignis, grando, nix, fumus, *
spíritus procellárum, qui facit verbum eius,
9 montes et omnes colles, *
ligna fructífera et omnes cedri,
10 béstiæ et univérsa pécora, *
serpéntes et vólucres pennátæ.

11 Reges terræ et omnes pópuli, *
príncipes et omnes iúdices terræ,
12 iúvenes et vírgines, *
senes cum iunióribus,
13 laudent nomen Dómini, *
quia exaltátum est nomen eius solíus.

Magnificéntia eius super cælum et terram, *
14 et exaltávit cornu pópuli sui.

Psalm 148

1 Praise the LORD!
Praise the LORD from the heavens,
praise him in the heights!
2 Praise him, all his angels,
praise him, all his host!

3 Praise him, sun and moon,
praise him, all you shining stars!
4 Praise him, you highest heavens,
and you waters above the heavens!

5 Let them praise the name of the Lord!
For he commanded and they were created.
6 And he established them for ever and ever;
he fixed their bounds which cannot be passed.

7 Praise the LORD from the earth,
you sea monsters and all deeps,
8 fire and hail, snow and frost,
stormy wind fulfilling his command!

9 Mountains and all hills,
fruit trees and all cedars!
10 Beasts and all cattle,
creeping things and flying birds!

11 Kings of the earth and all peoples,
princes and all rulers of the earth!
12 Young men and maidens together,
old men and children!

13 Let them praise the name of the Lord,
for his name alone is exalted;
His glory is above earth and heaven.

Hymnus ómnibus sanctis eius, *
filiis Israel, pópulo, qui propínquus est ei.

Ant. Laudáte Dóminum de cælis, allelúia.

LECTIO BREVIS Ez 37, 12B–14

Hæc dicit Dóminus Deus: Ecce ego apériam túmulos vestros et edúcam vos de sepúlcris vestris, pópulus meus, et indúcam vos in terram Israel; et sciétis quia ego Dóminus, cum aperúero sepúlcra vestra et edúxero vos de túmulis vestris, pópulus meus. Et dabo spíritum meum in vobis, et vivétis, et collocábo vos super humum vestram, et sciétis quia ego Dóminus. Locútus sum et fácio, ait Dóminus Deus.

RESPONSORIUM BREVE

℟. Christe, Fili Dei vivi, * Miserére nobis. Christe.
℣. Qui sedes ad déxteram Patris. * Miserére nobis.
Glória Patri. Christe.

PRECES

Deum, qui misit Spíritum Sanctum, ut fíeret lux beatíssima ómnium córdium, deprecémur instántes: *Illúmina pópulum tuum, Dómine.*

Benedíctus es, Deus, lux nostra,
—qui propter glóriam tuam ad diem novum nos perveníre fecísti.

Tu, qui per resurrectiónem Fílii tui mundum illuminásti,
—per Ecclésiam tuam in omnes hómines hoc lumen effúnde.

14 He has raised up a horn for his people,
praise for all his saints,
for the people of Israel who are near to him.
Praise the Lord!

Ant. 3 Praise the Lord from the heavens, alleluia.

SHORT READING Ezekiel 37:12b–14

Thus says the Lord God: Behold, I will open your graves, and raise you from your graves, O my people; and I will bring you home into the land of Israel. And you shall know that I am the Lord, when I open your graves, and raise you from your graves, O my people. And I will put my Spirit within you, and you shall live, and I will place you in your own land; then you shall know that I, the Lord, have spoken, and I have done it, says the Lord.

SHORT RESPONSORY

℣. Christ, Son of the living God, have mercy on us.
℟. You that are seated at the right hand of the Father.

Benedictus ant. as in Proper of the Time.

INTERCESSIONS

Let us intently beseech God, Who sent the Holy Spirit, that He might be the most blessed light of all hearts: *Enlighten your people, O Lord.*

Blessed are You, O God, our light,
—Who for the sake of Your glory have brought us to a new day.

You, Who through the resurrection of Your Son have enlightened the world,
—shed this light on all men through Your Church.

Qui Unigéniti tui discípulos per tuum Spíritum clarificásti,
—hunc emítte in Ecclésiam tuam, quæ sit tibi fidélis.

O lumen géntium, meménto eórum, qui adhuc in ténebris commorántur,
—óculos áperi cordis eórum, ut te solum Deum verum agnóscant.

Pater noster.

ORATIO

You, Who have glorified the disciples of Your only-begotten Son through Your Spirit,
—send forth this Spirit into Your Church, that She may be faithful to You.

O light of the nations, remember those who even now dwell in darkness,
—open the eyes of their hearts, that they may recognize You as the one true God.

Our Father.

Oration

As in Proper of the Time.

Hebdomada III

Dominica, ad II Vesperas

HYMNUS

Lucís creátor óptime,
lucem diérum próferens,
primórdiis lucis novæ
mundi parans oríginem;

Qui mane iunctum vésperi
diem vocári præcipis:
tætrum chaos illábitur;
audi preces cum flétibus.

Ne mens graváta crímine
vitæ sit exsul múnere,
dum nil perénne cógitat
seséque culpis ílligat.

Cælórum pulset íntimum,
vitále tollat præmium;
vitémus omne nóxium,
purgémus omne péssimum.

Præsta, Pater piíssime,
Patríque compar Unice,
cum Spíritu Paráclito
regnans per omne sæculum. Amen.

PSALMODIA

Ant. 1 Dixit Dóminus Dómino meo: Sede a dextris meis, allelúia. †

Week III

Sunday, Vespers II

HYMN Trans. J. H. Newman

Father of Lights, by whom each day
 Is kindled out of night,
Who, when the heavens were made, didst lay
 Their rudiments in light;

Thou, who didst bind and blend in one
 The glistening morn and evening pale,
Hear Thou our plaint, when light is gone,
 And lawlessness and strife prevail.

Hear, lest the whelming weight of crime
 Wreck us with life in view;
Lest thoughts and schemes of sense and time
 Earn us a sinner's due.

So may we knock at Heaven's door,
 And strive the immortal prize to win,
Continually and evermore
 Guarded without and pure within.

Grant this, O Father, Only Son,
 And Spirit, God of grace,
To whom all worship shall be done
 In every time and place.

PSALMODY

Ant. 1 The Lord says to my Lord: "Sit at My right hand," alleluia.

Psalmus 109 (110), 1–5. 7

1 Dixit Dóminus Dómino meo: *
« Sede a dextris meis,
† donec ponam inimícos tuos *
scabéllum pedum tuórum ».

2 Virgam poténtiæ tuæ emíttet Dóminus ex Sion: *
domináre in médio inimicórum tuórum.
3 Tecum principátus in die virtútis tuæ, †
in splendóribus sanctis, *
ex útero ante lucíferum génui te.

4 Iurávit Dóminus et non pænitébit eum: *
« Tu es sacérdos in ætérnum secúndum órdinem
Melchísedech ».
5 Dóminus a dextris tuis, *
conquassábit in die iræ suæ reges.

7 De torrénte in via bibet, *
proptérea exaltábit caput.

Ant. Dixit Dóminus Dómino meo: Sede a dextris meis, allelúia.
Ant. 2 Memóriam fecit mirabílium suórum miserátor Dóminus, allelúia.

Psalmus 110 (111)

1 Confitébor Dómino in toto corde meo, *
in consílio iustórum et congregatióne.

2 Magna ópera Dómini, *
exquirénda ómnibus, qui cúpiunt ea.

Psalm 110:1–5, 7

1 The LORD says to my lord:
"Sit at my right hand,
till I make your enemies your footstool."

2 The LORD sends forth from Zion
your mighty scepter.
Rule in the midst of your foes!
3 Your people will offer themselves freely
on the day you lead your host
upon the holy mountains.
From the womb of the morning
like dew your youth will come to you.
4 The Lord has sworn
and will not change his mind,
"You are a priest for ever
after the order of Melchizedek."

5 The Lord is at your right hand;
he will shatter kings on the day of his wrath.
7 He will drink from the brook by the way;
therefore he will lift up his head.

Ant. 1 The Lord says to my Lord: "Sit at My right hand," alleluia.
Ant. 2 The compassionate Lord has caused His wonderful works to be remembered, alleluia.

Psalm 111

1 I will give thanks to the Lord with all my heart,
in the company of the upright, in the
congregation.
2 Great are the works of the Lord,
studied by all who have pleasure in them.

3 Decor et magnificéntia opus eius, *
et iustítia eius manet in sæculum sæculi.

4 Memóriam fecit mirabílium suórum, *
misericors et miserátor Dóminus.
5 Escam dedit timéntibus se; *
memor erit in sæculum testaménti sui.

6 Virtútem óperum suórum annuntiávit pópulo suo, †
ut det illis hereditátem géntium; *
7 ópera mánuum eius véritas et iudícium.
Fidélia ómnia mandáta eius, †
8 confirmáta in sæculum sæculi, *
facta in veritáte et æquitáte.
9 Redemptiónem misit pópulo suo, *
mandávit in ætérnum testaméntum suum.

Sanctum et terríbile nomen eius. *
10 Inítium sapiéntiæ timor Dómini,
intelléctus bonus ómnibus faciéntibus ea; *
laudátio eius manet in sæculum sæculi.

Ant. Memóriam fecit mirabílium suórum miserátor Dóminus, allelúia.

Ant. 3 Regnávit Dóminus Deus noster omnípotens, allelúia.

Canticum CF. AP 19, 1–2. 5–7

Allelúia.
1 Salus et glória et virtus Deo nostro, *
(℟. Allelúia.)
2 quia vera et iusta iudícia eius.
℟. Allelúia (allelúia).

3 Full of honor and majesty is his work,
and his righteousness endures for ever.
4 He has caused his wonderful works to be remembered;
the LORD is gracious and merciful.
5 He provides food for those who fear him;
he is ever mindful of his covenant.
6 He has shown his people the power of his works,
in giving them the heritage of the nations.
7 The works of his hands are faithful and just;
all his precepts are trustworthy,
8 they are established for ever and ever,
to be performed with faithfulness and uprightness.
9 He sent redemption to his people;
he has commanded his covenant for ever.
Holy and terrible is his name!
10 The fear of the Lord is beginning of wisdom;
a good understanding have all those who practice it.
His praise endures for ever!

Ant. 2 The compassionate Lord has caused His wonderful works to be remembered, alleluia.
Ant. 3 The Lord our God the Almighty reigns, alleluia.

Canticle See Revelation 19:1–7

Alleluia.
Salvation and glory and power belong to our God;
(℟. Alleluia.)
for his judgments are true and just;
℟. Alleluia (alleluia).

Allelúia.
5 Laudem dícite Deo nostro, omnes servi eius *
(℟. Allelúia.)
et qui timétis eum, pusílli et magni!
℟. Allelúia (allelúia).

Allelúia.
6 Quóniam regnávit Dóminus, Deus noster omnípotens. *
(℟. Allelúia.)
7 Gaudeámus et exsultémus et demus glóriam ei.
℟. Allelúia (allelúia).

Allelúia.
Quia venérunt núptiæ Agni, *
(℟. Allelúia.)
et uxor eius præparávit se.
℟. Allelúia (allelúia).

Ant. Regnávit Dóminus Deus noster omnípotens, allelúia.

LECTIO BREVIS 1 PETR 1, 3-5

Benedíctus Deus et Pater Dómini nostri Iesu Christi, qui secúndum magnam misericórdiam suam regenerávit nos in spem vivam per resurrectiónem Iesu Christi ex mórtuis, in hereditátem incorruptíbilem et incontaminátam et immarcescíbilem, conservátam in cælis propter vos, qui in virtúte Dei custodímini per fidem in salútem parátam revelári in témpore novíssimo.

Alleluia.
Praise our God, all you his servants,
(℟. Alleluia.)
you that fear him, small and great.
℟. Alleluia (alleluia).

Alleluia.
For, the Lord our God the Almighty reigns;
(℟. Alleluia.)
let us rejoice and exult and give him glory.
℟. Alleluia (alleluia).

Alleluia.
For the marriage of the Lamb has come,
(℟. Alleluia.)
and his Bride has made Herself ready.
℟. Alleluia (alleluia).

Ant. 3 The Lord our God the Almighty reigns, alleluia.

SHORT READING 1 Peter 1:3–5

Blessed be the God and Father of our Lord Jesus Christ! By his great mercy we have been born anew to a living hope through the resurrection of Jesus Christ from the dead, and to an inheritance which is imperishable, undefiled, and unfading, kept in heaven for you, who by God's power are guarded through faith for a salvation ready to be revealed in the last time.

Responsorium Breve

℟. Benedíctus es, Dómine, * In firmaménto cæli. Benedíctus.
℣. Et laudábilis et glóriosus in sǽcula. * In firmaménto cæli. Glória Patri. Benedíctus.

Preces

Deum, qui mundum, olim creátum, redemptióne recreávit et semper rénovat amóre, lætántibus ánimis invocémus: *Rénova mirabília amóris tui, Dómine.*

Grátias tibi, Deus, qui poténtiam tuam in univérsa creatióne revélas,
—et in mundi cursu providéntiam maniféstas.

Per Fílium tuum, pacis præcónem et in cruce victórem,
—ab ináni timóre ac desperatióne nos líbera.

Omnibus, qui iustítiam díligunt atque colunt,
—concéde, ut sine dolo ad ædificándum mundum in vera pace cooperéntur.

Adésto oppréssis, captívos líbera, míseros consoláre, panem tríbue esuriéntibus, firmitátem concéde debílibus,
—victóriam crucis in ómnibus osténde.

Qui Fílium tuum post mortem et sepultúram ad glóriam mirabíliter suscitásti,
—defúnctos ad vitam cum eo perveníre concéde.

Pater noster.

Oratio

Short Responsory

℟. Blessed are You, O Lord, in the firmament of heaven.
℣. Praiseworthy and glorious forever.

Magnificat ant. as in Proper of the Time.

Intercessions

God, Who having once created the world recreated it in redemption, and always renews it in love, we invoke with joyful spirits: *Renew the marvels of Your love, O Lord.*

Thanks be to You, O God, Who reveal Your power in all creation
—and in the course of the world manifest Your providence.

Through Your Son, the Herald of peace and the Victor on the cross,
—free us from vain fear and despair.

For all who love and cultivate Your justice,
—grant that things may work together without sorrow to the building up of the world in true peace.

Be present to the oppressed, free the captives, console the sorrowful, bestow bread on the hungry, grant strength to the weak,
—show the victory of the cross in all.

You, Who marvelously raised up Your Son to glory after death and the grave,
—grant the departed to enter into life with Him.

Our Father.

Oration

As in Proper of the Time.

Hebdomada III

Feria II, ad Laudes matutinas

Hymnus

Splendor patérnæ glóriæ,
de luce lucem próferens,
lux lucis et fons lúminis,
diem dies illúminans,

Verúsque sol, illábere
micans nitóre pérpeti,
iubárque Sancti Spíritus
infúnde nostris sénsibus.

Votis vocémus et Patrem,
Patrem perénnis glóriæ,
Patrem poténtis grátiæ,
culpam reléget lúbricam.

Infórmet actus strénuos,
dentem retúndat ínvidi,
casus secúndet ásperos,
donet geréndi grátiam.

Mentem gubérnat et regat
casto, fidéli córpore;
fides calóre férveat,
fraudis venéna nésciat.

Christúsque nobis sit cibus,
potúsque noster sit fides;
læti bibámus sóbriam
ebrietátem Spíritus.

Week III

Monday, Lauds

Hymn

Trans. J. H. Newman

Of the Father Effluence bright,
Out of Light evolving light,
Light from Light, unfailing Ray,
Day creative of the day:

Truest Sun, upon us stream
With Thy calm perpetual beam,
In the Spirit's still sunshine
Making sense and thought divine.

Seek we too the Father's face
Father of almighty grace,
And of majesty excelling,
Who can purge our tainted dwelling;

Who can aid us, who can break
Teeth of envious foes, and make
Hours of loss and pain succeed,
Guiding safe each duteous deed,

And infusing self-control,
Fragrant chastity of soul,
Faith's keen flame to soar on high,
Incorrupt simplicity.

Christ Himself for food be given,
Faith become the cup of Heaven,
Out of which the joy is quaff'd
Of the Spirit's sobering draught.

Lætus dies hic tránseat;
pudor sit ut dilúculum,
fides velut merídies,
crepúsculum mens nésciat.

Auróra cursus próvehit;
Auróra totus pródeat,
in Patre totus Fílius
et totus in Verbo Pater. Amen.

PSALMODIA

Ant. 1 Beáti qui hábitant in domo tua, Dómine.

Psalmus 83 (84)

2 Quam diléсta tabernácula tua, Dómine,
virtútum! *
3 Concupíscit et déficit ánima mea in átria
Dómini.
Cor meum et caro mea *
exsultavérunt in Deum vivum.
4 Etenim passer invénit sibi domum, †
et turtur nidum sibi, ubi ponat pullos suos: *
altária tua, Dómine virtútum, rex meus et Deus
meus.
5 Beáti, qui hábitant in domo tua: *
in perpétuum laudábunt te.

With that joy replenishèd,
Morn shall glow with modest red,
Noon with beaming faith be bright,
Eve be soft without twilight.

It has dawn'd;—upon our way,
Father in Thy Word, this day,
In Thy Father Word Divine,
From Thy cloudy pillar shine.

To the Father, and the Son,
And the Spirit, Three and One,
As of old, and as in Heaven,
Now and here be glory given.

PSALMODY

Ant. 1 Blessed are those who dwell in Thy house, O Lord.

Psalm 84

1 How lovely is thy dwelling place,
O LORD of hosts!
2 My soul longs, yea, faints
for the courts of the LORD;
my heart and flesh sing for joy
to the living God.

3 Even the sparrow finds a home,
and the swallow a nest for herself,
where she may lay her young,
at thy altars, O LORD of hosts,
my King and my God.
4 Blessed are those who dwell in thy house,
ever singing thy praise!

6 Beátus vir, cuius est auxílium abs te, *
ascensiónes in corde suo dispósuit.
7 Transeúntes per vallem sitiéntem in fontem
ponent eam, *
étenim benedictiónibus véstiet eam plúvia
matutína.
8 Ibunt de virtúte in virtútem, *
vidébitur Deus deórum in Sion.

9 Dómine Deus virtútum, exáudi oratiónem
meam; *
áuribus pércipe, Deus Iacob.
10 Protéctor noster áspice, Deus, *
et réspice in fáciem christi tui.

11 Quia mélior est dies una in átriis tuis super
mília, †
elégi ad limen esse in domo Dei mei *
magis quam habitáre in tabernáculis
peccatórum.

12 Quia sol et scutum est Dóminus Deus, †
grátiam et glóriam dabit Dóminus; *
non privábit bonis eos, qui ámbulant in
innocéntia.
13 Dómine virtútum, *
beátus homo, qui sperat in te.

Ant. Beáti qui hábitant in domo tua, Dómine.
Ant. 2 Veníte, et ascendámus ad montem Dómini.

5 Blessed are the men whose strength is in thee,
in whose heart are the highways to Zion.
6 As they go through the valley of Baca
they make it a place of springs;
the early rain also covers it with pools.
7 They go from strength to strength;
the God of gods will be seen in Zion.

8 O LORD God of hosts, hear my prayer;
give ear, O God of Jacob!
9 Behold our shield, O God;
look upon the face of thine anointed!

10 For a day in thy courts is better
than a thousand elsewhere.
I would rather be a doorkeeper in the house of my God
than dwell in the tents of wickedness.
11 For the LORD God is a sun and shield;
He bestows favor and honor.
No good thing does the LORD withhold
from those who walk uprightly.
12 O LORD of hosts,
blessed is the man who trusts in thee!

Ant. 1 Blessed are those who dwell in Thy house, O Lord.
Ant. 2 Come, let us go up to the mountain of the Lord.

Canticum Is 2, 2–5

2 Erit in novíssimis diébus *
præparátus mons domus Dómini in vértice móntium,
et elevábitur super colles, *
et fluent ad eum omnes gentes.

3 Et ibunt pópuli multi et dicent: †
« Veníte et ascendámus ad montem Dómini, *
ad domum Dei Iacob,
ut dóceat nos vias suas, *
et ambulémus in sémitis eius »;
quia de Sion exíbit lex *
et verbum Dómini de Ierúsalem.
4 Et iudicábit gentes *
et árguet pópulos multos,
et conflábunt gládios suos in vómeres *
et lánceas suas in falces;
non levábit gens contra gentem gládium, *
nec exercebúntur ultra ad prœlium.

5 Domus Iacob, veníte, *
et ambulémus in lúmine Dómini.

Ant. Veníte, et ascendámus ad montem Dómini.
Ant. 3 Cantáte Dómino, benedícite nómini eius.

Canticle Isaiah 2:2–5

2 It shall come to pass in the latter days
that the mountain of the house of the LORD
shall be established as the highest of the mountains,
and shall be raised above the hills;
and all the nations shall flow to it.
3 and many peoples shall come, and say:
"Come, let us go up to the mountain of the LORD,
to the house of the God of Jacob;
that he may teach us his ways
and that we may walk in his paths."
For out of Zion shall go forth the law,
and the word of the LORD from Jerusalem.
4 He shall judge between the nations,
and shall decide for many peoples;
and they shall beat their swords into plowshares,
and their spears into pruning hooks;
nation shall not lift up sword against nation,
neither shall they learn war any more.

5 O house of Jacob,
come, let us walk
in the light of the LORD.

Ant. 2 Come, let us go up to the mountain of the Lord.

Ant. 3 Sing to the Lord, bless His name.

Psalmus 95 (96)

1 Cantáte Dómino cánticum novum, *
cantáte Dómino, omnis terra.
2 Cantáte Dómino, benedícite nómini eius, *
annuntiáte de die in diem salutáre eius.
3 Annuntiáte inter gentes glóriam eius, *
in ómnibus pópulis mirabília eius.

4 Quóniam magnus Dóminus et laudábilis nimis, *
terríbilis est super omnes deos.
5 Quóniam omnes dii géntium inánia, *
Dóminus autem cælos fecit.
6 Magnificéntia et pulchritúdo in conspéctu eius, *
poténtia et decor in sanctuário eius.

7 Afférte Dómino, famíliæ populórum, †
afférte Dómino glóriam et poténtiam, *
8 afférte Dómino glóriam nóminis eius.
Tóllite hóstias et introíte in átria eius, *
9 adoráte Dóminum in splendóre sancto.
Contremíscite a fácie eius, univérsa terra, *
10 dícite in géntibus: « Dóminus regnávit! ».
Etenim corréxit orbem terræ, qui non commovébitur; *
iudicábit pópulos in æquitáte.

11 Læténtur cæli et exsúltet terra, †
sonet mare et plenitúdo eius; *
12 gaudébunt campi et ómnia, quæ in eis sunt.
Tunc exsultábunt ómnia ligna silvárum †
13 a fácie Dómini, quia venit, *
quóniam venit iudicáre terram.
Iudicábit orbem terræ in iustítia *
et pópulos in veritáte sua.

Psalm 96

1 O sing to the Lord a new song;
sing to the Lord, all the earth!
2 Sing to the Lord, bless his name;
tell of his salvation from day to day.
3 Declare his glory among the nations;
his marvelous works among all the peoples!
4 For great is the Lord, and greatly to be praised;
he is to be feared above all gods.
5 For all the gods of the peoples are idols;
but the Lord made the heavens.
6 Honor and majesty are before him;
strength and beauty are in his sanctuary.

7 Ascribe to the Lord, O families of the peoples,
ascribe to the Lord the glory due his name;
8 Ascribe to the Lord the glory due his name;
bring an offering, and come into His courts!
9 Worship the Lord in holy array;
tremble before him, all the earth!

10 Say among the nations, "The Lord reigns!
Yea, the world is established, it shall never be moved;
he will judge the peoples with equity."
11 Let the heavens be glad, and let the earth rejoice;
let the sea roar, and all that fills it;
12 let the field exult, and everything in it!
Then shall all the trees of the wood sing for joy
13 before the Lord, for he comes,
for he comes to judge the earth.
He will judge the world with righteousness,
and the peoples with his truth.

Ant. Cantáte Dómino, benedícite nómini eius.

LECTIO BREVIS IAC 2, 12–13

Sic loquímini et sic fácite sicut per legem libertátis iudicándi. Iudícium enim sine misericórdia illi, qui non fecit misericórdiam; superexsúltat misericórdia iudício.

RESPONSORIUM BREVE

℟. Benedíctus Dóminus * A sǽculo et usque in sǽculum. Benedíctus.

℣. Qui facit mirabília solus. * A sǽculo et usque in sǽculum. Glória Patri. Benedíctus.

Ad Benedictus, ant. Benedíctus Dóminus Deus noster.

PRECES

Deum, qui hómines in mundo pósuit, ut concórditer ad suam glóriam opus fíeret ab illis, eníxe rogémus: *Fac nos te glorificáre, Dómine.*

Creátor universórum Deus, benedícimus tibi,
—qui nobis mundi bona dedísti vitámque nostram hucúsque servásti.

Réspice nos, qui labórem cotidiánum suscípimus,
—et óperis tui partícipes nos tuæ voluntáti confórma.

Opus nostrum hodiérnum sic redde nostris frátribus fructuósum,
—ut cum eis et pro eis terrénam civitátem, quæ tibi pláceat, ædificémus.

Nobis et ómnibus, quibus hódie occurrémus, adésto,
—gáudium largíre et pacem.

Pater noster.

Ant. 3 Sing to the Lord, bless His name.

SHORT READING James 2:12–13

So speak and so act as those who are to be judged under the law of liberty. For judgment is without mercy to one who has shown no mercy; yet mercy triumphs over judgment.

SHORT RESPONSORY

℟. Blessed be the Lord, from age to age.
℣. Who alone has done marvelous deeds.

Benedictus ant. Blessed be the Lord our God.

INTERCESSIONS

Let us eagerly beseech God, Who placed men in the world, that they might work harmoniously unto His glory: *Make us to glorify You, O Lord.*

O God, Creator of all, we bless You,
—Who have given us the good things of the world and preserved our life to this moment.

Look upon us, who take up our daily labor,
—and conform us to Your will as we share in Your work.

So make our daily work fruitful for our brothers,
—that with them and for them we might build an earthly city pleasing to You.

To us and to all whom we meet today be present,
—granting Your joy and Your peace.

Our Father.

ORATIO

Dirígere et sanctificáre, régere et gubernáre dignáre, Dómine Deus, Rex cæli et terræ, hódie corda et córpora nostra, sensus, sermónes, et actus nostros in lege tua et in opéribus mandatórum tuórum, ut hic et in ætérnum, te auxiliánte, salvi et líberi esse mereámur. Per Dóminum.

Oration

Deign this day to direct and sanctify, rule and govern, O Lord God, King of heaven and earth, our hearts and bodies, our thoughts, words and actions in Your law and in the works of Your commandments, that here and unto eternity, with Your assistance, we might merit salvation and freedom. Through our Lord.

Hebdomada III

Feria II, ad Vesperas

HYMNUS

Imménse cæli cónditor,
qui, mixta ne confúnderent,
aquæ fluénta dívidens,
cælum dedísti límitem,

Firmans locum cæléstibus
simúlque terræ rívulis,
ut unda flammas témperet,
terræ solum ne dissipet:

Infúnde nunc, piíssime,
donum perénnis grátiæ,
fraudis novæ ne cásibus
nos error átterat vetus

Lucem fides invéniat,
sic lúminis iubar ferat;
hæc vana cuncta térreat,
hanc falsa nulla cómprimant.

Præsta, Pater piíssime,
Patríque compar Unice,
cum Spíritu Paráclito
regnans oper omne sǽculum. Amen.

PSALMODIA

Ant. 1 Oculi nostri semper ad Dóminum, donec misereátur nostri.

Week III

Monday, Vespers

HYMN Trans. J. H. Newman

Lord of unbounded space,
  Who, lest the sky and main
Should mix, and heaven should lose its place,
  Didst the rude waters chain;

Parting the moist and rare,
  That rills on earth might flow
To soothe the angry flame, whene'er
  It ravens from below;

Pour on us of Thy grace
  The everlasting spring;
Lest our frail steps renew the trace
  Of ancient wandering.

May faith in lustre grow,
  And rear her star in heaven,
Paling all sparks of earth below,
  Unquenched by damps of even.

Grant it, O Father, Son,
  And Holy Spirit of grace,
To whom be glory, Three on One,
  In every time and place.

PSALMODY

Ant. 1 Our eyes look to the Lord, till He have mercy upon us.

Psalmus 122 (123)

1 Ad te levávi óculos meos, *
qui hábitas in cælis.

2 Ecce sicut óculi servórum ad manus dominórum suórum, *
sicut óculi ancíllæ ad manus dóminæ suæ,
ita óculi nostri ad Dóminum Deum nostrum, *
donec misereátur nostri.

3 Miserére nostri, Dómine, miserére nostri, *
quia multum repléti sumus despectióne;
4 quia multum repléta est ánima nostra *
derisióne abundántium et despectióne superbórum.

Ant. Oculi nostri semper ad Dóminum, donec misereátur nostri.
Ant. 2 Adiutórium nostrum in nómine Dómini, qui fecit cælum et terram.

Psalmus 123 (124)

1 Nisi quia Dóminus erat in nobis, dicat nunc Israel, †
2 nisi quia Dóminus erat in nobis, *
cum exsúrgerent hómines in nos:
3 forte vivos deglutíssent nos, *
cum irascerétur furor eórum in nos.

4 Fórsitan aqua absorbuísset nos, †
torrens pertransísset ánimam nostram; *
5 fórsitan pertransíssent ánimam nostram aquæ intumescéntes.

Psalm 123

1 To thee I lift up my eyes,
O thou who art enthroned in the heavens!
2 Behold, as the eyes of servants
look to the hand of their master,
as the eyes of a maid
to the hand of her mistress,
so our eyes look to the LORD our God,
till he have mercy upon us.

3 Have mercy upon us, O LORD, have mercy upon us,
for we have had more than enough of contempt.
4 Too long our soul has been sated
with the scorn of those who are at ease,
the contempt of the proud.

Ant. 1 Our eyes look to the Lord, till He have mercy upon us.
Ant. 2 Our help is in the name of the Lord, Who made heaven and earth.

Psalm 124

1 If it had not been the LORD who was on our side,
let Israel now say—
2 if it had not been the Lord who was on our side,
when men rose up against us,
3 then they would have swallowed us up alive,
when their anger was kindled against us;
4 then the flood would have swept us away,
the torrent would have gone over us;
5 then over us would have gone
the raging waters.

6 Benedíctus Dóminus, *
qui non dedit nos in direptiónem déntibus eórum.
7 Anima nostra sicut passer erépta est *
de láqueo venántium:
láqueus contrítus est, *
et nos erépti sumus.

8 Adiutórium nostrum in nómine Dómini, *
qui fecit cælum et terram.

Ant. Adiutórium nostrum in nómine Dómini, qui fecit cælum et terram.
Ant. 3 In Fílio suo elégit nos Deus in adoptiónem filiórum.

Canticum Eph 1, 3-10

3 Benedíctus Deus et Pater Dómini nostri Iesu Christi, *
qui benedíxit nos in omni benedictióne spiritáli in cæléstibus in Christo,
4 sicut elégit nos in ipso ante mundi constitutiónem, †
ut essémus sancti et immaculáti *
in conspéctu eius in caritáte,

5 qui prædestinávit nos in adoptiónem filiórum †
per Iesum Christum in ipsum, *
secúndum beneplácitum voluntátis suæ,
6 in laudem glóriæ grátiæ suæ, *
in qua gratificávit nos in Dilécto,

7 in quo habémus redemptiónem per sánguinem eius, *
remissiónem peccatórum,

6 Blessed be the Lord,
who has not given us
as prey to their teeth!
7 We have escaped as a bird
from the snare of the fowlers;
the snare is broken,
and we have escaped!

8 Our help is in the name of the Lord,
who made heaven and earth.

Ant. 2 Our help is in the name of the Lord, Who made heaven and earth.

Ant. 3 God chose us in His Son to be His adopted sons.

Canticle Ephesians 1:3–10

3 Blessed be the God and Father of our Lord Jesus Christ, who has blessed us in Christ with every spiritual blessing in the heavenly places,
4 even as he chose us in him before the foundation of the world, that we should be holy and blameless before him.
5 He destined us in love to be his sons through Jesus Christ, according to the purpose of his will,
6 to the praise of his glorious grace which he freely bestowed on us in the Beloved.
7 In him we have redemption through his blood, the forgiveness of our trespasses, according to the riches of his grace

secúndum divítias grátiæ eius, †
8 qua superabundávit in nobis *
in omni sapiéntia et prudéntia

9 notum fáciens nobis mystérium voluntátis suæ, *
secúndum beneplácitum eius,

quod propósuit in eo, *
10 in dispensatiónem plenitúdinis témporum:
recapituláre ómnia in Christo, *
quæ in cælis et quæ in terra.

Ant. In Fílio suo elégit nos Deus in adoptiónem filiórum.

LECTIO BREVIS Iac 4, 11–12

Nolíte detráhere altérutrum, fratres; qui détrahit fratri aut qui iúdicat fratrem suum, détrahit legi et iúdicat legem; si autem iúdicas legem, non es factor legis sed iudex. Unus est legislátor et iudex, qui potest salváre et pérdere; tu autem quis es, qui iúdicas próximum?

RESPONSORIUM BREVE

℟. Sana ánimam meam, * Quia peccávi tibi. Sana.
℣. Ego dixi: Dómine, miserére mei, * Quia peccávi tibi. Glória Patri. Sana.

Ad Magnificat, ant. Magníficat ánima mea Dóminum, quia respéxit Deus humilitátem meam.

8 which he lavished upon us.
9 For he has made known to us in all wisdom and insight the mystery of his will, according to his purpose which he set forth in Christ
10 as a plan for the fulness of time, to unite all things in him, things in heaven and things on earth.

Ant. 3 God chose us in His Son to be His adopted sons.

SHORT READING James 4:11–12

Do not speak evil against one another, brethren. He that speaks evil against a brother or judges his brother, speaks evil against the law and judges the law. But if you judge the law, you are not a doer of the law but a judge.

There is one lawgiver and judge, he who is able to save and to destroy. But who are you that you judge your neighbor?

SHORT RESPONSORY

℟. Heal my soul, for I have sinned against You.
℣. I said: Lord, have mercy upon me.

Magnificat ant. My soul magnifies the Lord, for God has regarded the low estate of His handmaiden.

Preces

Christus omnes hómines ad salútem vult perdúcere. Ideo eum sincéro ánimi afféctu exorémus: *Trahe ómnia ad te, Dómine.*

Benedíctus es, Dómine, qui redemísti nos per pretiósum sánguinem tuum a servitúte peccáti;
—libertátem glóriæ nobis tríbue filiórum.

Grátiam tuam concéde antístiti nostro N. et ómnibus Ecclésiæ epíscopis,
—ut mystéria tua læto spíritus fervóre minístrent.

Da ómnibus, qui veritátem investígant, ut eam quæréndo invéniant,
—et inveniéndo semper requírant.

Adésto, Dómine, órphanis, víduis et ómnibus derelíctis,
—ut propínquum te séntiant tibíque magis adhæreant.

Defúnctos fratres in cæléstem civitátem benígnus accípias,
—in qua cum Patre et Spíritu Sancto eris ómnia in ómnibus.

Pater noster.

Oratio

Deus, qui lumen indefíciens mérito prædicáris, nobis, ad hanc horam addúctis, et ténebras, quæsumus, illumináre, et delícta dignáre propitiátus ignóscere. Per Dóminum.

INTERCESSIONS

Christ wishes to lead all men to salvation. Let us entreat Him, then, with a sincere disposition of spirit: *Draw all things to Yourself, O Lord.*

Blessed are You, O Lord, Who have redeemed us from the slavery of sin through Your precious blood;
—grant to us the freedom of the sons of glory.

Bestow Your grace on our Bishop, N., and on all bishops of the Church,
—that they may administer Your mysteries with joyful fervor of spirit.

Grant to all who search for truth, that in seeking they may find it,
—and in finding it may yet seek for more.

Be present, O Lord, to orphans, widows, and all who have been abandoned,
—that they may sense Your closeness to them and cling more closely to You.

May You graciously receive our deceased brethren into the heavenly city,
—in which, with the Father and the Holy Spirit, You will be all in all.

Our Father.

ORATION

O God, Who are truly proclaimed the unfailing Light, as we come to this hour, we beseech you: illumine the darkness and mercifully deign to forgive our offenses. Through our Lord.

Hebdomada III

Feria III, ad Laudes matutinas

Hymnus

Pergráta mundo núntiat
auróra solis spícula,
res et colóre véstiens
iam cuncta dat nitéscere.

Qui sol per ævum prænites,
o Christe, nobis vívidus,
ad te canéntes vértimur,
te gestiéntes pérfrui.

Tu Patris es sciéntia
Verbúmque per quod ómnia
miro refúlgent órdine
mentésque nostras áttrahunt.

Da lucis ut nos fílii
sic ambulémus ímpigri,
ut Patris usque grátiam
mores et actus éxprimant.

Sincéra præst*a* ut prófluant
ex ore nostro iúgiter,
et veritátis dúlcibus
ut excitémur gáudiis.

Sit, Christe, rex piíssime,
tibi Patríque glória
cum Spíritu Paráclito,
in sempitérna sǽcula. Amen.

Week III

Tuesday, Lauds

HYMN — Trans. The Benedictine Nuns, St. Cecilia's Abbey

The beauty of the rising sun
Begins to tint the world with light,
Awakened nature glows with life
As form and colour disappear.

Lord Jesus Christ, You far surpass
The sun that shines since time began;
We turn to You with joyous song
That You may bless us with Your smile.

You are God's knowledge infinite,
His Word, through Whom all things were made;
Their wondrous order speaks to us
And draws our hearts and minds to You.

Give us Your light that like true sons
Intrepid we may tread life's path.
May all our ways and actions show
The gift of God the Father's grace.

Let every word our lips may say
Prove our sincerity and truth,
That our serenity of soul
May radiate our inward joy.

O Christ our King and tender Lord,
All glory ever be to You,
Who with the Holy Spirit reign
With God the Father's might supreme. Amen.

Psalmodia

Ant. 1 Benedixísti, Dómine, terram tuam; remisísti iniquitátem plebis tuæ.

Psalmus 84 (85)

2 Complacuísti tibi, Dómine, in terra tua, *
convertísti captivitátem Iacob.
3 Remisísti iniquitátem plebis tuæ, *
operuísti ómnia peccáta eórum.
4 Contraxísti omnem iram tuam, *
revertísti a furóre indignatiónis tuæ.

5 Convérte nos, Deus, salutáris noster, *
et avérte iram tuam a nobis.
6 Numquid in ætérnum irascéris nobis *
aut exténdes iram tuam a generatióne in generatiónem?
7 Nonne tu convérsus vivificábis nos, *
et plebs tua lætábitur in te?
8 Osténde nobis, Dómine, misericórdiam tuam *
et salutáre tuum da nobis.

9 Audiam, quid loquátur Dóminus Deus, †
quóniam loquétur pacem ad plebem suam et sanctos suos *
et ad eos, qui convertúntur corde.
10 Vere prope timéntes eum salutáre ipsíus, *
ut inhábitet glória in terra nostra.
11 Misericórdia et véritas obviavérunt sibi, *
iustítia et pax osculátæ sunt.
12 Véritas de terra orta est, *
et iustítia de cælo prospéxit.

PSALMODY

Ant. 1 Lord, Thou wast favorable to Thy land; Thou didst forgive the iniquity of Thy people.

Psalm 85

1 Lord, thou wast favorable to thy Land;
thou didst restore the fortunes of Jacob.
2 Thou didst forgive the iniquity of thy people;
thou didst pardon all their sin.
3 Thou didst withdraw all thy wrath;
thou didst turn from thy hot anger.

4 Restore us again, O God of our salvation,
and put away thy indignation toward us!
5 Wilt thou be angry with us for ever?
Wilt thou prolong thy anger to all generations?
6 Wilt thou not revive us again,
that thy people may rejoice in thee?
7 Show us thy steadfast love, O Lord,
and grant us thy salvation.

8 Let me hear what God the Lord will speak,
for he will speak peace to his people,
to his saints, to those who turn to him in their hearts.
9 Surely his salvation is at hand for those who fear him,
that glory may dwell in our land.

10 Steadfast love and faithfulness will meet;
righteousness and peace will kiss each other.
11 Faithfulness will spring up from the ground,
and righteousness will look down from the sky.

13 Etenim Dóminus dabit benignitátem, *
et terra nostra dabit fructum suum.
14 Iustítia ante eum ambulábit, *
et ponet in via gressus suos.

Ant. Benedixísti, Dómine, terram tuam; remisísti iniquitátem plebis tuæ.
Ant. 2 Anima mea desiderávit te in nocte, de mane vígilans ad te.

Canticum Is 26, 1-4. 7-9. 12

1 Urbs fortis nobis in salútem; *
pósuit muros et antemurále.
2 Aperíte portas, et ingrediátur gens iusta, *
quæ servat fidem.
3 Propósitum eius est firmum; *
servábis pacem, quia in te sperávit.
4 Speráte in Dóminum in sæculis ætérnis, *
Dóminus est petra ætérna.

7 Sémita iusti recta est; *
rectum callem iusti complánas.
8 Et in sémita iudiciórum tuórum, Dómine,
sperávimus in te; *
ad nomen tuum et ad memoriále tuum
desidérium ánimæ.

12 Yea, the Lord will give what is good,
and our land will yield its increase.
13 Righteousness will go before him,
and make his footsteps a way.

Ant. 1 Lord, Thou wast favorable to Thy land; Thou didst forgive the iniquity of Thy people.
Ant. 2 My soul has yearned for Thee in the night, keeping watch for Thee in the morning.

Canticle Isaiah 26:1–4,7–9,12

1 "We have a strong city;
he sets up salvation
as walls and bulwarks.
2 Open the gates,
that the righteous nation which keeps faith
may enter in.
3 Thou dost keep him in perfect peace,
whose mind is stayed on thee,
because he trusts in thee.
4 Trust in the LORD for ever,
for the LORD God
is an everlasting rock.

7 The way of the righteous is level;
thou dost make smooth the path of the
righteous.
8 In the path of thy judgments,
O LORD, we wait for thee;
thy memorial name
is the desire of our soul

9 Anima mea desíderat te in nocte, *
sed et spíritu meo in præcórdiis meis te quæro.
Cum resplendúerint iudícia tua in terra, *
iustítiam discent habitatóres orbis.

12 Dómine, dabis pacem nobis; *
ómnia enim ópera nostra operátus es nobis.

Ant. Anima mea desiderávit te in nocte, de mane vígilans ad te.

Ant. 3 Illúmina, Dómine, vultum tuum super nos.

Psalmus 66 (67)

2 Deus misereátur nostri et benedícat nobis; *
illúminet vultum suum super nos,
3 ut cognoscátur in terra via tua, *
in ómnibus géntibus salutáre tuum.

4 Confiteántur tibi pópuli, Deus; *
confiteántur tibi pópuli omnes.
5 Lætántur et exsúltent gentes, †
quóniam iúdicas pópulos in æquitáte *
et gentes in terra dírigis.

6 Confiteántur tibi pópuli, Deus, *
confiteántur tibi pópuli omnes.
7 Terra dedit fructum suum; *
benedícat nos Deus, Deus noster,
8 benedícat nos Deus, *
et métuant eum omnes fines terræ.

Ant. Illúmina, Dómine, vultum tuum super nos.

9 My soul yearns for thee in the night,
my spirit within me earnestly seeks thee.
For when thy judgments are in the earth,
the inhabitants of the world learn righteousness.

12 O Lord, thou wilt ordain peace for us,
thou hast wrought for us all our works.

Ant. 2 My soul has yearned for Thee in the night, keeping watch for Thee in the morning.
Ant. 3 Make Thy face to shine upon us, O Lord.

Psalm 67

1 May God be gracious to us and bless us
and make his face to shine upon us,

2 that thy way may be known upon earth,
thy saving power among all nations.
3 Let the peoples praise thee, O God;
let all the peoples praise thee!

4 Let the nations be glad and sing for joy,
for thou dost judge the peoples with equity
and guide the nations upon earth.
5 Let the peoples praise thee, O God;
let all the peoples praise thee!

6 The earth has yielded its increase;
God our God, has blessed us.
7 God has blessed us;
let all the ends of the earth fear him!

Ant. 3 Make Thy face to shine upon us, O Lord.

LECTIO BREVIS 1 Io 4, 14-15

Nos vídimus et testificámur quóniam Pater misit Fílium salvatórem mundi. Quisque conféssus fúerit: Iesus est Fílius Dei, Deus in ipso manet, et ipse in Deo.

RESPONSORIUM BREVE

℟. Deus meus, adiútor meus, * Et sperábo in eum. Deus meus.

℣. Refúgium meum et liberátor meus. * Et sperábo in eum. Gloria Patri. Deus meus.

Ad Benedictus, ant. Eréxit nobis Dóminus cornu salútis, sicut locútus est per os prophetárum suórum.

PRECES

Christum, qui sibi pópulum novum acquisívit in sánguine suo, adorémus et rogémus supplíciter:
Meménto pópuli tui, Dómine.

Rex et Redémptor noster, audi Ecclésiam tuam, huius diéi inítio te laudántem,
—doce eam sine intermissióne glorificáre maiestátem tuam.

Spes et fírmitas nostra, in te confídimus,
—neque umquam confundémur.

Infirmitátem nostram réspice et in adiutórium nostrum festína,
—quia sine te nihil póssumus fácere.

Páuperum et derelictórum meménto, ne dies novus sit eis pondus,
—sed solámen et gáudium.

Pater noster.

Short Reading

1 John 4:14–15

We have seen and testify that the Father has sent his Son as the Savior of the world. Whoever confesses that Jesus is the Son of God, God abides in him, and he in God.

Short Responsory

℟. My God, my helper, in Whom I shall hope.
℣. My refuge and my liberator.

Benedictus ant. The Lord has raised up a horn of salvation for us, as He spoke by the mouth of His prophets.

Intercessions

Christ, Who acquired for Himself a new people by His blood, let us adore and humbly ask Him praying: *Remember Your people, Lord.*

Our King and Redeemer, hear Your Church, praising You at the beginning of this day,
—teach Her to glorify Your majesty without ceasing.

Our hope and strength, in You we trust,
—that we might never be confounded.

Look upon our weakness and hasten to our aid,
—for without You we can do nothing.

Remember the poor and the downtrodden, that the new day might not be a burden to them,
—but a consolation and a joy.

Our Father.

Oratio

Deus omnípotens, cuius est bona rerum et speciósa creátio, da nobis hunc diem in nómine tuo lætánter incípere, et in operósa tui fratrúmque dilectióne complére. Per Dóminum.

ORATION

Almighty God, Whose is the good and beautiful creation of all things, grant us to begin this day joyfully in Your name, and to complete it lovingly in service to You and our brothers. Through our Lord.

Hebdomada III

Feria III, ad Vesperas

HYMNUS

Tellúris ingens cónditor,
mundi solum qui éruens,
pulsis aquæ moléstiis,
terram dedísti immóbilem,

Ut germen aptum próferens,
fulvis decóra flóribus,
fecúnda fructu sísteret
pastúmque gratum rédderet:

Mentis perústæ vúlnera
munda viróre grátiæ
ut facta fletu díluat
motúsque pravos átterat,

Iussis tuis obtémperet,
nullis malis appróximet,
bonis repléri gáudeat
et mortis actum nésciat.

Præsta, Pater piíssime,
Patríque compar Unice,
cum Spíritu Paráclito
regnans per omne sæculum. Amen.

PSALMODIA

Ant. 1 Dóminus in circuitu populi sui.

Tuesday, Vespers

Hymn

Trans. J. H. Newman

All-bountiful Creator, who,
  When Thou didst mould the world, didst drain
The waters from the mass, that so
  Earth might immovable remain;

That its dull clods it might transmute
  To golden flowers in vale or wood,
To juice of thirst-allaying fruit,
  And grateful herbage spread for food;

Wash Thou our smarting wounds and hot,
  In the cool freshness of Thy grace;
Till tears start forth the past to blot,
  And cleanse and calm Thy holy place;

Till we obey Thy full behest,
  Shun the world's tainted touch and breath,
Joy in what highest is and best,
  And gain a spell to baffle death.

Grant it, O Father, Only Son,
  And Holy Spirit, God of Grace;
To whom all glory, Three in One,
  Be given in every time and place.

Psalmody

Ant. 1 The Lord is round about His people.

Psalmus 124 (125)

1 Qui confídunt in Dómino sicut mons Sion: *
non commovébitur, in ætérnum manet.

2 Ierúsalem, montes in circúitu eius, †
et Dóminus in circúitu pópuli sui *
ex hoc nunc et usque in sæculum.
3 Quia non requiéscet virga iniquitátis super sortem iustórum, *
ut non exténdant iusti ad iniquitátem manus suas.

4 Bénefac, Dómine, bonis. *
et rectis corde.
5 Declinántes autem per vias pravas †
addúcet Dóminus cum operántibus iniquitátem. *
Pax super Israel!

Ant. Dóminus in circúitu pópuli sui.
Ant. 2 Nisi efficiámini sicut párvuli, non intrábitis in regnum cælórum.

Psalmus 130 (131)

1 Dómine, non est exaltátum cor meum, *
neque eláti sunt óculi mei,
neque ambulávi in magnis, *
neque in mirabílibus super me.

2 Vere pacátam et quiétam *
feci ánimam meam;
sicut ablactátus in sinu matris suæ, *
sicut ablactátus, ita in me est ánima mea.

3 Speret Israel in Dómino *
ex hoc nunc et usque in sæculum.

Psalm 125

1 Those who trust in the Lord are like Mount Zion,
which cannot be moved, but abides for ever.
2 As the mountains are round about Jerusalem,
so the Lord is round about his people,
from this time forth and for evermore.
3 For the scepter of wickedness shall not rest
upon the land allotted to the righteous,
lest the righteous put forth
their hands to do wrong.
4 Do good, O Lord, to those who are good,
and to those who are upright in their hearts!
5 But those who turn aside upon their crooked ways
the Lord will lead away with evildoers!
Praise be in Israel!

Ant. 1 The Lord is round about His people.
Ant. 2 Unless you become like little children, you shall not enter the kingdom of heaven.

Psalm 131

1 O LORD, my heart is not lifted up,
my eyes are not raised too high;
I do not occupy myself with things
too great and too marvelous for me.
2 But I have calmed and quieted my soul,
like a child quieted at its mother's breast;
like a child that is quieted is my soul.

3 O Israel, hope in the LORD
from this time forth and for evermore.

Ant. Nisi efficiámini sicut párvuli, non intrábitis in regnum cælórum.

Ant. 3 Fecísti nos, Dómine, regnum et sacerdótes Deo nostro.

Canticum Ap 4, 11; 5, 9. 10. 12

4,11 Dignus es, Dómine et Deus noster, *
accípere glóriam et honórem et virtútem,
quia tu creásti ómnia, *
et propter voluntátem tuam erant et creáta sunt.

5,9 Dignus es, Dómine, accípere librum *
et aperíre signácula eius,
quóniam occísus es †
et redemísti Deo in sánguine tuo *
ex omni tribu et lingua et pópulo et natióne
10 et fecísti eos Deo nostro regnum et sacerdótes, *
et regnábunt super terram.

12 Dignus est Agnus, qui occísus est, †
accípere virtútem et divítias et sapiéntiam *
et fortitúdinem et honórem et glóriam et benedictiónem.

Ant. Fecísti nos, Dómine, regnum et sacerdótes Deo nostro.

LECTIO BREVIS Rom 12, 9–12

Diléctio sine simulatióne. Odiéntes malum, adhæréntes bono; caritáte fraternitátis ínvicem diligéntes, honóre ínvicem præveniéntes, sollicitúdine non pigri, spíritu fervéntes, Dómino serviéntes, spe gaudéntes, in tribulatióne patiéntes, oratióni instántes.

Ant. 2 Unless you become like little children, you shall not enter the kingdom of heaven.
Ant. 3 Thou hast made us, O Lord, a kingdom and priests to our God.

Canticle Revelation 4:11; 5:9, 10, 12

11 "Worthy art thou, our Lord and God, to receive glory and honor and power,
for thou didst create all things, and by thy will they existed and were created.
9 "Worthy art thou to take the scroll and to open its seals,
for thou wast slain and by thy blood didst ransom men for God
from every tribe and tongue and people and nation,
10 and hast made them a kingdom and priests to our God,
and they shall reign on earth.
12 "Worthy is the Lamb who was slain,
to receive power and wealth and wisdom
and might and honor and glory and blessing!"

Ant. 3 Thou hast made us, O Lord, a kingdom and priests to our God.

SHORT READING Romans 12:9–12

Let love be genuine; hate what is evil, hold fast to what is good; love one another with brotherly affection; outdo one another in showing honor. Never flag in zeal, be aglow with the Spirit, serve the Lord. Rejoice in your hope, be patient in tribulation, be constant in prayer.

Responsorium Breve

℟. In ætérnum, Dómine, * Pérmanet verbum tuum. In ætérnum.

℣. In sæculum sæculi véritas tua. * Pérmanet verbum tuum. Gloria Patri. In ætérnum.

Ad Benedictus, ant. Exsúltet spíritus meus in Dómino Deo, salutári meo.

Preces

Deus pópulum suum in spe constítuit. Quare cum lætítia acclamémus: *Tu es spes pópuli tui, Dómine.*

Grátias ágimus tibi, Dómine, quod per ómnia dívites in Christo facti sumus,
—in omni verbo et in omni sciéntia.

Deus, in cuius manu sunt corda poténtium, rei públicæ moderatóribus régimen sapiéntia tua concéde,
—ut haustis de tuo fonte consíliis, tibi corde et ópere pláceant.

Tu, qui artes coléntibus præstas ut splendórem tuum suo ingénio maniféstent,
—mundum per eórum ópera cum spe gaudióque illústra.

Qui non páteris nos tentári supra id quod póssumus,
—débiles róbora, érige lapsos.

Qui per Fílium tuum promisísti hómines ad vitam in die novíssimo surrectúros,
—córpore iam exútos ne obliviscáris in perpétuum.

Pater noster.

Short Responsory

℟. Through all eternity, O Lord, Your word endures,
℣. and Your faithfulness forever.

Benedictus ant. May my spirit rejoice in the Lord God, my Savior.

Intercessions

God established His people in hope. Let us, therefore, cry out with joy: *You are the hope of Your people, O Lord.*

We give You thanks, O Lord, because through all things we are made rich in Christ,
—in every word and in all knowledge.

O God, in Whose hand are the hearts of the powerful, bestow on heads of State guidance by Your wisdom,
—that drawing from Your fount of counsels, they may be pleasing to You in heart and in work.

You, Who show to those who cultivate the arts, that, by their talent, they might reflect Your splendor,
—may their works illuminate the world with hope and joy.

You, Who do not allow us to be tempted beyond our ability,
—strengthen the weak, raise the fallen.

Who, through Your Son have promised to raise men to life on the final day,
—now do not forget the dead forever.

Our Father.

ORATIO

Ascéndat ad cleméntiam tuam nostra, Dómine, orátio vespertína, et descéndat super nos benedíctio tua, ut hic et in ætérnum, te auxiliánte, salvi esse mereámur. Per Dóminum.

ORATION
May our evening prayer ascend to Your mercy, O Lord, and may Your blessing descend upon us, that now and always, with Your help, we may merit salvation. Through our Lord.

Hebdomada III

Feria IV, ad Laudes matutinas

HYMNUS

Nox et tenébr*æ* et núbila,
confúsa mund*i* et túrbida,
lux intrat, albéscit polus:
Christus venit; discédite.

Calígo terræ scínditur
percússa solis spículo,
rebúsque iam color redit
vultu niténtis síderis.

Sic nostra mox obscúritas
fraudísque pectus cónscium,
ruptis retéctum núbibus,
regnánte palléscet Deo.

Te, Christe, solum nóvimus,
te mente pur*a* et símplici
rogáre curváto genu
flend*o* et canéndo díscimus.

Inténde nostris sénsibus
vitámque totam díspice:
sunt multa fucis íllita
quæ luce purgéntur tua.

Sit, Christe, rex piíssime,
tibi Patríque glória
cum Spíritu Paráclito,
in sempitérna sæcula. Amen.

Week III

Wednesday, Lauds

HYMN Trans. J. H. Newman

Haunting gloom and flitting shades,
Ghastly shapes, away!
Christ is rising, and pervades
Highest Heaven with day.

He with His bright spear the night
Dazzles and pursues:
Earth wakes up and glows with light
Of a thousand hues.

Thee, O Christ, and Thee alone,
With a single mind,
We with chant and plaint would own:
To Thy flock be kind.

Much it needs Thy light divine.
Spot and stain to clean;
Light of Angels, on us shine
With Thy face serene.

To the Father, and the Son,
And the Holy Ghost,
Here be glory, as is done
By the angelic host.

PSALMODIA

Ant. 1 Lætífica ánimam servi tui: ad te, Dómine, ánimam meam levávi.

Psalmus 85 (86)

1 Inclína, Dómine, aurem tuam et exáudi me, *
quóniam inops et pauper sum ego.
2 Custódi ánimam meam, quóniam sanctus sum; *
salvum fac servum tuum, Deus meus,
sperántem in te.
3 Miserére mei, Dómine, *
quóniam ad te clamávi tota die.
4 Lætífica ánimam servi tui, *
quóniam ad te, Dómine, ánimam meam levávi.
5 Quóniam tu, Dómine, suávis et mitis *
et multæ misericórdiæ ómnibus invocántibus te.
6 Auribus pércipe, Dómine, oratiónem meam *
et inténde voci deprecatiónis meæ.
7 In die tribulatiónis meæ clamávi ad te, *
quia exáudies me.

8 Non est símilis tui in diis, Dómine, *
et nihil sicut ópera tua.
9 Omnes gentes, quascúmque fecísti, vénient †
et adorábunt coram te, Dómine, *
et glorificábunt nomen tuum,
10 quóniam magnus es tu et fáciens mirabília: *
tu es Deus solus.

11 Doce me, Dómine, viam tuam, *
et ingrédiar in veritáte tua;
simplex fac cor meum, *
ut tímeat nomen tuum.

PSALMODY

Ant. 1 Gladden the soul of Thy servant, for to Thee, O Lord, do I lift up my soul.

Psalm 86

1 Incline thy ear, O LORD, and answer me,
for I am poor and needy.
2 Preserve my life, for I am godly;
save thy servant who trusts in thee.
Thou art my God; 3 be gracious to me, O Lord,
for to thee do I cry all the day.
4 Gladden the soul of thy servant,
for to thee, O Lord, do I lift up my soul.
5 For thou, O Lord, art good and forgiving,
abounding in steadfast love to all who call on thee.
6 Give ear, O LORD, to my prayer;
hearken to my cry of supplication.
7 In the day of my trouble I call on thee,
for thou dost answer me.

8 There is none like thee among the gods, O Lord,
nor are there any works like thine.
9 All the nations thou hast made shall come
and bow down before thee, O Lord,
and shall glorify thy name.
10 For thou art great and doest wondrous things,
thou alone art God.
11 Teach me thy way, O LORD,
that I may walk in thy truth;
unite my heart to fear thy name.

12 Confitébor tibi, Dómine Deus meus, in toto corde meo *
et glorificábo nomen tuum in ætérnum,
13 quia misericórdia tua magna est super me, *
et eruísti ánimam meam ex inférno inferióri.

14 Deus, supérbi insurrexérunt super me, †
et synagóga poténtium quæsiérunt ánimam meam, *
et non proposuérunt te in conspéctu suo.
15 Et tu, Dómine, Deus miserátor et miséricors, *
pátiens et multæ misericórdiæ et veritátis,
16 réspice in me et miserére mei; †
da fortitúdinem tuam púero tuo *
et salvum fac fílium ancíllæ tuæ.
17 Fac mecum signum in bonum, †
ut vídeant, qui odérunt me, et confundántur, *
quóniam tu, Dómine, adiuvísti me et consolátus es me.

Ant. Lætífica ánimam servi tui: ad te, Dómine, ánimam meam levávi.

Ant. 2 Beátus vir, qui ámbulat in iustítia et lóquitur veritátem.

Canticum Is 33, 13-16

13 Audíte, qui longe estis, quæ fécerim, *
et cognóscite, vicíni, fortitúdinem meam.
14 Contérriti sunt in Sion peccatóres, *
possédit tremor ímpios.

12 I give thanks to thee, O LORD my God, with my whole heart,
and I will glorify thy name for ever.
13 For great is thy steadfast love toward me;
thou hast delivered my soul from the depths of Sheol.

14 O God, insolent men have risen up against me;
a band of ruthless men seek my life,
and they do not set thee before them.
15 But thou, O Lord, art a God merciful and gracious,
slow to anger and abounding in steadfast love and faithfulness.
16 Turn to me and take pity on me;
give thy strength to thy servant,
and save the son of thy handmaid.
17 Show me a sign of thy favor,
that those who hate me may see and be put to shame
because thou, LORD, hast helped me and comforted me.

Ant. 1 Gladden the soul of Thy servant, for to Thee, O Lord, do I lift up my soul.
Ant. 2 Blessed is the man, who walks righteously and speaks uprightly.

Canticle Isaiah 33:13–16

13 Hear, you who are far off, what I have done;
and you who are near, acknowledge my might.
14 The sinners in Zion are afraid;
trembling has seized the godless:

Quis póterit habitáre de vobis cum igne
devoránte? *
Quis habitábit ex vobis cum ardóribus
sempitérnis?

15 Qui ámbulat in iustítiis *
et lóquitur æquitátes,
qui réicit lucra ex rapínis *
et éxcutit manus suas, ne múnera accípiat,
qui obtúrat aures suas, ne áudiat sánguinem, *
et claudit óculos suos, ne vídeat malum:

16 iste in excélsis habitábit, *
muniménta saxórum refúgium eius;
panis ei datus est, *
aquæ eius fidéles sunt.

Ant. Beátus vir, qui ámbulat in iustítia et lóquitur veritátem.

Ant. 3 Iubiláte in conspéctu regis Dómini.

Psalmus 97 (98)

1 Cantáte Dómino cánticum novum, *
quia mirabília fecit.

Salvávit sibi déxtera eius, *
et bráchium sanctum eius.
2 Notum fecit Dóminus salutáre suum, *
in conspéctu géntium revelávit iustítiam suam.
3 Recordátus est misericórdiæ suæ *
et veritátis suæ dómui Israel.
Vidérunt omnes términi terræ *
salutáre Dei nostri.

"Who among us can dwell with the devouring
fire?
Who among us can dwell with everlasting
burnings?"
15 He who walks righteously and speaks uprightly,
who despises the gain of oppressions
who shakes his hands, lest they hold a bribe,
who stops his ears from hearing of bloodshed
and shuts his eyes from looking upon evil,
16 he will dwell on the heights;
his place of defense will be the fortresses of
rocks;
his bread will be given him, his water will be
sure.

Ant. 2 Blessed is the man, who walks righteously and speaks uprightly.

Ant. 3 Rejoice in the sight of the King, the Lord.

Psalm 98

1 O sing to the LORD a new song,
for he has done marvelous things!
His right hand and his holy arm
have gotten him victory.
2 The LORD has made known his victory,
he has revealed his vindication in the sight of
the nations.
3 He has remembered his steadfast love and
faithfulness
to the house of Israel.
All the ends of the earth have seen
the victory of our God.

4 Iubiláte Deo, omnis terra, *
erúmpite, exsultáte et psállite.
5 Psállite Dómino in címthara, *
in címthara et voce psalmi;
6 in tubis ductílibus et voce tubæ córneæ, *
iubiláte in conspéctu regis Dómini.

7 Sonet mare et plenitúdo eius, *
orbis terrárum, et qui hábitant in eo.
8 Flúmina plaudent manu, †
simul montes exsultábunt 9 a conspéctu Dómini, *
quóniam venit iudicáre terram.
Iudicábit orbem terrárum in iustítia *
et pópulos in æquitáte.

Ant. Iubiláte in conspéctu regis Dómini.

LECTIO BREVIS — IOB 1, 21; 2, 10B

Nudus egréssus sum de útero matris meæ et nudus revértar illuc. Dóminus dedit, Dóminus ábstulit; sicut Dómino plácuit, ita factum est: sit nomen Dómini benedíctum. Si bona suscépimus de manu Dei, mala quare non suscipiámus?

RESPONSORIUM BREVE

℟. Inclína cor meum, Deus, * In testimónia tua. Inclína.
℣. In via tua vivífica me. * In testimónia tua. Glória Patri. Inclína.

Ad Benedictus, ant. Fac nobíscum misericórdiam, Dómine, et memoráre testaménti tui sancti.

4 Make a joyful noise to the LORD, all the earth;
break forth into joyous song and sing praises!
5 Sing praises to the LORD with the lyre,
with the lyre and the sound of melody!
6 With trumpets and the sound of the horn
make a joyful noise before the King, the LORD!

7 Let the sea roar, and all that fills it;
the world and those who dwell in it!
8 Let the floods clap their hands;
let the hills sing for joy together
9 before the LORD, for he comes
to judge the earth.
He will judge the world with righteousness,
and the peoples with equity.

Ant. 3 Rejoice in the sight of the King, the Lord.

SHORT READING — Job 1:21; 2:10b

"Naked I came from my mother's womb, and naked shall I return; the Lord gave, and the Lord has taken away; blessed be the name of the Lord.

"Shall we receive good at the hand of God, and shall we not receive evil?"

SHORT RESPONSORY

℟. Incline my heart according to Your will, O God.
℣. Give me life according to Your way.

Benedictus ant. Be merciful with us, O Lord, and remember Your holy covenant.

Preces

Christum, qui nutrit et fovet Ecclésiam pro qua seípsum trádidit, hac deprecatióne rogémus:
Réspice Ecclésiam tuam, Dómine.

Pastor Ecclésiæ tuæ, benedíctus es, qui nobis hódie tríbuis lucem et vitam,
—nos gratos redde pro múnere tam iucúndo.

Gregem tuum misericórditer réspice, quem in tuo nómine congregásti,
—ne quis péreat eórum, quos Pater dedit tibi.

Ecclésiam tuam duc in via mandatórum tuórum,
—fidélem tibi Spíritus Sanctus eam effíciat.

Ecclésiam ad mensam verbi tui panísque vivífica,
—ut in fortitúdine huius cibi te læta sequátur.

Pater noster.

Oratio

Sénsibus nostris, quæsumus, Dómine, lumen sanctum tuum benígnus, infúnde, ut tibi semper simus conversatióne devóti, cuius sapiéntia creáti sumus et providéntia gubernámur. Per Dóminum.

INTERCESSIONS

With this prayer, let us ask Christ, Who nourishes and supports the Church for which He gave himself: *Look upon Your Church, Lord.*

Shepherd of Your Church, blessed are You, Who give us light and life today,
—make us grateful for such a pleasing gift.

Look mercifully upon Your flock, which You have gathered in Your name,
—that none of them might perish, whom the Father gave to You.

Lead Your Church in the way of Your laws,
—May the Holy Spirit make Her faithful to You.

Make the Church live at the table of Your Word and bread,
—that She might joyfully follow You in the strength of this food.

Our Father.

ORATION

Lord, we ask, kindly pour out Your holy light on our senses, that in our life we might always be devoted to You, by Whose providence we are governed. Through our Lord.

Hebdomada III

Feria IV, ad Vesperas

HYMNUS

Cæli Deus sanctíssime,
qui lúcidum centrum poli
candóre pingis igneo
augens decóri lúmina,

Quarto die qui flámmeam
solis rotam constítuens,
lunæ minístras órdini
vagos recúrsus síderum,

Ut nóctibus vel lúmini
diremptiónis términum,
primórdiis et ménsium
signum dares notíssimum:

Illúmina cor hóminum,
abstérge sordes méntium,
resólve culpæ vínculum,
evérte moles críminum.

Præsta, Pater piíssime,
Patríque compar Unice,
cum Spíritu Paráclito
regnans per omne sæculum. Amen.

PSALMODIA

Ant. 1 Qui séminant in lácrimis, in exsultatióne metent.

Week III

Wednesday, Vespers

HYMN

Trans. J. H. Newman

O Lord, who, thron'd in the holy height,
Through plains of ether didst diffuse
The dazzling beams of light,
In soft transparent hues;

Who didst, on the fourth day, in heaven
Light the fierce cresset of the sun,
And the meek moon at even,
And stars that wildly run;

That they might mark and arbitrate
'Twixt alternating night and day,
And tend the train sedate
Of months upon their way;

Clear, Lord, the brooding night within,
And clean these hearts for Thy abode,
Unlock the spell of sin,
Crumble its giant load.

Grant it, O Father, Only Son,
And Holy Spirit, God of Grace,
To whom all praise be done
In every time and place.

PSALMODY

Ant. 1 May those who sow in tears reap with shouts of joy!

Psalmus 125 (126)

1 In converténdo Dóminus captivitátem Sion, *
facti sumus quasi somniántes.
2 Tunc replétum est gáudio os nostrum, *
et lingua nostra exsultatióne.
Tunc dicébant inter gentes: *
« Magnificávit Dóminus fácere cum eis ».
3 Magnificávit Dóminus fácere nobíscum; *
facti sumus lætántes.
4 Convérte, Dómine, captivitátem nostram, *
sicut torréntes in austro.
5 Qui séminant in lácrimis, *
in exsultatióne metent.

6 Eúntes ibant et flebant *
semem spargéndum portántes;
veniéntes autem vénient in exsultatióne *
portántes manípulos suos.

Ant. Qui séminant in lácrimis, in exsultatióne metent.
Ant. 2 Dóminus ædíficet nobis domum et custódiat civitátem.

Psalmus 126 (127)

1 Nisi Dóminus ædificáverit domum, *
in vanum labórant, qui ædíficant eam.
Nisi Dóminus custodíerit civitátem, *
frustra vígilat, qui custódit eam.
2 Vanum est vobis ante lucem súrgere et sero quiéscere, †
qui manducátis panem labóris, *
quia dabit diléctis suis somnum.

Psalm 126

1 When the LORD restored the fortunes of Zion,
we were like those who dream.
2 Then our mouth was filled with laughter,
and our tongue with shouts of joy;
then they said among the nations,
"The LORD has done great things for them."
3 The LORD has done great things for us;
we are glad.

4 Restore our fortunes, O LORD,
like the watercourses in the Negeb!
5 May those who sow in tears
reap with shouts of joy!
6 He that goes forth weeping,
bearing the seed for sowing,
shall come home with shouts of joy,
bringing his sheaves with him.

Ant. 1 May those who sow in tears reap with shouts of joy!
Ant. 2 May the Lord build the house and watch over our city for us.

Psalm 127

1 Unless the Lord builds the house,
those who build it labor in vain.
Unless the Lord watches over the city,
the watchman stays awake in vain.
2 It is in vain that you rise up early
and go late to rest,
eating the bread of anxious toil;
for he gives to his beloved sleep.

3 Ecce heréditas Dómini fílii, *
merces fructus ventris.
4 Sicut sagíttæ in manu poténtis, *
ita fílii iuventútis.
5 Beátus vir, qui implévit pháretram suam ex ipsis: *
non confundétur, cum loquétur inimícis suis in porta.

Ant. Dóminus ædíficet nobis domum et custódiat civitátem.

Ant. 3 Ipse primogénitus omnis creatúræ, in ómnibus primátum tenens.

Canticum Cf. Col 1, 12–20

12 Grátias agámus Deo Patri, *
qui idóneos nos fecit in partem sortis sanctórum in lúmine;
13 qui erípuit nos de potestáte tenebrárum *
et tránstulit in regnum Fílii dilectiónis suæ,
14 in quo habémus redemptiónem, *
remissiónem peccatórum;

15 qui est imágo Dei invisíbilis, *
primogénitus omnis creatúræ,
16 quia in ipso cóndita sunt univérsa †
in cælis et in terra, *
visibília et invisibília,
sive throni sive dominatiónes *
sive principátus sive potestátes.

Omnia per ipsum et in ipsum creáta sunt, †
17 et ipse est ante ómnia, *
et ómnia in ipso constant.

3 Lo, sons are a heritage from the Lord,
the fruit of the womb a reward.
4 Like arrows in the hand of a warrior
are the sons of one's youth.
5 Happy is the man who has
his quiver full of them!
He shall not be put to shame
when he speaks with his enemies in the gate.

Ant. 2 May the Lord build the house and watch over our city for us.

Ant. 3 He is the first-born of all creation; in every thing He is pre-eminent.

Canticle Colossians 1:12–20

12 Let us give thanks to the Father, Who has qualified us to share in the inheritance of the saints in light.
13 He has delivered us from the dominion of darkness and transferred us to the kingdom of his beloved Son,
14 in whom we have redemption, the forgiveness of sins.
15 He is the image of the invisible God, the first-born of all creation;
16 for in him all things were created, in heaven and on earth, visible and invisible, whether thrones or dominions or principalities or authorities—all things were created through him and for him.
17 He is before all things, and in him all things hold together.

18 Et ipse est caput córporis ecclésiæ; †
qui est princípium, primogénitus ex mórtuis, *
ut sit in ómnibus ipse primátum tenens,
19 quia in ipso complácuit omnem plenitúdinem
habitáre *
20 et per eum reconciliáre ómnia in ipsum,
pacíficans per sánguinem crucis eius, *
sive quæ in terris sive quæ in cælis sunt.

Ant. Ipse primogénitus omnis creatúræ, in ómnibus primátum tenens.

LECTIO BREVIS Eph 3, 20–21

Deo, qui potens est supra ómnia fácere superabundánter quam pétimus aut intellégimus, secúndum virtútem, quæ operátur in nobis, ipsi glória in ecclésia et in Christo Iesu in omnes generatiónes sæculi sæculórum. Amen.

RESPONSORIUM BREVE

℟. Rédime me, Dómine, * Et miserére mei. Rédime.
℣. Ne perdas cum ímpiis ánimam meam. * Et miserére mei. Glória Patri. Rédime.

Ad Magnificat, ant. Fecit mihi magna qui potens est, et sanctum nomen eius.

PRECES

Deum, qui Fílium suum misit salvatórem et exémplar pópuli sui, humíliter implorémus: *Sit laus tua in pópulo tuo, Dómine.*

Grátias ágimus tibi, qui elegísti nos primítias in salútem,
—et vocásti nos in acquisitiónem glóriæ Dómini nostri Iesu Christi.

18 He is the head of the body, the church; He is the beginning, the first-born from the dead, that in everything he might be pre-eminent.
19 For in him all the fulness of God was pleased to dwell,
20 and through him to reconcile to himself all things, whether on earth or in heaven, making peace by the blood of his cross.

Ant. 3 He is the first-born of all creation; in every thing He is pre-eminent.

SHORT READING Ephesians 3:20–21

Now to him who by the power at work within us is able to do far more abundantly than all that we ask or think, to him be glory in the church and in Christ Jesus to all generations, for ever and ever. Amen.

SHORT RESPONSORY

℟. Redeem me, O Lord, and have mercy on me.
℣. Do not abandon my soul to the wicked.

Magnificat ant. He Who is mighty has done great things for me, and holy is His name.

INTERCESSIONS

Let us humbly implore God, Who sent His Son as Savior and Example to His people: *May Your praise be in Your people, O Lord.*

We give You thanks Who have elected us as the first-fruits unto salvation,
—and Who have called us to the adoption of the glory of our Lord, Jesus Christ.

Fiant omnes, qui sanctum nomen tuum confiténtur,
in verbi tui veritáte concórdes,
—et tua semper caritáte fervéntes.
Creátor universórum, cuius Fílius inter hómines et
cum homínibus mánibus suis vóluit operári,
—operariórum meménto, qui in sudóre vultus sui
victum quærunt.
Meménto étiam eórum, qui fratérno se dévovent
servítio,
—ne infelíci éxitu vel aliórum neglegéntia a suo
propósito removeántur.
Misericórdiam tuam frátribus nostris concéde
defúnctis,
—neque in potestátem malígni spíritus tradas eos.

Pater noster.

Oratio

Vox clamántis Ecclésiæ ad aures, Dómine, quǽsumus, tuæ pietátis ascéndat, ut percépta vénia peccatórum, plebs tua te fiat operánte devóta, te protegénte secúra. Per Dóminum.

May all who confess Your holy name be united in the truth of Your word,
—and always fervent in Your love.
Creator of all, Whose Son wished to work among men and with men by His own hands,
—remember the workers who seek gain by the sweat of their brow.
Remember those who devote themselves to the service of their brethren,
—let them not withdraw from their goal because of an unfruitful result or the negligence of others.
Bestow Your mercy on our deceased brothers,
—and do not hand them over into the power of the evil spirit.

Our Father.

ORATION

May the voice of Your Church crying out reach the ears of Your love, O Lord, that, perceiving the pardon of sins, Your people might become devout by Your work and secure in Your protection. Through our Lord.

Hebdomada III

Feria V, ad Laudes matutinas

HYMNUS

Sol ecce surgit ígneus:
piget, pudéscit, pænitet,
nec teste quisquam lúmine
peccáre constánter potest.

Tandem facéssat cæcitas,
quae nosmet in praeceps diu
lapsos sinístris gréssibus
erróre traxit dévio.

Haec lux serénum cónferat
purósque nos præstet sibi;
nihil loquámur súbdolum,
volvámus obscúrum nihil.

Sic tota decúrrat dies,
ne lingua mendax, ne manus
oc*u*líve peccent lúbrici,
ne noxa corpus ínquinet.

Spec*u*látor astat désuper,
qui nos diébus ómnibus
actúsque nostros próspicit
a luce prim*a* in vésperum.

Deo Patri sit glória
eiúsque soli Fílio
cum Spíritu Paráclito,
in sempitérna sǽcula. Amen.

Week III

Thursday, Lauds

HYMN

Trans. J. H. Newman

See, the fiery sun is glowing
While the paly shades are going,
Which have led us far and long,
In a labyrinth of wrong.

May it bring us peace serene;
May it cleanse, as it is clean;
Plain and clear our words be spoke,
And our thoughts without a cloak;

So the day's account shall stand.
Guileless tongue and holy hand,
Steadfast eyes and unbeguiled,
"Flesh as of a little child."

There is One who from above
Watches how the still hours move
Of our day of service done,
From the dawn to setting sun.

To the Father, and the Son,
And the Spirit, Three and One,
As of old, and as in Heaven,
Now and here be glory given.

PSALMODIA

Ant. 1 Gloriósa dicta sunt de te, cívitas Dei.

Psalmus 86 (87)

1 Fundaménta eius in móntibus sanctis; †
2 díligit Dóminus portas Sion *
super ómnia tabernácula Iacob.
3 Gloriósa dicta sunt de te, *
cívitas Dei!
4 Memor ero Rahab et Babylónis inter sciéntes me; †
ecce Philistǽa et Tyrus cum Æthiópia: *
hi nati sunt illic.
5 Et de Sion dicétur: « Hic et ille natus est in ea; *
et ipse firmávit eam Altíssimus ».

6 Dóminus réferet in librum populórum: *
« Hi nati sunt illic ».
7 Et cantant sicut choros ducéntes: *
« Omnes fontes mei in te ».

Ant. Gloriósa dicta sunt de te, cívitas Dei.

Ant. 2 Dóminus in fortitúdine véniet, et merces eius cum eo.

Canticum Is 40, 10–17

10 Ecce Dóminus Deus in virtúte venit, *
et bráchium eius dominátur:
ecce merces eius cum eo *
et prǽmium illíus coram illo.

PSALMODY

Ant. 1 Glorious things are spoken of you, O city of God.

Psalm 87

1 On the holy mount stands the city he founded;
2 the Lord loves the gates of Zion
more than all the dwelling places of Jacob.
3 Glorious things are spoken of you,
O city of God.

4 Among those who know me I mention Rahab and Babylon;
behold, Philistia and Tyre, with Ethiopia—
"This one was born there," they say.
5 And of Zion it shall be said,
"This one and that one were born in her";
for the Most High himself will establish her.
6 The Lord records as he registers the peoples,
"This one was born there."

7 Singers and dancers alike say,
"All my springs are in you."

Ant. 1 Glorious things are spoken of you, O city of God.

Ant. 2 The Lord God comes with might, and His reward is with Him.

Canticle Isaiah 40:10–17

10 Behold, the Lord God comes with might, and his arm rules for him; behold, his reward is with him, and his recompense before him.

11 Sicut pastor gregem suum pascit, †
in bráchio suo cóngregat agnos et in sinu suo levat; *
fetas ipse portat.

12 Quis mensus est pugíllo aquas et cælos palmo dispósuit, †
módio contínuit púlverem terræ
et librávit in póndere montes *
et colles in statéra?
13 Quis diréxit spíritum Dómini? *
Aut quis consílium suum osténdit illi?
14 Cum quo íniit consílium et instrúxit eum *
et dócuit eum sémitam iustítiæ
et erudívit eum sciéntiam *
et viam prudéntiæ osténdit illi?

15 Ecce gentes quasi stilla sítulæ †
et quasi moméntum púlveris in statéra reputántur; *
ecce ínsulæ quasi pulvis exíguus.
16 Et Líbanus non sufficiet ad succendéndum, *
et animália eius non suffícient ad holocáustum.
17 Omnes gentes, quasi non sint, coram eo; *
quasi níhilum et ináne reputántur ab eo.

Ant. Dóminus in fortitúdine véniet, et merces eius cum eo.
Ant. 3 Exaltáte Dóminum Deum nostrum, et adoráte ad montem sanctum eius.

11 He will feed his flock like a shepherd, He will gather the lambs in his arms, He will carry them in his bosom, and gently lead those that are with young.
12 Who has measured the waters in the hollow of his hand and marked off the heavens with a span, enclosed the dust of the earth in a measure and weighed the mountains in scales and the hills in a balance?
13 Who has directed the Spirit of the Lord, or as his counselor has instructed him?
14 Whom did he consult for his enlightenment, and who taught him the path of justice, and taught him knowledge, and showed him the way of understanding?
15 Behold, the nations are like a drop from a bucket, and are accounted as the dust on the scales; behold, he takes up the isles like fine dust.
16 Lebanon would not suffice for fuel, nor are its beasts enough for a burnt offering.
17 All the nations are as nothing before him, they are accounted by him as less than nothing and emptiness.

Ant. 2 The Lord God comes with might, and His reward is with Him.
Ant. 3 Extol the Lord our God; worship at His holy mountain.

Psalmus 98 (99)

1 Dóminus regnávit! Commoveántur pópuli; *
sedet super chérubim, moveátur terra.
2 Dóminus in Sion magnus *
et excélsus super omnes pópulos.

3 Confiteántur nómini tuo magno et terríbili, *
quóniam sanctum est.
4 Rex potens iudícium díligit: †
tu statuísti, quæ recta sunt, *
iudícium et iustítiam in Iacob tu fecísti.

5 Exaltáte Dóminum Deum nostrum †
et adoráte ad scabéllum pedum eius, *
quóniam sanctus est.
6 Móyses et Aaron in sacerdótibus eius *
et Sámuel inter eos, qui ínvocant nomen eius.
Invocábant Dóminum, et ipse exaudiébat eos, *
7 in colúmna nubis loquebátur ad eos.
Custodiébant testimónia eius *
et præcéptum, quod dedit illis.
8 Dómine Deus noster, tu exaudiébas eos; †
Deus, tu propítius fuísti eis, *
ulcíscens autem adinventiónes eórum.

9 Exaltáte Dóminum Deum nostrum †
et adoráte ad montem sanctum eius, *
quóniam sanctus Dóminus Deus noster.

Ant. Exaltáte Dóminum Deum nostrum, et adoráte ad montem sanctum eius.

Psalm 99

1 The LORD reigns; let the peoples tremble!
He sits enthroned upon the cherubim; let the earth quake!
2 The LORD is great in Zion;
He is exalted over all the peoples.
3 Let them praise thy great and terrible name!
Holy is he!
4 Mighty King, lover of justice,
thou hast established equity;
thou hast executed justice
and righteousness in Jacob.
5 Extol the LORD our God;
worship at his footstool!
Holy is he!

6 Moses and Aaron were among his priests,
Samuel also was among those who called on his name.
They cried to the LORD, and he answered them.
7 He spoke to them in the pillar of cloud;
they kept his testimonies,
and the statutes that he gave them.

8 O LORD our God, thou didst answer them;
thou wast a forgiving God to them,
but an avenger of their wrong-doings.
9 Extol the LORD our God,
and worship at his holy mountain;
for the LORD our God is holy!.

Ant. 3 Extol the Lord our God; worship at His holy mountain.

LECTIO BREVIS 1 Petr 4, 10-11

Unusquísque, sicut accépit donatiónem, in altérutrum illam administrántes sicut boni dispensatóres multifórmis grátiæ Dei. Si quis lóquitur, quasi sermónes Dei; si quis minístrat, tamquam ex virtúte, quam largítur Deus, ut in ómnibus glorificétur Deus per Iesum Christum.

RESPONSORIUM BREVE

℟. Clamávi in toto corde meo: * Exáudi me, Dómine. Clamávi.
℣. Iustificatiónes tuas servábo. * Exáudi me, Dómine. Glória Patri. Clamávi.

Ad Benedictus, ant. In sanctitáte serviámus Dómino, et liberábit nos ab inimícis nostris.

PRECES

Grátias agámus Deo Patri, qui amóre suo dedúcit et nutrit pópulum suum, lætíque clamémus: *Glória tibi, Dómine, in sǽcula.*

Pater clementíssime, de tuo nos te laudámus amóre,
—quia nos mirabíliter condidísti et mirabílius, reformásti.

In huius diéi princípio serviéndi tibi stúdium córdibus nostris infúnde,
—ut cogitatiónes et actiónes nostræ te semper gloríficent.

Ab omni desidério malo corda nostra purífica,
—ut tuæ voluntáti simus semper inténti.

Fratrum omniúmque necessitátibus corda résera nostra,
—ne fratérna nostra dilectióne privéntur.

Short Reading
1 Peter 4:10–11a

As each has received a gift, employ it for one another, as good stewards of God's varied grace: whoever speaks, as one who utters oracles of God; whoever renders service, as one who renders it by the strength which God supplies; in order that in everything God may be glorified through Jesus Christ.

Short Responsory
℟. From the depths of my heart have I cried to you; hear me, O Lord.
℣. Your righteous decrees I shall keep.

Benedictus ant. May we serve the Lord in holiness, and He will deliver us from our enemies.

Intercessions
Let us give thanks to God the Father, Who by His love leads and nourishes His people, and in joy let us cry out: *Glory to You, O Lord unto the ages.*

Most merciful Father, for Your love for us, we praise You,
—for You have wonderfully created and more wonderfully molded us.

At the beginning of this day, fill our hearts with eagerness for serving You,
—that our thoughts and actions might always glorify You.

Purify our hearts of every evil desire,
—that we might always be directed by Your will.

Open our hearts to the needs of all our brothers,
—that they might not be deprived of our brotherly love.

Pater noster.

ORATIO

Omnípotens ætérne Deus, pópulos, qui in umbra mortis sedent, lúmine tuæ claritátis illústra, qua visitávit nos Oriens ex alto, Iesus Christus Dóminus noster. Qui tecum.

Our Father.

ORATION

All-powerful and ever-living God, enlighten the people who sit in the shadow of death by the light of Your brightness, which has visited us rising from on high, Jesus Christ our Lord. Who with You.

Hebdomada III

Feria V, ad Vesperas

Hymnus

Magnæ Deus poténtiæ,
qui ex aquis ortum genus
partim remíttis gúrgiti,
partim levas in áera,

Demérsa lymphis ímprimens,
subvécta cælis írrogans,
ut, stirpe una pródita,
divérsa répleant loca:

Largíre cunctis sérvulis,
quos mundat unda sánguinis,
nescíre lapsus críminum
nec ferre mortis tædium,

Ut culpa nullam déprimat,
nullum levet iactántia,
elísa mens ne cóncidat,
eláta mens ne córruat.

Præsta, Pater piísime,
Patríque compar Unice,
cum Spíritu Paráclito
regnans per omne sæculum. Amen.

Psalmodia

Ant. 1 Sancti tui exsúltent, Dómine, intrántes in tabernáculum tuum.

Week III

Thursday, Vespers

Hymn — Trans. J. H. Newman

O God, who hast given
 the sea and the sky,
To fish and to bird
 for dwelling to keep,
Both sons of the waters,
 one low and one high,
Ambitious of heaven,
 yet sunk in the deep;

Save, Lord, Thy servants,
 whom Thou hast new made
In a laver of blood,
 lest they trespass and die;
Lest pride should elate,
 or the flesh should degrade,
And they stumble on earth,
 or be dizzied on high.

To the Father and the Son
And the Spirit be done,
Now and always,
Glory and praise.

Psalmody

Ant. 1 Let Thy saints shout for joy, O Lord, as they enter Thy dwelling place.

Psalmus 131 (132)

I

1 Meménto, Dómine, David *
et omnis mansuetúdinis eius,
2 quia iurávit Dómino, *
votum vovit Poténti Iacob:

3 « Non introíbo in tabernáculum domus meæ, *
non ascéndam in lectum strati mei,
4 non dabo somnum óculis meis *
et pálpebris meis dormitatiónem,
5 donec invéniam locum Dómino, *
tabernáculum Poténti Iacob ».

6 Ecce audívimus eam esse in Ephratha, *
invénimus eam in campis Iaar.
7 Ingrediámur in tabernáculum eius, *
adorémus ad scabéllum pedum eius.

8 Surge, Dómine, in réquiem tuam, *
tu et arca fortitúdinis tuæ.
9 Sacerdótes tui induántur iustítiam, *
et sancti tui exsúltent.
10 Propter David servum tuum *
non avértas fáciem christi tui.

Ant. Sancti tui exsúltent, Dómine, intrántes in tabernáculum tuum.
Ant. 2 Elégit Dóminus Sion in habitatiónem sibi.

II

11 Iurávit Dóminus David veritátem *
et non recédet ab ea:

Psalm 132

I

1 Remember, O LORD, in David's favor,
all the hardships he endured;
2 how he swore to the LORD
and vowed to the Mighty One of Jacob,
3 "I will not enter my house
or get into my bed;
4 I will not give sleep to my eyes
or slumber to my eyelids,
5 until I find a place for the LORD,
a dwelling place for the Mighty One of Jacob."

6 Lo, we heard of it in Ephrathah,
we found it in the fields of Jaar.
7 "Let us go to his dwelling place;
let us worship at his footstool!"

8 Arise, O LORD, and go to thy resting place,
thou and the ark of thy might.
9 Let thy priests be clothed with righteousness
and let thy saints shout for joy.
10 For thy servant David's sake
do not turn away the face of thy anointed one.

Ant. 1 Let Thy saints shout for joy, O Lord, as they enter Thy dwelling place.
Ant. 2 The Lord has chosen Zion for His habitation.

II

11 The Lord swore to David a sure oath
from which he will not turn back;

« De fructu ventris tui *
ponam super sedem tuam.
12 Si custodíerint fílii tui testaméntum meum *
et testimónia mea, quæ docébo eos,
fílii eórum usque in sǽculum *
sedébunt super sedem tuam ».

13 Quóniam elégit Dóminus Sion, *
desiderávit eam in habitatiónem sibi:
14 « Hæc réquies mea in sǽculum sǽculi; *
hic habitábo, quóniam desirerávi eam.

15 Cibária eius benedícens benedícam, *
páuperes eius saturábo pánibus.
16 Sacerdótes eius índuam salutári, *
et sancti eius exsultatióne exsultábunt.

17 Illic germináre fáciam cornu David, *
parábo lucérnam christo meo.
18 Inimícos eius índuam confusióne, *
super ipsum autem efflorébit diadéma eius ».

Ant. Elégit Dóminus Sion in habitatiónem sibi.
Ant. 3 Dedit ei Dóminus potestátem et honórem et regnum, et omnes pópuli ipsi sérvient.

Canticum Ap 11, 17–18; 12, 10b–12a

11,17 Grátias ágimus tibi, *
Dómine Deus omnípotens,
qui es et qui eras, *
quia accepísti virtútem tuam magnam et regnásti.

"One of the sons of your body
I will set on your throne.
12 If your sons keep my covenant
and my testimonies which I shall teach them,
their sons also for ever
shall sit upon your throne."

13 For the Lord has chosen Zion;
he has desired it for his habitation:
14 "This is my resting place for ever;
here I will dwell, for I have desired it.
15 I will abundantly bless her provisions;
I will satisfy her poor with bread.
16 Her priests I will clothe with salvation,
and her saints will shout for joy.
17 There I will make a horn to sprout for David;
I have prepared a lamp for my anointed.
18 His enemies I will clothe with shame,
but upon himself his crown will shed its luster.

Ant. 2 The Lord has chosen Zion for His habitation.
Ant. 3 The Lord has given Him all power, honor and kingship; all peoples will serve Him.

Canticle

Revelation 11:17–18;12:10b–12a

17 "We give thanks to thee, Lord God Almighty, who art and who wast, that thou hast taken thy great power and begun to reign.

18 Et irátæ sunt gentes, *
et advénit ira tua, et tempus mortuórum iudicári,
et réddere mercédem servis tuis prophétis et sanctis *
et timéntibus nomen tuum, pusíllis et magnis.
12,10 Nunc facta est salus et virtus et regnum Dei nostri *
et potéstas Christi eius,
quia proiéctus est accusátor fratrum nostrórum, *
qui accusábat illos ante conspéctum Dei nostri die ac nocte.

11 Et ipsi vicérunt illum propter sánguinem Agni, *
et propter verbum testimónii sui;
et non dilexérunt ánimam suam *
usque ad mortem.
12 Proptérea lætámini, cæli *
et qui habitátis in eis.

Ant. Dedit ei Dóminus potestátem et honórem et regnum, et omnes pópuli ipsi sérvient.

LECTIO BREVIS 1 PETR 3, 8-9

Omnes unánimes, compatiéntes, fraternitátis amatóres, misericórdes, humiles, non reddéntes malum pro malo vel maledíctum pro maledícto, sed e contrário benedicéntes, quia in hoc vocáti estis, ut benedictiónem hereditáte accipiátis.

RESPONSORIUM BREVE

℟. Cibávit nos Dóminus * Ex ádipe fruménti. Cibávit.
℣. Et de petra melle saturávit nos. * Ex ádipe fruménti. Glória Patri. Cibávit.

18 The nations raged, but thy wrath came, and the time for the dead to be judged, for rewarding thy servants, the prophets and saints, and those who fear thy name, both small and great, and for destroying the destroyers of the earth.
10 Now the salvation and the power and the kingdom of our God and the authority of his Christ have come, for the accuser of our brethren has been thrown down, who accuses them day and night before our God.
11 And they have conquered him by the blood of the Lamb and by the word of their testimony, for they loved not their lives even unto death.
12 Rejoice then, O heaven, and you that dwell therein!

Ant. 3 The Lord has given Him all power, honor and kingship; all peoples will serve Him.

SHORT READING — 1 Peter 3:8–9

All of you, have unity of spirit, sympathy, love of the brethren, a tender heart and a humble mind. Do not return evil for evil or reviling for reviling; but on the contrary bless, for to this you have been called, that you may obtain a blessing.

SHORT RESPONSORY

℟. The Lord has fed us with the finest wheat.
℣. And with honey from the rock has He filled us.

Ad Magnificat, ant. Depósuit Dóminus poténtes de sede, et exaltávit húmiles.

Preces

Christum, pastórem, adiutórem et consolatórem pópuli sui, devótis méntibus deprecémur: *Deus, refúgium nostrum, exáudi nos.*

Benedíctus es, Dómine, qui nos ad tuam sanctam Ecclésiam vocáre dignátus es:
—in ea iúgiter nos consérva.

Tu, qui sollicitúdinem ómnium ecclesiárum Papæ nostro N. tradidísti,
—fidem indeficiéntem, spem vivam, atténtam illi tríbue caritátem.

Da peccatóribus conversiónem lapsísque virtútem:
—ómnibus pæniténtiam et salútem concéde.

Tu, qui in regióne aliéna habitáre voluísti,
—meménto illórum, qui procul a família et pátria degunt.

Omnibus defúnctis, qui in te speravérunt,
—pacem tríbue sempitérnam.

Pater noster.

Oratio

Grátias tibi, Dómine, transácto diéi cursu deférimus, tuámque misericórdiam súpplices implorámus, ut, quæ per fragilitátem carnis contráximus, benígnus ignóscas. Per Dóminum.

Magnificat ant. The Lord has put down the mighty from their thrones, and exalted those of low degree.

INTERCESSIONS

With devout minds, let us beseech Christ, the Shepherd, Helper, and Consolation of His people:
O God, our Refuge, hear us.

Blessed are You, O Lord, Who deign to call us into Your holy Church,
—continually preserve us in Her.

You that have given over the care of all the churches to our Pope, N.,
—grant to him unfailing faith, living hope, and loving concern.

Give conversion to the sinners, and strength to the fallen,
—and bestow on all repentance and salvation.

You that willed to dwell in a foreign land,
—remember those who are far from family and country.

To all the deceased who have hoped in You,
—grant eternal peace.

Our Father.

ORATION

We give You thanks, O Lord, as the day has run its course, and humbly we implore Your mercy, that You would kindly overlook what we have done through the frailty of our flesh. Through our Lord.

Hebdomada III

Feria VI, ad Laudes matutinas

Hymnus

Ætérna cæli glória,
beáta spes mortálium,
celsi Paréntis Unice
castǽque proles Vírginis,

Da déxteram surgéntibus,
exsúrgat et mens sóbria
flagrans et in laudem Dei
grates repéndat débitas.

Ortus refúlget lúcifer
ipsámque lucem núntiat,
cadit calígo nóctium,
lux sancta nos illúminet,

Manénsque nostris sénsibus
noctem repéllat sǽculi
omníque fine témporis
purgáta servet péctora.

Quæsíta iam primum fides
radícet altis sénsibus,
secúnda spes congáudeat;
tunc maior exstat cáritas.

Sit, Christe, rex piísime,
tibi Patríque glória
cum Spíritu Paráclito,
in sempitérna sǽcula. Amen.

Week III

Friday, Lauds

HYMN Trans. J. H. Newman

Glory of the eternal Heaven,
Blessed hope to mortals given,
Of the Almighty Only Son,
And the Virgin's Holy One;
Raise us, Lord, and we shall rise
  In a sober mood,
And a zeal, which glorifies
  Thee from gratitude.

Now the day-star, keenly glancing,
Tells us of the Sun's advancing;
While the unhealthy shades decline,
Rise within us, Light Divine!
Rise, and, risen, go not hence,
  Stay, and make us bright,
Streaming through each cleansèd sense,
  On the outward night.

Then the foot of faith shall spread
In the heart new fashionèd;
Gladsome hope shall spring above,
And shall bear the fruit of love.
To the Father, and the Son.
  And the Holy Ghost,
Here be glory, as is done
  By the angelic host.

Psalmodia

Ant. 1 Tibi soli peccávi, Dómine; miserére mei.

Psalmus 50 (51)

3 Miserére mei, Deus, *
secúndum misericórdiam tuam;
et secúndum multitúdinem miseratiónum tuárum *
dele iniquitátem meam.
4 Amplius lava me ab iniquitáte mea *
et a peccáto meo munda me.

5 Quóniam iniquitátem meam ego cognósco, *
et peccátum meum contra me est semper.

6 Tibi, tibi soli peccávi *
et malum coram te feci,
ut iustus inveniáris in senténtia tua *
et æquus in iudício tuo.

7 Ecce enim in iniquitáte generátus sum, *
et in peccáto concépit me mater mea.
8 Ecce enim veritátem in corde dilexísti *
et in occúlto sapiéntiam manifestásti mihi.

9 Aspérges me hyssópo, et mundábor; *
lavábis me, et super nivem dealbábor.
10 Audíre me fácies gáudium et lætítiam, *
et exsultábunt ossa, quæ contrivísti.

11 Avérte fáciem tuam a peccátis meis *
et omnes iniquitátes meas dele.
12 Cor mundum crea in me, Deus, *
et spíritum firmum ínnova in viscéribus meis.

PSALMODY

Ant. 1 Against Thee, Thee only, have I sinned, O Lord; have mercy on me.

Psalm 51

1 Have mercy on me, O God,
according to thy steadfast love;
according to thy abundant mercy blot out my transgressions.
2 Wash me thoroughly from my iniquity,
and cleanse me from my sin!

3 For I know my transgressions,
and my sin is ever before me.
4 Against thee, thee only, have I sinned,
and done that which is evil in thy sight,
so that thou art justified in Thy sentence
and blameless in thy judgment.
5 Behold, I was brought forth in iniquity,
and in sin did my mother conceive me.

6 Behold, thou desirest truth in the inward being;
therefore teach me wisdom in my secret heart.
7 Purge me with hyssop, and I shall be clean;
wash me, and I shall be whiter than snow.
8 Fill me with joy and gladness;
let the bones which thou hast broken rejoice.
9 Hide thy face from my sins,
and blot out all my iniquities.

10 Create in me a clean heart, O God,
and put a new and right spirit within me.

13 Ne proícias me a fácie tua *
et spíritum sanctum tuum ne áuferas a me.
14 Redde mihi lætítiam salutáris tui *
et spíritu promptíssimo confírma me.

15 Docébo iníquos vias tuas, *
et ímpii ad te converténtur.
16 Líbera me de sanguínibus, Deus, Deus salútis meæ, *
et exsultábit lingua mea iustítiam tuam.

17 Dómine, lábia mea apéries, *
et os meum annuntiábit laudem tuam.
18 Non enim sacrifício delectáris, *
holocáustum, si ófferam, non placébit.
19 Sacrifícium Deo spíritus contribulátus, *
cor contrítum et humiliátum, Deus, non despícies.

20 Benígne fac, Dómine, in bona voluntáte tua Sion, *
ut ædificéntur muri Ierúsalem.
21 Tunc acceptábis sacrifícium iustítiæ, oblatiónes et holocáusta; *
tunc impónent super altáre tuum vítulos.

Ant. Tibi soli peccávi, Dómine; miserére mei.
Ant. 2 Cognóvimus, Dómine, iniquitátes nostras, quia peccávimus tibi.

11 Cast me not away from thy presence,
and take not thy holy Spirit from me.
12 Restore to me the joy of thy salvation,
and uphold me with a willing spirit.
13 Then I will teach transgressors thy ways,
and sinners will return to thee.
14 Deliver me from bloodguiltiness, O God,
thou God of my salvation,
and my tongue will sing aloud of thy
deliverance.

15 O Lord, open thou my lips,
and my mouth shall show forth thy praise.
16 For thou hast no delight in sacrifice;
were I to give a burnt offering, thou wouldst not
be pleased.
17 The sacrifice acceptable to God is a broken spirit;
a broken and contrite heart, O God, thou wilt
not despise.
18 Do good to Zion in thy good pleasure;
rebuild the walls of Jerusalem,
19 then wilt thou delight in right sacrifices,
in burnt offerings and whole burnt offerings;
then bulls will be offered on thy altar.

Ant. 1 Against Thee, Thee only, have I sinned, O Lord; have mercy on me.
Ant. 2 We acknowledge our wickedness, O Lord, for we have sinned against Thee.

Canticum IER 14, 17–21

17 Dedúcant óculi mei lácrimam per noctem et
diem, *
et non táceant,
quóniam contritióne magna contríta est virgo fília
pópuli mei, *
plaga péssima veheménter.

18 Si egréssus fúero ad agros, ecce occísi gládio; *
et si introíero in civitátem, ecce attenuáti fame:
prophéta quoque et sacérdos *
abiérunt per terram nesciéntes.

19 Numquid proíciens abiecísti, Iudam *
aut Sion abomináta est ánima tua?
Quare ergo percussísti nos, *
ita ut nulla sit sánitas?
Exspectávimus pacem, et non est bonum, *
et tempus curatiónis, et ecce turbátio.

20 Cognóvimus, Dómine, impietátes nostras, †
iniquitátes patrum nostrórum, *
quia peccávimus tibi.
21 Ne des nos in oppróbrium propter nomen tuum, *
ne fácias contuméliam sólio glóriæ tuæ;
recordáre, *
ne írritum fácias fœdus tuum nobíscum.

Ant. Cognóvimus, Dómine, iniquitátes nostras, quia peccávimus tibi.
Ant. 3 Dóminus ipse est Deus; nos pópulus eius et oves páscuæ eius.

Canticle Jeremiah 14:17–21

17 "Let my eyes run down with tears night and day
and let them not cease,
for the virgin daughter of my people is smitten
with a great wound,
with a very grievous blow.
18 If I go out into the field,
behold, those slain by the sword!
And if I enter the city,
behold, the diseases of famine!
For both prophet and priest ply their trade through
the land,
and have no knowledge."

19 Hast thou utterly rejected Judah?
Does thy soul loathe Zion?
Why hast thou smitten us
so that there is no healing for us?
We looked for peace, but no good came;
for a time of healing, but behold, terror.
20 We acknowledge our wickedness, O LORD,
and the iniquity of our fathers,
for we have sinned against thee.
21 Do not spurn us, for thy name's sake;
do not dishonor thy glorious throne;
remember and do not break thy covenant with
us.

Ant. 2 We acknowledge our wickedness, O Lord, for we have sinned against Thee.
Ant. 3 The Lord is God; we are His people and the sheep of His pasture.

Psalmus 99 (100)

2 Iubiláte Dómino, omnis terra, *
servíte Dómino in lætítia;
introíte in conspéctu eius *
in exsultatióne.

3 Scitóte quóniam Dóminus ipse est Deus; †
ipse fecit nos, et ipsíus sumus, *
pópulus eius et oves páscuæ eius.

4 Introíte portas eius in confessióne, †
átria eius in hymnis, *
confitémini illi, benedícite nómini eius.
5 Quóniam suávis est Dóminus; †
in ætérnum misericórdia eius, *
et usque in generatiónem et generatiónem
véritas eius.

Ant. Dóminus ipse est Deus; nos pópulus eius et oves páscuæ eius.

LECTIO BREVIS 2 COR 12, 9B–10

Libentíssime gloriábor in infirmitátibus meis, ut inhábitet in me virtus Christi. Propter quod pláceo mihi in infirmitátibus, in contuméliis, in necessitátibus, in persecutiónibus et in angústiis, pro Christo: cum enim infírmor, tunc potens sum.

RESPONSORIUM BREVE

℟. Audítam fac mihi mane * Misericórdiam tuam. Audítam.
℣. Notam fac mihi viam in qua ámbulem. * Misericórdiam tuam. Glória Patri. Audítam.

Psalm 100

1 Make a joyful noise to the LORD, all the lands!
2 Serve the LORD with gladness!
Come into his presence with singing!

3 Know that the LORD is God!
It is he that made us, and we are his;
we are his people and the sheep of his pasture.

4 Enter his gates with thanksgiving,
and his courts with praise!
Give thanks to him, bless his name!

5 For the LORD is good;
his steadfast love endures for ever,
and his faithfulness to all generations.

Ant. 3 The Lord is God; we are His people and the sheep of His pasture.

SHORT READING 2 Corinthians 12:9b–10

I will all the more gladly boast of my weaknesses, that the power of Christ may rest upon me. For the sake of Christ, then, I am content with weaknesses, insults, hardships, persecutions, and calamities; for when I am weak, then I am strong.

SHORT RESPONSORY

℟. At daybreak, make me to hear of your mercy.
℣. Make known to me the path in which I should walk.

Ad Benedictus, ant. Visitávit et fecit redemptiónem Dóminus plebis suæ.

Preces

Ad Christum óculos levémus, qui pro pópulo suo natus et mórtuus est ac resurréxit. Itaque eum fidénter deprecémur: *Salva, Dómine, quos tuo sánguine redemísti.*

Benedíctus es, Iesu hóminum salvátor, qui passiónem et crucem pro nobis subíre non dubitásti,
—et sánguine tuo pretióso nos redemísti.

Qui promisísti te aquam esse datúrum saliéntem in vitam ætérnam,
—Spíritum tuum effúnde super omnes hómines.

Qui discípulos misísti ad Evangélium géntibus prædicándum,
—eos ádiuva, ut victóriam tuæ crucis exténdant.

Infírmis et míseris quos cruci tuæ sociásti,
—virtútem et patiéntiam concéde.

Pater noster.

Oratio

Illábere sénsibus nostris, omnípotens Pater, ut in præceptórum tuórum lúmine gradiéntes, te ducem semper sequámur et príncipem. Per Dóminum.

Benedictus ant. The Lord has visited and redeemed His people.

INTERCESSIONS

Let us raise our eyes to Christ, Who for His people was born and died and rose. And so, let us faithfully pray to Him: *Save, O Lord, those whom You have redeemed by Your blood.*

Blessed are You, Jesus, Savior of men, Who did not hesitate to undergo the passion and the cross for us,

—and have redeemed us by Your precious blood.

You that promised to give water springing unto eternal life,

—pour out Your Spirit on all men.

You that sent the disciples to preach the Gospel to the nations,

—help them, that they might extend the victory of Your cross.

To the sick and those in misery whom you have united to Your cross,

—grant strength and patience.

Our Father.

ORATION

Illuminate our senses, All-powerful Father, that walking in the light of Your precepts, we might always follow You as our leader and sovereign. Through our Lord.

Hebdomada III

Feria VI, ad Vesperas

HYMNUS

Plasmátor hóminis, Deus,
qui, cuncta solus órdinans,
humum iubes prodúcere
reptántis et feræ genus;

Qui magna rerum córpora,
dictu iubéntis vívida,
ut sérviant per órdinem
subdens dedísti hómini:

Repélle a servis tuis
quicquid per immundítiam
aut móribus se súggerit,
aut áctibus *se* intérserit.

Da gaudiórum prǽmia,
da gratiárum múnera;
dissólve litis víncula,
astrínge pacis fœ́dera.

Præsta, Pater piísime,
Patríque compar Unice,
cum Spíritu Paráclito
regnans per omne sǽculum. Amen.

Week III

Friday, Vespers

HYMN
Trans. J. H. Newman

Whom all obey,—
Maker of man! who from Thy height
Badest the dull earth bring to light
All creeping things, and the fierce might
Of beasts of prey;—

And the huge make
Of wild or gentler animal,
Springing from nothing at Thy call,
To serve in their due time, and all
For sinners' sake;

Shield us from ill!
Come it by passion's sudden stress,
Lurk in our mind's habitual dress,
Or through our actions seek to press
Upon our will.

Vouchsafe the prize
Of sacred joy's perpetual mood,
And service-seeking gratitude,
And love to quell each strife or feud,
If it arise.

Grant it, O Lord!
To whom, the Father, Only Son,
And Holy Spirit, Three in One,
In heaven and earth all praise be done,
With one accord.

Psalmodia

Ant. 1 Magnus est Dóminus, et Deus noster præ ómnibus diis.

Psalmus 134 (135)

I

1 Laudáte nomen Dómini, *
laudáte, servi Dómini,
2 qui statis in domo Dómini, *
in átriis domus Dei nostri.

3 Laudáte Dóminum, quia bonus Dóminus; *
psállite nómini eius, quóniam suáve.
4 Quóniam Iacob elégit sibi Dóminus, *
Israel in pecúlium sibi.

5 Quia ego cognóvi quod magnus est Dóminus *
et Deus noster præ ómnibus diis.
6 Omnia, quæcúmque vóluit, †
Dóminus fecit in cælo et in terra, *
in mari et in ómnibus abýssis.
7 Addúcens nubes ab extrémo terræ, †
fúlgura in plúviam facit, *
prodúcit ventos de thesáuris suis.

8 Qui percússit primogénita Ægýpti *
ab hómine usque ad pecus.
9 Misit signa et prodígia in médio tui, Ægýpte, *
in pharaónem et in omnes servos eius,
10 Qui percússit gentes multas *
et occídit reges fortes:

PSALMODY

Ant. 1 Great is the Lord, and our God is greater than all other gods.

Psalm 135

I

1 Praise the LORD!
Praise the name of the LORD,
give praise, O servants of the LORD,
2 you that stand in the house of the LORD,
in the courts of the house of our God!
3 Praise the LORD, for the LORD is good;
sing to his name, for he is gracious!
4 For the LORD has chosen Jacob for himself,
Israel as his own possession.

5 For I know that the LORD is great,
and that our Lord is above all gods.
6 Whatever the LORD pleases he does,
in heaven and on earth,
in the seas and all deeps.
7 He it is who makes the clouds rise
at the end of the earth,
who makes lightnings for the rain
and brings forth the wind from his storehouses.

8 He it was who smote the first-born of
Eqypt, both of man and of beast;
9 Who in thy midst, O Egypt,
sent signs and wonders
against Pharaoh and all his servants;
10 Who smote many nations
and slew mighty kings,

11 Sehon regem Amorræórum et Og regem Basan *
et ómnia regna Chánaan.
12 Et dedit terram eórum hereditátem, *
hereditátem Israel pópulo suo.

Ant. Magnus est Dóminus, et Deus noster præ ómnibus diis.

Ant. 2 Domus Israel, benedícite Dómino; psállite nómini eius, quóniam suáve.

II

13 Dómine, nomen tuum in ætérnum; *
Dómine, memoriále tuum in generatiónem et generatiónem.
14 Quia iudicábit Dóminus pópulum suum *
et servórum suórum miserébitur.

15 Simulácra géntium argéntum et aurum, *
ópera mánuum hóminum:
16 os habent et non loquéntur; *
óculos habent et non vidébunt;
17 aures habent et non áudient; *
neque enim est spíritus in ore ipsórum.
18 Símiles illis erunt, qui fáciunt ea, *
et omnes, qui confídunt in eis.

19 Domus Israel, benedícite Dómino; *
domus Aaron, benedícite Dómino;
20 domus Levi, benedícite Dómino; *
qui timétis Dóminum, benedícite Dómino.

21 Benedíctus Dóminus ex Sion, *
qui hábitat in Ierúsalem.

11 Sihon, king of the Amorites,
and Og, king of Bashan,
and all the kingdoms of Canaan,
12 and gave their land as a heritage,
a heritage to his people Israel.

Ant. 1 Great is the Lord, and our God is greater than all other gods.
Ant. 2 O house of Israel, bless the Lord; praise Him, for such is delightful.

II

13 Thy name, O LORD, endures for ever,
thy renown, O LORD, throughout all ages.
14 For the LORD will vindicate his people,
and have compassion on his servants.

15 The idols of the nations are silver
and gold, the work of men's hands.
16 They have mouths, but they speak not,
they have eyes, but they see not,
17 they have ears, but they hear not,
nor is there any breath in their mouths.
18 Like them be those who make them!—-
yea, every one who trusts in them!

19 O house of Israel, bless the LORD!
O house of Aaron, bless the Lord!
20 O house of Levi, bless the LORD!
You that fear the LORD, bless the Lord!
21 Blessed be the LORD from Zion,
he who dwells in Jerusalem!
Praise the LORD!

Ant. Domus Israel, benedícite Dómino; psállite nómini eius, quóniam suáve.
Ant. 3 Omnes gentes vénient et adorábunt coram te, Dómine.

Canticum Ap 15, 3-4

3 Magna et mirabília ópera tua, *
Dómine Deus omnípotens;
iustæ et veræ viæ tuæ, *
Rex géntium!
4 Quis non timébit, Dómine, *
et glorificábit nomen tuum?
Quia solus Sanctus, †
quóniam omnes gentes vénient et adorábunt in conspéctu tuo, *
quóniam iudícia tua manifestáta sunt.

Ant. Omnes gentes vénient et adorábunt coram te, Dómine.

LECTIO BREVIS Iac 1, 2-4

Omne gáudium existimáte, fratres mei, cum in tentatiónibus váriis incidéritis, sciéntes quod probátio fídei vestræ patiéntiam operátur; patiéntia autem opus perféctum hábeat, ut sitis perfécti et íntegri, in nullo deficiéntes.

RESPONSORIUM BREVE

℟. Christus diléxit nos et lavit nos * In sánguine suo. Christus.
℣. Et fecit nos Deo regnum et sacerdótium. * In sánguine suo. Glória Patri. Christus.

Ad Magníficat, ant. Suscépit nos Dóminus púeros suos, recordátus misericórdiæ suæ.

Ant. 2 O house of Israel, bless the Lord; praise Him, for such is delightful.
Ant. 3 All nations shall come and worship before Thee, O Lord.

Canticle Revelation 15:3–4

3 "Great and wonderful are thy deeds,
O Lord God the Almighty!
Just and true are thy ways,
O King of the Ages!
4 Who shall not fear and glorify thy name, O Lord?
For Thou alone art holy.
All nations shall come and worship thee,
for thy judgments have been revealed."

Ant. 3 All nations shall come and worship before Thee, O Lord.

SHORT READING James 1:2–4
Count it all joy, my brethren, when you meet various trials, for you know that the testing of your faith produces steadfastness. And let steadfastness have its full effect, that you may be perfect and complete, lacking in nothing.

SHORT RESPONSORY
℟. Christ has loved us and washed us in His own blood.
℣. And has made us a kingdom and a priesthood for God.

Magnificat ant. The Lord has helped us, His children, in remembrance of His mercy.

PRECES

Dóminum Iesum, quem Pater propter delícta nostra trádidit et propter iustificatiónem nostram resúrgere vóluit, deprecémur dicéntes: *Miserére pópuli tui, Dómine.*

Exáudi, quæsumus, Dómine, súpplicum preces et confiténtium tibi parce peccátis,
—ut páriter nobis indulgéntiam tríbuas benígnus et pacem.

Qui per Apóstolum dixísti: « Ubi abundávit peccátum, superabundávit grátia »,
—multa débita nostra lárgiter dimítte.

Multum quidem peccávimus, Dómine, sed tuam confitémur misericórdiam infinítam:
—convérte nos et convertémur.

Salvum fac pópulum tuum, Dómine, a peccátis eius,
—et beneplácitum tibi sit in ipso.

Qui latróni, te salvatórem confiténti, paradísum aperuísti,
—noli defúnctis nostris cæli cláudere portas.

Pater noster.

ORATIO

Dómine, sancte Pater, qui Christum Fílium tuum nostræ salútis prétium fíeri voluísti, da nobis ita vívere, ut, per societátem passiónum ipsíus, virtútem resurrectiónis cónsequi valeámus. Qui tecum.

Intercessions

Let us beseech the Lord Jesus, Whom the Father handed over because of our crimes and Whom He willed to raise for our justification, saying: *Have mercy on Your people, Lord.*

We ask that You hear, O Lord, the prayers of those who implore You and that You forgive the sins of those who confess to You,
—that in Your kindness You may grant us forgiveness and peace.

You that said through the Apostle: Where sin abounded, grace abounded all the more,
—graciously forgive our many debts.

We have sinned much, O Lord, but we trust in Your infinite mercy:
—convert us and we shall be converted.

Save Your people, Lord, from their sins,
—and may they be most pleasing to You.

You that opened paradise to the thief who confessed You to be the Savior,
—close not the gates of heaven to our departed.

Our Father.

Oration

O Lord, Holy Father, Who willed Christ Your Son to become the price of our salvation, grant us so to live, that through sharing in His passion, we may experience the power of His resurrection. Who with You.

Hebdomada III

Sabbato, ad Laudes matutinas

Hymnus

Auróra iam spargit polum,
terris dies illábitur,
lucis resúltat spículum:
discédat omne lúbricum.

Iam vana noctis décidant,
mentis reátus súbruat,
quicquid tenébris hórridum
nox áttulit culpæ, cadet,

Ut mane illud últimum,
quod præstolámur cérnui,
in lucem nobis éffluat,
dum hoc canóre cóncrepat.

Deo Patri sit glória
eiúsque soli Fílio
cum Spíritu Paráclito,
in sempitérna sǽcula. Amen.

Psalmodia

Ant. 1 Prope es tu, Dómine, et omnes viæ tuæ véritas.

Week III

Saturday, Lauds

HYMN Trans. J. H. Newman

The dawn is sprinkled o'er the sky,
  The day steals softly on;
Its darts are scatter'd far and nigh,
And all that fraudful is, shall fly
  Before the brightening sun;
Spectres of ill, that stalk at will,
  And forms of guilt that fright,
And hideous sin, that ventures in
  Under the cloak of night.

And of our crimes the tale complete,
  Which bows us in Thy sight,
Up to the latest, they shall fleet,
Out-told by our full members sweet,
  And melted by the light.
To Father, Son, and Spirit, One,
  Whom we adore and love,
Be given all praise now and always,
  Here as in Heaven above.

PSALMODY

Ant. 1 Thou art near, O Lord, and all Thy ways are true.

Psalmus 118 (119), 145–152

145 Clamávi in toto corde, exáudi me, Dómine; *
iustificatiónes tuas servábo.
146 Clamávi ad te, salvum me fac, *
ut custódiam testimónia tua.

147 Prævéni dilúculo et clamávi, *
in verba tua supersperávi.
148 Prævenérunt óculi mei vigílias, *
ut meditárer elóquia tua.

149 Vocem meam audi secúndum misericórdiam
tuam, Dómine, *
secúndum iudícium tuum vivífica me.
150 Appropinquavérunt persequéntes me in malítia, *
a lege autem tua longe facti sunt.

151 Prope es tu, Dómine, *
et ómnia præcépta tua véritas.
152 Ab inítio cognóvi de testimóniis tuis, *
quia in ætérnum fundásti ea.

Ant. Prope es tu, Dómine, et omnes viæ tuæ véritas.
Ant. 2 Mecum sit, Dómine, sapiéntia tua et mecum labóret.

Canticum — Sap 9, 1–6. 9–11

1 Deus patrum meórum et Dómine misericórdiæ, *
qui fecísti ómnia verbo tuo
2 et sapiéntia tua constituísti hóminem *
ut dominarétur creatúris, quæ a te factæ sunt,
3 et dispóneret orbem terrárum in sanctitáte et
iustítia *

Psalm 119:145–152

145 With my whole heart I cry; answer me, O LORD!
I will keep thy statutes.
146 I cry to thee; save me
that I may observe thy testimonies.
147 I rise before dawn and cry for help;
I hope in thy words.
148 My eyes are awake before the watches of the night,
that I may meditate upon thy promise.
149 Hear my voice in thy steadfast love;
O Lord, in thy justice preserve my life.
150 They draw near who persecute me with evil purpose;
they are far from thy law.
151 But thou art near, O Lord,
and all thy commandments are true.
152 Long have I known from thy testimonies
that thou hast founded them for ever.

Ant. 1 Thou art near, O Lord, and all Thy ways are true.

Ant. 2 May Thy wisdom be with me, O Lord, and may it always work with me.

Canticle Wisdom 9:1–6, 9–11

1 "O God of my fathers and Lord of mercy,
who hast made all things by thy word,
2 and by thy wisdom hast formed man,
to have dominion over the creatures thou hast made,
3 and rule the world in holiness and righteousness,

et in directióne cordis iudícium iudicáret,
4 da mihi sédium tuárum assistrícem sapiéntiam *
et noli me reprobáre a púeris tuis,
5 quóniam servus tuus sum ego et fílius ancíllæ tuæ, †
homo infírmus et exígui témporis *
et minor ad intelléctum iudícii et legum.

6 Nam, et si quis erit consummátus inter fílios hóminum, †
si ab illo abfúerit sapiéntia tua, *
in níhilum computábitur.

9 Et tecum sapiéntia, quæ novit ópera tua, *
quæ et áffuit tunc, cum orbem terrárum fáceres,
et sciébat quid esset plácitum in óculis tuis *
et quid diréctum in præcéptis tuis *

10 Emítte illam de cælis sanctis tuis *
et a sede magnitúdinis tuæ mitte illam,
ut mecum sit et mecum labóret, *
ut sciam quid accéptum sit apud te.

11 Scit enim illa ómnia et intéllegit †
et dedúcet me in opéribus meis sóbrie *
et custódiet me in sua glória.

Ant. Mecum sit, Dómine, sapiéntia tua et mecum labóret.
Ant. 3 Véritas Dómini manet in ætérnum.

and pronounce judgment in uprightness of soul,
4 give me the wisdom that sits by thy throne,
and do not reject me from among thy servants.
5 For I am thy slave and the son of thy maidservant,
a man who is weak and short-lived,
with little understanding of judgment and laws;
6 for even if one is perfect among the sons of men,
yet without the wisdom that comes from thee
he will be regarded as nothing.

9 With thee is wisdom, who knows thy works
and was present when Thou didst make the world,
and who understands what is pleasing in thy sight
and what is right according to thy commandments.
10 Send her forth from the holy heavens,
and from the throne of thy glory send her,
that she may be with me and toil,
and that I may learn what is pleasing to thee.
11 For she knows and understands all things,
and she will guide me wisely in my actions
and guard me with her glory.

Ant. 2 May Thy wisdom be with me, O Lord, and may it always work with me.
Ant. 3 The faithfulness of the Lord endures for ever.

Psalmus 116 (117)

1 Laudáte Dóminum, omnes gentes, *
collaudáte eum, omnes pópuli.

2 Quóniam confirmáta est super nos misericórdia eius, *
et véritas Dómini manet in ætérnum.

Ant. Véritas Dómini manet in ætérnum.

LECTIO BREVIS — PHIL 2, 14–15

Omnia fácite sine murmuratiónibus et hæsitatiónibus, ut efficiámini sine queréla et símplices, fílii Dei sine reprehensióne in médio generatiónis pravæ et persérsæ, inter quos lucétis sicut luminária in mundo.

RESPONSORIUM BREVE

℟. Clamávi ad te, Dómine; * Tu es refúgium meum. Clamávi.
℣. Pórtio mea in terra vivéntium. * Tu es refúgium meum. Glória Patri. Clamávi.

Ad Benedictus, ant. Illúmina, Dómine, sedéntes in ténebris et umbra mortis.

PRECES

Deum, qui Maríam matrem Christi ómnibus creatúris cæléstibus et terréstribus antecéllere vóluit, cum fidúcia implorémus: *Réspice Matrem Fílii tui et exáudi nos.*

Pater misericordiárum, grátias tibi reférimus quod nobis Maríam matrem et exémplum dedísti,
—per eius intercessiónem corda nostra sanctífica.

Psalm 117

1 Praise the LORD, all nations!
Extol him, all peoples!
2 For great is his steadfast love toward us;
and the faithfulness of the LORD endures for ever.
Praise the Lord!

Ant. 3 The faithfulness of the Lord endures for ever.

SHORT READING Philippians 2:14–15

Do all things without grumbling or questioning, that you may be blameless and innocent, children of God without blemish in the midst of a crooked and perverse generation, among whom you shine as lights in the world.

SHORT RESPONSORY

℟. I have cried to You, O Lord; You are my refuge.
℣. You are my portion in the land of the living.

Benedictus ant. Give light, O Lord, to those who sit in darkness and in the shadow of death.

INTERCESSIONS

God, Who wished Mary the Mother of Christ to be above all creatures in the heavens and on the earth, with confidence let us implore Him: *Look upon the Mother of Your Son and hear us.*

Father of mercies, we return thanks to You that have given us Mary as Mother and example,
—through her intercession sanctify our hearts.

Qui Maríam tuo inténtam reddidísti verbo et ancíllam tuam fidélem effecísti,
—per eius intercessiónem fructus Sancti Spíritus nobis concéde.

Qui Maríam iuxta crucem stantem roborásti et in resurrectióne Fílii tui replésti lætítia,
—per eius intercessiónem tribulatiónes súbleva nostras spemque nostram confírma.

Pater noster.

ORATIO

Deus, nostræ fons et orígo salútis, ita nos fac semper vita nostra tuam glóriam profitéri, ut et in cælis a tua numquam laude cessémus. Per Dóminum.

You that have made Mary intent on Your word, and have made her Your faithful handmaid,
—through her intercession grant us the fruits of the Holy Spirit.

You that strengthened Mary standing by the cross and, in the resurrection of Your Son, filled her with joy,
—through her intercession, support us in our tribulations and confirm our hope.

Our Father.

ORATION

God, the fountain and source of our salvation, so make our life always to profess Your glory, that we might never cease praising You in heaven. Through our Lord.

Hebdomada IV

Dominica, ad I Vesperas

HYMN

Rerum, Deus, fons ómnium,
qui, rebus actis ómnibus,
totíus orbis ámbitum
censu replésti múnerum,

Ac, mole tanta cóndita,
tandem quiétem díceris
sumpsísse, dans labóribus
ut nos levémur grátius:

Concéde nunc mortálibus
deflére vitæ crímina,
instáre iam virtútibus
et munerári prósperis,

Ut cum treméndi iúdicis
horror suprémus cœperit,
lætémur omnes ínvicem
pacis repléti múnere.

Præsta, Pater piíssime,
Patríque compar Unice,
cum Spíritu Paráclito
regnans per omne sæculum. Amen.

PSALMODIA

Ant. 1 Rogáte quæ ad pacem sunt Ierúsalem.

Week IV

Sunday, Vespers I

HYMN Trans. The Benedictine Nuns, St. Cecilia's Abbey

O God, the Source and Fount of life,
  Creating all things by Your will,
To give us joy You never cease
  The earth with wondrous gifts to fill.

And when creation was complete,
  Repose for man You also blessed
By resting on the seventh day,
  That he might toil again refreshed.

To fallen mortals grant the grace
  Of sorrow for each sin's offence,
And courage to begin anew
  And strive for virtue's recompense.

When Christ the Judge supreme appears
  To sift the present and the past,
May we His servants thrill with joy
  And peace to gaze on Him at last.

Most tender Father, hear our prayer,
  Whom we adore, with Christ the Lord,
And Holy Spirit of them both;
  Bless us who praise Your Trinity.
    Amen.

PSALMODY

Ant. 1 Pray for the peace of Jerusalem.

Psalmus 121 (122)

1 Lætátus sum in eo quod dixérunt mihi: *
« In domum Dómini íbimus ».
2 Stantes iam sunt pedes nostri *
in portis tuis, Ierúsalem.

3 Ierúsalem, quæ ædificáta est ut cívitas, *
sibi compácta in idípsum.
4 Illuc enim ascendérunt tribus, tribus Dómini, *
testimónium Israel, ad confiténdum nómini Dómini.
5 Quia illic sedérunt sedes ad iudícium, *
sedes domus David.

6 Rogáte, quæ ad pacem sunt Ierúsalem: *
« Secúri sint diligéntes te!
7 Fiat pax in muris tuis, *
et secúritas in túrribus tuis! ».

8 Propter fratres meos et próximos meos *
loquar: « Pax in te! ».
9 Propter domum Dómini Dei nostri *
exquíram bona tibi.

Ant. Rogáte quæ ad pacem sunt Ierúsalem.
Ant. 2 A custódia matutína usque ad noctem, sperávit ánima mea in Dómino.

Psalmus 129 (130)

1 De profúndis clamávi ad te, Dómine; *
2 Dómine, exáudi vocem meam.
Fiant aures tuæ intendéntes *
in vocem deprecatiónis meæ.

Psalm 122

1 I was glad when they said to me,
"Let us go to the house of the LORD!"
2 Our feet have been standing
within your gates, O Jerusalem!

3 Jerusalem, built as a city
which is bound firmly together,
4 to which the tribes go up,
the tribes of the LORD,
as was decreed for Israel,
to give thanks to the name of the LORD.
5 There thrones for judgment were set,
the thrones of the house of David.

6 Pray for the peace of Jerusalem!
"May they prosper who love you!
7 Peace be within your walls,
and security within your towers!"
8 For my brethren and companions' sake
I will say, "Peace be within you!"
9 For the sake of the house of the LORD our God,
I will seek your good.

Ant. 1 Pray for the peace of Jerusalem.
Ant. 2 From the morning watch until night, my soul waits, and in His word I hope.

Psalm 130

1 Out of the depths I cry to thee, O LORD!
2 Lord, hear my voice!
Let thy ears be attentive
to the voice of my supplications!

3 Si iniquitátes observáveris, Dómine, *
Dómine, quis sustinébit?
4 Quia apud te propitiátio est, *
ut timeámus te.
5 Sustínui te, Dómine, *
sustínuit ánima mea in verbo eius;
sperávit 6ánima mea in Dómino *
magis quam custódes auróram.

Magis quam custódes auróram †
7 speret Israel in Dómino,
quia apud Dóminum misericórdia, *
et copiósa apud eum redémptio.
8 Et ipse rédimet Israel *
ex ómnibus iniquitátibus eius.

Ant. A custódia matutína usque ad noctem, sperávit ánima mea in Dómino.

Ant. 3 In nómine Iesu omne genu flectátur in cælo et in terra, allelúia.

Canticum PHIL 2, 6–11

6 Christus Iesus, cum in forma Dei esset, *
non rapínam arbitrátus est esse se æquálem Deo,
7 sed semetípsum exinanívit formam servi
accípiens, †
in similitúdinem hóminum factus; *
et hábitu invéntus ut homo,
8 humiliávit semetípsum †
factus obœ́diens usque ad mortem, *
mortem autem crucis.

3 If thou, O LORD, shouldst mark iniquities,
Lord, who could stand?
4 But there is forgiveness with thee,
that thou mayest be feared.

5 I wait for the LORD, my soul waits,
and in his word I hope;
6 my soul waits for the LORD
more than watchmen for the morning,
more than watchmen for the morning.

7 O Israel, hope in the LORD!
For with the LORD there is steadfast love,
and with him is plenteous redemption.
8 And he will redeem Israel
from all his iniquities.

Ant. 2 From the morning watch until night, my soul waits, and in His word I hope.
Ant. 3 At the name of Jesus every knee should bow, in heaven and on earth, alleluia.

Canticle Philippians 2:6–11

6 Christ, though he was in the form of God, did not
count equality with God a thing to be grasped,
7 but emptied himself, taking the form of a servant,
being born in the likeness of men.
8 And being found in human form he humbled
himself and became obedient unto death, even
death on a cross.

9 Propter quod et Deus illum exaltávit †
et donávit illi nomen, *
quod est super omne nomen,
10 ut in nómine Iesu omne genu flectátur *
cæléstium et terréstrium et infernórum
11 et omnis lingua confiteátur: *
« Dóminus Iesus Christus! », in glóriam Dei Patris.

Ant. In nómine Iesu omne genu flectátur in cælo et in terra, allelúia.

LECTIO BREVIS — 2 PETR 1, 19–21

Habémus firmiórem prophéticum sermónem, cui bene fácitis attendéntes quasi lucérnæ lucénti in caliginóso loco, donec dies illucéscat et lúcifer oriátur in córdibus vestris, hoc primum intellegéntes quod omnis prophetía Scriptúræ própria interpretatióne non fit; non enim voluntáte humána proláta est prophetía aliquándo, sed a Spíritu Sancto ducti locúti sunt a Deo hómines.

RESPONSORIUM BREVE

℟. A solis ortu usque ad occásum, * Laudábile nomen Dómini. A solis.
℣. Super cælos glória eius. * Laudábile nomen Dómini. Glória Patri. A solis.

PRECES

Christum, in quo lætántur omnes, qui sperant in eum deprecémur: *Réspice et exáudi nos, Dómine.*

Testis fidélis et primogénite mortuórum, qui lavásti nos a peccátis nostris in sánguine tuo,
—mirabílium tuórum redde nos mémores.

9 Therefore, God has highly exalted him and
bestowed on him the name which is above
every name,
10 that at the name of Jesus every knee should bow,
in heaven and on earth and under the earth,
11 and every tongue confess that Jesus Christ is
Lord, to the glory of God the Father.

Ant. 3 At the name of Jesus every knee should bow, in heaven and on earth, alleluia.

Short Reading

2 Peter 1:19–21

And we have the prophetic word more sure. You will do well to pay attention to this as to a lamp shining in a dark place, until the day dawns and the morning star rises in your hearts. First of all you must understand this, that no prophecy of scripture is a matter of one's own interpretation, because no prophecy ever came by the impulse of man, but men moved by the Holy Spirit spoke from God.

Short Responsory

℟. From the rising of the sun to its setting,
may the name of the Lord be praised.
℣. His glory is above the heavens.

Magnificat ant. as in Proper of the Time.

Intercessions

Let us, who hope in Christ, beseech Him, in Whom all rejoice: *Look upon us and hear us, O Lord.*

O faithful witness and First-born of the dead, Who have cleansed us from our sins in Your blood,
—make us mindful of Your wonders.

Quos Evangélii vocásti præcónes,
—strénui et fidéles dispensatóres mystérii regni tui inveniántur.
Rex pacífice, véniat Spíritus tuus in illos, qui pópulos regunt,
—ut óculos in páuperes miserósque convértant.
Cónsule iis, qui discrímen ob genus, colórem, condiciónem, sermónem aut religiónem patiúntur,
—ut iúrium suórum ac dignitátis agnitiónem consequántur.
Omnes, qui in tuo amóre decessérunt, beatitúdinis redde partícipes,
—cum beáta María Vírgine et ómnibus sanctis tuis.

Pater noster.

ORATIO

May those whom You have called to be heralds of the gospel,
—be found strong stewards of the mysteries of Your kingdom.

O Peaceful King, let Your Spirit come into those who rule the peoples,
—that they might turn their eyes to the poor and the suffering.

Assist those who suffer discrimination because of color, class, language, or religion,
—that they might obtain recognition of their rights and dignity.

Make all who have departed in Your love to be partakers of your blessedness,
—with the Blessed Virgin Mary and all Your saints.

Our Father.

Oration

As in Proper of the Time.

Hebdomada IV

Dominica, ad Laudes matutinas

HYMN

Ecce iam noctis tenuátur umbra,
lucis auróra rútilans corúscat;
nísibus totis rogitémus omnes cunctipoténtem,

Ut Deus, nostri miserátus, omnem
pellat angórem, tríbuat salútem,
donet et nobis pietáte patris regna polórum.

Præstet hoc nobis Déitas beáta
Patris ac Nati, paritérque Sancti
Spíritus, cuius résonat per omnem glória
mundum. Amen.

PSALMODIA

Ant. 1. Confitémini Dómino, quóniam in sæculum misericórdia eius, allelúia.

Week IV

Sunday, Lauds

HYMN Trans. The Benedictine Nuns, St. Cecilia's Abbey

Out of the darkness
  in which night has held us;
See, dawn arises,
  shining now in splendour;
All our fresh ardour
  let us use in praising
God the Almighty.

That in His mercy
  He may always keep us,
Eager not slothful
  in His holy service
Then may He give us
  with a Father's bounty
Joy in His Kingdom.

May the assistance
  and the love protect us,
Of the great Godhead
  Father, Son, and Spirit,
Whose wondrous glory
  in the world around us
Ever finds echo. Amen.

PSALMODY

Ant. 1 O give thanks to the Lord, for His steadfast love endures forever, alleluia.

Psalmus 117 (118)

1 Confitémini Dómino, quóniam bonus, *
quóniam in sæculum misericórdia eius.

2 Dicat nunc Israel, quóniam bonus, *
quóniam in sæculum misericórdia eius.
3 Dicat nunc domus Aaron, *
quóniam in sæculum misericórdia eius.
4 Dicant nunc, qui timent Dóminum, *
quóniam in sæculum misericórdia eius.

5 De tribulatióne invocávi Dóminum, *
et exaudívit me edúcens in latitúdinem
Dóminus.
6 Dóminus mecum, *
non timébo, quid fáciat mihi homo.
7 Dóminus mecum adiútor meus, *
et ego despíciam inimícos meos.

8 Bonum est confúgere ad Dóminum *
quam confídere in hómine.
9 Bonum est confúgere ad Dóminum *
quam confídere in princípibus.
10 Omnes gentes circuiérunt me, *
et in nómine Dómini excídi eos.
11 Circumdántes circumdedérunt me, *
et in nómine Dómini excídi eos.
12 Circumdedérunt me sicut apes †
et exarsérunt sicut ignis in spinis, *
et in nómine Dómini excídi eos.
13 Impelléntes impulérunt me, ut cáderem, *
et Dóminus adiúvit me.
14 Fortitúdo mea et laus mea Dóminus *
et factus est mihi in salútem.

Psalm 118

1 O give thanks to the LORD, for he is good;
his steadfast love endures for ever!

2 Let Israel say,
"His steadfast love endures for ever."
3 Let the house of Aaron say,
"His steadfast love endures for ever."
4 Let those who fear the LORD say,
"His steadfast love endures for ever."

5 Out of my distress I called on the LORD;
the LORD answered me and set me free.
6 With the LORD on my side I do not fear.
What can man do to me?
7 The LORD is on my side to help me;
I shall look in triumph on those who hate me.
8 It is better to take refuge in the LORD
than to put confidence in man.
9 It is better to take refuge in the LORD
than to put confidence in princes.

10 All nations surrounded me;
in the name of the LORD I cut them off!
11 They surrounded me, surrounded me on every side;
in the name of the LORD I cut them off!
12 They surrounded me like bees,
they blazed like a fire of thorns;
in the name of the LORD I cut them off!
13 I was pushed hard, so that I was falling,
but the LORD helped me.
14 The LORD is my strength and my song;
he has become my salvation.

15 Vox iubilatiónis et salútis *
in tabernáculis iustórum:
16 « Déxtera Dómini fecit virtútem! †
Déxtera Dómini exaltávit me; *
déxtera Dómini fecit virtútem! ».

17 Non móriar, sed vivam *
et narrábo ópera Dómini.
18 Castígans castigávit me Dóminus *
et morti non trádidit me.

19 Aperíte mihi portas iustítiæ; *
ingréssus in eas confitébor Dómino.

20 Hæc porta Dómini; *
iusti intrábunt in eam.

21 Confitébor tibi, quóniam exaudísti me *
et factus es mihi in salútem.

22 Lápidem, quem reprobavérunt ædificántes, *
hic factus est in caput ánguli;
23 a Dómino factum est istud *
et est mirábile in óculis nostris.

24 Hæc est dies, quam fecit Dóminus: *
exsultémus et lætémur in ea. *

25 O Dómine, salvum me fac; *
o Dómine, da prosperitátem!

26 Benedíctus, qui venit in nómine Dómini. *
Benedícimus vobis de domo Dómini.
27 Deus Dóminus et illúxit nobis. *
Instrúite sollemnitátem in ramis condénsis
usque ad córnua altáris.

15 Hark, glad songs of victory
in the tents of the righteous;
"The right hand of the LORD does valiantly,
16 the right hand of the LORD is exalted,
the right hand of the LORD does valiantly!"
17 I shall not die, but I shall live,
and recount the deeds of the Lord.
18 The LORD has chastened me sorely,
but he has not given me over to death.

19 Open to me the gates of righteousness,
that I may enter through them
and give thanks to the LORD.

20 This is the gate of the LORD;
the righteous shall enter through it.

21 I thank thee that thou hast answered me
and hast become my salvation.
22 The stone which the builders rejected
has become the head of the corner.
23 This is the Lord's doing;
it is marvelous in our eyes.
24 This is the day which the LORD has made;
let us rejoice and be glad in it.
25 Save us, we beseech thee, O LORD!
O LORD, we beseech thee, give us success!

26 Blessed be he who enters in the name of the LORD!
We bless you from the house of the LORD.
27 The LORD is God,
and he has given us light.
Bind the festal procession with branches,
up to the horns of the altar!

28 Deus meus es tu, et confitébor tibi, *
Deus meus, et exaltábo te.

29 Confitémini Dómino, quóniam bonus, *
quóniam in sæculum misericórdia eius.

Ant. Confitémini Dómino, quóniam in sæculum misericórdia eius, allelúia.

Ant. 2 Allelúia, benedícite, ómnia ópera Dómini, Dómino, allelúia.

Canticum *Dan 3, 52–57*

52 Benedíctus es, Dómine Deus patrum nostrórum, *
et laudábilis et superexaltátus in sæcula;
et benedíctum nomen glóriæ tuæ sanctum *
et superlaudábile et superexaltátum in sæcula.
53 Benedíctus es in templo sanctæ glóriæ tuæ *
et superlaudábilis et supergloriósus in sæcula.
54 Benedíctus es in throno regni tui *
et superlaudábilis et superexaltátus in sæcula.
55 Benedíctus es, qui intuéris abýssos †
sedens super chérubim, *
et laudábilis et superexaltátus in sæcula.
56 Benedíctus es in firmaménto cæli *
et laudábilis et gloriósus in sæcula.
57 Benedícite, ómnia ópera Dómini, Dómino, *
laudáte et superexaltáte eum in sæcula.

Ant. Allelúia, benedícite, ómnia ópera Dómini, Dómino, allelúia.

Ant. 3 Omnis spíritus laudet Dóminum, allelúia.

28 Thou art my God, and I will give thanks to thee;
thou art my God, I will extol thee.

29 O give thanks to the Lord, for he is good;
for his steadfast love endures for ever!

Ant. 1 O give thanks to the Lord, for His steadfast love endures forever, alleluia.
Ant. 2 Alleluia! Bless the Lord, all works of the Lord, alleluia!

Canticle Daniel 3:29–35

29 "Blessed art thou, O Lord, God of our fathers,
and to be praised and highly exalted for ever;
30 And blessed is thy glorious, holy name
and to be highly praised and highly exalted for ever;
31 Blessed art thou in the temple of thy holy glory
and to be extolled and highly glorified for ever.
32 Blessed art thou, who sittest upon cherubim and lookest upon the deeps,
and to be praised and highly exalted for ever.
33 Blessed art thou upon the throne of thy kingdom,
and to be extolled and highly exalted for ever.
34 Blessed art thou in the firmament of heaven
and to be sung and glorified for ever.

35 "Bless the Lord, all works of the Lord,
sing praise to him and highly exalt him for ever."

Ant. 2 Alleluia! Bless the Lord, all works of the Lord, alleluia!
Ant. 3 Let everything that breathes praise the Lord, alleluia.

Psalmus 150

1 Laudáte Dóminum in sanctuário eius, *
laudáte eum in firmaménto virtútis eius.
2 Laudáte eum in magnálibus eius, *
laudáte eum secúndum multitúdinem
magnitúdinis eius.

3 Laudáte eum in sono tubæ, *
laudáte eum in psaltério et cíthara,
4 laudáte eum in týmpano et choro, *
laudáte eum in chordis et órgano,
5 laudáte eum in cýmbalis benesonántibus, †
laudáte eum in cýmbalis iubilatiónis: *
omne quod spirat, laudet Dóminum.

Ant. Omnis spíritus laudet Dóminum, allelúia.

LECTIO BREVIS 2 TIM 2, 8. 11–13

Memor esto Iesum Christum resuscitátum esse a mórtuis, ex sémine David. Fidélis sermo: Nam si commórtui sumus, et convivémus; si sustinémus, et conregnábimus; si negábimus, et ille negábit nos; si non crédimus, ille fidélis manet, negáre enim seípsum non potest.

RESPONSORIUM BREVE

℟. Confitébimur tibi, Deus, * Et invocábimus nomen tuum. Confitébimur.

℣. Narrábimus mirabília tua. * Et invocábimus nomen tuum. Glória Patri. Confitébimur.

Psalm 150

1 Praise the LORD!
Praise God in his sanctuary;
praise him in his mighty firmament!
2 Praise him for his mighty deeds;
praise him according to his exceeding greatness!
3 Praise him with trumpet sound;
praise him with lute and harp!
4 Praise him with timbrel and dance;
praise him with strings and pipe!
5 Praise him with sounding cymbals;
praise him with loud clashing cymbals!
6 Let everything that breathes praise the Lord!
Praise the LORD!

Ant. 3 Let everything that breathes praise the Lord, alleluia.

SHORT READING 2 Timothy 2:8, 11–13

Remember Jesus Christ, risen from the dead, descended from David. The saying is sure:
If we have died with him, we shall also live with him;
if we endure, we shall also reign with him;
if we deny him, he also will deny us;
if we are faithless, he remains faithful—
for he cannot deny himself.

SHORT RESPONSORY

℟. We shall confess you, O God, and call upon your name.

℣. We shall proclaim your marvelous deeds.

Preces

Deo poténtiæ et bonitátis, qui nos amat et novit quibus rebus indigémus, cum láudibus corda nostra læti pandámus: *Te laudámus, in te confídimus, Dómine.*

Benedícimus tibi, omnípotens Deus, Rex univérsi, qui nos iniústos et peccatóres vocásti,
—ut cognoscámus veritátem tuam et maiestáti tuæ serviámus.

Deus, qui nobis misericórdiæ iánuam patére voluísti,
—fac ut a vitæ numquam sémitis inveniámur dévii.

Resurrectiónem dilectíssimi Fílii tui celebrántes,
—fac nos hunc diem in gáudio spiritáli transígere.

Da fidélibus tuis, Dómine, spíritum oratiónis et laudis,
—ut in ómnibus tibi grátias semper agámus.

Pater noster.

Oratio

Magnificat ant. as in Proper of the Time.

Intercessions

To the God of power and goodness, Who loves us and knows what we need, with praises let us joyfully open our hearts: *We praise You, and in You we trust, O Lord.*

We bless You, almighty God, King of the universe, Who called us, the unjust and the sinners,
—that we might know Your truth and serve Your majesty.

God, Who wished to open the gate of mercy to us,
—grant that we might never be found straying from the paths of life.

Celebrating the resurrection of Your most beloved Son,
—make us pass through this day in spiritual joy.

Give to Your faithful, Lord, the spirit of prayer and praise,
—that in all things we might always give thanks to You.

Our Father.

Oration

As in Proper of the Time.

Hebdomada IV

Dominica, ad II Vesperas

Hymn

O lux, beáta Trínitas
et principális Unitas,
iam sol recédit ígneus:
infúnde lumen córdibus.

Te mane laudem cármine,
te deprecémur véspere;
te nostra supplex glória
per cuncta laudet sǽcula.

Christum rogámus et Patrem,
Christi Patrísque Spíritum;
unum potens per ómnia,
fove precántes, Trínitas. Amen.

Psalmodia

Ant. 1 In splendóribus sanctis, ante lucíferum génui te, allelúia.

Psalmus 109 (110), 1–5. 7

1 Dixit Dóminus Dómino meo: *
« Sede a dextris meis,
donec ponam inimícos tuos *
scabéllum pedum tuórum ».

2 Virgam poténtiæ tuæ emíttet Dóminus ex Sion: *
domináre in médio inimicórum tuórum.

Week IV

Sunday, Vespers II

HYMN Trans. J. M. Neale

O Trinity of blessed light,
O Unity of princely might,
The fiery sun now goes his way;
Shed Thou within our hearts Thy ray.

To Thee our morning song of praise,
To Thee our evening prayer we raise;
Thy glory suppliant we adore
For ever and for evermore.

All laud to God the Father be;
All praise, eternal Son, to Thee;
All glory, as is ever meet,
To God the Holy Paraclete. Amen.

PSALMODY

Ant. 1 In eternal splendor, before the dawn, I have begotten Thee, alleluia.

Psalm 110:1–5, 7

1 The LORD says to my lord:
"Sit at my right hand,
till I make your enemies your footstool."

2 The Lord sends forth from Zion
your mighty scepter.
Rule in the midst of your foes!

3 Tecum principátus in die virtútis tuæ, †
in splendóribus sanctis, *
ex útero ante lucíferum génui te.
4 Iurávit Dóminus et non pænitébit eum: *
« Tu es sacérdos in ætérnum secúndum órdinem Melchísedech ».
5 Dóminus a dextris tuis, *
conquassábit in die iræ suæ reges.

7 De torrénte in via bibet, *
proptérea exaltábit caput.

Ant. In splendóribus sanctis, ante lucíferum génui te, allelúia.
Ant. 2 Beáti qui esúriunt et sítiunt iustítiam, quóniam ipsi saturabúntur.

Psalmus III (112)

1 Beátus vir, qui timet Dóminum, *
in mandátis eius cupit nimis.
2 Potens in terra erit semen eius, *
generátio rectórum benedicétur.
3 Glória et divítiæ in domo eius, *
et iustítia eius manet in sæculum sæculi.

4 Exórtum est in ténebris lumen rectis, *
miséricors et miserátor et iustus.
5 Iucúndus homo, qui miserétur et cómmodat, †
dispónet res suas in iudício, *
6 quia in ætérnum non commovébitur.

3 Your people will offer themselves freely
on the day you lead your host
upon the holy mountains.
From the womb of the morning
like dew your youth will come to you.
4 The Lord has sworn
and will not change his mind,
"You are a priest for ever
according to the order of Melchizedek."

5 The Lord is at your right hand;
he will shatter kings on the day of his wrath.

7 He will drink from the brook by the way;
therefore he will lift up his head.

Ant. 1 In eternal splendor, before the dawn, I have begotten Thee, alleluia.
Ant. 2 Blessed are they who hunger and thirst for justice, for they will be satisfied.

Psalm 112

1 Praise the LORD!
Blessed is the man who fears the LORD,
who greatly delights in his commandments!
2 His descendants will be mighty in the land;
the generation of the upright will be blessed.
3 Wealth and riches are in his house;
and his righteousness endures for ever.
4 Light rises in the darkness for the upright;
the LORD is gracious, merciful, and righteous.
5 It is well with the man who deals generously and lends,
who conducts his affairs with justice.

In memória ætérna erit iustus, *
7 ab auditióne mala non timébit.
Parátum cor eius, sperans in Dómino, †
8 confirmátum est cor eius, non timébit, *
donec despíciat inimícos suos.
9 Distríbuit, dedit paupéribus; †
iustítia eius manet in sæculum sæculi, *
cornu eius exaltábitur in glória.
10 Peccátor vidébit et irascétur, †
déntibus suis fremet et tabéscet. *
Desidérium peccatórum períbit.

Ant. Beáti qui esúriunt et sítiunt iustítiam, quóniam ipsi saturabúntur.

Ant. 3 Laudem dícite Deo, omnes servi eius, pusílli et magni, allelúia.

Canticum Cf. Ap 19, 1-2. 5-7

Allelúia.
1 Salus et glória et virtus Deo nostro, *
(℟. Allelúia.)
2 quia vera et iusta iudícia eius.
℟. Allelúia (allelúia).

Allelúia.
5 Laudem dícite Deo nostro, omnes servi eius *
(℟. Allelúia.)
et qui timétis eum, pusílli et magni!
℟. Allelúia (allelúia).

6 For the righteous will never be moved;
he will be remembered for ever.
7 He is not afraid of evil tidings;
his heart is firm, trusting in the LORD.
8 His heart is steady, he will not be afraid,
until he sees his desire on his adversaries.
9 He has distributed freely, he has given to the poor;
his righteousness endures for ever;
his horn is exalted in honor.
10 The wicked man sees it and is angry;
he gnashes his teeth and melts away;
the desire of the wicked man comes to nought.

Ant. 2 Blessed are they who hunger and thirst for justice, for they will be satisfied.
Ant. 3 Praise our God, all you His servants, small and great, alleluia.

Canticle See Revelation 19:1–7

Alleluia.
Salvation and glory and power belong to our God;
(℟. Alleluia.)
for his judgments are true and just;
℟. Alleluia (alleluia).

Alleluia.
Praise our God, all you his servants,
(℟. Alleluia.)
you that fear him, small and great.
℟. Alleluia (alleluia).

Allelúia.
6 Quóniam regnávit Dóminus, Deus noster
omnípotens. *
(℟. Allelúia.)
7 Gaudeámus et exsultémus et demus glóriam ei.
℟. Allelúia (allelúia).

Allelúia.
Quia venérunt núptiæ Agni, *
(℟. Allelúia.)
et uxor eius præparávit se.
℟. Allelúia (allelúia).

Ant. Laudem dícite Deo, omnes servi eius, pusílli et magni, allelúia.

LECTIO BREVIS HEBR 12, 22–24

Accessístis ad Sion montem et civitátem Dei vivéntis, Ierúsalem cæléstem, et multa mília angelórum, frequéntiam et ecclésiam primogenitórum, qui conscrípti sunt in cælis, et iúdicem Deum ómnium, et spíritus iustórum, qui consummáti sunt, et testaménti novi mediatórem Iesum, et sánguinem aspersiónis, mélius loquéntem quam Abel.

RESPONSORIUM BREVE

℟. Magnus Dóminus noster, * Et magna virtus eius. Magnus.
℣. Et sapiéntiæ eius non est númerus. * Et magna virtus eius. Glória Patri. Magnus.

Alleluia.
For, the Lord our God the Almighty reigns;
(℟. Alleluia.)
let us rejoice and exult and give him glory.
℟. Alleluia (alleluia).

Alleluia.
For the marriage of the Lamb has come,
(℟. Alleluia.)
and his Bride has made Herself ready.
℟. Alleluia (alleluia).

Ant. 3 Praise our God, all you His servants, small and great, alleluia.

SHORT READING Hebrews 12:22–24

But you have come to Mount Zion and to the city of the living God, the heavenly Jerusalem, and to innumerable angels in festal gathering, and to the assembly of the first-born who are enrolled in heaven, and to a Judge who is God of all, and to the spirits of just men made perfect, and to Jesus, the Mediator of a new covenant, and to the sprinkled blood that speaks more graciously than the blood of Abel.

SHORT RESPONSORY

℟. Our Lord is great, mighty is His power.
℣. To His wisdom there is no limit.

Magnificat ant. as in Proper of the Time.

Preces

Gaudéntes in Dómino, a quo omne bonum descéndit, ipsum sincéris méntibus deprecémur:
Dómine, exáudi oratiónem nostram.

Universórum Pater et Dómine, qui Fílium tuum in mundum misísti, ut nomen tuum glorificarétur in omni loco,
—testimónium Ecclésiæ tuæ róbora apud gentes.

Fac nos Apostolórum prædicatióni dóciles,
—et fídei nostræ veritáti confórmes.

Qui díligis iustos,
—iudícium fac iniúriam patiéntibus.

Compedítos solve, cæcos illúmina,
—elísos érige, ádvenas custódi.

In tua iam dormiéntium pace votum complére dignéris:
—da eos per Fílium tuum ad resurrectiónem sanctam perveníre.

Pater noster.

Oratio

Intercessions

Rejoicing in the Lord, from Whom every good thing comes, with a sincere mind, let us beseech Him:
Lord, hear our prayer.

Father and Lord of all, Who sent Your Son into the world that Your name might be glorified in every place,
—strengthen the witness of Your Church among the nations.

Make us obedient to the preaching of the Apostles,
—and conformed to the truth of our faith.

You that love the just,
—render judgment on behalf of those who suffer injury.

Liberate the captives, grant sight to the blind,
—lift up the fallen, protect the strangers.

Deign to fulfill Your vow to those who are already asleep in Your peace,
—grant them, through Your Son, to come to the holy resurrection.

Our Father.

Oration

As in Proper of the Time.

Hebdomada IV

Feria II, ad Laudes matutinas

Hymn

Lucis largítor spléndide,
cuius seréno lúmine
post lapsa noctis témpora
dies refúsus pánditur,

Tu verus mundi lúcifer,
non is qui parvi síderis
ventúræ lucis núntius
angústo fulget lúmine,

Sed toto sole clárior,
lux ipse totus et dies,
intérna nostri péctoris
illúminans præcórdia.

Evíncat mentis cástitas
quæ caro cupit árrogans,
sanctúmque puri córporis
delúbrum servet Spíritus.

Sit, Christe, rex piíssime,
tibi Patríque glória
cum Spíritu Paráclito
in sempitérna sǽcula. Amen.

Psalmodia

Ant. 1 Repléti sumus mane misericórdia tua, Dómine.

Week IV

Monday, Lauds

HYMN Trans. The Benedictine Nuns, St. Cecilia's Abbey

O lavish Giver of the light
That bathes the world in dawning glow;
The daylight cheers our hearts again
When sombre hours of night are past.

You are the world's true Morning Star,
Compared with whom the eager gleam
That heralds in the dawning light
Is but a timid, narrow ray.

True Light itself, Eternal Day,
You are far brighter than the sun,
Illuminating with your grace
The deep recesses of each heart.

And may our purity of mind
Suppress what lower nature claims,
So that our bodies too may be
The Holy Spirit's spotless shrine,

O Christ our King and tender Lord,
All glory ever be to you,
Who with the Holy Spirit reign
With God the Father's might supreme.
Amen.

PSALMODY

Ant. 1 We have been satisfied in the morning with Thy steadfast love, O Lord.

Psalmus 89 (90)

1 Dómine, refúgium factus es nobis *
a generatióne in generatiónem.
2 Priúsquam montes nasceréntur †
aut gignerétur terra et orbis, *
a sǽculo et usque in sǽculum tu es Deus.

3 Redúcis hóminem in púlverem; *
et dixísti: « Revertímini, fílii hóminum ».
4 Quóniam mille anni ante óculos tuos tamquam
dies hestérna, quæ prætériit, *
et custódia in nocte.
5 Auferes eos, sómnium erunt: *
6 mane sicut herba succréscens,
mane floret et crescit, *
véspere décidit et aréscit.

7 Quia defécimus in ira tua *
et in furóre tuo turbáti sumus.
8 Posuísti iniquitátes nostras in conspéctu tuo, *
occúlta nostra in illuminatióne vultus tui.

9 Quóniam omnes dies nostri evanuérunt in ira
tua, *
consúmpsimus ut suspírium annos nostros.
10 Dies annórum nostrórum sunt septuagínta anni *
aut in valéntibus octogínta anni,
et maior pars eórum labor et dolor, *
quóniam cito tránseunt, et avolámus.
11 Quis novit potestátem iræ tuæ *
et secúndum timórem tuum indignatiónem
tuam?
12 Dinumeráre dies nostros sic doce nos, *
ut inducámus cor ad sapiéntiam.

Psalm 90

1 LORD, thou hast been our dwelling place
in all generations.
2 Before the mountains were brought forth,
or ever thou hadst formed the earth and the world,
from everlasting to everlasting thou art God.

3 Thou turnest man back to the dust,
and sayest, "Turn back, O children of men!"
4 For a thousand years in thy sight
are but as yesterday when it is
past, or as a watch in the night.

5 Thou dost sweep men away; they are like a dream
like grass which is renewed in the morning:
6 in the morning it flourishes and is renewed;
in the evening it fades and withers.

7 For we are consumed by thy anger;
by thy wrath we are overwhelmed.
8 Thou hast set our iniquities before thee,
our secret sins in the light of thy countenance.

9 For all our days pass away under thy wrath,
our years come to an end like a sigh.
10 The years of our life are threescore and ten,
or even by reason of strength fourscore;
yet their span is but toil and trouble;
they are soon gone, and we fly away.

11 Who considers the power of thy anger,
and thy wrath according to the fear of thee?
12 So teach us to number our days
that we may get a heart of wisdom.

13 Convértere, Dómine, úsquequo? *
Et deprecábilis esto super servos tuos.
14 Reple nos mane misericórdia tua, *
et exsultábimus et delectábimur ómnibus diébus nostris.
15 Lætífica nos pro diébus, quibus nos humiliásti, *
pro annis, quibus vídimus mala.

16 Appáreat servis tuis opus tuum *
et decor tuus fíliis eórum.
17 Et sit splendor Dómini Dei nostri super nos, †
et ópera mánuum nostrárum confírma super nos *
et opus mánuum nostrárum confírma.

Ant. Repléti sumus mane misericórdia tua, Dómine.
Ant. 2 Laus Dómini ab extrémis terræ.

Canticum Is 42, 10–16

10 Cantáte Dómino cánticum novum, *
laus eius ab extrémis terræ;
qui descénditis in mare et plenitúdo eius, *
ínsulæ et habitatóres eárum.

11 Exsúltent desértum et civitátes eius, *
vici, quos hábitat Cedar.
Iúbilent habitatóres Petræ, *
de vértice móntium clament.
12 Ponant Dómino glóriam *
et laudem eius in ínsulis núntient.

13 Dóminus sicut fortis egrediétur *
sicut vir prœliátor suscitábit zelum;

13 Return, O LORD! How long?
Have pity on thy servants!
14 Satisfy us in the morning with thy steadfast love,
that we may rejoice and be glad all our days.
15 Make us glad as many days as thou hast afflicted us,
and as many years as we have seen evil.
16 Let thy work be manifest to thy servants,
and thy glorious power to their children.
17 Let the favor of the Lord our God be upon us,
and establish thou the work of our hands upon us,
yea, the work of our hands establish thou it.

Ant. 1 We have been satisfied in the morning with Thy steadfast love, O Lord.
Ant. 2 The Lord's praise is from the end of the earth.

Canticle Isaiah 42:10–16

10 Sing to the Lord a new song,
his praise from the end of the earth!
Let the sea roar and all that fills it,
the coastlands and their inhabitants.
11 Let the desert and its cities lift up their voice,
the villages that Kedar inhabits;
let the inhabitants of Sela sing for joy,
let them shout from the top of the mountains.
12 Let them give glory to the Lord,
and declare his praise in the coastlands.
13 The Lord goes forth like a mighty man,
like a man of war he stirs up his fury;

vociferábitur et conclamábit, *
super inimícos suos prævalébit.
14 « Tácui semper, sílui, pátiens fui; †
sicut partúriens ululábo, *
gemam et fremam simul.
15 Desértos fáciam montes et colles *
et omne gramen eórum exsiccábo;
et ponam flúmina in ínsulas *
et stagna arefáciam.
16 Et ducam cæcos in viam, quam nésciunt, *
et in sémitis, quas ignoravérunt, ambuláre eos fáciam;
ponam ténebras coram eis in lucem *
et prava in recta ».

Ant. Laus Dómini ab extrémis terræ.
Ant. 3 Laudáte nomen Dómini, qui statis in domo Dómini.

Psalmus 134 (135), 1–12

1 Laudáte nomen Dómini, *
laudáte, servi Dómini,
2 qui statis in domo Dómini, *
in átriis domus Dei nostri.

3 Laudáte Dóminum, quia bonus Dóminus; *
psállite nómini eius, quóniam suáve.

he cries out, he shouts aloud,
he shows himself mighty against his foes.

14 For a long time I have held my peace,
I have kept still and restrained myself;
now I will cry out like a woman in travail,
I will gasp and pant.
15 I will lay waste mountains and hills,
and dry up all their herbage;
I will turn the rivers into islands,
and dry up the pools.
16 And I will lead the blind
in a way that they know not,
in paths that they have not known
I will guide them.
I will turn the darkness before them into light,
the rough places into level ground.
These are the things I will do,
and I will not forsake them.

Ant. 2 The Lord's praise is from the end of the earth.
Ant. 3 Praise the name of the Lord, you that stand in the house of the Lord.

Psalm 135:1–12

1 Praise the LORD!
Praise the name of the LORD,
give praise, O servants of the LORD,
2 you that stand in the house of the LORD,
in the courts of the house of our God!
3 Praise the LORD, for the LORD is good;
sing to his name, for he is gracious!

4 Quóniam Iacob elégit sibi Dóminus, *
Israel in pecúlium sibi.

5 Quia ego cognóvi quod magnus est Dóminus *
et Deus noster præ ómnibus diis.
6 Omnia, quæcúmque vóluit, †
Dóminus fecit in cælo et in terra, *
in mari et in ómnibus abýssis.
7 Addúcens nubes ab extrémo terræ, †
fúlgura in plúviam facit, *
prodúcit ventos de thesáuris suis.
8 Qui percússit primogénita Ægýpti *
ab hómine usque ad pecus.
9 Misit signa et prodígia in médio tui, Ægýpte, *
in pharaónem et in omnes servos eius.
10 Qui percússit gentes multas *
et occídit reges fortes:
11 Sehon regem Amorræórum et Og regem Basan *
et ómnia regna Chánaan.
12 Et dedit terram eórum hereditátem, *
hereditátem Israel pópulo suo.

Ant. Laudáte nomen Dómini, qui statis in domo Dómini.

LECTIO BREVIS — IUDT 8, 25–26A. 27

Grátias agámus Dómino Deo nostro, qui temptat nos sicut et patres nostros. Mémores estóte quanta fécerit cum Abraham et Isaac, et quanta facta sint Iacob. Quia

4 For the LORD has chosen Jacob for himself,
Israel as his own possession.

5 For I know that the LORD is great,
and that our Lord is above all gods.
6 Whatever the LORD pleases he does,
in heaven and on earth,
in the seas and all deeps.
7 He it is who makes the clouds rise at the end of the earth,
who makes lightnings for the rain
and brings forth the wind from his storehouses.

8 He it was who smote the first-born of Egypt,
both of man and of beast;
9 who in thy midst, O Egypt,
sent signs and wonders
against Pharaoh and all his servants;
10 who smote many nations
and slew mighty kings,
11 Sihon, king of the Amorites,
and Og, king of Bashan,
and all the kingdoms of Canaan,
12 and gave their land as a heritage,
a heritage to his people Israel.

Ant. 3 Praise the name of the Lord, you that stand in the house of the Lord.

SHORT READING Judith 8:25–26a, 27

Let us give thanks to the Lord our God, who is putting us to the test as he did our forefathers. Remember what he did with Abraham, and how he tested Isaac, and

non sicut illos combússit in inquisitiónem cordis illórum et in nos non ultus est, sed in monitiónem flagéllat Dóminus appropinquántes sibi.

Responsorium Breve

℟. Exsultáte, iusti, in Dómino; * Rectos decet collaudátio. Exsultáte.
℣. Cantáte ei cánticum novum. * Rectos decet collaudátio. Glória Patri. Exsultáte.

Ad Benedictus, ant. Benedíctus Dóminus, quia visitávit et liberávit nos.

Preces

Christum, qui exáudit et salvos facit sperántes in se, precémur acclamántes: *Te laudámus, in te sperámus, Dómine.*

Grátias ágimus tibi, qui dives es in misericórdia,
—propter nímiam caritátem, qua dilexísti nos.

Qui omni témpore in mundo cum Patre operáris,
—nova fac ómnia per Spíritus Sancti virtútem.

Aperi óculos nostros et fratrum nostrórum,
—ut videámus hódie mirabília tua.

Qui nos hódie ad tuum servítium vocas,
—nos erga fratres multifórmis grátiæ tuæ facinístros.

Pater noster.

what happened to Jacob. For he has not tried us with fire, as he did them, to search their hearts, nor has he taken revenge upon us; but the Lord scourges those who draw near to him, in order to admonish them.

SHORT RESPONSORY

℞. Rejoice, you just, in the Lord; praise befits the upright.
℣. Sing to Him a new song.

Benedictus ant. Blessed be the Lord, for He has visited and freed us.

INTERCESSIONS

To Christ, Who hears and saves those who hope in Him, let us pray acclaiming: *We praise You; in You we hope, O Lord.*

We give thanks to You, Who are rich in mercy,
—on account of Your abundant charity, with which You love us.

You that work with the Father at all times in the world,
—make all things new through the strength of the Holy Spirit.

Open our eyes and those of our brothers,
—that today we might see your wonders.

You that call us today to Your service,
—make us ministers of Your manifold grace toward our brothers.

Our Father.

Oratio

Deus, qui custodiéndam colendámque terram homínibus commisísti, ac solem fecísti eórum úsui deservíre, concéde nos hódie in tuam glóriam et proximórum bonum, te donánte, fidéliter operári. Per Dóminum.

ORATION

O God, Who have committed the earth to the keeping and cultivation of men, and Who made the sun to serve their use, grant us today, by Your grace, to work faithfully, for Your glory and for the good of our neighbors. Through our Lord.

Hebdomada IV

Feria II, ad Vesperas

Hymn

Lúminis fons, lux et orígo lucis,
tu pius nostris précibus favéto,
luxque, peccáti ténebris fugátis,
nos tu*a* adórnet.

Ecce transáctus labor est diéi,
teque nos tuti sumus adnuénte;
en tibi grates ágimus libéntes
tempus in omne.

Solis abscéssus ténebras redúxit:
ille sol nobis rádiet corúscus
luce qui fulva fovet angelórum
ágmina sancta.

Quas dies culpas hodiérna texit,
Christus deléto pius atque mitis,
pectus et puro rútilet nitóre
témpore noctis.

Laus tibi Patri, decus atque Nato,
Flámini Sancto párilis potéstas,
cuncta qui sceptro régitis suprémo
omne per ævum. Amen.

Psalmodia

Ant. 1 Confitémini Dómino, quóniam in ætérnum misericórdia eius.

Monday, Vespers

HYMN Trans. The Benedictine Nuns, St. Cecilia's Abbey

O Fount of light, True Light itself,
Smile down on us as here we pray.
May Your bright splendor shine on us,
When shades of sin are cast away

We thank you for Your loving care
While work and toil have been our lot,
And now that day its near its close,
Dear Lord, we pray, forsake us not.

Though sun declines and shadows fall,
Our souls draw light from those fair rays
The Sun of Justice ne'er withholds,
On Whom the hosts of angels gaze.

May all the faults which we deplore,
Be washed away by Christ our Light,
And may He purify our hearts
Throughout the hours of coming night.

All glory, Father, be to You,
Praise to the Spirit and the Son,
Who rule all things with pow'r supreme
Till all created time is done. Amen.

PSALMODY

Ant. 1 O give thanks to the Lord, for His steadfast love endures forever.

Psalmus 135 (136)

I

1 Confitémini Dómino, quóniam bonus, *
quóniam in ætérnum misericórdia eius.
2 Confitémini Deo deórum, *
quóniam in ætérnum misericórdia eus.
3 Confitémini Dómino dominórum, *
quóniam in ætérnum misericórdia eius.
4 Qui facit mirabília magna solus, *
quóniam in ætérnum misericórdia eius.
5 Qui fecit cælos in intelléctu, *
quóniam in ætérnum misericórdia eius.
6 Qui expándit terram super aquas, *
quóniam in ætérnum misericórdia eius.
7 Qui fecit luminária magna, *
quóniam in ætérnum misericórdia eius;
8 solem, ut præésset diéi, *
quóniam in ætérnum misericórdia eius;
9 lunam et stellas, ut præéssent nocti, *
quóniam in ætérnum misericórdia eius.

Ant. Confitémini Dómino, quóniam in ætérnum misericórdia eius.
Ant. 2 Magna et mirabília sunt ópera tua, Dómine Deus omnípotens.

II

10 Qui percússit Ægýptum in primogénitis eórum, *
quóniam in ætérnum misericórdia eius.
11 Qui edúxit Israel de médio eórum, *
quóniam in ætérnum misericórdia eius;

Psalm 136

I

1 O give thanks to the Lord, for he is good,
for his steadfast love endures for ever.
2 O give thanks to the God of gods,
for his steadfast love endures for ever.
3 O give thanks to the Lord of lords,
for his steadfast love endures for ever;

4 to him who alone does great wonders,
for his steadfast love endures for ever;
5 to him who by understanding made the heavens,
for his steadfast love endures for ever;
6 to him who spread out the earth upon the waters,
for his steadfast love endures for ever;
7 to him who made the great lights,
for his steadfast love endures for ever;
8 the sun to rule over the day,
for his steadfast love endures for ever;
9 the moon and stars to rule over the night,
for his steadfast love endures for ever;

Ant. 1 O give thanks to the Lord, for his steadfast love endures forever.
Ant. 2 Great and wonderful are Thy works, O Lord God almighty.

II

10 to him who smote the first-born of Egypt,
for his steadfast love endures for ever;
11 and brought Israel out from among them,
for his steadfast love endures for ever;

12 in manu poténti et bráchio exténto, *
quóniam in ætérnum misericórdia eius.
13 Qui divísit mare Rubrum in divisiónes, *
quóniam in ætérnum misericórdia eius.
14 Et tradúxit Israel per médium eius, *
quóniam in ætérnum misericórdia eius.
15 Et excússit pharaónem et virtútem eius in mari Rubro, *
quóniam in ætérnum misericórdia eius.
16 Qui tradúxit pópulum suum per desértum, *
quóniam in ætérnum misericórdia eius.
17 qui percússit reges magnos, *
quóniam in ætérnum misericórdia eius;
18 et occídit reges poténtes, *
quóniam in ætérnum misericórdia eius.
19 Sehon regem Amorræórum, *
quóniam in ætérnum misericórdia eius;
20 et Og regem Basan, *
quóniam in ætérnum misericórdia eius.
21 Et dedit terram eórum hereditátem, *
quóniam in ætérnum misericórdia eius;
22 hereditátem Israel servo suo *,
quóniam in ætérnum misericórdia eius.
23 Qui in humilitáte nostra memor fuit nostri, *
quóniam in ætérnum misericórdia eius;
24 et redémit nos ab inimícis nostris, *
quóniam in ætérnum misericórdia eius.
25 Qui dat escam omni carni, *
quóniam in ætérnum misericórdia eius.
26 Confitémini Deo cæli, *
quóniam in ætérnum misericórdia eius.

12 with a strong hand and an outstretched arm,
for his steadfast love endures for ever;
13 to him who divided the Red Sea in sunder,
for his steadfast love endures for ever;
14 and made Israel pass through the midst of it,
for his steadfast love endures for ever;
15 but overthrew Pharaoh and his host in the Red
Sea,
for his steadfast love endures for ever;
16 to him who led his people through the wilderness,
for his steadfast love endures for ever;
17 to him who smote great kings,
for his steadfast love endures for ever;
18 and slew famous kings,
for his steadfast love endures for ever;
19 Sihon, king of the Amorites,
for his steadfast love endures for ever;
20 and Og, king of Bashan,
for his steadfast endures for ever;
21 and gave their land as a heritage,
for his steadfast endures for ever;
22 a heritage to Israel his servant,
for his steadfast love endures for ever.

23 It is he who remembered us in our low estate,
for his steadfast love endures for ever;
24 and rescued us from our foes,
for his steadfast love endures for ever;
25 he who gives food to all flesh,
for his steadfast love endures for ever.
26 O give thanks to the God of heaven,
for his steadfast love endures for ever.

Ant. Magna et mirabília sunt ópera tua, Dómine Deus omnípotens.

Ant. 3 Propósuit Deum in plenitúdine témporum instauráre ómnia in Christo.

Canticum Eph 1, 3–10

3 Benedíctus Deus et Pater Dómini nostri Iesu Christi, *
qui benedíxit nos in omni benedictióne spiritáli in cæléstibus in Christo,
4 sicut elégit nos in ipso ante mundi constitutiónem, †
ut essémus sancti et immaculáti *
in conspéctu eius in caritáte,
5 qui prædestinávit nos in adoptiónem filiórum †
per Iesum Christum in ipsum, *
secúndum beneplácitum voluntátis suæ,
6 in laudem glóriæ grátiæ suæ, *
in qua gratificávit nos in Dilécto,
7 in quo habémus redemptiónem per sánguinem eius, *
remissiónem peccatórum,
secúndum divítias grátiæ eius, †
8 qua superabundávit in nobis *
in omni sapiéntia et prudéntia
9 notum fáciens nobis mystérium voluntátis suæ, *
secúndum beneplácitum eius,
quod propósuit in eo, *
10 in dispensatiónem plenitúdinis témporum:
recapituláre ómnia in Christo, *
quæ in cælis et quæ in terra.

Ant. 2 Great and wonderful are Thy works, O Lord God almighty.
Ant. 3 God planned to restore all things in Christ in the fulness of time.

Canticle Ephesians 1:3–10

3 Blessed be the God and Father of our Lord Jesus Christ, who has blessed us in Christ with every spiritual blessing in the heavenly places,
4 even as he chose us in him before the foundation of the world, that we should be holy and blameless before him.
5 He destined us in love to be his sons through Jesus Christ, according to the purpose of his will,
6 to the praise of his glorious grace which he freely bestowed on us in the Beloved.
7 In him we have redemption through his blood, the forgiveness of our trespasses, according to the riches of his grace
8 which he lavished upon us.
9 For he has made known to us in all wisdom and insight the mystery of his will, according to his purpose which he set forth in Christ
10 as a plan for the fulness of time, to unite all things in him, things in heaven and things on earth.

Ant. Propósuit Deus in plenitúdine témporum instauráre ómnia in Christo.

LECTIO BREVIS 1 TH 3, 12–13

Vos Dóminus abundáre et superabundáre fáciat caritáte in ínvicem et in omnes, quemádmodum et nos in vos, ad confirmánda corda vestra sine queréla in sanctitáte ante Deum et Patrem nostrum, in advéntu Dómini nostri Iesu cum ómnibus sanctis eius.

RESPONSORIUM BREVE

℟. Dirigátur, Dómine, * Ad te orátio mea. Dirigátur.
℣. Sicut incénsum in conspéctu tuo. * Ad te orátio mea. Glória Patri. Dirigátur.

Ad Magnificat, ant. Magníficet te semper ánima mea, Deus meus.

PRECES

Iesum, qui sperántes in se non derelínquit, húmili deprecatióne rogémus: *Deus noster, exáudi nos.*

Illuminátor noster, Christe Dómine, Ecclésiam tuam illústra lúmine tuo,
—ut géntibus prædicet te, magnum pietátis sacraméntum, manifestátum in carne.

Sacerdótes et minístros Ecclésiæ tuæ serva,
—ut, cum áliis prædicáverint, ipsi fidéles in tuo servítio inveniántur.

Qui pacem mundo præstitísti per sánguinem tuum,
—discórdiæ peccátum et belli flagéllum avérte.

Ant. 3 God planned to restore all things in Christ in the fulness of time.

SHORT READING 1 Thessalonians 3:12–13

And may the Lord make you increase and abound in love to one another and to all men, as we do to you, so that he may establish your hearts unblamable in holiness before our God and Father, at the coming of our Lord Jesus with all his saints.

SHORT RESPONSORY

℟. May my prayer, O Lord, come before You.

℣. Like incense in Your sight.

Magnificat ant. May my soul always magnify You, my God.

INTERCESSIONS

To Jesus, Who deserts not those who hope in Him, let us humbly make our prayer: *Our God, hear us.*

O Christ our Lord, Who enlighten us, illuminate Your Church with Your light,
—that she might proclaim to the nations the great sacrament of loving-kindness made manifest in the flesh.

Protect the priests and ministers of Your Church,
—that having preached to others, they may be found faithful in Your service.

You that have given peace to the world through Your blood,
—turn away the sin of discord and the scourge of war.

Grátiæ tuæ cópia coniugátis auxiliáre,
—quo perféctius signíficent Ecclésiæ tuæ mystérium.
Omnibus concéde defúnctis véniam peccatórum,
—ut per misericórdiam tuam inter sanctos respírent.

Pater noster.

Oratio

Mane nobíscum, Dómine Iesu, quóniam advesperáscit, et nos cómitans in via, réfove corda, spem éxcita miserátus, ut te in Scriptúris et in fractióne panis cum nostris frátribus agnoscámus. Qui vivis.

By the fullness of Your grace, come to the aid of married couples,
—that they may signify more perfectly the mystery of Your Church.
Grant pardon of sins to all the deceased,
—that through Your mercy, they may rest among the saints.

Our Father.

ORATION

Stay with us, Lord Jesus, for evening approaches, and as You accompany us on the way, in Your mercy, refresh our hearts and mercifully stir up hope, so that we, with our brothers, may recognize You in the Scriptures and in the breaking of the bread. Through our Lord.

Hebdomada IV

Feria III, ad Laudes matutinas

Hymn

Ætérne lucis cónditor,
lux ipse totus et dies,
noctem nec ullam séntiens
natúra lucis pérpeti,

Iam cedit pallens próximo
diéi nox advéntui,
obtúndens lumen síderum
adest et clarus lúcifer.

Iam stratis læti súrgimus
grates canéntes et tuas,
quod cæcam noctem vícerit
revéctans rursus sol diem.

Te nunc, ne carnis gáudia
blandis subrépant æstibus,
dolis ne cedat sǽculi
mens nostra, sancte, quǽsumus.

Ira ne rixas próvocet,
gulam ne venter íncitet,
opum pervértat ne famis,
turpis ne luxus óccupet,

Sed firma mente sóbrii,
casto manéntes córpore
totum fidéli spíritu
Christo ducámus hunc diem.

Week IV

Tuesday, Lauds

HYMN Trans. The Benedictine Nuns, St. Cecilia's Abbey

Eternal Maker of the light,
True Light itself, surpassing day,
No gloom or darkness can you know,
In your own light which has no end.

Pale shades of night are yielding fast,
Before the bold advance of day;
Resplendent shines the morning star
While other constellations fade.

We gladly rise to sing Your praise,
And thank You with renewed delight,
That rising sun brings back the day,
To conquer night's obscurity.

Most Holy One, we beg of You
Let not our souls be led astray,
By nature's pleasures and desires
Or by the world's deceiving glare.

Let no contention raise disputes,
Nor greed disgrace a Christian's name,
Nor greed for riches be a snare,
Nor evil thoughts corrupt our minds.

But let us show well-governed souls,
Within a body chaste and pure,
To spend this day in work and prayer,
For Christ our Leader and our Lord.

Præsta, Pater piíssime,
Patríque compar Unice,
cum Spíritu Paráclito
regnans per omne sæculum. Amen.

PSALMODIA

Ant. 1 Tibi, Dómine, psallam, et intéllegam in via immaculáta.

Psalmus 100 (101)

1 Misericórdiam et iudícium cantábo; *
tibi, Dómine, psallam.
2 Intéllegam in via immaculáta; *
quando vénies ad me?

Perambulábo in innocéntia cordis mei, *
in médio domus meæ.
3 Non propónam ante óculos meos rem iniústam, †
faciéntem prævaricatiónes ódio habébo, *
non adhærébit mihi.

4 Cor pravum recédet a me, *
malígnum non cognóscam.
5 Detrahéntem secréto próximo suo, *
hunc cessáre fáciam;
supérbum óculo et inflátum corde, *
hunc non sustinébo.

6 Oculi mei ad fidéles terræ, ut sédeant mecum; *
qui ámbulat in via immaculáta, hic mihi ministrábit.

Most loving Father, hear our prayer
Through Jesus Christ Your only Son,
Who, with the Spirit, reigns with You,
Eternal Trinity in one. Amen.

PSALMODY

Ant. 1 To Thee, O Lord, I will sing and I will give heed to the way that is blameless.

Psalm 101

1 I will sing of loyalty and of justice;
to thee, O LORD, I will sing.
2 I will give heed to the way that is blameless.
Oh, when wilt thou come to me?
I will walk with integrity of heart
within my house;
3 I will not set before my eyes
anything that is base.

I hate the work of those who fall away;
it shall not cleave to me.
4 Perverseness of heart shall be far from me;
I will know nothing of evil.

5 Him who slanders his neighbor secretly
I will destroy.
The man of haughty looks and arrogant heart
I will not endure.

6 I will look with favor on the faithful in the land,
that they may dwell with me;
he who walks in the way that is blameless
shall minister to me.

7 Non habitábit in médio domus meæ, qui facit superbiam; *
qui lóquitur iníqua, non stabit in conspéctu oculórum meórum.
8 In matutíno cessáre fáciam omnes peccatóres terræ, *
ut dispérdam de civitáte Dómini omnes operántes iniquitátem.

Ant. Tibi, Dómine, psallam, et intéllegam in via immaculáta.
Ant. 2 Ne áuferas, Dómine, misericórdiam tuam a nobis.

Canticum DAN 3, 26. 27. 29. 34–41

26 Benedíctus es, Dómine, Deus patrum nostrórum, *
et laudábilis et gloriósum nomen tuum in sǽcula,
27 quia iustus es in ómnibus, *
quæ fecísti nobis.
29 Peccávimus enim et iníque égimus recedéntes a te *
et delíquimus in ómnibus.
34 Ne, quǽsumus, tradas nos in perpétuum propter nomen tuum *
et ne díssipes testaméntum tuum,
35 neque áuferas misericórdiam tuam a nobis †
propter Abraham diléctum tuum *
et Isaac servum tuum et Israel sanctum tuum,

7 No man who practices deceit
shall dwell in my house;
no man who utters lies
shall continue in my presence.

8 Morning by morning I will destroy
all the wicked in the land,
cutting off all the evildoers
from the city of the Lord.

Ant. 1 To Thee, O Lord, I will sing, and I will give heed to the way that is blameless.
Ant. 2 Do not withdraw Thy mercy from us, O Lord.

Canticle Daniel 3:3, 4, 6, 11–18

3 "Blessed art thou, O Lord, God of our fathers, and worthy of praise;
and thy name is glorified for ever.
4 For thou art just in all that thou hast done to us,
and all thy works are true and thy ways right,
and all thy judgments are truth.

6 For we have sinfully and lawlessly departed from thee,
and have sinned in all things and have not obeyed thy commandments;

11 For thy name's sake do not give us up utterly,
and do not break thy covenant,
12 and do not withdraw thy mercy from us,
for the sake of Abraham, thy beloved,
and for the sake of Isaac, thy servant,
and Israel, thy holy one,

36 quibus dixísti quod multiplicáres semen eórum *
sicut stellas cæli et sicut arénam, quæ est in lítore
maris,

37 quia, Dómine, imminúti sumus plus quam omnes
gentes *
sumúsque húmiles in univérsa terra hódie
propter peccáta nostra;

38 et non est in témpore hoc †
princeps et prophéta et dux, *
neque holocáustum neque sacrifícium,
neque oblátio neque incénsum, †
neque locus primitiárum coram te, *
ut possímus inveníre misericórdiam;
39 sed in ánima contríta et spíritu humilitátis
suscipiámur †
sicut in holocáusto aríetum et taurórum *
40 et sicut in mílibus agnórum pínguium, sic fiat
sacrifícium nostrum
in conspéctu tuo hódie, †
et pérfice subsequéntes te, *
quóniam non est confúsio confidéntibus in te.

41 Et nunc séquimur te in toto corde *
et timémus te et quærimus fáciem tuam.

Ant. Ne áuferas, Dómine, misericórdiam tuam a nobis.
Ant. 3 Deus, cánticum novum cantábo tibi.

13 to whom thou didst promise
to make their descendants as many as the stars of heaven
and as the sand on the shore of the sea.
14 For we, O Lord, have become fewer than any nation,
and are brought low this day in all the world because of our sins.
15 And at this time there is no prince, or prophet, or leader,
no burnt offering, or sacrifice, or oblation, or incense
no place to make an offering before thee or to find mercy.
16 Yet with a contrite heart and a humble spirit may we be accepted,
as though it were with burnt offerings of rams and bulls,
and with tens of thousands of fat lambs;
17 such may our sacrifice be in thy sight this day,
and may we wholly follow thee,
for there will be no shame for those who trust in thee.
18 And now with all our heart we follow thee,
we fear thee and seek thy face.

Ant. 2 Do not withdraw Thy mercy from us, O Lord.

Ant. 3 O God, to Thee will I sing a new song.

Psalmus 143 (144), 1–10

1 Benedíctus Dóminus, adiútor meus, †
qui docet manus meas ad prœlium *
et dígitos meos ad bellum.
2 Misericórdia mea et fortitúdo mea, *
refúgium meum et liberátor meus;
scutum meum, et in ipso sperávi, *
qui subdit pópulum meum sub me.

3 Dómine, quid est homo, quod agnóscis eum, *
aut fílius hóminis, quod réputas eum?
4 Homo vanitáti símilis factus est, *
dies eius sicut umbra prætériens.

5 Dómine, inclína cælos tuos et descénde; *
tange montes, et fumigábunt.
6 Fúlgura coruscatiónem et díssipa eos; *
emítte sagíttas tuas et contúrba eos.
7 Emítte manum tuam de alto; *
éripe me et líbera me de aquis multis,
de manu filiórum alienigenárum, †
8 quorum os locútum est vanitátem, *
et déxtera eórum déxtera mendácii.

9 Deus, cánticum novum cantábo tibi, *
in psaltério decachórdo psallam tibi,
10 qui das salútem régibus, *
qui rédimis David servum tuum de gládio malígno.

Ant. Deus, cánticum novum cantábo tibi.

Psalm 144:1–10

1 Blessed be the LORD, my rock,
who trains my hands for war,
and my fingers for battle;
2 my rock and my fortress,
my stronghold and my deliverer,
my shield and he in whom I take refuge,
who subdues the peoples under him.

3 O Lord, what is man that thou dost regard him,
or the son of man that thou dost think of him?
4 Man is like a breath,
his days are like a passing shadow.

5 Bow thy heavens, O LORD, and come down!
Touch the mountains that they smoke!
6 Flash forth the lightning and scatter them,
send out thy arrows and rout them!
7 Stretch forth thy hand from on high,
rescue me and deliver me from the many
waters,
from the hand of aliens,
8 whose mouths speak lies,
and whose right hand is a right hand of
falsehood.

9 I will sing a new song to thee, O God;
upon a ten-stringed harp I will play to thee,
10 who givest victory to kings,
who rescuest David thy servant.

Ant. 3 O God, to Thee will I sing a new song.

LECTIO BREVIS Is 55, 1

Omnes sitiéntes, veníte ad aquas; et, qui non habétis argéntum, properáte, émite et comédite, veníte, émite absquo argénto et absquo ulla commutatióne vinum et lac.

RESPONSORIUM BREVE

℟. Vocem meam audi, Dómine; * In verba tua supersperávi. Vocem.

℣. Prævéni dilúculo et clamávi. * In verba tua supersperávi. Glória Patri. Vocem.

Ad Benedictus, ant. De manu ómnium qui odérunt nos, salva nos, Dómine.

PRECES

Deus, lætítiam nobis concédens hoc matutíno témpore eum laudándi, spem róborat nostram. Ideo fidénter ipsi supplicémus: *Ad glóriam nóminis tui, audi nos, Dómine.*

Grátias ágimus tibi, Deus et Pater Salvatóris nostri Iesu,
—pro cognitióne et immortalitáte, quas dedísti nobis per ipsum.

Concéde humilitátem córdibus nostris,
—ut subiécti simus ínvicem in timóre Christi.

Spíritum tuum nobis fámulis tuis infúnde,
—ut diléctio nostra fratérna sine simulatióne fiat.

SHORT READING

Isaiah 55:1

1 "Ho, every one who thirsts,
come to the waters;
and he who has no money,
come, buy and eat!
Come, buy wine and milk
without money and without price."

SHORT RESPONSORY

℟. Lord, hear my voice; I have trusted in Your words.
℣. At dawn I watched and cried out.

Benedictus ant. From the hand of all who hate us, save us, O Lord.

INTERCESSIONS

God, granting us the joy of praising Him this morning time, strengthens our hope. So let us faithfully entreat Him: *To the glory of Your name, hear us, O Lord.*

We give You thanks, God and Father of our Savior, Jesus,
—for the knowledge and immortality which You have given us through Him.

Grant humility to our hearts,
—that in turn, we might be subjected to one another in the fear of Christ.

Pour out Your Spirit on us Your servants,
—that our fraternal love might be without pretense.

Qui hómini labórem præcepísti in mundi dominatiónem,
—concéde, ut labor noster te célebret fratrésque nostros sanctíficet.

Pater noster.

ORATIO

Auge in nobis, quǽsumus, Dómine, fidem tuam, ut in ore nostro perfécta laus tua cæléstes iúgiter áfferat fructus. Per Dóminum.

You that prescribed for man work in the dominion of the world,
—grant that our work might celebrate You and sanctify our brothers.

Our Father.

ORATION

Increase in us, we ask, O Lord, Your faith, that Your perfect praise in our mouth might constantly bear heavenly fruit. Through our Lord.

Feria III, ad Vesperas

Hymn

Sator princépsque témporum,
clarum diem labóribus
Noctémque qui sopóribus
fixo distínguis órdine,

Mentem tu castam dírige,
obscúra ne siléntia
ad dira cordis vúlnera
telis patéscant ínvidi.

Vacent ardóre péctora,
faces nec ullas pérferant,
quæ nostr*o* hæréntes sénsui
mentis vigórem sáucient.

Præsta, Pater piíssime,
Patríque compar Unice,
Cum Spíritu Paráclito
regnans per omne sǽculum. Amen.

Psalmodia

Ant. 1 Si oblítus fúero tui, Ierúsalem, oblivióni detur déxtera mea.

Week IV

Tuesday, Vespers

HYMN Trans. The Benedictine Nuns, St. Cecilia's Abbey

Great Ruler of all space and time,
  You give us daylight to employ
In work for You, that with the night
  Refreshing sleep we may enjoy.

While silence and the darkness reign
  Preserve our souls from sin and harm,
Let nothing evil venture near
  To cause us panic or alarm.

And while we thus renew our strength,
  Quite free from taint of sinful fire
Let hearts and minds find rest in You,
  Untroubled by ill-timed desire.

Most tender Father, hear our prayer,
  Whom we adore with Christ the Lord,
And Holy Spirit of them both;
  Bless us who praise Your Trinity.
          Amen.

PSALMODY

Ant. 1 If I forget you, O Jerusalem, let my right hand wither!

Psalmus 136 (137), 1–6

1 Super flúmina Babylónis, illic sédimus et
flévimus, *
cum recordarémur Sion.
2 In salícibus in médio eius *
suspéndimus cítharas nostras.

3 Quia illic rogavérunt nos, qui captívos duxérunt
nos, *
verba cantiónum
et, qui affligébant nos, lætítiam: *
« Cantáte nobis de cánticis Sion ».

4 Quómodo cantábimus cánticum Dómini *
in terra aliéna?
5 Si oblítus fúero tui, Ierúsalem, *
oblivióni detur déxtera mea;
6 adhæreat lingua mea fáucibus meis, *
si non memínero tui,
si non præposúero Ierúsalem *
in cápite lætítiæ meæ.

Ant. Si oblítus fúero tui, Ierúsalem, oblivióni detur déxtera mea.

Ant. 2 In conspéctu angelórum psallam tibi, Deus meus.

Psalmus 137 (138)

1 Confitébor tibi, Dómini, in toto corde meo, *
quóniam audísti verba oris mei.
In conspéctu angelórum psallam tibi, *
2 adorábo ad templum sanctum tuum;

Psalm 137:1–6

1 By the waters of Babylon, there we sat down and wept,
when we remembered Zion.
2 On the willows there
we hung up our lyres.
3 For there our captors
required of us songs,
and our tormentors, mirth, saying,
"Sing us one of the songs of Zion!"

4 How shall we sing the Lord's song
in a foreign land?
5 If I forget you, O Jerusalem,
let my right hand wither!
6 Let my tongue cleave to the roof of my mouth,
if I do not remember you,
if I do not set Jerusalem
above my highest joy!

Ant. 1 If I forget you, O Jerusalem, let my right hand wither!
Ant. 2 In the sight of the angels I will sing to You, my God.

Psalm 138

1 I give thee thanks, O LORD, with my whole heart;
before the gods I sing thy praise;
2 I bow down toward thy holy temple
and give thanks to thy name for thy steadfast love and thy faithfulness;

et confitébor nómini tuo †
propter misericórdiam tuam et veritátem tuam, *
quóniam magnificásti super omne nomen elóquium tuum.

3 In quacúmque die invocávero te, exáudi, me; *
multiplicábis in ánima mea virtútem.
4 Confitebúntur tibi, Dómine, omnes reges terræ, *
quia audiérunt elóquia oris tui.
5 Et cantábunt vias Dómini, *
quóniam magna est glória Dómini;
6 quóniam excélsus Dóminus, †
et húmilem réspicit, *
et supérbum a longe cognóscit.

7 Si ambulávero in médio tribulatiónis, vivificábis me; †
et contra iram inimicórum meórum exténdes manum tuam, *
et salvum me fáciet déxtera tua.
8 Dóminus perfíciet pro me; †
Dómine, misericórdia tua in sǽculum: *
ópera mánuum tuárum ne despícias.

Ant. In conspéctu angelórum psallam tibi, Deus meus.
Ant. 3 Dignus est Agnus qui occísus est accípere glóriam et honórem.

for thou hast exalted above everything
thy name and thy word.
3 On the day I called, thou didst answer me,
my strength of soul thou didst increase.

4 All the kings of the earth shall praise thee, O Lord,
for they have heard the words of thy mouth;
5 and they shall sing of the ways of the Lord,
for great is the glory of the LORD.
6 For though the LORD is high, he regards the lowly;
but the haughty he knows from afar.

7 Though I walk in the midst of trouble,
thou dost preserve my life;
thou dost stretch out thy hand against the wrath of my enemies,
and thy right hand delivers me.
8 The LORD will fulfil his purpose for me;
thy steadfast love, O LORD, endures for ever.
Do not forsake the work of thy hands.

Ant. 2 In the sight of the angels I will sing to You, my God.
Ant. 3 Worthy is the Lamb Who was slain to receive glory and honor.

Canticum Ap 4, 11; 5, 9. 10. 12

4,11 Dignus es, Dómine et Deus noster, *
accípere glóriam et honórem et virtútem,
quia tu creásti ómnia, *
et propter voluntátem tuam erant et creáta sunt.
5,9 Dignus es, Dómine, accípere librum *
et aperíre signácula eius,
quóniam occísus es †
et redemísti Deo in sánguine tuo *
ex omni tribu et lingua et pópulo et natióne
10 et fecísti eos Deo nostro regnum et sacerdótes, *
et regnábunt super terram.
12 Dignus est Agnus, qui occísus est, †
accípere virtútem et divítias et sapiéntiam *
et fortitúdinem et honórem et glóriam et
benedictiónem.

Ant. Dignus est Agnus qui occísus est accípere glóriam et honórem.

Lectio Brevis Col 3, 16

Verbum Christi hábitet in vobis abundánter, in omni sapiéntia docéntes et commonéntes vosmetípsos psalmis, hymnis, cánticis spiritálibus, in grátia cantántes in córdibus vestris Deo.

Responsorium Breve

℟. Adimplébis me lætítia * Cum vultu tuo, Dómine. Adimplébis.
℣. Delectatiónes in déxtera tua usque in finem. * Cum vultu tuo, Dómine. Glória Patri. Adimplébis.

Canticle Revelation 4:11; 5:9, 10, 12

11 "Worthy art thou, our Lord and God,
to receive glory and honor and power,
for thou didst create all things,
and by thy will they existed and were created.

9 "Worthy art thou to take the scroll and to open its seals,
for thou wast slain and by thy blood didst ransom men for God
from every tribe and tongue and people and nation,
10 and hast made them a kingdom and priests to our God,
and they shall reign on earth.

12 "Worthy is the Lamb who was slain, to receive power and wealth and wisdom and might and honor and glory and blessing!"

Ant. 3 Worthy is the Lamb Who was slain to receive glory and honor.

SHORT READING Colossians 3:16

Let the word of Christ dwell in you richly, as you teach and admonish one another in all wisdom, and as you sing psalms and hymns and spiritual songs with thankfulness in your hearts to God.

SHORT RESPONSORY

℟. You shall fill me with joy in Your presence, O Lord.

℣. Delight at Your right hand forever.

Ad Magnificat, ant. Fac nobíscum, Dómine, magna, quia potens es, et sanctum nomen tuum.

Preces

Christum, qui poténtiam et robur dat pópulo suo, exaltémus et sincéris ánimis exorémus: *Exáudi nos, Dómine, et te semper laudábimus.*

Christe, fortitúdo nostra, fidélibus tuis, quos ad tuam veritátem vocásti,
—fidem et constántiam tríbue miserátus.

Dírige secúndum cor tuum, Dómine, omnes, qui nos in potestáte regunt,
—eórum mentes dispóne, ut in pace nos ducant.

Qui turbas pánibus satiásti,
—doce nos ópibus nostris esuriéntibus subveníre.

Fac ut regéntes non ad solam suam natiónem ánimos inténdant,
—sed cunctos revereántur ac de ómnibus sint sollíciti.

Frátribus, qui dormiérunt, resurrectiónem vitámque beátam concéde,
—dum véneris glorificári in ómnibus, qui credidérunt.

Pater noster.

Oratio

Orántes in conspéctu tuo, Dómine, tuam cleméntiam implorámus, ut ea semper meditémur in córdibus, quæ tibi labiórum vócibus profitémur. Per Dóminum.

Magnificat ant. Do great things for us, O Lord, for You are mighty, and holy is Your name.

INTERCESSIONS

Let us exalt Christ, Who gives power and strength to His people, and with sincere spirits let us pray:
Hear us, O Lord, and we will praise You always.

O Christ our Strength, to Your faithful ones whom You called to Your truth,
—mercifully grant faith and constancy.

Direct according to Your heart, O Lord, all who rule over us in power,
—guide their minds that they may lead us in peace.

You that satisfied the crowds with bread,
—teach us to relieve the hungry with our own resources.

Make rulers to direct their minds not only to their own nations,
—but that they may show respect and have concern for all.

Grant to our brethren who have fallen asleep life and blessed resurrection,
—until You come to be glorified in all who have believed.

Our Father.

ORATION

Praying in Your sight, O Lord, we implore Your mercy, that we may always meditate in our hearts what we profess to You with our lips. Through our Lord.

Hebdomada IV

Feria IV, ad Laudes matutinas

HYMN

Fulgéntis auctor ætheris,
qui lunam lumen nóctibus,
solem diérum cúrsibus
certo fundásti trámite,

Nox atra iam depéllitur,
mundi nitor renáscitur,
novúsque iam mentis vigor
dulces in actus érigit.

Laudes sonáre iam tuas
dies relátus ádmonet,
vultúsque cæli blándior
nostra serénat péctora.

Vitémus omne lúbricum,
declínet prava spíritus,
vitam facta non ínquinent,
linguam culpa non ímplicet;

Sed, sol diem dum cónficit,
fides profúnda férveat,
spes ad promissa próvocet,
Christo coniúngat cáritas.

Præsta, pater piíssime,
Patrique compar Unice,
cum Spíritu Paráclito
regnans per omne sæculum. Amen.

Week IV

Wednesday, Lauds

HYMN Trans. The Benedictine Nuns, St. Cecilia's Abbey

Creator of the skies above,
The wisdom of Your plan decreed
That sun should give us light by day,
And moon should rule the hours of night.

The darkness is dispelled at last,
The world's great beauty is revealed;
Our strength of soul is fresh and keen
To spur us on to kindly deeds.

Returning day calls us to prayer,
And bids us sing Your praise anew;
The bright'ning aspect of the sky
Gives courage and serenity.

May we avoid all stain of sin,
No evil mar our thoughts this day,
No sinful action spoil our lives,
No wrong or idle words offend.

But while the sun draws on the day,
May our firm faith grow deeper yet
With hope that presses to the goal,
And love unites us all to Christ.

Most loving Father, hear our prayer
Through Jesus Christ, Your only Son,
Who, with the Spirit reigns with You,
Eternal Trinity in One. Amen.

PSALMODIA

Ant. 1 Parátum cor meum, Deus, parátum cor meum. †

Psalmus 107 (108)

2 Parátum cor meum, Deus, †
parátum cor meum, *
† cantábo et psallam. Euge, glória mea!
3 Exsúrge, psaltérium et cíthara, *
excitábo auróram.

4 Confitébor tibi in pópulis, Dómine, *
et psallam tibi in natiónibus,
5 quia magna est usque ad cælos misericórdia tua *
et usque ad nubes véritas tua.
6 Exaltáre super cælos, Deus, *
et super omnem terram glória tua.
7 Ut liberéntur dilécti tui, *
salvum fac déxtera tua et exáudi me.

8 Deus locútus est in sancto suo: †
« Exsultábo et dívidam Síchimam *
et convállem Succoth dimétiar;
9 meus est Gálaad et meus est Manásses †
et Ephraim fortitúdo cápitis mei, *
Iuda sceptrum meum.
10 Moab lebes lavácri mei; †
super Idumǽam exténdam calceaméntum meum, *
super Philistǽam vociferábor ».

11 Quis dedúcet me in civitátem munítam? *
Quis dedúcet me usque in Idumǽam?

PSALMODY

Ant. 1 My heart is steadfast, O God, my heart is steadfast!

Psalm 108

1 My heart is steadfast, O God, my heart is
steadfast!
I will sing and make melody!
Awake, my soul!
2 Awake, O harp and lyre!
I will awake the dawn!
3 I will give thanks to thee, O LORD, among the
peoples,
I will sing praises to thee among the nations.
4 For thy steadfast love is great above the heavens,
thy faithfulness reaches to the clouds.

5 Be exalted, O God, above the heavens!
Let thy glory be over all the earth!

6 That thy beloved may be delivered
give help by thy right hand, and answer me!

7 God has promised in his sanctuary:
"With exultation I will divide up Shechem,
and portion out the Vale of Succoth.
8 Gilead is mine; Manasseh is mine;
Ephraim is my helmet;
Judah my scepter.
9 Moab is my washbasin;
upon Edom I cast my shoe;
over Philistia I shout in triumph."

10 Who will bring me to the fortified city?
Who will lead me to Edom?

12 Nonne, Deus, qui reppulísti nos? *
Et non exíbis, Deus, in virtútibus nostris?
13 Da nobis auxílium de tribulatióne, *
quia vana salus hóminis.
14 In Deo faciémus virtútem, *
et ipse conculcábit inimícos nostros.

Ant. Parátum cor meum, Deus, parátum cor meum.
Ant. 2 Induit me Dóminus induménto salútis et iustítiæ.

Canticum Is 61, 10—62, 5

61,10 Gaudens gaudébo in Dómino, *
et exsultábit ánima mea in Deo meo,
quia índuit me vestiméntis salútis *
et induménto iustítiæ circúmdedit me,
quasi sponsum decorátum coróna *
et quasi sponsam ornátam monílibus suis.

11 Sicut enim terra profert germen suum †
et sicut hortus semen suum gérminat, *
sic Dóminus Deus germinábit iustítiam et
laudem coram univérsis géntibus.

62,1 Propter Sion non tacébo *
et propter Ierúsalem non quiéscam,
donec egrediátur ut splendor iustítia eius, *
et salus eius ut lampas accendátur.

2 Et vidébunt gentes iustítiam tuam *
et cuncti reges glóriam tuam;

11 Hast thou not rejected us, O God?
Thou dost not go forth, O God, with our armies.
12 O grant us help against the foe,
for vain is the help of man!
13 With God we shall do valiantly;
it is he who will tread down our foes.

Ant. 1 My heart is steadfast, O God, my heart is steadfast.
Ant. 2 The Lord has clothed me with the robe of salvation and righteousness.

Canticle Isaiah 61:10—62:5

10 I will greatly rejoice in the Lord,
my soul shall exult in my God;
for he has clothed me with the garments of salvation,
he has covered me with the robe of righteousness,
as a bridegroom decks himself with a garland,
and as a bride adorns herself with her jewels.
11 For as the earth brings forth its shoots,
and as a garden causes what is sown in it to spring up,
so the Lord God will cause righteousness and praise
to spring forth before all the nations.

62,1 For Zion's sake, I will not keep silent,
and for Jerusalem's sake I will not rest,
until her vindication goes forth as brightness,
and her salvation as a burning torch.
2 The nations shall see your vindication,
and all the kings your glory;

et vocáberis nómine novo, *
quod os Dómini nominábit.
3 Et eris coróna glóriæ in manu Dómini *
et diadéma regni in manu Dei tui.

4 Non vocáberis ultra Derelícta, *
et terra tua non vocábitur ámplius Desoláta;
sed vocáberis Beneplácitum meum in ea, *
et terra tua Nupta,
quia complácuit Dómino in te, *
et terra tua erit nupta.
5 Nam ut iúvenis uxórem ducit vírginem, *
ita ducent te fílii tui;
ut gaudet sponsus super sponsam, *
ita gaudébit super te Deus tuus.

Ant. Induit me Dóminus induménto salútis et iustítiæ.

Ant. 3 Laudábo Deum meum in vita mea.

Psalmus 145 (146)

1 Lauda, ánima mea, Dóminum; †
2 laudábo Dóminum in vita mea, *
psallam Deo meo, quámdiu fúero.

3 Nolíte confídere in princípibus, *
in fíliis hóminum, in quibus non est salus.
4 Exíbit spíritus eius et revertétur in terram suam; *
in illa die períbunt cogitatiónes eórum.

5 Beátus, cuius Deus Iacob est adiútor, *
cuius spes in Dómino Deo suo,

and you shall be called by a new name
which the mouth of the Lord will give.
3 You shall be a crown of beauty in the hand of the Lord,
and a royal diadem in the hand of your God.
4 You shall no more be termed Forsaken,
and your land shall no more be termed Desolate;
but you shall be called My delight is in her
and your land Married;
for the Lord delights in you,
and your land shall be married.
5 For as a young man marries a virgin,
so shall your sons marry you,
and as the bridegroom rejoices over the bride,
so shall your God rejoice over you.

Ant. 2 The Lord has clothed me with the robe of salvation and righteousness.

Ant. 3 I will praise the Lord as long as I live.

Psalm 146

1 Praise the LORD, O my soul!
2 I will praise the LORD as long as I live;
I will sing praises to my God while I have being.

3 Put not your trust in princes,
in a son of man, in whom there is no help.
4 When his breath departs he returns to his earth;
on that very day his plans perish.

5 Happy is he whose help is the God of Jacob,
whose hope is in the LORD his God,

6 qui fecit cælum et terram, *
mare et ómnia, quæ in eis sunt;
qui custódit veritátem in sæculum, †
7 facit iudícium oppréssis, *
dat escam esuriéntibus.

Dóminus solvit compedítos, *
8 Dóminus illúminat cæcos,
Dóminus érigit depréssos, *
Dóminus díligit iustos,
9 Dóminus custódit ádvenas, †
pupíllum et víduam susténtat *
et viam peccatórum dispérdit.
10 Regnábit Dóminus in sæcula, *
Deus tuus, Sion, in generatiónem et
generatiónem.

Ant. Laudábo Deum meum in vita mea.

LECTIO BREVIS — DEUT 4, 39-40A

Scito hódie et cogitáto in corde tuo quod Dóminus ipse sit Deus in cælo sursum et in terra deórsum, et non sit álius. Custódi præcépta eius atque mandáta, quæ ego præcípio tibi hódie.

RESPONSORIUM BREVE

℟. Benedícam Dóminum. * In omni témpore. Benedícam.
℣. Semper laus eius in ore meo. * In omni témpore. Glória Patri. Benedícam.

Ad Benedictus, ant. In sanctitáte serviámus Dómino ómnibus diébus nostris.

6 who made heaven and earth,
the sea, and all that is in them;
who keeps faith for ever;
7 who executes justice for the oppressed;
who gives food to the hungry.

The Lord sets the prisoners free;
8 the LORD opens the eyes of the blind.
The LORD lifts up those who are bowed down;
the LORD loves the righteous.
9 The LORD watches over the sojourners,
he upholds the widow and the fatherless;
but the way of the wicked he brings to ruin.

10 The LORD will reign for ever,
thy God, O Zion, to all generations.

Ant. 3 I will praise the Lord as long as I live.

SHORT READING Deuteronomy 4:39–40a

Know therefore this day, and lay it to your heart, that the Lord is God in heaven above and on the earth beneath; there is no other. Therefore, you shall keep his statutes and his commandments, which I command you this day.

SHORT RESPONSORY

℟. I shall bless the Lord at all times.
℣. His praise shall be ever on my lips.

Benedictus ant. In holiness, let us serve the Lord all the days of our life.

Preces

Christus, splendor patérnæ glóriæ, verbo suo nos illúminat. Eum amánter invocémus dicéntes:
Exáudi nos, Rex ætérnæ glóriæ.

Benedíctus es, auctor fídei nostræ et consummátor,
—qui de ténebris vocásti nos in admirábile lumen tuum.

Qui cæcórum óculos aperuísti, et surdos fecísti audíre,
—ádiuva incredulitátem nostram.

Dómine, in dilectióne tua iúgiter maneámus,
—ne ab ínvicem separémur.

Da nobis in tentatióne resístere, in tribulatióne sustinére,
—et in prósperis grátias ágere.

Pater noster.

Oratio

Memoráre, Dómine, testaménti tui sancti, quod sanguis Agni novo fœdere consecrávit, ut pópulus tuus et remissiónem obtíneat peccatórum, et ad redemptiónis indesinénter profíciat increméntum. Per Dóminum.

INTERCESSIONS

Christ, the splendor of the Father's glory, illumines us by His Word. Let us lovingly invoke Him saying: *Hear us, King of eternal glory.*

Blessed are You, author of our faith and its consummator,
—Who have called us from the darkness into Your marvelous light.

You Who opened the eyes of the blind, and made the deaf to hear,
—help our unbelief.

Lord, may we remain constantly in Your love,
—lest we be separated from one another.

Grant us to resist temptation, to stand firm in tribulation,
—and to give thanks in prosperity.

Our Father.

ORATION

Remember, O Lord, Your holy covenant, which the blood of the Lamb consecrated by a new pact, that Your people might both obtain the remission of their sins and progress unceasingly toward the increase of redemption. Through our Lord.

Hebdomada IV

Feria IV, ad Vesperas

Hymn

Sol, ecce, lentus óccidens
montes et arv*a* et ǽquora
mæstus relínquit, ínnovat
sed lucis omen crástinæ,

Mirántibus mortálibus
sic te, Creátor próvide,
leges vicésque témporum
umbris dedíss*e* et lúmini.

Ac dum, tenébris ǽthera
siléntio preméntibus,
vigor labórum déficit,
quies cupíta quǽritur,

Spe nos fidéque dívites
tui beámur lúmine
Verbi, quod est a sǽculis
splendor patérnæ gloriæ.

Est ille sol qui nésciat
ortum vel umquam vésperum;
quo terra gestit cóntegi,
quo cæl*i* in ævum iúbilant.

Hac nos seréna pérpetim
da luce tandem pérfrui
cum Nat*o* et almo Spíritu
tibi novántes cántica. Amen.

Week IV

Wednesday, Vespers

HYMN — Trans. The Benedictine Nuns, St. Cecilia's Abbey

As sun declines and shadows fall,
  The sea and hills will fade from sight;
Its fiery orb bids us farewell
  But promises tomorrow's light.

And thus, O God, Creator wise,
  You regulate in wondrous way
The laws of this great universe
  At which we marvel night and day.

While darkness rides across the sky,
  And stars their silent watches keep,
Your children leave their constant toil,
  Regaining strength by peaceful sleep.

Made rich in hope and solid faith,
  May we be blest throughout the night,
By Christ, the Word Who timeless reigns,
  True splendour of the Father's light.

He is the sun that never sets,
  No dusk can make His lustre die,
The kind Protector of the earth,
  The joy of all the saints on high.

O Father, Son, and Spirit too
  Grant us at last that light to see,
And full of joy Your praises sing,
  Bathed in Your love eternally. Amen.

PSALMODIA

Ant. 1 Mirábilis facta est sciéntia tua super me, Dómine.

Psalmus 138 (139), 1–18. 23–24

I

1 Dómine, scrutátus es et cognovísti me, *
2 tu cognovísti sessiónem meam et
resurrectiónem meam.
Intellexísti cogitatiónes meas de longe, *
3 sémitam meam et accúbitum meum investigásti.
Et omnes vias meas perspexísti, †
4 quia nondum est sermo in lingua mea, *
et ecce, Dómine, tu novísti ómnia.

5 A tergo et a fronte coartásti me *
et posuísti super me manum tuam.
6 Mirábilis nimis facta est sciéntia tua super me, *
sublímis, et non attíngam eam.

7 Quo ibo a spíritu tuo *
et quo a fácie tua fúgiam?
8 Si ascéndero in cælum, tu illic es; *
si descéndero in inférnum, ades.
9 Si súmpsero pennas auróræ *
et habitávero in extrémis maris,
10 étiam illuc manus tua dedúcet me, *
et tenébit me déxtera tua.
11 Si díxero: « Fórsitan ténebræ cómpriment me, *
et non illuminátio erit circa me »,
12 étiam ténebræ non obscurabúntur a te, †
et nox sicut dies illuminábitur *
—sicut ténebræ eius ita et lumen eius—.

PSALMODY

Ant. 1 Such knowledge is too wonderful for me, O Lord.

Psalm 139:1–18, 23–24

I

1 O LORD, thou hast searched me and known me!
2 Thou knowest when I sit down and when I rise up;
thou discernest my thoughts from afar.
3 Thou searchest out my path and my lying down,
and art acquainted with all my ways.
4 Even before a word is on my tongue,
lo, O LORD, thou knowest it altogether.

5 Thou dost beset me behind and before,
and layest thy hand upon me.
6 Such knowledge is too wonderful for me;
it is high, I cannot attain it.

7 Whither shall I go from thy Spirit?
Or whither shall I flee from thy presence?
8 If I ascend to heaven, thou art there!
If I make my bed in Sheol, thou art there!
9 If I take the wings of the morning
and dwell in the uttermost parts of the sea,
10 even there thy hand shall lead me,
and thy right hand shall hold me.
11 If I say, "Let only darkness cover me,
and the light about me be night,"
12 even the darkness is not dark to thee,
the night is bright as the day;
for darkness is as light with thee.

Ant. Mirábilis facta est sciéntia tua super me, Dómine.

Ant. 2 Ego Dóminus scrutans cor et probans renes, qui do unicuíque secúndum viam suam.

II

13 Quia tu formásti renes meos, *
contexuísti me in útero matris meæ.
14 Confitébor tibi, quia mirabíliter plasmátus sum; †
mirabília ópera tua, *
et ánima mea cognóscit nimis.

15 Non sunt abscóndita ossa mea a te, †
cum factus sum in occúlto, *
contéxtus in inferióribus terræ.
16 Imperféctum adhuc me vidérunt óculi tui, †
et in libro tuo scripti erant omnes dies: *
ficti erant, et nondum erat unus ex eis.
17 Mihi autem nimis pretiósæ cogitatiónes tuæ, Deus; *
nimis gravis summa eárum.
18 Si dinumerábo eas, super arénam multiplicabúntur; *
si ad finem pervénerim, adhuc sum tecum.

23 Scrutáre me, Deus, et scito cor meum; *
proba me et cognósce sémitas meas
24 et vide, si via vanitátis in me est, *
et deduc me in via ætérna.

Ant. Ego Dóminus scrutans cor et probans renes, qui do unicuíque secúndum viam suam.

Ant. 3 In ipso cóndita sunt univérsa, et ómnia in ipso constant.

Ant. 1 Such knowledge is too wonderful for me, O Lord.

Ant. 2 I, the Lord, search the heart and probe the mind; I give to each one as his deeds deserve.

II

13 For thou didst form my inward parts,
thou didst knit me together in my mother's womb.
14 I praise thee, for thou art fearful and wonderful.
Wonderful are thy works!
Thou knowest me right well;
15 my frame was not hidden from thee,
when I was being made in secret,
intricately wrought in the depths of the earth.
16 Thy eyes beheld my unformed substance;
in thy book were written, every one of them,
the days that were formed for me,
when as yet there was none of them.
17 How precious to me are thy thoughts, O God!
How vast is the sum of them!
18 If I would count them, they are more than the sand.
When I awake, I am still with thee.

23 Search me, O God, and know my heart!
Try me and know my thoughts!
24 And see if there be any wicked way in me,
and lead me in the way everlasting!

Ant. 2 I, the Lord, search the heart and probe the mind; I give to each one as his deeds deserve.

Ant. 3 In him all things were created, and in Him all things hold together.

Canticum CF. COL 1, 12–20

12 Grátias agámus Deo Patri, *
qui idóneos nos fecit in partem sortis sanctórum
in lúmine;
13 qui erípuit nos de potestáte tenebrárum *
et tránstulit in regnum Fílii dilectiónis suæ,
14 in quo habémus redemptiónem, *
remissiónem peccatórum;
15 qui est imágo Dei invisíbilis, *
primogénitus omnis creatúræ,
16 quia in ipso cóndita sunt univérsa †
in cælis et in terra, *
visibília et invisibília,
sive throni sive dominatiónes *
sive principátus sive potestátes.

Omnia per ipsum et in ipsum creáta sunt, †
17 et ipse est ante ómnia, *
et ómnia in ipso constant.

18 Et ipse est caput córporis ecclésiæ; †
qui est princípium, primogénitus ex mórtuis, *
ut sit in ómnibus ipse primátum tenens,
19 quia in ipso complácuit omnem plenitúdinem
habitáre *
20 et per eum reconciliáre ómnia in ipsum,
pacíficans per sánguinem crucis eius, *
sive quæ in terris sive quæ in cælis sunt.

Ant. In ipso cóndita sunt univérsa, et ómnia in ipso constant.

Canticle Colossians 1:12–20

12 Let us give thanks to the Father, who has qualified us to share in the inheritance of the saints in light.
13 He has delivered us from the dominion of darkness and transferred us to the kingdom of his beloved Son,
14 in whom we have redemption, the forgiveness of sins.
15 He is the image of the invisible God, the first-born of all creation;
16 for in him all things were created, in heaven and on earth, visible and invisible, whether thrones or dominions or principalities or authorities—all things were created through him and for him.
17 He is before all things, and in him all things hold together.
18 He is the head of the body, the church; he is the beginning, the first-born from the dead, that in everything he might be pre-eminent.
19 For in him all the fulness of God was pleased to dwell,
20 and through him to reconcile to himself all things whether on earth or in heaven, making peace by the blood of his cross.

Ant. 3 In him all things were created, and in Him all things hold together.

LECTIO BREVIS 1 Io 2, 3-6

In hoc cognóscimus quóniam nóvimus Christum: si mandáta eius servémus. Qui dicit: « Novi eum, » et mandáta eius non servat, mendax est, et in isto véritas non est; qui autem servat verbum eius, vere in hoc cáritas Dei consummáta est. In hoc cognóscimus quóniam in ipso sumus. Qui dicit se in ipso manére, debet, sicut ille ambulávit, et ipse ambuláre.

RESPONSORIUM BREVE

℟. Custódi nos, Domine, * Ut pupíllam óculi. Custódi.

℣. Sub umbra alárum tuárum prótege nos. * Ut pupíllam óculi. Glória Patri. Custódi.

Ad Magnificat, ant. Fac, Deus, poténtiam in brácchio tuo, dispérde supérbos et exálta húmiles.

PRECES

Ætérno Patri, cuius misericórdia in pópulum suum magnificáta est usque ad cælos, exsultántibus córdibus acclamémus: *Læténtur omnes, qui sperant in te, Dómine.*

Dómine, qui misísti Fílium tuum non ut iúdicet mundum, sed ut salvétur mundus per ipsum,
—da ut mors eius gloriósa in nobis fructum suum áfferat copiósum.

Qui sacerdótes tuos minístros Christi et tuórum constituísti mysteriórum dispensatóres,
—ipsis concéde cor fidéle, sciéntiam et caritátem.

SHORT READING

1 John 2:3–6

And by this we can be sure that we know Christ, if we keep his commandments. He who says "I know him" but disobeys his commandments is a liar, and the truth is not in him; but whoever keeps his word, in him truly love for God is perfected. By this we may be sure that we are in him: he who says he abides in him ought to walk in the same way in which he walked.

SHORT RESPONSORY

℟. Keep us, O Lord, as the apple of Your eye.
℣. Protect us under the shadow of Your wings.

Magnificat ant. Show strength, O God, with Your arm; scatter the proud and exalt those of low degree.

INTERCESSIONS

To the eternal Father, Whose mercy for His people is magnified even to the heavens, with rejoicing hearts let us give acclaim: *May all rejoice who hope in You, O Lord.*

O Lord, Who sent Your Son not that He might judge the world, but that the world might be saved through Him,
—grant that His glorious death may bear the fulness of His fruit within us.

You that established Your priests as ministers of Christ and stewards of Your mysteries,
—bestow on them knowledge, love, and a heart which is faithful.

Quos vocásti ad castitátem propter regnum cælórum,
—fac ut intemeráta fidelitáte Fílium tuum sequántur.
Qui hóminem ab inítio másculum et féminam creásti,
—omnes serva famílias in amóre sincéro.
Qui, per Christi oblatiónem, hóminum peccáta abstulísti.
—ómnibus defúnctis remissiónem tríbue peccatórum.

Pater noster.

ORATIO

Recordáre, Dómine, misericórdiæ tuæ, ut qui esuriéntes bonis cæléstibus implére dignáris, indigéntiæ nostræ tríbuas tuis abundáre divítiis. Per Dóminum.

To those whom You have called to chastity for the sake of the kingdom of heaven,
—make them to follow Your Son with unblemished fidelity.

You that from the beginning created man male and female,
—protect all families in sincere love.

You that, through Christ's oblation, absolved the sins of men,
—grant to all the deceased the remission of their sins.

Our Father.

Oration

Remember, O Lord, Your mercy, that as You deign to fill the hungry with the good things of heaven, You would make our poverty to abound in Your riches. Through our Lord.

Hebdomada IV

Feria V, ad Laudes matutinas

HYMN

Iam lucis orto sídere
Deum precémur súpplices,
ut in diúrnis áctibus
nos servet a nocéntibus.

Linguam refrénans témperet,
ne litis horror ínsonet;
visum fovéndo cóntegat,
ne vanitátes háuriat.

Sint pura cordis íntima,
absístat et vecórdia;
carnis terat supérbiam
potus cibíque párcitas;

Ut, cum dies abscésserit
noctémque sors redúxerit,
mundi per abstinéntiam
ipsi canámus glóriam.

Deo Patri sit glória
eiúsque soli Filio
cum Spíritu Paráclito,
in sempitérna sǽcula. Amen.

PSALMODIA

Ant. 1 Audítam fac mihi mane misericórdiam tuam, Dómine.

Week IV

Thursday, Lauds

HYMN Trans. J. M. Neale

Now that the daylight fills the sky,
We lift our hearts to God on high,
That He, in all we do or say,
Would keep us free from harm today:

Would guard our hearts and tongues from strife;
From anger's din would hide our life;
From all ill sights would turn our eyes;
Would close our ears from vanities:

Would keep our inmost conscience pure;
Our souls from folly would secure;
Would bid us check the pride of sense
With due and holy abstinence.

So we, when this new day is gone,
And night in turn is drawing on,
With conscience by the world unstained
Shall praise His name for victory gained.

All laud to God the Father be;
All praise, eternal Son, to Thee;
All glory as is ever meet,
To God the holy Paraclete. Amen.

PSALMODY

Ant. 1 Let me hear in the morning of thy steadfast love.

Psalmus 142 (143), 1–11

1 Dómine, exáudi oratiónem meam, †
áuribus pércipe obsecratiónem meam in veritáte tua; *
exáudi me in tua iustítia.
2 Et non intres in iudícium cum servo tuo, *
quia non iustificábitur in conspéctu tuo omnis vivens.

3 Quia persecútus est inimícus ánimam meam, †
contrívit in terra vitam meam, *
collocávit me in obscúris sicut mórtuos a sǽculo.
4 Et anxiátus est in me spíritus meus, *
in médio mei obríguit cor meum.
5 Memor fui diérum antiquórum, †
meditátus sum in ómnibus opéribus tuis, *
in factis mánuum tuárum recogitábam.
6 Expándi manus meas ad te, *
ánima mea sicut terra sine aqua tibi.

7 Velóciter exáudi me, Dómine; *
defécit spíritus meus.
Non abscóndas fáciem tuam a me, *
ne símilis fiam descendéntibus in lacum.
8 Audítam fac mihi mane misericórdiam tuam, *
quia in te sperávi.
Notam fac mihi viam, in qua ámbulem, *
quia ad te levávi ánimam meam.
9 Eripe me de inimícis meis, *
Dómine, ad te confúgi.
10 Doce me fácere voluntátem tuam, *
quia Deus meus es tu.

Psalm 143:1–11

1 Hear my prayer, O LORD; give ear to my supplications!
In thy faithfulness answer me, in thy righteousness!
2 Enter not into judgment with thy servant;
for no man living is righteous before thee.

3 For the enemy has pursued me;
he has crushed my life to the ground;
he has made me sit in darkness like those long dead.
4 Therefore my spirit faints within me;
my heart within me is appalled.

5 I remember the days of old,
I meditate on all that thou hast done;
I muse on what thy hands have wrought.
6 I stretch out my hands to thee;
my soul thirsts for thee like a parched land.

7 Make haste to answer me, O LORD!
My spirit fails!
Hide not thy face from me,
lest I be like those who go down to the Pit.
8 Let me hear in the morning of thy steadfast love,
for in thee I put my trust.
Teach me the way I should go,
for to thee I lift up my soul.

9 Deliver me, O LORD, from my enemies!
I have fled to thee for refuge!
10 Teach me to do thy will,
for thou art my God!

Spíritus tuus bonus dedúcet me in terram,
rectam; *
11 propter nomen tuum, Dómine, vivificábis me.
In iustítia tua *
edúces de tribulatióne ánimam meam.

Ant. Audítam fac mihi mane misericórdiam tuam, Dómine.

Ant. 2 Declinábit Dóminus super Ierúsalem flúvium pacis.

Canticum Is 66, 10–14A

10 Lætámini cum Ierúsalem et exsultáte in ea, *
omnes, qui dilígitis eam;
gaudéte cum ea gáudio, *
univérsi, qui lugebátis super eam,
11 ut sugátis et repleámini *
ab úbere consolatiónis eius,
ut mulgeátis et delíciis affluátis *
ex ubéribus glóriæ eius.
12 Quia hæc dicit Dóminus: †
« Ecce ego dírigam ad eam quasi flúvium
pacem *
et quasi torréntem inundántem glóriam
géntium.
Sugétis, in ulnis portabímini, *
et super génua blandiéntur vobis.

13 Quómodo si quem mater consolátur, †
ita ego consolábor vos; *
et in Ierúsalem consolabímini.
14 Vidébitis, et gaudébit cor vestrum, *
et ossa vestra quasi herba germinábunt ».

Let thy good spirit lead me
on a level path!

11 For thy name's sake, O Lord, preserve my life!
In thy righteousness bring me out of trouble!

Ant. 1 Let me hear in the morning of thy steadfast love.
Ant. 2 The Lord will make a river of peace to flow over Jerusalem.

Canticle Isaiah 66:10–14a

10 "Rejoice with Jerusalem, and be glad for her,
all you who love her;
rejoice with her in joy,
all you who mourn over her;
11 that you may suck and be satisfied with her consoling breasts;
that you may drink deeply with delight
from the abundance of her glory."

12 For thus says the Lord:
"Behold, I will extend prosperity to her like a river,
and the wealth of the nations like an overflowing stream;
and you shall suck, you shall be carried upon her hip,
and dandled upon her knees.
13 As one whom his mother comforts,
so I will comfort you;
you shall be comforted in Jerusalem.
14 You shall see, and your heart shall rejoice;
your bones shall flourish like the grass.

Ant. Declinábit Dóminus super Ierúsalem flúvium pacis.

Ant. 3 Deo nostro iucúnda sit laudátio.

Psalmus 146 (147 A)

1 Laudáte Dóminum, quóniam bonum est psállere
Deo nostro, *
quóniam iucúndum est celebráre laudem.

2 Ædíficans Ierúsalem Dóminus, *
dispérsos Israélis congregábit.
3 Qui sanat contrítos corde *
et álligat plagas eórum;
4 qui númerat multitúdinem stellárum *
et ómnibus eis nómina vocat.
5 Magnus Dóminus noster et magnus virtúte, *
sapiéntiæ eius non est númerus.
6 Susténtat mansuétos Dóminus, *
humílians autem peccatóres usque ad terram.

7 Præcínite Dómino in confessióne, *
psállite Deo nostro in cíthara.
8 Qui óperit cælum núbibus *
et parat terræ plúviam.
Qui prodúcit in móntibus fenum *
et herbam servitúti hóminum.
9 Qui dat iuméntis escam ipsórum *
et pullis corvórum invocántibus eum.
10 Non in fortitúdine equi delectátur, *
nec in tíbiis viri beneplácitum est ei.
11 Beneplácitum est Dómino super timéntes eum *
et in eis, qui sperant super misericórdia eius.

Ant. Deo nostro iucúnda sit laudátio.

Ant. 2 The Lord will make a river of peace to flow over Jerusalem.
Ant. 3 Praise is pleasing to our God.

Psalm 147:1–11

1 Praise the LORD!
For it is good to sing praises to our God;
for he is gracious, and a song of praise is seemly.
2 The LORD builds up Jerusalem;
he gathers the outcasts of Israel.
3 He heals the brokenhearted,
and binds up their wounds.
4 He determines the number of the stars,
he gives to all of them their names.
5 Great is our LORD, and abundant in power;
his understanding is beyond measure.
6 The LORD lifts up the downtrodden,
he casts the wicked to the ground.

7 Sing to the LORD with thanksgiving;
make melody to our God upon the lyre!
8 He covers the heavens with clouds,
he prepares rain for the earth.
he makes grass grow upon the hills.
9 He gives to the beasts their food,
and to the young ravens which cry.
10 His delight is not in the strength of the horse,
nor his pleasure in the legs of a man;
11 but the LORD takes pleasure in those who fear him,
in those who hope in his steadfast love.

Ant. 3 Praise is pleasing to our God.

Lectio Brevis

Rom 8, 18–21

Non sunt condígnæ passiónes huius témporis ad futúram glóriam, quæ revelánda est in nobis. Nam expectátio creatúræ revelatiónem filiórum Dei expéctat; vanitáti enim creatúra subiécta est, non volens sed propter eum, qui subiécit, in spem, quia et ipsa creatúra liberábitur a servitúte corruptiónis in libertátem glóriæ filiórum Dei.

Responsorium Breve

℟. In matutínis, Dómine, * Meditábor de te. In matutínis.
℣. Quia factus es adiútor meus. * Meditábor de te. * Glória Patri. In matutínis.

Ad Benedictus, ant. Da sciéntiam salútis plebi tuæ, Dómine, et dimítte nobis peccáta nostra.

Preces

Deum, a quo óbvenit salus pópulo suo, celebrémus ita dicéntes: *Tu es vita nostra, Dómine.*

Benedíctus es, Pater Dómini nostri Iesu Christi, qui secúndum misericórdiam tuam regenerásti nos in spem vivam,
—per resurrectiónem Iesu Christi ex mórtuis.

Qui hóminem, ad imáginem tuam creátum, in Christo renovásti,
—fac nos confórmes imágini Fílii tui.

In córdibus nostris invídia et ódio vulnerátis,
—caritátem per Spíritum Sanctum datam effúnde.

SHORT READING Romans 8:18–21

I consider that the sufferings of this present time are not worth comparing with the glory that is to be revealed to us. For the creation waits with eager longing for the revealing of the sons of God; for the creation was subjected to futility, not of its own will but by the will of him who subjected it in hope; because the creation itself will be set free from its bondage to decay and obtain the glorious liberty of the children of God.

SHORT RESPONSORY

℟. In the morning hours, I shall meditate on You, O Lord.
℣. For You have become my Helper.

Benedictus ant. Give knowledge of salvation to Your people, O Lord, and the forgiveness of our sins.

INTERCESSIONS

Let us celebrate God, from Whom salvation comes to His people, thus saying: *You are our life, O Lord.*

Blessed are You, Father of our Lord Jesus Christ, Who according to Your mercy have recreated us unto a lively hope,
—through the resurrection of Jesus Christ from the dead.

You Who, in Christ, renewed man created in Your image,
—make us conform to the image of Your Son.

In our hearts wounded by envy and hatred,
—pour out Your charity given through the Holy Spirit.

Da hódie operáriis labórem, esuriéntibus panem, mæréntibus gáudium,
—ómnibus homínibus grátiam atque salútem.

Pater noster.

ORATIO

Sciéntiam salútis, Dómine, nobis concéde sincéram, ut sine timóre, de manu inimicórum nostrórum liberáti, ómnibus diébus nostris tibi fidéliter serviámus. Per Dóminum.

Grant work to our laborers today, bread to the hungry, joy to the sorrowful,
—and to all men grace and salvation.

Our Father.

ORATION
Knowledge of salvation, Lord, grant us sincerely, that without fear, freed from the hands of our enemies, we might serve You faithfully all our days. Through our Lord.

Hebdomada IV

Feria V, ad Vesperas

HYMN

Deus, qui claro lúmine
diem fecísti, Dómine,
tuam rogámus glóriam
dum pronus dies vólvitur.

Iam sol urgénte véspero
occásum suum gráditur,
mundum conclúdens ténebris,
suum obsérvans órdinem.

Tu ver*o*, excélse Dómine,
precántes tuos fámulos
diúrno lassos ópere
ne sinas umbris ópprimi,

Ut non fuscátis méntibus
dies abscédat sǽculi,
sed tua tecti grátia
cernámus lucem prósperam.

Præsta, Pater piíssme,
Patrique compar Unice,
cum Spíritu Paráclito
regnans per omne sǽculum. Amen.

PSALMODIA

Ant. 1 Misericórdia mea et refúgium meum Dóminus: in ipso sperávi.

Week IV

Thursday, Vespers

HYMN Trans. The Benedictine Nuns, St. Cecilia's Abbey

O Lord our God, Who made the day
 To gladden us with its fair light,
We praise Your name, imploring aid,
 For day will soon give place to night.

The evening shadows grow apace,
 Advancing, they will hide the sun,
As darkness creeps upon the earth
 When daylight hours their course have run.

We beg You, Lord and God Most High,
 Protect us with Your presence blessed,
Though weary, keep our souls in peace
 And not by gloom of night oppressed.

Let not Your lovely sun go down
 On hearts distressed with sin, and sore,
But sheltered by Your gentle grace,
 May we perceive the day once more.

Most tender Father, hear our prayer,
 Whom we adore, with Christ the Lord,
And Holy Spirit of them both;
 Bless us who praise Your Trinity. Amen.

PSALMODY

Ant. 1 The Lord is my rock and my fortress; in Him have I hoped.

Psalmus 143 (144)

I

1 Benedíctus Dóminus, adiútor meus, †
qui docet manus meas ad prœlium *
et dígitos meos ad bellum.
2 Misericórdia mea et fortitúdo mea, *
refúgium meum et liberátor meus;
scutum meum, et in ipso sperávi, *
qui subdit pópulum meum sub me.

3 Dómine, quid est homo, quod agnóscis eum, *
aut fílius hóminis, quod réputas eum?
4 Homo vanitáti símilis factus est, *
dies eius sicut umbra prætériens.

5 Dómine, inclína cælos tuos et descénde; *
tange montes, et fumigábunt.
6 Fúlgura coruscatiónem et díssipa eos; *
emítte sagíttas tuas et contúrba eos.
7 Emítte manum tuam de alto; *
éripe me et líbera me de aquis multis,
de manu filiórum alienigenárum, †
8 quorum os locútum est vanitátem, *
et déxtera eórum déxtera mendácii.

Ant. Misericórdia mea et refúgium meum Dóminus: in ipso sperávi.
Ant. 2 Beátus pópulus cuius Dóminus Deus eius.

Psalm 144

I

1 Blessed be the LORD, my rock,
who trains my hands for war,
and my fingers for battle;
2 my rock and my fortress,
my stronghold and my deliverer,
my shield and he in whom I take refuge,
who subdues the peoples under him.

3 O LORD, what is man that thou dost regard him,
or the son of man that thou dost think of him?
4 Man is like a breath,
his days are like a passing shadow.

5 Bow thy heavens, O Lord, and come down!
Touch the mountains that they smoke!
6 Flash forth the lightning and scatter them,
send out thy arrows and rout them!
7 Stretch forth thy hand from on high,
rescue me and deliver me from the many
waters,
from the hand of aliens,
8 whose mouths speak lies,
and whose right hand is a right hand of
falsehood.

Ant. 1 The Lord is my rock and my fortress; in Him have I hoped.
Ant. 2 Happy the people whose God is the Lord.

II

9 Deus, cánticum novum cantábo tibi, *
in psaltério decachórdo psallam tibi,
10 Qui das salútem régibus *
qui rédimis David servum tuum de gládio malígno.
11 Eripe me et líbera me *
de manu filiórum alienigenárum,
quorum os locútum est vanitátem, *
et déxtera eórum déxtera mendácii.

12 Fílii nostri sicut novéllæ crescéntes *
in iuventúte sua;
fíliæ nostræ sicut colúmnæ anguláres, *
sculptæ ut structúra templi.
13 Promptuária nostra plena, *
redundántia ómnibus bonis;
oves nostræ in mílibus †
innumerábiles in campis nostris, *
14 boves nostræ crassæ.
Non est ruína macériæ neque egréssus, *
neque clamor in platéis nostris.
15 Beátus pópulus, cui hæc sunt; *
beátus pópulus, cuius Dóminus Deus eius.

Ant. Beátus pópulus cuius Dóminus Deus eius.
Ant. 3 Nunc facta est salus et regnum Dei nostri.

II

9 I will sing a new song to thee, O God;
upon a ten-stringed harp I will play to thee,
10 who givest victory to kings,
who rescuest David thy servant.
11 Rescue me from the cruel sword,
and deliver me from the hand of aliens,
whose mouths speak lies,
and whose right hand is a right hand of falsehood.

12 May our sons in their youth
be like plants full grown,
our daughters like corner pillars
cut for the structure of a palace;
13 may our garners be full,
providing all manner of store;
may our sheep bring forth thousands
and ten thousands in our fields;
14 may our cattle be heavy with young
suffering no mischance or failure in bearing;
may there be no cry of distress in our streets!
15 Happy the people to whom such blessings fall!
Happy the people whose God is the LORD!

Ant. 2 Happy the people whose God is the Lord.
Ant. 3 Now the salvation and kingdom of our God have come.

Canticum Ap 11, 17–18; 12, 10b–12a

11,17 Grátias ágimus tibi, *
Dómine Deus omnípotens,
qui es et qui eras, *
quia accepísti virtútem tuam magnam et regnásti.
18 Et irátæ sunt gentes, *
et advénit ira tua, et tempus mortuórum iudicári,
et réddere mercédem servis tuis prophétis et sanctis *
et timéntibus nomen tuum, pusíllis et magnis.

12,10 Nunc facta est salus et virtus et regnum Dei nostri *
et potéstas Christi eius,
quia proiéctus est accusátor fratrum nostrórum, *
qui accusábat illos ante conspéctum Dei nostri die ac nocte.
11 Et ipsi vicérunt illum propter sánguinem Agni *
et propter verbum testimónii sui;
et non dilexérunt ánimam suam *
usque ad mortem.
12 Proptérea lætámini, cæli *
et qui habitátis in eis.

Ant. Nunc facta est salus et regnum Dei nostri.

Lectio Brevis — Cf. Col 1, 23

Permanéte in fide fundáti et stábiles et immóbiles a spe evangélii, quod audístis, quod prædicátum est in univérsa creatúra, quæ sub cælo est.

Canticle

Revelation 11:17–18; 12:10b–12a

17 "We give thanks to thee, Lord God Almighty, who art and who wast,
that thou hast taken thy great power and begun to reign.
18 The nations raged, but thy wrath came,
and the time for the dead to be judged,
for rewarding thy servants, the prophets and saints,
and those who fear thy name, both small and great,
and for destroying the destroyers of the earth.

10 "Now the salvation and the power and the kingdom of our God and the authority of his Christ have come, for the accuser of our brethren has been thrown down, who accuses them day and night before our God.
11 And they have conquered him by the blood of the Lamb and by the word of their testimony, for they loved not their lives even unto death.
12 Rejoice then, O heaven and you that dwell therein!"

Ant. 3 Now the salvation and kingdom of our God have come.

SHORT READING — Colossians 1:23

Continue in the faith, stable and steadfast, not shifting from the hope of the gospel which you heard, which has been preached to every creature under heaven.

RESPONSORIUM BREVE

℟. Dóminus pascit me, * Et nihil mihi déerit. Dóminus.

℣. In páscuis viréntibus me collocávit. * Et nihil mihi déerit. Glória Patri. Dóminus.

Ad Magnificat, ant. Esuriéntes iustítiam Dóminus saturávit et implévit bonis.

PRECES

Christum, lumen gentium et gaudium omnium viventium, læta devotione rogemus: *Da lucem, pacem et salutem, Domine.*

Lux indefíciens et Verbum Patris, qui ad omnes hómines salvándos venísti,
—dírige catechúmenos Ecclésiæ tuæ, ut in te illuminéntur.

Iniquitátes nostras, Dómine, ne consíderes,
—quia apud te propitiátio est.

Qui voluísti ut hómines ingénio suo secréta naturália investigárent ad mundum regéndum,
—da ut sciéntia et artes ad glóriam tuam et ómnium felicitátem dirigántur.

Eos tuére, qui servítio fratrum suórum in mundo sese mancipavérunt,
—ut líbere et sine detriménto opus suum perfícere váleant.

Dómine, qui áperis et nemo claudit,
—educ in lumen tuum defúnctos qui in spe resurrectiónis dormiérunt.

Pater noster.

Short Responsory

℟. The Lord is my shepherd, there is nothing I shall want.
℣. He has made me to lie down in green pastures.

Magnificat ant. The Lord has satisfied those who hunger for justice and has filled them with good things.

Intercessions

With joyful devotion, let us implore Christ, the Light of the nations and the Joy of all the living: *Grant Your light, peace, and salvation, O Lord.*

O unfailing Light and Word of the Father, Who came to save all men,
—direct the catechumens of Your Church, that they might be enlightened in You.

Do not regard our iniquities, O Lord,
—for with You there is mercy.

You that willed that men should seek with their minds the secrets of nature so as to rule the world,
—grant that knowledge and the arts may be directed to Your glory and the happiness of all.

Look upon those who have dedicated themselves to the service of their brothers in the world,
—that they might be able to perfect their work with freedom and without complication.

O Lord, Who open and no one closes,
—lead into Your light the deceased who have fallen asleep in the hope of the resurrection.

Our Father.

Oratio

Nostris propitiáre, Dómine, supplicatiónibus vespertínis, et præsta, ut Fílii tui vestígia sequéntes, in patiéntia fructum bonórum óperum afferámus. Per Dóminum.

Oration

Accept, O Lord, our evening supplications, and grant that, following the example of Your Son, we may bear the fruit of good works in patience. Through our Lord.

Hebdomada IV

Feria VI, ad Laudes matutinas

HYMN

Deus, qui cæli lumen es
satórque lucis, qui polum
patérno fultum brácchio
præclára pandis déxtera,

Auróra stellas iam tegit
rubrum sustóllens gúrgitem,
uméctis atque flátibus
terram baptízans róribus.

Iam noctis umbra línquitur,
polum calígo déserit,
typúsque Christi, lúcifer
diem sopítum súscitat.

Dies diérum tu, Deus,
lucísque lumen ipse es,
Unum potens per ómnia,
potens in unum Trínitas.

Te nunc, Salvátor, quǽsumus
tibíque genu fléctimus,
Patrem cum Sancto Spíritu
totis laudántes vócibus. Amen.

PSALMODIA

Ant. 1 Cor mundum crea in me, Deus, et spíritum rectum ínnova in viscéribus meis.

Week IV

Friday, Lauds

HYMN — Trans. The Benedictine Nuns, St. Cecilia's Abbey

O God, the Light of Heaven's home,
You scatter light like golden grain;
Your fatherly right hand protects
The earth depending on Your pow'r.

The stars are hidden by the dawn,
That casts a red glow on the sky,
And with its moist, refreshing breeze
Bathes soil and plants in sparkling dew.

The shadows of the night are gone,
While fogs and mist disperse and flee;
The type of Christ, the morning star
Bestirs to life the drowsy day.

O God, You are the Day of days,
And very Light of light itself,
One and Almighty in Your works,
And mighty Trinity in One.

Our Saviour kind, we call to You
At daybreak, as we bow in prayer;
With newborn strength we sing our praise
To Father and Spirit too. Amen.

PSALMODY

Ant. 1 Create in me a clean heart, O God, and put a new and right spirit within me.

Psalmus 50 (51)

3 Miserére mei, Deus, *
secúndum misericórdiam tuam;
et secúndum multitúdinem miseratiónum
tuárum *
dele iniquitátem meam.
4 Amplius lava me ab iniquitáte mea *
et a peccáto meo munda me.

5 Quóniam iniquitátem meam ego cognósco, *
et peccátum meum contra me est semper.
6 Tibi, tibi soli peccávi *
et malum coram te feci,
ut iustus inveniáris in senténtia tua *
et æquus in iudício tuo.

7 Ecce enim in iniquitáte generátus sum, *
et in peccáto concépit me mater mea.
8 Ecce enim veritátem in corde dilexísti *
et in occúlto sapiéntiam manifestásti mihi.

9 Aspérges me hyssópo, et mundábor; *
lavábis me, et super nivem dealbábor.
10 Audíre me fácies gáudium et lætítiam, *
et exsultábunt ossa, quæ contrivísti.

11 Avérte fáciem tuam a peccátis meis *
et omnes iniquitátes meas dele.
12 Cor mundum crea in me, Deus, *
et spíritum firmum ínnova in viscéribus meis.

13 Ne proícias me a fácie tua *
et spíritum sanctum tuum ne áuferas a me.
14 Redde mihi lætítiam salutáris tui *
et spíritu promptíssimo confírma me.

Psalm 51

1 Have mercy on me, O God,
according to thy steadfast love;
according to thy abundant mercy blot out my
transgressions.
2 Wash me thoroughly from my iniquity,
and cleanse me from my sin!

3 For I know my transgressions,
and my sin is ever before me.
4 Against thee, thee only, have I sinned,
and done that which is evil in thy sight,
so that thou art justified in thy sentence
and blameless in thy judgment.
5 Behold, I was brought forth in iniquity,
and in sin did my mother conceive me.

6 Behold, thou desirest truth in the inward being;
therefore teach me wisdom in my secret heart,
7 Purge me with hyssop, and I shall be clean;
wash me, and I shall be whiter than snow.
8 Fill me with joy and gladness;
let the bones which thou hast broken rejoice.
9 Hide thy face from my sins,
and blot out all my iniquities.

10 Create in me a clean heart, O God,
and put a new and right spirit within me.
11 Cast me not away from thy presence,
and take not thy holy Spirit from me.
12 Restore to me the joy of thy salvation,
and uphold me with a willing spirit.

15 Docébo iníquos vias tuas, *
et ímpii ad te converténtur.
16 Líbera me de sanguínibus, Deus, Deus salútis meæ, *
et exsultábit lingua mea iustítiam tuam.

17 Dómine, lábia mea apéries, *
et os meum annuntiábit laudem tuam.
18 Non enim sacrifício delectáris, *
holocáustum, si ófferam, non placébit.
19 Sacrifícium Deo spíritus contribulátus, *
cor contrítum et humiliátum, Deus, non despícies.

20 Benígne fac, Dómine, in bona voluntáte tua Sion, *
ut ædificéntur muri Ierúsalem.
21 Tunc acceptábis sacrifícium iustítiæ, oblatiónes et holocáusta; *
tunc impónent super altáre tuum vítulos.

Ant. Cor mundum crea in me, Deus, et spíritum rectum ínnova in viscéribus meis.
Ant. 2 Lætáre, Ierúsalem, quia per te omnes congregabúntur ad Dóminum.

Canticum

TOB 13, 8–11. 13–14AB. 15–16AB

8 Benedícite Dóminum, omnes elécti, *
et omnes laudáte maiestátem illíus.
Agite dies lætítiæ *
et confitémini illi.

13 Then I will teach transgressors thy ways,
and sinners will return to thee.
14 Deliver me from bloodguiltiness, O God,
thou God of my salvation,
and my tongue will sing aloud of thy deliverance.

15 O Lord, open thou my lips,
and my mouth shall show forth thy praise.
16 For thou hast no delight in sacrifice;
were I to give a burnt offering, thou wouldst not be pleased.
17 The sacrifice acceptable to God is a broken spirit;
a broken and contrite heart, O God, thou wilt not despise.
18 Do good to Zion in thy good pleasure;
rebuild the walls of Jerusalem,
19 then wilt thou delight in right sacrifices,
in burnt offerings and whole burnt offerings;
then bulls will be offered on thy altar.

Ant. 1 Create in me a clean heart, O God, and put a new and right spirit within me.
Ant. 2 Rejoice, Jerusalem, for through you all men will be gathered to the Lord.

Canticle Tobit 13:8–11, 13–16

8 Let all men speak,
and give him thanks in Jerusalem.
9 O Jerusalem, the holy city,
he will afflict you for the deeds of your sons,
but again he will show mercy to the sons of the righteous.

9 Ierúsalem, cívitas sancta, *
flagellábit te in opéribus mánuum tuárum.

10 Confitére Dómino in bono ópere *
et bénedic regem sæculórum,
ut íterum tabernáculum tuum ædificétur in te cum gáudio *
et lætos fáciat in te omnes captívos
et díligat in te omnes míseros *
in ómnia sǽcula sæculórum.
11 Lux spléndida fulgébit *
in ómnibus fínibus terræ;
natiónes multæ vénient tibi ex longínquo †
et a novíssimis pártibus terræ ad nomen sanctum tuum *
et múnera sua in mánibus suis habéntes regi cæli.
Generatiónes generatiónum dabunt in te lætítiam, *
et nomen eléctæ erit in sǽcula sæculórum.

13 Tunc gaude et lætáre in fíliis iustórum, †
quóniam omnes colligéntur *
et benedícent Dómino ætérno.

14 Felíces, qui díligunt te, *
et felíces, qui gaudébunt in pace tua.

15 Anima mea, bénedic Dómino regi magno, *
16 quia in Ierúsalem civitáte ædificábitur
domus illíus *
in ómnia sǽcula.

10 Give thanks worthily to the Lord, and praise the
King of the ages, that his tent may be raised
for you again with joy.
May he cheer those within you who are captives,
and love those within you who are distressed,
to all generations for ever.
11 Many nations will come from afar to the name of
the Lord God,
bearing gifts in their hands, gifts for the King of
heaven.
Generations of generations will give you joyful
praise.
13 Rejoice and be glad for the sons of the righteous;
for they will be gathered together,
and will praise the Lord of the righteous.
14 How blessed are those who love you!
They will rejoice in your peace.
Blessed are those who grieved over all your
afflictions;
for they will rejoice for you upon seeing all
your glory,
and they will be made glad for ever.
15 Let my soul praise God the great King.
16 For Jerusalem will be built with sapphires and
emeralds,
her walls with precious stones,
and her towers and battlements with pure gold.

Ant. Lætáre, Ierúsalem, quia per te omnes congregabúntur ad Dóminum.

Ant. 3 Lauda Deum tuum, Sion, qui emíttit elóquium suum terræ.

Psalmus 147 (147B)

12 Lauda, Ierúsalem, Dóminum; *
colláuda Deum tuum, Sion.

13 Quóniam confortávit seras portárum tuárum, *
benedíxit fíliis tuis in te.
14 Qui ponit fines tuos pacem *
et ádipe fruménti sátiat te.
15 Qui emíttit elóquium suum terræ, *
velóciter currit verbum eius.
16 Qui dat nivem sicut lanam, *
pruínam sicut cínerem spargit.
17 Mittit crystállum suam sicut buccéllas; *
ante fáciem frígoris eius quis sustinébit?
18 Emíttet verbum suum et liquefáciet ea, *
flabit spíritus eius, et fluent aquæ.
19 Qui annúntiat verbum suum Iacob, *
iustítias et iudícia sua Israel.
20 Non fecit táliter omni natióni, *
et iudícia sua non manifestávit eis.

Ant. Lauda Deum tuum, Sion, qui emíttit elóquium suum terræ.

LECTIO BREVIS GAL 2, 19B–20

Christo confíxus sum cruci: vivo autem iam non ego, vivit vero in me Christus; quod autem nunc vivo in carne, in fide vivo Fílii Dei, qui diléxit me et trádidit seípsum pro me.

Ant. 2 Rejoice, Jerusalem, for through you all men will be gathered to the Lord.
Ant. 3 O Zion, praise your God, Who sends forth His command to the earth.

Psalm 147:12–20

12 Praise the Lord, O Jerusalem!
   Praise your God, O Zion!
13 For he strengthens the bars of your gates;
   he blesses your sons within you.
14 He makes peace in your borders;
   he fills you with the finest of the wheat.
15 He sends forth his command to the earth;
   his word runs swiftly.
16 He gives snow like wool;
   he scatters hoarfrost like ashes.
17 He casts forth his ice like morsels;
   who can stand before his cold?
18 He sends forth his word, and melts them;
   he makes his wind blow, and the waters flow.
19 He declares his word to Jacob,
   his statutes and ordinances to Israel.
20 He has not dealt thus with any other nation;
   they do not know his ordinances.

Ant. 3 O Zion, praise your God, Who sends forth His command to the earth.

SHORT READING Galatians 2:20
I have been crucified with Christ; it is no longer I who live, but Christ who lives in me; and the life I now live in the flesh I live by faith in the Son of God, who loved me and gave himself for me.

RESPONSORIUM BREVE
℟. Clamábo ad Dóminum altíssimum, * Qui benefécit mihi. Clamábo.
℣. Mittet de cælo et liberábit me. * Qui benefécit mihi. Glória Patri. Clamábo.

Ad Benedictus, ant. Per víscera misericórdiæ Dei nostri, visitávit nos Oriens ex alto.

PRECES
Fidúciam habéntes in Deum, qui sollícitus est ómnium, quos creávit et redémit per Fílium suum, oratiónem nostram innovémus: *Confírma, quod operátus es in nobis, Dómine.*
Deus misericórdiæ, gressus nostros in sanctitáte cordis dírige,
—ut, quæ sunt vera, iusta et amabília, cogitémus.
Ne derelínquas nos in perpétuum propter nomen tuum,
—ne díssipes, Dómine, testaméntum tuum.
In ánimo contríto et spíritu humilitátis suscipiámur,
—quóniam non est confúsio confidéntibus in te.
Qui nos in Christo ad munus prophéticum vocásti,
—da nos tuas annuntiáre virtútes.

Pater noster.

ORATIO
Grátiæ tuæ, quǽsumus, Dómine, supplícibus tuis tríbue largitátem, ut mandáta tua, te operánte, sectántes, consolatiónem vitæ præséntis accípiant, et futúra gáudia comprehéndant. Per Dóminum.

SHORT RESPONSORY

℟. I shall cry out to the Lord Most High, Who has done good to me.

℣. He shall send from heaven and save me.

Benedictus ant. Through the tender mercy of our God, the Dawn from on high has visited us.

INTERCESSIONS

Having trust in God, Who watches over all, which He created and redeemed through His Son, let us renew our prayer: *Confirm what You have worked in us, O Lord.*

God of mercy, direct our steps in sanctity of heart,
—that we might think those things which are true, just and lovely.

For the sake of Your name, do not forsake us for ever,
—lest You break up Your covenant, Lord.

May we be accepted with a contrite heart and a spirit of humility,
—because there is no confusion for those who trust in You.

You that have called us to a prophetic duty in Christ,
—Grant us to announce Your mighty deeds.

Our Father.

ORATION

Grant to Your suppliants, we beseech You, O Lord, the bounty of Your grace that, by Your help, following Your commandments, they might receive consolation in the present life and grasp the joys to come. Through our Lord.

Feria VI, ad Vesperas

Hymn

Horis peráctis úndecim
ruit dies in vésperum;
solvámus omnes débitum
mentis libénter cánticum.

Labor diúrnus tránsiit
quo, Christe, nos condúxeras;
da iam colónis víneæ
promíssa dona glóriæ.

Mercéde quos nunc ádvocas,
quos ad futúrum múneras,
nos in labóre ádiuva
et post labórem récrea.

Sit, Christe, rex piíssime,
tibi Patríque glória
cum Spíritu Paráclito,
in sempitérna sæcula. Amen.

Psalmodia

Ant. 1 Per síngulos dies benedícam tibi, Dómine, et mirabília tua narrábo.

Week IV

Friday, Vespers

Hymn Trans. The Benedictine Nuns, St. Cecilia's Abbey

The hours are passing swiftly by,
  And into night the shades will flow,
So let us sing to God with joy
  The grateful hymn of praise we owe.

The burden and the heat of day
  Have passed in working for our Lord,
So may His vineyard workers all
  Receive from Him the great reward.

Lord Jesus Christ, You call us now
  To labor for our recompense,
Assist our work, then grant us rest,
  Until Your love shall call us hence.

O Christ our King and tender Lord,
  All glory ever be to You,
Who with the Holy Spirit reign
  With God the Father's might supreme.
    Amen.

Psalmody

Ant. 1 Every day I will bless Thee, O Lord, I shall declare Thy mighty acts.

Psalmus 144 (145)

I

1 Exaltábo te, Deus meus rex, †
et benedícam nómini tuo *
in sǽculum et in sǽculum sǽculi.
2 Per síngulos dies benedícam tibi †
et laudábo nomen tuum *
in sǽculum et in sǽculum sǽculi.

3 Magnus Dóminus et laudábilis nimis, *
et magnitúdinis eius non est investigátio.
4 Generátio generatióni laudábit ópera tua, *
et poténtiam tuam pronuntiábunt.
5 Magnificéntiam glóriæ maiestátis tuæ loquéntur *
et mirabília tua enarrábunt.
6 Et virtútem terribílium tuórum dicent *
et magnitúdinem tuam narrábunt.
7 Memóriam abundántiæ suavitátis tuæ
eructábunt *
et iustítia tua exsultábunt.
8 Miserátor et miséricors Dóminus, *
longánimis et multæ misericórdiæ.
9 Suávis Dóminus univérsis, *
et miseratiónes eius super ómnia ópera eius.

10 Confiteántur tibi, Dómine, ómnia ópera tua; *
et sancti tui benedícant tibi.
11 Glóriam regni tui dicant *
et poténtiam tuam loquántur,
12 ut notas fáciant fíliis hóminum poténtias tuas *
et glóriam magnificéntiæ regni tui.

Psalm 145

I

1 I will extol thee, my God and King,
and bless thy name for ever and ever.
2 Every day I will bless thee,
and praise thy name for ever and ever.

3 Great is the LORD, and greatly to be praised,
and his greatness is unsearchable.
4 One generation shall laud thy works to another,
and shall declare thy mighty acts.
5 On the glorious splendor of thy majesty,
and on thy wondrous works, I will meditate.
6 Men shall proclaim the might of thy terrible acts,
and I will declare thy greatness.
7 They shall pour forth the fame of thy abundant goodness,
and shall sing aloud of thy righteousness.

8 The LORD is gracious and merciful,
slow to anger and abounding in steadfast love.
9 The LORD is good to all,
and his compassion is over all that he has made.

10 All thy works shall give thanks to thee, O LORD,
and all thy saints shall bless thee!
11 They shall speak of the glory of thy kingdom,
and tell of thy power,
12 To make known thy to the sons of men thy mighty deeds,
and the glorious splendor of thy kingdom.

13 Regnum tuum regnum ómnium sæculórum, *
et dominátio tua in omnem generatiónem et generatiónem.

Ant. Per síngulos dies benedícam tibi, Dómine, et mirabília tua narrábo.

Ant. 2 Oculi ómnium in te sperant, Dómine; prope es ómnibus invocántibus te.

II

13b Fidélis Dóminus in ómnibus verbis suis *
et sanctus in ómnibus opéribus suis.
14 Allevat Dóminus omnes qui córruunt *
et érigit omnes depréssos.
15 Oculi ómnium in te sperant, *
et tu das illis escam in témpore opportúno.
16 Aperis tu manum tuam *
et imples omne ánimal in beneplácito.

17 Iustus Dóminus in ómnibus viis suis *
et sanctus in ómnibus opéribus suis.
18 Prope est Dóminus ómnibus invocántibus eum, *
ómnibus invocántibus eum in veritáte.
19 Voluntátem timéntium se fáciet †
et deprecatiónem eórum exáudiet *
et salvos fáciet eos.
20 Custódit Dóminus omnes diligéntes se *
et omnes peccatóres dispérdet.

21 Laudatiónem Dómini loquétur os meum, †
et benedícat omnis caro nómini sancto eius *
in sæculum et in sæculum sæculi.

13 Thy kingdom is an everlasting kingdom,
and thy dominion endures throughout all generations.

Ant. 1 Every day I will bless Thee, O Lord, and declare Thy mighty acts.
Ant. 2 The eyes of all look to Thee, O Lord; Thou art near to all Who call upon Thee.

II

The LORD is faithful in all his words,
and gracious in all his deeds.
14 The LORD upholds all who are falling,
and raises up all who are bowed down.
15 The eyes of all look to thee,
and thou givest them their food in due season.
16 Thou openest thy hand,
thou satisfiest the desire of every living thing.
17 The LORD is just in all his ways,
and kind in all his doings.
18 The LORD is near to all who call upon him,
to all who call upon him in truth.
19 He fulfils the desire of all who fear him,
he also hears their cry, and saves them.
20 The LORD preserves all who love him;
but all the wicked he will destroy.

21 My mouth will speak the praise of the LORD,
and let all flesh bless his holy name for ever and ever.

Ant. Oculi ómnium in te sperant, Dómine; prope es ómnibus invocántibus te.
Ant. 3 Iustæ et veræ sunt viæ tuæ, Rex sæculórum.

Canticum Ap 15, 3-4

3 Magna et mirabília ópera tua, *
Dómine Deus omnípotens;
iustæ et veræ viæ tuæ, *
Rex géntium!
4 Quis non timébit, Dómine, *
et glorificábit nomen tuum?
Quia solus Sanctus, †
quóniam omnes gentes vénient et adorábunt in conspéctu tuo, *
quóniam iudícia tua manifestáta sunt.

Ant. Iustæ et veræ sunt viæ tuæ, Rex sæculórum.

Lectio Brevis Rom 8, 1-2

Nihil nunc damnatiónis est his, qui sunt in Christo Iesu; lex enim Spíritus vitæ in Christo Iesu liberávit te a lege peccáti et mortis.

Responsorium Breve

℟. Christus mórtuus est pro peccátis nostris, * Ut nos offéret Deo. Christus.
℣. Mortificátus quidem carne, vivificátus autem Spíritu. * Ut nos offéret Deo. Glória Patri. Christus.

Ad Magnificat, ant. Recordáre, Dómine, misericórdiæ tuæ, sicut locútus es ad patres nostros.

Ant. 2 The eyes of all look to Thee, O Lord; Thou art near to all who call upon Thee.
Ant. 3 Just and true are Thy ways, O King of the ages!

Canticle Revelation 15:3–4

3 "Great and wonderful are thy deeds,
O Lord God the Almighty!
Just and true are thy ways,
O King of the ages!
4 Who shall not fear and glorify thy name, O Lord?
For thou alone art holy.
All nations shall come and worship thee,
for thy judgments have been revealed."

Ant. 3 Just and true are thy ways, O King of the Ages!

SHORT READING Romans 8:1–2

There is now no condemnation for those who are in Christ Jesus. For the law of the Spirit of life in Christ Jesus has set me free from the law of sin and death.

SHORT RESPONSORY

℟. Christ died for our sins to offer us to God.
℣. He died to this world of sin, and rose in the power of the Spirit.

Magnificat ant. Remember, O Lord, Your mercy, as You spoke to our fathers.

Preces

Christum, in quem sperant qui novérunt nomen eius, fidénter acclamántes rogémus: *Kyrie, eléison.*

Da, Christe, ut humána fragílitas, quæ per se proclívis est ad lapsum,
—per te semper firmétur.

Quæ per se prona est ad offénsam,
—per te semper reparétur ad véniam.

Qui culpa offénderis et pæniténtia placáris,
—flagélla tuæ iracúndiæ, quæ pro peccátis nostris merémur, avérte.

Qui mulíeris pæniténtis remisísti peccáta, et ovem errántem in úmeros tuos imposuísti,
—ne avértas misericórdiam tuam a nobis.

Omnes, qui in te, cum in terris dégerent, speravérunt,
—ad cæli portas admítte, quas crucis tuæ mérito reserásti.

Pater noster.

Oratio

Omnípotens et misericors Deus, qui Christum tuum pati pro totíus mundi salúte voluísti, concéde plebi tuæ, ut in hóstiam vivam tibi conténdat offérri, et amóris tui váleat plenitúdine satiári. Per Dóminum.

INTERCESSIONS

Faithfully acclaiming Christ, the Hope of those who have known His name, let us ask: *Kyrie, eleison.*

Grant, O Lord, that human frailty which inclines us to fall,

—may be strengthened continually through You.

May that which by itself is prone to offense,

—be restored to favor by You.

You that are displeased by sin and pleased with repentance,

—avert the scourges of Your wrath which we merit for our sins.

You that forgave the sins of the penitent woman and placed the wandering sheep on Your shoulders,

—do not turn away Your mercy from us.

All who, while they abode on earth, hoped in You,

—admit to the gates of heaven, which You opened by the merit of Your Cross.

Our Father.

ORATION

All-powerful and merciful God, Who willed that Your Christ suffer for the salvation of the whole world, grant to Your people, that they might be able to offer themselves as a living victim and be filled with the fullness of Your love. Through our Lord.

Hebdomada IV

Sabbato, ad Laudes matutinas

Hymn

Diéi luce réddita,
lætis gratísque vócibus
Dei canámus glóriam,
Christi faténtes grátiam,

Per quem creátor ómnium
diem noctémque cóndidit,
ætérna lege sánciens
ut semper succédant sibi.

Tu vera lux fidélium,
quem lex vetérna non tenet,
noctis nec ortu súccidens,
ætérno fulgens lúmine.

Præsta, Pater ingénite,
totum ducámus iúgiter
Christo placéntes hunc diem
Sancto repléti Spíritu. Amen.

Psalmodia

Ant. 1 Bonum est psállere nómini tuo, Altíssime, annuntiáre mane misericórdiam tuam.

Week IV

Saturday, Morning prayer

HYMN Trans. The Benedictine Nuns, St. Cecilia's Abbey

As light of day returns once more,
With joyful voices let us sing
To God of glory infinite,
To Christ our Lord for all His grace.

Through Whom the great Creator's will
Called day and night from nothingness,
Appointing them successive law,
Till time itself shall pass away.

True Light of every faithful soul
Unfettered by the claims of law;
No shades of night can fall that dim
Your dazzling and undying light.

O Father, uncreated Light,
Be with us as the hours go by,
That we may please Your Son our Lord,
Filled with the Spirit of Your love.
Amen.

PSALMODY

Ant. 1 It is good to sing praises to Thy name, O Most High, and to declare Thy steadfast love in the morning.

Psalmus 91 (92)

2 Bonum est confitéri Dómino *
et psállere nómini tuo, Altíssime,
3 annuntiáre mane misericórdiam tuam *
et veritátem tuam per noctem,
4 in decachórdo et psaltério, *
cum cántico in cíthara.

5 Quia delectásti me, Dómine, in factúra tua, *
et in opéribus mánuum tuárum exsultábo.

6 Quam magnificáta sunt ópera tua, Dómine: *
nimis profúndæ factæ sunt cogitatiónes tuæ.
7 Vir insípiens non cognóscet, *
et stultus non intélleget hæc.
8 Cum germináverint peccatóres sicut fenum, *
et florúerint omnes, qui operántur iniquitátem,
hoc tamen erit ad intéritum in sæculum sæculi; *
9 tu autem altíssimus in ætérnum, Dómine.

10 Quóniam ecce inimíci tui, Dómine, †
quóniam ecce inimíci tui períbunt, *
et dispergéntur omnes, qui operántur iniquitátem.
11 Exaltábis sicut unicórnis cornu meum, *
perfúsus sum óleo úberi.
12 Et despíciet óculus meus inimícos meos, *
et in insurgéntibus in me malignántibus áudiet auris mea.

13 Iustus ut palma florébit, *
sicut cedrus Líbani succréscet.
14 Plantáti in domo Dómini, *
in átriis Dei nostri florébunt.

Psalm 92

1 It is good to give thanks to the LORD,
to sing praises to thy name, O Most High;
2 to declare thy steadfast love in the morning,
and thy faithfulness by night,
3 to the music of the lute and the harp,
to the melody of the lyre.
4 For thou, O LORD, hast made me glad by thy work;
at the works of thy hands I sing for joy.

5 How great are thy works, O LORD!
Thy thoughts are very deep!
6 The dull man cannot know,
the stupid cannot understand this:
7 that, though the wicked sprout like grass
and all evildoers flourish,
they are doomed to destruction for ever,
8 but thou, O LORD, art on high for ever.
9 For lo, thy enemies, O LORD,
for lo, thy enemies shall perish;
all evildoers shall be scattered.

10 But thou hast exalted my horn like that of the wild ox;
thou hast poured over me fresh oil.
11 My eyes have seen the downfall of my enemies,
my ears have heard the doom of my evil assailants.

12 The righteous flourish like the palm tree.
and grow like a cedar in Lebanon.
13 They are planted in the house of the LORD,
they flourish in the courts of our God.

15 Adhuc fructus dabunt in senécta, *
úberes et bene viréntes erunt,
16 ut annúntient quóniam rectus Dóminus refúgium meum, *
et non est iníquitas in eo.

Ant. Bonum est psállere nómini tuo, Altíssime, annuntiáre mane misericórdiam tuam.

Ant. 2 Dabo vobis cor novum et spíritum novum in médio vestri.

Canticum Ez 36, 24-28

24 Tollam quippe vos de géntibus †
et congregábo vos de univérsis terris *
et addúcam vos in terram vestram;
25 et effúndam super vos aquam mundam, †
et mundabímini ab ómnibus inquinaméntis vestris, *
et ab univérsis idólis vestris mundábo vos.

26 Et dabo vobis cor novum *
et spíritum novum ponam in médio vestri
et áuferam cor lapídeum de carne vestra *
et dabo vobis cor cárneum;
27 et spíritum meum ponam in médio vestri †
et fáciam, ut in præcéptis meis ambulétis *
et iudícia mea custodiátis et operémini.

28 Et habitábitis in terra, quam dedi pátribus vestris, †
et éritis mihi in pópulum, *
et ego ero vobis in Deum.

14 They still bring forth fruit in old age,
they are ever full of sap and green,
15 to show that the LORD is upright;
he is my rock, and there is no unrighteousness
in him.

Ant. 1 It is good to sing praises to Thy name, O Most High, and to declare Thy steadfast love in the morning.

Ant. 2 A new heart I will give you, I will put a new spirit within you.

Canticle Ezekiel 36:24–28

24 "For I will take you from the nations, and gather
you from all the countries, and bring you into
your own land.
25 I will sprinkle clean water upon you, and you
shall be clean from all your uncleannesses,
and from all your idols I will cleanse you.
26 A new heart I will give you, and a new spirit I will
put within you; and I will take out of your
flesh the heart of stone and give you a heart of
flesh.
27 And I will put my spirit within you, and cause you
to walk in my statutes and be careful to
observe my ordinances.
28 You shall dwell in the land which I gave to your
fathers; and you shall be my people, and I will
be your God."

Ant. Dabo vobis cor novum et spíritum novum in médio vestri.

Ant. 3 Ex ore infántium et lacténtium, Dómine, perfecísti laudem.

Psalmus 8

2 Dómine, Dóminus noster, *
quam admirábile est nomen tuum in univérsa terra,
quóniam eleváta est magnificéntia tua *
super cælos.

3 Ex ore infántium et lactántium †
perfecísti laudem propter inimícos tuos, *
ut déstruas inimícum et ultórem.

4 Quando vídeo cælos tuos, ópera digitórum tuórum, *
lunam et stellas, quæ tu fundásti,
5 quid est homo, quod memor es eius, *
aut fílius hóminis quóniam vísitas eum?

6 Minuísti eum paulo minus ab ángelis, †
glória et honóre coronásti eum *
7 et constituísti eum super ópera mánuum tuárum.

Omnia subiecísti sub pédibus eius, †
8 oves et boves univérsas, *
ínsuper et pécora campi,
9 vólucres cæli et pisces maris, *
quæcúmque perámbulant sémitas maris.

10 Dómine, Dóminus noster, *
quam admirábile est nomen tuum in univérsa terra!

Ant. 2 A new heart I will give you, I will put a new spirit within you.
Ant. 3 On the lips of children and of babes, Thou hast fashioned perfect praise.

Psalm 8

1 O LORD, our Lord
how majestic is thy name in all the earth!
Thou whose glory above the heavens is chanted
2 by the mouth of babes and infants,
thou hast founded a bulwark because of thy foes,
to still the enemy and the avenger.
3 When I look at thy heavens, the work of thy fingers,
the moon and the stars which thou hast established;
4 what is man that thou art mindful of him,
and the son of man that thou dost care for him?
5 Yet thou hast made him little less than God,
and dost crown him with glory and honor.
6 Thou hast given him dominion over the works of thy hands;
thou hast put all things under his feet,
7 all sheep and oxen,
and also the beasts of the field,
8 the birds of the air, and the fish of the sea,
whatever passes along the paths of the sea.

9 O LORD, our Lord,
how majestic is thy name in all the earth!

Ant. Ex ore infántium et lacténtium, Dómine, perfecísti laudem.

LECTIO BREVIS 2 PETR 3, 13–15A

Novos cælos et terram novam secúndum promíssum Dómini exspectámus, in quibus iustítia hábitat. Propter quod, caríssimi, hæc exspectántes satágite immaculáti et invioláti ei inveníri in pace et Dómini nostri longanimitátem salútem arbitrámini.

RESPONSORIUM BREVE

℟. Exsultábunt lábia mea, * Cum cantávero tibi. Exsultábunt.

℣. Lingua mea meditábitur iustítiam tuam. * Cum cantávero tibi. Glória Patri. Exsultábunt.

Ad Benedictus, ant. Dírige, Dómine, pedes nostros in viam pacis.

PRECES

Adorémus Deum, qui per Fílium suum spem mundo et vitam dedit, et humíliter deprecémur: *Dómine, audi nos.*

Dómine, Pater ómnium, qui nos ad princípium huius diéi perveníre fecísti,
—ad laudem glóriæ tuæ fac nos cum Christo vívere.

Fidem, spem et caritátem tuam, quæ córdibus nostris infudísti,
—in nobis semper manére concéde.

Ad te, semper, Dómine, óculi nostri levéntur,
—ut tibi vocánti alácriter respondeámus.

Ab insídiis nos et illécebris iniquitátis avérte,
—et gressus nostros ab omni offensióne defénde.

Ant. 3 On the lips of children and of babes, Thou hast fashioned perfect praise.

SHORT READING 2 Peter 3:13–15a

But according to his promise we wait for new heavens and a new earth in which righteousness dwells.

Therefore, beloved, since you wait for these, be zealous to be found by him without spot or blemish and at peace. And count the forbearance of our Lord as salvation.

SHORT RESPONSORY

℟. My lips will rejoice when I sing to You.
℣. My tongue will meditate on Your justice.

Benedictus ant. Guide our feet, O Lord, into the way of peace.

INTERCESSIONS

Let us adore God, Who through His Son gave hope and life to the world, and humbly let us entreat Him: *Lord, hear us.*

Lord, Father of all, Who have made us to come to the beginning of this day,
—to the praise of Your glory make us to live with Christ.

Your faith, hope and charity, which You have poured into our hearts,
—grant to remain in us always.

To You, O Lord, may our eyes be raised always,
—that we might respond eagerly to Your call.

Turn us from the deceits and all lures of iniquity,
—and defend our steps from every stumbling.

Pater noster.

ORATIO

Omnípotens ætérne Deus, qui splendor es veri lúminis et dies perpétuus, te, matutíni, témporis redeúnte círculo, deprecámur, ut nostras quoque mentes, vitiórum nocte discússa, advéntus tui fulgor illústret. Per Dóminum.

Our Father.

ORATION

All-powerful and ever-living God, Who are the splendor of true light and the everlasting day, we beseech You at the coming around of morning time, that as You have scattered the night of our sins, so the brightness of Your advent might enlighten our minds. Through our Lord.

III

Proprium de Tempore / Proper of the Time

Dominica II

per annum

Ad I Vesperas

Anno A

Ecce Agnus Dei, ecce qui tollit peccátum mundi, allelúia.

Anno B

Audiérunt Ioánnem duo discípuli, et secúti sunt Iesum, dicéntes: Rabbi, ubi manes? Dicit eis: Veníte et vidéte.

Anno C

Núptiæ factæ sunt in Cana Galilǽæ, et erat ibi Iesus cum María matre sua.

Oratio

Omnípotens sempitérne Deus, qui cæléstia simul et terréna moderáris, supplicatiónes pópuli tui cleménter exáudi, et pacem tuam nostris concéde tempóribus. Per Dóminum.

Ad Laudes matutinas

Anno A

Hoc est testimónium quod perhíbuit Ioánnes: Post me venit vir, qui ante me factus est, quia prior me erat.

Anno B

Venérunt discípuli et vidérunt ubi manéret Iesus, et apud eum mansérunt die illo.

2nd Sunday

throughout the year

First Vespers

Year A

Behold the Lamb of God, behold Him Who takes away the sin of the world, alleluia.

Year B

The two disciples heard John, and were following Jesus, saying: Rabbi, where are You staying? He said to them: Come and see.

Year C

There was a marriage at Cana in Galilee, and Jesus was there with Mary His mother.

Oration

Almighty and everlasting God, Who govern all things in heaven and on earth, mercifully hear the supplications of Your people and grant us Your peace in our times.

Lauds

Year A

This is the testimony which John gave: After me comes a man who ranks before me, for He was before me.

Year B

The disciples came and saw where Jesus was staying, and they stayed with Him that day.

Anno C

Dicit mater Iesu minístris: Quodcúmque díxerit vobis, facite. Et iussit Iesus impléri hýdrias aqua, quæ in vinum convérsa est.

Ad II Vesperas

Anno A

Descéndit Spíritus quasi colúmba de cælo, et mansit super Iesum: Hic est qui baptízat in Spíritu Sancto.

Anno B

Dixit Andréas Simóni fratri: Invénimus Messíam. Et addúxit eum ad Iesum.

Anno C

Hoc fecit inítium signórum Iesus in Cana Galilǽæ, et manifestávit glóriam suam, et credidérunt in eum discípuli eius.

Year C

The mother of Jesus said to the servants: Do whatever He tells you. And Jesus ordered the water-jars to be filled with water, which was turned into wine.

Second Vespers

Year A

The Spirit descended from heaven as a dove, and remained on Jesus: This is He Who baptizes in the Holy Spirit.

Year B

Andrew said to his brother Simon: We have found the Messiah. And he led him to Jesus.

Year C

This, the first of His signs, Jesus did at Cana in Galilee, and manifested His glory; and His disciples believed in Him.

Dominica III

per annum

Ad I Vesperas

Anno A

Dicit Dóminus: Pæniténtiam ágite: appropinquávit enim regnum cælórum.

Anno B

Venit Iesus in Galilǽam prǽdicans Evangélium Dei, et dicens: Implétum est tempus et appropinquávit regnum Dei: pænitémini et crédite Evangélio.

Anno C

Venit Iesus in virtúte Spíritus, et docébat die sábbati in synagógis, et magnificábitur ab ómnibus.

Oratio

Omnípotens sempitérne Deus, dírige actus nostros in beneplácito tuo, ut in nómine dilécti Fílii tui mereámur bonis opéribus abundáre. Per Dóminum.

Ad Laudes matutinas

Anno A

Ámbulans iuxta mare Galilǽæ vidit duos fratres, mitténtes retes in mare, et vocávit eos. Illi autem contínuo, relíctis rétibus, secúti sunt eum.

3rd Sunday

throughout the year

First Vespers

Year A

The Lord says: Repent, for the kingdom of heaven is at hand.

Year B

Jesus came into Galilee preaching the Gospel of God, and saying: The time is fulfilled, and the kingdom of God is at hand; repent, and believe in the Gospel.

Year C

Jesus came in the power of the Spirit, and He taught on the sabbath day in the synagogues, and was glorified by all.

Oration

Almighty and everlasting God, direct our actions according to Your good pleasure, so that in the name of Your beloved Son, we may merit to abound in good works.

Lauds

Year A

Walking next to the Sea of Galilee, He saw two brothers, casting nets into the sea, and He called them. And, immediately abandoning the nets, they followed Him.

Anno B

Veníte post me, dicit Dóminus; fáciam vos fíeri piscatóres hóminum.

Anno C

Spíritus Dómini super me, evangelizáre paupéribus misit me.

Ad II Vesperas

Anno A

Prædicábat Iesus Evangélium regni, et sanábat omnem infirmitátem in pópulo.

Anno B

Relíctis rétibus suis, secúti sunt Dóminum et Redemptórem, allelúia.

Anno C

Cum plicuísset librum, cœpit Iesus dícere ad illos: Hódie impléta est hæc Scriptúra in áuribus vestris.

Year B

Follow me, says the Lord; I will make you become fishers of men.

Year C

The Spirit of the Lord is upon me, He sent me to preach good news to the poor.

Second Vespers

Year A

Jesus preached the Gospel of the kingdom, and healed every infirmity among the people.

Year B

Abandoning their nets, they followed the Lord and Redeemer, alleluia.

Year C

When He had closed the book, Jesus began to say to them: Today this Scripture is fulfilled in your hearing.

Dominica IV

per annum

Ad I Vesperas

Anno A

Cum vidísset Iesus turbas, ascéndit in montem; et accessérunt ad eum discípuli eius; et apériens os suum docébat eos, dicens: Beáti páuperes spíritu, quóniam ipsórum est regnum cælórum.

Anno B

Stupébant omnes super doctrína Iesu; erat enim docens eos tamquam potestátem habens.

Anno C

Mirabántur omnes in verbis grátiæ quæ procedébant de ore Iesu.

Oratio

Concéde nobis, Dómine Deus noster, ut te tota mente venerémur, et omnes hómines rationábili diligámus afféctu. Per Dóminum.

Ad Laudes matutinas

Anno A

Beáti mundo corde, quóniam ipsi Deum vidébunt, dicit Dóminus.

4th Sunday

throughout the year

First Vespers

Year A

When Jesus saw the crowds, He went up the mountain; and His disciples came to Him; and opening His mouth He taught them, saying: Blessed are the poor in spirit, for theirs is the kingdom of heaven.

Year B

They all wondered at Jesus' teaching; for He was teaching them as one having power.

Year C

They all wondered at the words of grace which proceeded from the mouth of Jesus.

Oration

Grant to us, O Lord our God, that we may venerate You with our whole mind and that all men may love You with an ordered affection.

Lauds

Year A

Blessed are the pure in heart, for they shall see God, says the Lord.

Anno B

Conquirébant inter se dicéntes: Quidnam est hoc? Doctrína nova cum potestáte; et spirítibus immúndis ímperat et obœ́diunt ei.

Anno C

Amen dico vobis: Nemo prophéta accéptus est in pátria sua.

Ad II Vesperas

Anno A

Beáti pacífici, quóniam fílii Dei Vocabúntur, dicit Dóminus.

Anno B

Miráti sunt omnes, et procéssit rumor eius statim ubíque in omnem regiónem Galilǽæ.

Anno C

Eiecérunt Iesum extra civitátem, ut præcipitárent eum. Ipse autem tránsiens per médium illórum ibat.

Year B

They questioned among themselves, saying: What is this? A new teaching with power; and He commands the unclean spirits and they obey Him.

Year C

Amen I say to you: No prophet is accepted in his own country.

Second Vespers

Year A

Blessed are the peacemakers, for they shall be called sons of God, says the Lord.

Year B

They all wondered, and at once His fame spread everywhere throughout all the region of Galilee.

Year C

They threw Jesus out of the city, so that they might throw Him down headlong. But passing through the midst of them, He went away.

Dominica V

per annum

Ad I Vesperas

Anno A

Vos estis sal terræ: quod si sal evanúerit, in quo saliétur? dicit Dóminus discípulis suis.

Anno B

Véspere autem facto, afferébant ad eum omnes male habéntes, et curávit multos qui vexabántur váriis languóribus.

Anno C

Ascéndens Iesus in navim, et sedens, docébat turbas.

Oratio

Famíliam tuam, quæsumus, Dómine, contínua pietáte custódi, ut, quæ in sola spe grátiæ cæléstis innítitur, tua semper protectióne muniátur. Per Dóminum.

Ad Laudes matutinas

Anno A

Vos estis lux mundi: lúceat lux vestra coram homínibus, ut vídeant ópera vestra bona et gloríficent Patrem vestrum, qui in cælis est.

5th Sunday

throughout the year

First Vespers

Year A

You are the salt of the earth; but if salt has lost its taste, how shall its saltness be restored? says the Lord to His disciples.

Year B

In the evening they brought to Him all who were sick, and He healed many who were sick with various diseases.

Year C

Getting into the boat and sitting down, Jesus taught the crowds.

Oration

We beseech You, O Lord, to keep Your family in continual devotion, that what is begun solely in the hope of heavenly grace, may always be guarded by Your protection.

Lauds

Year A

You are the light of the world: let your light shine before men, that they may see your good works and give glory to your Father Who is in heaven.

Anno B

Dilúculo valde surgens, egréssus Iesus ábiit in desértum locum, ibíque orábat.

Anno C

Præcéptor, per totam noctem laborántes nihil cépimus; in verbo autem tuo laxábo rete.

Ad II Vesperas

Anno A

Lúceat lux vestra sicut lucérna, quæ pónitur super candelábrum, ut lúceat ómnibus, qui in domo sunt.

Anno B

Simon et qui cum illo erant dicébant: Omnes quærunt te! Et ait illis: Eámus álibi ut et ibi prǽdicem: ad hoc enim veni.

Anno C

Exi a me, quia homo peccátor sum, dixit Petrus ad Iesum. Noli timére, ex hoc iam hómines eris cápiens.

Year B

Rising early in the morning, Jesus went out and went into a desert place, and there He prayed.

Year C

Teacher, we took nothing laboring through the whole night; but at Your word I will let down the net.

Second Vespers

Year A

Let your light shine as a lamp which is placed upon a stand, that it may shine for all who are in the house.

Year B

Simon and those who were with him said: Everyone is looking for You! And He said to them: Let us go on to another place that I may preach there; for that is why I came.

Year C

Depart from me, for I am a sinful man, said Peter to Jesus. Do not be afraid, henceforth you will be catching men.

Dominica VI

per annum

Ad I Vesperas

Anno A

Qui fécerit et docúerit, hic magnus vocábitur in regno cælórum, dicit Dóminus.

Anno B

Dómine, si vis, potes me mundáre. Et ait Iesus: Volo, mundáre.

Anno C

Beáti páuperes, quia vestrum est regnum Dei. Beáti, qui nunc esurítis, quia saturabímini.

Oratio

Deus, qui te in rectis et sincéris manére pectóribus ásseris, da nobis tua grátia tales exístere, in quibus habitáre dignéris. Per Dóminum.

Ad Laudes matutinas

Anno A

Nisi abundáverit iustítia vestra plus quam scribárum et pharisæórum, non intrábitis in regnum cælórum.

6th Sunday

throughout the year

First Vespers

Year A

He who does and teaches [these commandments] will be called great in the kingdom of heaven, says the Lord.

Year B

Lord, if You will, You can make me clean. And Jesus said: I will; be clean.

Year C

Blessed are the poor, for yours is the kingdom of heaven. Blessed are you that hunger now, for you shall be satisfied.

Oration

O God, Who proclaim that You remain in upright and sincere hearts, grant to us that these in whom you deign to dwell may have our existence by Your grace.

Lauds

Year A

Unless your righteousness exceeds that of the scribes and Pharisees, you will never enter the kingdom of heaven.

Anno B

Iesus misértus exténdens manum suam tétigit leprósum, et statim discéssit ab eo lepra, et mundátus est.

Anno C

Beáti qui nunc fletis, quia ridébitis, dicit Dóminus.

Ad II Vesperas

Anno A

Si offers munus tuum ante altáre et recordátus fúeris quia frater tuus habet áliquid advérsus te, relínque ibi munus tuum ante altáre et vade prius reconciliári fratri tuo; et tunc véniens offer munus tuum, allelúia.

Anno B

Vide némini quidquam díxeris, sed vade, osténde te sacerdóti, in testimónium illis. At ille egréssus cœpit prædicáre multum et diffamáre sermóne.

Anno C

Beáti éritis, cum vos óderint hómines propter Fílium hóminis: gaudéte et exsultáte, ecce enim merces vestra multa est in cælo.

Year B

Moved with pity, Jesus stretched out His hand and touched the leper, and immediately the leprosy left him, and he was made clean.

Year C

Blessed are you that weep now, for you shall laugh, says the Lord.

Second Vespers

Year A

If you are offering your gift at the altar, and there remember that your brother has something against you, leave your gift there before the altar and go; first be reconciled to your brother, and then come and offer your gift, alleluia.

Year B

See that you say nothing to anyone; but go, show yourself to the priest, in testimony to him. But he went out and began to talk freely about it, and to spread the news.

Year C

Blessed are you when men hate you on account of the Son of Man; rejoice and exsult, for behold, your reward is great in heaven.

Dominica VII

per annum

Ad I Vesperas

Anno A

Dilígite inimícos vestros et oráte pro persequéntibus vos, ut sitis fílii Patris vestri, qui in cælis est.

Anno B

Véniunt feréntes ad Iesum paralýticum. Cum vidísset fidem illórum, ait Iesus paralýtico: fili, dimittúntur peccáta tua.

Anno C

Prout vultis ut fáciant vobis hómines, fácite illis simíliter, dicit Dóminus.

Oratio

Præsta, quæsumus, omnípotens Deus, ut, semper rationabília meditántes, quæ tibi sunt plácita, et dictis exsequámur et factis. Per Dóminum.

Ad Laudes matutinas

Anno A

Pater vester solem suum oríri facit super malos et bonos et pluit super iustos et iniústos.

7th Sunday

throughout the year

First Vespers

Year A

Love your enemies and pray for those who persecute you, so that you may be sons of your Father Who is in heaven.

Year B

They came bringing a paralytic to Jesus. When He saw their faith, Jesus said to the paralytic: Son, your sins are forgiven.

Year C

As you wish that men would do to you, do so to them, says the Lord.

Oration

Grant, we beseech You, almighty God, that always meditating on those things which accord with reason, as such things are pleasing to You, we may carry them out both by our words and by our deeds.

Lauds

Year A

Your Father makes His sun rise on the evil and the good, and sends rain on the just and the unjust.

Anno B

Dixit Iesus: Ut sciátis quia potestátem habet Fílius hóminis in terra dimitténdi peccáta, ait paralýtico: Tibi dico: Surge, tolle grabátum tuum et vade in domum tuam.

Anno C

Nolíte iudicáre, ut non iudicémini: in quo enim iudício iudicavéritis iudicabímini, dicit Dóminus.

Ad II Vesperas

Anno A

Estóte vos perfécti sicut Pater vester cæléstis perféctus est, dicit Dóminus.

Anno B

Tulit paralýticus lectum suum, in quo iacébat, magníficans Deum; et omnis plebs, ut vidit, dedit laudem Deo.

Anno C

Dimíttite et dimittémini; date, et dábitur vobis. Eádem quippe mensúra qua mensi fuéritis, remetiétur vobis.

Year B

Jesus said: So that you may know that the Son of Man has authority on earth to forgive sins—He said to the paralytic—I say to you, rise, take up your pallet and go home.

Year C

Do not judge, so that you will not be judged; for by the judgment that you judge you will be judged, says the Lord.

Second Vespers

Year A

You must be perfect as your heavenly Father is perfect, says the Lord.

Year B

The paralytic, glorifying God, took up his pallet on which he had lain; and all the people, as they saw this, gave praise to God.

Year C

Forgive, and you will be forgiven; give, and it will be given to you. For the measure you give will be the measure you get back.

Dominica VIII

per annum

Ad I Vesperas

Anno A

Respícite volatília cæli, quóniam non serunt neque metunt, et Pater vester cæléstis pascit illa. Nonne vos magis pluris estis illis?

Anno B

Quanto témpore habent secum convívæ sponsum, non possunt ieiunáre, dicit Dóminus.

Anno C

Éice primum trabem de óculo tuo, et tunc perspícies ut edúcas festúcam quæ est in óculo fratris tui, dicit Dóminus.

Oratio

Da nobis, quæsumus, Dómine, ut et mundi cursus pacífico nobis tuo órdine dirigátur, et Ecclésia tua tranquílla devotióne lætétur. Per Dóminum.

Lauds

Anno A

Nolíte sollíciti esse dicéntes: Quid manducábimus, aut quid bibémus? Scit enim Pater vester cæléstis quid vobis necésse sit!

8th Sunday

throughout the year

First Vespers

Year A

Look at the birds of the air: they neither sow nor reap, and yet your heavenly Father feeds them. Are you not of more value than they?

Year B

As long as they have the bridegroom with them, they cannot fast, says the Lord.

Year C

First take the log out of your own eye, then you will see clearly to take out the speck that is in your brother's eye, says the Lord.

Oration

Grant us, we beseech you, O Lord, that as the course of the world is directed by your peaceful order, so too Your Church may rejoice in tranquillity and devotion.

Lauds

Year A

Do not be anxious, saying: What shall we eat, or what shall we drink? For your heavenly Father knows what you need!

Anno B

Loquar ad cor tuum: Sponsábo te mihi in fide, et cognósces Dóminum.

Anno C

Non potest arbor bona fructus malos fácere, neque arbor mala fructus bonos fácere.

Ad II Vesperas

Anno A

Quǽrite primum regnum Dei et iustítiam eius, et hæc ómnia adiciéntur vobis.

Anno B

Nemo mittit vinum novum in utres véteres, sed vinum novum in utres novos mitti debet.

Anno C

Bonus homo de bono thesáuro cordis profert bonum: ex abundántia enim cordis os eius lóquitur.

Year B

I will speak to your heart: I will marry you to me in faith, and you will know the Lord.

Year C

For no good tree bears bad fruit, nor again does a bad tree bear good fruit.

Second Vespers

Year A

Seek first the kingdom of God and His righteousness, and all these things shall be yours as well.

Year B

No one puts new wine into old wineskins, but he ought to put new wine into new wineskins.

Year C

The good man out of the good treasure of his heart produces good; for out of the abundance of the heart his mouth speaks.

Dominica IX

per annum

Ad I Vesperas

Anno A

Non omnis qui dicit mihi: Dómine, Dómine, intrábit in regnum cælórum, sed qui facit voluntátem Patris mei, qui in cælis est, ipse intrábit in regnum cælórum.

Anno B

Sábbatum propter hóminem factum est, et non homo propter sábbatum, dicit Dóminus.

Anno C

Cum audísset centúrio de Iesu, misit ad eum senióres Iudæórum, rogans eum, ut veníret et salváret servum eius.

Oratio

Deus, cuius providéntia in sui dispositióne non fállitur, te súpplices exorámus, ut nóxia cuncta submóveas, et ómnia nobis profutúra concédas. Per Dóminum.

Ad Laudes matutinas

Anno A

Omnis qui audit verba mea hæc et facit ea, assimilábitur viro sapiénti, qui ædificávit domum suam supra petram.

9th Sunday

throughout the year

First Vespers

Year A

Not everyone who says to me: Lord, Lord, shall enter the kindgom of heaven, but he who does the will of my Father Who is in heaven, he will enter the kingdom of heaven.

Year B

The sabbath was made for man, not man for the sabbath, says the Lord.

Year C

When he heard of Jesus, he sent to Him elders of the Jews, asking Him to come and heal his slave.

Oration

O God, Whose providence does not fail in its governance, we humbly beseech You to remove all things which are harmful and to bestow on us all things which are profitable.

Lauds

Year A

Everyone who hears these words of mine and does them will be like a wise man who built his house upon the rock.

Anno B

Respóndit Iesus pharisǽis: Dóminus est Fílius hóminis étiam sábbati.

Anno C

Dómine, non sum dignus ut intres sub tectum meum; sed tantum dic verbo, et sanábitur puer meus.

Ad II Vesperas

Anno A

Flúmina et venti irruérunt in domum sapiéntis et non cécidit: fundáta enim erat supra petram.

Anno B

Dicit Iesus hómini habénti manum áridam: Exténde manum. Et exténdit, et restitúta est manus eius.

Anno C

Iesus mirátus est centuriónem, et ait: Dico vobis, nec in Israel tantum fidem invéni. Et revérsi qui missi fúerant domum, invenérunt servum sanum.

Year B

Jesus answered the Pharisees: The Son of Man is Lord even of the sabbath.

Year C

Lord, I am not worthy that You should enter under my roof; but only say the word, and my servant shall be healed.

Second Vespers

Year A

The floods and the winds beat upon the house of the wise man but it did not fall, because it had been founded on the rock.

Year B

Jesus said to the man with the withered hand: Extend your hand. And he extended it, and his hand was restored.

Year C

Jesus marveled at the centurion, and said: I say to you, not even in Israel have I found such faith. And when those who had been sent returned to the house, they found the slave well.

Dominica X

per annum

Ad I Vesperas

Anno A

Cum transíret Iesus, vidit hóminem sedéntem in telóneo, Matthǽo nómine, et ait illi: Séquere me. Et surgens secútus est eum.

Anno B

Si in dígito Dei eício dæmónia, profécto pervénit in vos regnum Dei.

Anno C

Cum vidísset Dóminus víduam, misericórdia motus super ea dixit illi: Noli flere.

Oratio

Deus, a quo bona cuncta procédunt, tuis largíre supplícibus, ut cogitémus, te inspiránte, quæ recta sunt, et, te gubernánte, éadem faciámus. Per Dóminum.

Ad Laudes matutinas

Anno A

Multi publicáni et peccatóres veniéntes simul discumbébant cum Iesu et discípulis eius.

Anno B

Cum fortis armátus custódit átrium suum, in pace sunt ómnia quæ póssidet.

10th Sunday

throughout the year

First Vespers

Year A

As Jesus passed on, He saw a man called Matthew sitting at the tax office, and He said to him: Follow me. And he rose and followed Him.

Year B

If I cast out demons by the finger of God, the kingdom of God has truly come among you.

Year C

When the Lord saw the widow, He had compassion on her and said to her: Do not weep.

Oration

O God, from Whom all good things do proceed, grant to Your suppliants that, by Your inspiration, we may think those things which are right and, by Your governance, do the same.

Lauds

Year A

Many tax collectors and sinners came and sat down at table together with Jesus and His disciples.

Year B

When an armed warrior guards his house, everything he posseses is in peace.

Anno C

Aduléscens, tibi dico, surge. Et resédit, qui erat mórtuus, et cœpit loqui; et dedit illum matri suæ.

Ad II Vesperas

Anno A

Misericórdiam volo et non sacrifícium. Non enim veni vocáre iustos, sed peccatóres.

Anno B

Qui fécerit voluntátem Dei, hic frater meus, et soror mea et mater est, dicit Dóminus.

Anno C

Prophéta magnus surréxit in nobis, et Deus visitávit plebem suam.

Year C

Young man, I say to you, arise. And the dead man sat up, and began to speak; and He gave him to his mother.

Second Vespers

Year A

I desire mercy and not sacrifice. For I came not to call the righteous, but sinners.

Year B

Whoever does the will of God is my brother, and my sister, and my mother, says the Lord.

Year C

A great prophet has arisen among us, and God has visited His people.

Dominica XI

per annum

Ad I Vesperas

Anno A

Videns Iesus turbas, misértus est eis, quia erant vexáti et iacéntes sicut oves non habéntes pastórem.

Anno B

Sic est regnum Dei, quemádmodum si homo iáciat seméntem in terram, et semen gérminet et incréscat, dum nescit ille.

Anno C

Múlier, quæ erat in civitáte peccátrix, áttulit alabástrum unguénti, et flens lácrimis rigábat pedes Iesu, et osculabátur, et unguénto ungébat.

Oratio

Deus, in te sperántium fortitúdo, invocatiónibus nostris adésto propítius, et, quia sine te nihil potest mortális infírmitas, grátiæ tuæ præsta semper auxílium, ut, in exsequéndis mandátis tuis, et voluntáte tibi et actióne placeámus. Per Dóminum.

11th Sunday

throughout the year

First Vespers

Year A

When Jesus saw the crowds, He had compassion for them, because they were harassed and helpless, like sheep without a shepherd.

Year B

The kingdom of God is as if a man should scatter seed upon the ground, and the seed should sprout and grow, he knows not how.

Year C

A woman of the city who was a sinner brought an alabaster flask of ointment, and, weeping, she began to wet Jesus' feet, and kissed His feet, and anointed them with the ointment.

Oration

O God, the strength of those who hope in You, graciously hear our prayers and, as our mortal weakness can do nothing without You, always bestow upon us the help of Your grace, that, in following Your commandments, we may please You in desire and action.

AD LAUDES MATUTINAS

Anno A

Duódecim apóstolos misit Iesus, præcípiens eis et dicens: Ite ad oves, quæ periérunt domus Israel.

Anno B

Símile est regnum cælórum grano sinápis, quod minus est ómnibus semínibus; et cum seminátum fúerit ascéndit et fit maius ómnibus holéribus.

Anno C

Remíssa sunt peccáta eius multa, quóniam diléxit multum; qui autem minus dimíttitur, minus díligit.

AD II VESPERAS

Anno A

Eúntes prædicáte Evangélium regni: gratis accepístis, gratis date.

Anno B

Multis parábolis loquebátur Iesus verbum. Seórsum autem discípulis suis disserébat ómnia.

Anno C

Dixit Iesus ad mulíerem: fides tua te salvam fecit; vade in pace.

Lauds

Year A

Jesus sent twelve apostles, charging them: Go to the lost sheep of the house of Israel.

Year B

The kingdom of heaven is like a grain of mustard seed, which is the smallest of all seeds; yet when it is sown, it grows up and becomes the greatest of all shrubs.

Year C

Her sins, which are many, are forgiven, for she loved much; but he who is forgiven little, loves little.

Second Vespers

Year A

Preach the Gospel of the kingdom as you go: You received freely, give freely.

Year B

With many parables Jesus spoke the word. But privately to His own disciples, He explained everything.

Year C

Jesus said to the woman: Your faith has saved you; go in peace.

Dominica XII

per annum

Ad I Vesperas

Anno A

Quod dico vobis in ténebris dícite in lúmine; et quod in aure audítis, prædicáte super tecta.

Anno B

Dómine, salva nos, perímus; ímpera et fac, Deus, tranquillitátem.

Anno C

Dixit Iesus discípulis suis: Vos autem quem me esse dícitis? Respóndens Petrus dixit: Christus Dei.

Oratio

Sancti nóminis tui, Dómine, timórem páriter et amórem fac nos habére perpétuum, quia numquam tua gubernatióne destítuis, quos in soliditáte tuæ dilectiónis instítuis. Per Dóminum.

Ad Laudes matutinas

Anno A

Vestri capílli cápitis omnes numeráti sunt. Nolíte ergo timére, dicit Dóminus.

Anno B

Exsúrgens Iesus comminátus est vento et dixit mari: Tace, obmutésce. Et cessávit ventus, et facta est tranquíllitas magna.

12th Sunday

throughout the year

First Vespers

Year A

What I tell you in the dark, utter in the light; and what you hear whispered, proclaim upon the housetops.

Year B

Lord, save us, we are perishing; O God, command and make tranquility.

Year C

Jesus said to His disciples: But who do you say that I am? And Peter answered: The Christ of God.

Oration

Make us, O Lord, to have at one and the same time a perpetual fear and love of Your holy name, since in Your governance You never abandon those whom You establish in the firmness of Your love.

Lauds

Year A

The hairs of your head are all numbered. Fear not, therefore, says the Lord.

Year B

Jesus rose and rebuked the wind, and said to the sea: Peace, be still. And the wind ceased, and there was a great calm.

Anno C

Opórtet Fílium hóminis multa pati et reprobári, et occídi, et tértia die resúrgere.

Ad II Vesperas

Anno A

Qui me confessus fúerit coram homínibus, confitébor et ego eum coram Patre meo, qui est in cælis.

Anno B

Timuérunt discípuli magno timóre et dicébant ad altérutrum: Quis putas est iste, quia et ventus et mare obœdiunt ei?

Anno C

Qui vult veníre post me, ábneget seípsum et tollat crucem suam et sequátur me, dicit Dóminus.

Year C

The Son of Man must suffer many things, and be rejected, and be killed, and on the third day be raised.

Second Vespers

Year A

Everyone who acknowledges Me before men, I also will acknowledge before My Father Who is in heaven.

Year B

The disciples feared with a great fear and said to one another: Who do you think this is, that even wind and sea obey Him?

Year C

Whoever wishes to come after Me, let him deny himself and take up his cross and follow me, says the Lord.

Dominica XIII

per annum

Ad I Vesperas

Anno A

Qui non áccipit crucem suam et séquitur me, non est me dignus, dicit Dóminus.

Anno B

Dicébat múlier intra se: Si vel vestiménta eius tetígero, salva ero.

Anno C

Vulpes fóveas habent et vólucres cæli nidos. Fílius autem hóminis non habet, ubi caput reclínet.

Oratio

Deus, qui, per adoptiónem grátiæ, lucis nos esse fílios voluísti, præsta, quæsumus, ut errórum non involvámur ténebris, sed in splendóre veritátis semper maneámus conspícui. Per Dóminum.

Ad Laudes matutinas

Anno A

Qui récipit vos me récipit; et qui me récipit, récipit eum qui me misit.

Anno B

Iesus convérsus et videns mulíerem dixit: Fília, fides tua te salvam fecit; vade in pace.

13th Sunday

throughout the year

First Vespers

Year A

He who does not take up his cross and follow me is not worthy of me, says the Lord.

Year B

The woman said to herself: If I touch even His garments, I shall be made well.

Year C

Foxes have holes, and birds of the air have nests; but the Son of Man has nowhere to lay His head.

Oration

O God, Who through the adoption of grace, willed us to be sons of light, grant, we beseech You, that we not be wrapped in the darkness of error but always remain visibly in the splendor of the truth.

Lauds

Year A

He who receives you receives Me, and he who receives Me receives Him Who sent Me.

Year B

Jesus turned, and seeing the woman, said: Daughter, your faith has made you well; go in peace.

Anno C

Sine, ut mórtui sepéliant mórtuos suos: tu autem vade, annúntia regnum Dei.

Ad II Vesperas

Anno A

Quicúmque potum déderit uni ex mínimis istis cálicem aquæ frígidæ tantum in nómine discípuli, amen dico vobis, non perdet mercédem suam.

Anno B

Puélla non est mórtua, sed dormit. Et tenens manum puéllæ ait illi: Puélla, tibi dico, surge.

Anno C

Nemo mittens manum suam in arátrum et aspíciens retro, aptus est regno Dei, dicit Dóminus.

Year C

Leave the dead to bury their own dead; but as for you, go and proclaim the kingdom of God.

Second Vespers

Year A

Whoever gives to one of these little ones even a cup of cold water because he is a disciple, amen I say to you, he shall not lose his reward.

Year B

The girl is not dead, but sleeping. And holding the girl's hand, He said: Little girl, I say to you, arise.

Year C

No one who puts his hand to the plow and looks back is fit for the kingdom of God, says the Lord.

Dominica XIV

per annum

Ad I Vesperas

Anno A

Confíteor tibi, Pater, Dómine cæli et terræ, quia abscondísti hæc a sapiéntibus et prudéntibus et revelásti ea párvulis.

Anno B

Multi audiéntes admirabántur in doctrína Iesu, dicéntes: Unde huic hæc ómnia? Nonne iste est faber, fílius Maríæ?

Anno C

Messis quidem multa, operárii autem pauci. Rogáte ergo Dóminum messis, ut mittat operários in messem suam.

Oratio

Deus, qui in Fílii tui humilitáte iacéntem mundum erexísti, fidélibus tuis sanctam concéde lætítiam, ut, quos eripuísti a servitúte peccáti, gáudiis fácias pérfrui sempitérnis. Per Dóminum.

Ad Laudes matutinas

Anno A

Tóllite iugum meum super vos et díscite a me quia mitis sum et húmilis corde; et inveniétis réquiem animábus vestris.

14th Sunday

throughout the year

First Vespers

Year A

I confess to You, Father, Lord of heaven and earth, that You have hidden these things from the wise and understanding and revealed them to babes.

Year B

Many who heard Him were astonished at the teaching of Jesus, saying: Where did this man get all this? Is this not the carpenter, the Son of Mary?

Year C

The harvest is plentiful, but the laborers are few; pray therefore the Lord of the harvest to send out laborers into His harvest.

Oration

O God, Who raised up a fallen world by the abasement of Your Son, grant to Your faithful holy joy, that those whom You have delivered from the bondage of sin, You would make to abound in eternal joys.

Lauds

Year A

Take My yoke upon you and learn from Me; for I am gentle and lowly in heart, and you will find rest for your souls.

Anno B

Amen dico vobis, quia nemo prophéta accéptus est in pátria sua.

Anno C

In quamcúmque domum intravéritis, primum dícite: Pax huic dómui. Et requiéscet super illam pax vestra.

Ad II Vesperas

Anno A

Iugum meum suáve est, et onus meum leve, dicit Dóminus.

Anno B

Egréssus Iesus e pátria sua, circumíbat castélla in circúitu docens.

Anno C

Gaudéte et exsultáte, quia nómina vestra scripta sunt in cælis, dicit Dóminus.

Year B

Amen I say to you, no prophet is accepted in his own country.

Year C

Whatever house you enter, first say: Peace be to this house. And your peace shall rest upon it.

Second Vespers

Year A

My yoke is sweet, and my burden light, says the Lord.

Year B

Jesus went out from His own country, and went about the villages teaching.

Year C

Rejoice and exsult, for your names are written in heaven, says the Lord.

Dominica XV

per annum

Ad I Vesperas

Anno A

Locútus est Iesus turbis in parábolis dicens: Ecce éxiit qui séminat semináre semen suum.

Anno B

Convocávit Iesus Duódecim et dedit illis potestátem in spíritus immúndos.

Anno C

Díliges Dóminum Deum tuum ex toto corde tuo et próximum tuum sicut teípsum.

Oratio

Deus, qui errántibus, ut in viam possint redíre, veritátis tuæ lumen osténdis, da cunctis qui christiána professióne censéntur, et illa respúere, quæ huic inimíca sunt nómini, et ea quæ sunt apta sectári. Per Dóminum.

Ad Laudes matutinas

Anno A

Vobis datum est nosse mystérium regni cælórum: céteris autem in parábolis, dixit Iesus discípulis suis.

Anno B

Exeúntes discípuli prædicavérunt, ut pæniténtiam ágerent.

15th Sunday

throughout the year

First Vespers

Year A

Jesus spoke to the crowds in parables, saying: Behold, a sower went out to sow his seed.

Year B

Jesus called together the Twelve and gave them authority over the unclean spirits.

Year C

You shall love the Lord your God with all your heart and your neighbor as yourself.

Oration

O God, Who show the light of Your truth to those who stray, that they may return to Your path, grant to all who are known by their Christian profession, that they may reject those things hostile to that name and follow those things appropriate to it.

Lauds

Year A

To you has been given to know the mystery of the kingdom of heaven; but [it is given] to the others in parables, said Jesus to His disciples.

Year B

Going out, the disciples preached that men should repent.

Anno C

Samaritánus quidam iter fáciens, venit secus illum qui incíderat in latrónes, et videns eum misericórdia motus est et curávit vúlnera eius.

Ad II Vesperas

Anno A

Semen est verbum Dei, sator autem est Christus; omnis qui audit eum, manébit in ætérnum.

Anno B

Dæmónia multa eiciébant discípuli et ungébant óleo multos ægrótos et sanábant.

Anno C

Quis tibi vidétur próximus fuísse illi, qui íncidit in latrónes? Et ait illi: Qui fecit misericórdiam in illum. Vade et tu fac simíliter.

Year C

A certain Samaritan making a journey came upon the man who fell among robbers, and seeing him was moved with compassion, and bound up his wounds.

Second Vespers

Year A

The seed is the word of God, and the sower is Christ; everyone who hears Him, will remain for ever.

Year B

The disciples cast out many demons and anointed with oil many that were sick and healed them.

Year C

Who was seen to be neighbor to him who fell among robbers? And he said to Him: He who had compassion on him. Go and do likewise.

Dominica XVI

per annum

Ad I Vesperas

Anno A

Collígite primum zizánia, et alligáte ea in fascículos ad comburéndum, tríticum autem congregáte in hórreum meum, dicit Dóminus.

Anno B

Conveniéntes apóstoli ad Iesum, renuntiavérunt ei ómnia quæ égerant et docúerant.

Anno C

Intrávit Iesus in quoddam castéllum, et múlier quædam, Martham nómine, excépit illum.

Oratio

Propitiáre, Dómine, fámulis tuis, et cleménter grátiæ tuæ super eos dona multíplica, ut, spe, fide et caritáte fervéntes, semper in mandátis tuis vígili custódia persevérent. Per Dóminum.

Ad Laudes matutinas

Anno A

Símile est regnum cælórum ferménto, quod accéptum múlier abscóndit in farínæ satis tribus, donec fermentátum est totum.

16th Sunday

throughout the year

First Vespers

Year A

Gather the weeds first and bind them in bundles to be burned, but gather the wheat into my barn, says the Lord.

Year B

The apostles returned to Jesus, and told Him all that they had done and taught.

Year C

Jesus entered a village, and a woman named Martha received Him.

Oration

Be gracious, O Lord, to Your servants, and in Your mercy multiply upon them the gifts of your grace, that fervent in faith, hope and charity, they may always persevere in Your commandments under Your watchful protection.

Lauds

Year A

The kingdom of heaven is like leaven which a woman took and hid in three measures of meal, till it was all leavened.

Anno B

Veníte vos ipsi seórsum in desértum locum et requiéscite pusíllum, dicit Dóminus.

Anno C

María sedens secus pedes Dómini audiébat verbum illíus.

Ad II Vesperas

Anno A

In consummatióne sǽculi, fulgébunt iusti sicut sol in regno Patris eórum.

Anno B

Vidit Iesus multam turbam et misértus est super eos, quia erant sicut oves non habéntes pastórem.

Anno C

Optimam partem elégit sibi María, quæ non auferétur ab ea in ætérnum.

Year B

Come away by yourselves to a lonely place, and rest a while, says the Lord.

Year C

Mary sat at the Lord's feet and listened to His word.

SECOND VESPERS

Year A

In the consummation of the age, the righteous will shine like the sun in the kingdom of their Father.

Year B

Jesus saw a great crowd and had compassion on them, because they were like sheep without a shepherd.

Year C

Mary has chosen for herself the best part, which shall not be taken away from her for ever.

Dominica XVII

per annum

Ad I Vesperas

Anno A

Símile est regnum cælórum hómini negotiatóri quærénti bonas margarítas. Invénta una pretiósa, ábiit et véndidit ómnia quæ hábuit, et emit eam.

Anno B

Cum sublevásset óculos Iesus, et vidísset máximam multitúdinem veniéntem ad se, dixit ad Philíppum: Unde emémus panes ut mandúcent hi? Hoc autem dicébat tentans eum: ipse enim sciébat quid esset factúrus.

Anno C

Cum esset Iesus in quodam loco orans, dixit unus ex discípulis suis ad eum: Dómine, doce nos oráre.

Oratio

Protéctor in te sperántium, Deus, sine quo nihil est válidum, nihil sanctum, multíplica super nos misericórdiam tuam, ut, te rectóre, te duce, sic bonis transeúntibus nunc utámur, ut iam possímus inhærére mansúris. Per Dóminum.

17th Sunday

throughout the year

First Vespers

Year A

The kingdom of heaven is like a merchant in search of fine pearls. Having found one of great value, he went and sold all that he had and bought it.

Year B

When Jesus lifted up His eyes and saw the great crowd coming to Him, He said to Philip: Where shall we buy bread so that these may eat? But He said this testing him; for He knew what He was going to do.

Year C

When Jesus was in a certain place praying, one of His disciples said to Him: Lord, teach us to pray.

Oration

O God, the Protector of those who hope in You, without Whom nothing is strong, nothing holy, multiply upon us Your mercy that, with You as our ruler and leader, we may so use now the good things which pass away, that we may then we able to cling to those things which shall remain.

Ad Laudes matutinas

Anno A

Símile est regnum cælórum sagénæ missæ in mare; quam cum impléta esset, educéntes secus litus et sedéntes collegérunt bonos in vasa, malos autem foras misérunt.

Anno B

Satiávit Dóminus quinque mília hóminum, de quinque pánibus et duóbus píscibus.

Anno C

Pétite, et dábitur vobis: quærite, et inveniétis; pulsáte, et aperiétur vobis.

Ad II Vesperas

Anno A

Omnis scriba doctus in regno cælórum símilis est hómini patri famílias, qui profert de thesáuro suo nova et vétera.

Anno B

Illi hómines, cum vidíssent, quod fécerat Iesus signum, dicébant: Hic est vere prophéta, qui venit in mundum!

Anno C

Si vos, cum sitis mali, nostis dona bona dare fíliis vestris, quanto magis Pater de cælo dabit Spíritum Sanctum peténtibus se!

Lauds

Year A

The kingdom of heaven is like a net which was thrown into the sea; when it was full, men drew it ashore and sat down and sorted the good into vessels but threw away the bad.

Year B

The Lord fed five thousand men from five loaves and two fish.

Year C

Ask, and it will be given you; seek, and you will find; knock, and it will be opened to you.

Second Vespers

Year A

Every scribe who has been trained for the kingdom of heaven is like a householder who brings out of his treasure what is new and what is old.

Year B

Those men, when they saw the sign which Jesus had done, said: This is indeed the prophet who is to come into the world!

Year C

If you then, who are evil, know how to give good gifts to your children, how much more will the Father in heaven give the Holy Spirit to those asking Him!

Dominica XVIII

per annum

AD I VESPERAS

Anno A

Cum turba multa esset cum Iesu, nec habérent quod manducárent, convocátis discípulis, ait illis: Miséreor super turbam.

Anno B

Operámini non cibum, qui perit, sed qui pérmanet in vitam ætérnam.

Anno C

Cavéte ab omni avarítia, quia vita vestra non est ex his, quæ possidétis.

Oratio

Adésto, Dómine, fámulis tuis, et perpétuam benignitátem largíre poscéntibus, ut his, qui te auctórem et gubernatórem gloriántur habére, et grata restáures, et restauráta consérves. Per Dóminum.

AD LAUDES MATUTINAS

Anno A

De quinque pánibus et duóbus píscibus satiávit Dóminus quinque míllia hóminum.

18th Sunday

throughout the year

First Vespers

Year A

When the great crowd was with Jesus, and they did not have anything to eat, Jesus, calling together the disciples, said to them: I have compassion for the crowd.

Year B

Do not labor for the food which perishes, but for the food which endures unto eternal life.

Year C

Beware of all covetousness, for your life does not consist in these things which you possess.

Oration

Be present, O Lord, to Your servants, and grant Your perpetual kindness to those who ask, that to these who glory to have You as their author and governor, You would restore those things which are pleasing and, once they are restored, preserve them.

Lauds

Year A

From five loaves and two fish the Lord fed five thousand men.

Anno B

Amen, amen dico vobis, non Móyses dedit vobis panem de cælo, sed Pater meus dat vobis panem de cælo verum.

Anno C

Thesaurizáte vobis thesáuros in cælo, ubi nec ærúgo, nec tínea demolítur.

AD II VESPERAS

Anno A

Manducavérunt omnes et saturáti sunt, et tulérunt relíquias fragmentórum duódecim cóphinos plenos.

Anno B

Ego sum panis vitæ. Qui venit ad me, non esúriet, et qui credit in me, non sítiet umquam.

Anno C

Si vere, fratres, dívites esse cúpitis, veras divítias amáte.

Year B

Amen, amen I say to you, Moses did not give you the bread from heaven, but My Father gives you the true bread from heaven.

Year C

Store up for yourselves treasures in heaven, where neither rust nor worm destroys.

SECOND VESPERS

Year A

They all ate and were satisfied, and they took up twelve baskets full of the the broken pieces left over.

Year B

I am the Bread of Life. He who comes to Me shall not hunger, and he who believes in Me shall never thirst.

Year C

Brothers, if you desire to be truly rich, love true riches.

Dominica XIX

per annum

Ad I Vesperas

Anno A

Dimíssis turbis, ascéndit Iesus in montem solus oráre. Véspere autem facto, solus erat ibi.

Anno B

Nemo potest veníre ad me, nisi Pater, qui misit me, tráxerit eum, et ego resuscitábo eum in novíssimo die.

Anno C

Ubi est thesáurus tuus, ibi est et cor tuum, dicit Dóminus.

Oratio

Omnípotens sempitérne Deus, quem patérno nómine invocáre præsúmimus, pérfice in córdibus nostris spíritum adoptiónis filiórum, ut promíssam hereditátem íngredi mereámur. Per Dóminum.

Ad Laudes matutinas

Anno A

Locútus est Iesus discípulis, qui erant turbáti: Habéte fidúciam, ego sum, nolíte timére.

Anno B

Amen, amen dico vobis: Qui credit in me, habet vitam ætérnam, allelúia.

19th Sunday

throughout the year

First Vespers

Year A

After He had dismissed the crowds, Jesus went up the mountain alone to pray. When evening came, He was there alone.

Year B

No one can come to Me, unless the Father Who sent Me draws him; and I will raise him up at the last day.

Year C

Where your treasure is, there will your heart be also, says the Lord.

Oration

Almighty and everlasting God, Whom we dare to call by the name of Father, perfect in our hearts the spirit of adoption as sons that we may merit to enter into the promised inheritance.

Lauds

Year A

Jesus spoke to the disciples who were afraid: Have confidence, I AM, do not fear.

Year B

Amen, amen I say to you: He who believes in Me will have eternal life, alleluia.

Anno C

Beáti illi servi, quos cum vénerit Dóminus, et pulsáverit iánuam, invénerit vigilántes.

Ad II Vesperas

Anno A

Dómine, iube me veníre ad te super aquas. Et exténdens Iesus manum apprehéndit Petrum; et ait illi: Módicæ fídei, quare dubitásti?

Anno B

Hic est panis de cælo descéndens, ut, si quis ex ipso manducáverit, non moriátur.

Anno C

Sint lumbi vestri præcíncti, et lucérnæ ardéntes in mánibus vestris.

Year C

Blessed are those servants whom the Lord finds awake when He comes and knocks on the door.

Second Vespers

Year A

Lord, command me to come to You across the waters. And reaching out, Jesus caught Peter's hand; and He said to him: O man of little faith, why did you doubt?

Year B

This is the bread which comes down from heaven, so that if anyone eats of it, he will not die.

Year C

Let your loins be girded and your lamps burning in your hands.

Dominica XX

per annum

Ad I Vesperas

Anno A

Múlier Chananǽa clamábat dicens: Fília mea male a dæmónio vexátur. Miserére mei, Dómine fili David!

Anno B

Ego sum panis vivus, qui de cælo descéndit: si quis manducáverit ex hoc pane, vivet in ætérnum.

Anno C

Ignem veni míttere in terram, et quid volo nisi ut accendátur?

Oratio

Deus, qui diligéntibus te bona invisibília præparásti, infúnde córdibus nostris tui amóris afféctum, ut, te in ómnibus et super ómnia diligéntes, promissiónes tuas, quæ omne desidérium súperant, consequámur. Per Dóminum.

Ad Laudes matutinas

Anno A

Múlier Chananǽa venit ad Iesum et adorávit eum dicens: Dómine, ádiuva me.

20th Sunday

throughout the year

First Vespers

Year A

A Canaanite woman shouted, saying: My daughter is badly disturbed by a demon. Have mercy on me, O Lord, Son of David!

Year B

I AM the Living Bread which came down from heaven; if anyone eats of this Bread, he will live forever.

Year C

I came to cast fire upon the earth; and would that it were already kindled.

Oration

O God, Who have prepared invisible goods for those who love You, fill our hearts with a desire for Your love that, loving You in all things and above all things, we may attain your promises which exceed every desire.

Lauds

Year A

The Canaanite woman came to Jesus and adored Him, saying: Lord, help me.

Anno B

Caro mea vere est cibus, et sanguis meus vere est potus. Qui mandúcat meam carnem et bibit meum sánguinem, habébit vitam ætérnam.

Anno C

Baptísmo hábeo baptizári, et quómodo coárctor usque dum perficiátur!

Ad II Vesperas

Anno A

O múlier, magna est fides tua: fiat tibi sicut petísti.

Anno B

Sicut misit me vivens Pater, et ego vivo propter Patrem, et qui mandúcat me, et ipse vivet propter me.

Anno C

Putátis quia pacem veni dare in terram? Non, dico vobis, sed separatiónem.

Year B

My flesh is food indeed, and My Blood is drink indeed. He who eats My flesh and drinks My Blood will have eternal life.

Year C

I have a baptism to be baptized with; and how I am constrained until it is accomplished!

Second Vespers

Year A

O woman, great is your faith; be it done to you as you desire.

Year B

As the living Father sent Me, and I live because of the Father, so he who eats Me will live because of Me.

Year C

Do you think that I have come to give peace on earth? No, I tell you, but rather division.

Dominica XXI

per annum

Ad I Vesperas

Anno A

Tu es Christus, Fílius Dei vivi. Et tu beátus, Simon Bar Iona.

Anno B

Spíritus est, qui vivíficat, caro non prodest quidquam; verba, quæ ego locútus sum vobis, Spíritus sunt et vita.

Anno C

Conténdite intráre per angústam portam, quia multi, dico vobis, quærent intráre et non póterunt.

Oratio

Deus, qui fidélium mentes unius éfficis voluntátis, da pópulis tuis id amáre quod præcipis, id desideráre quod promíttis, ut, inter mundánas varietátes, ibi nostra fixa sint corda, ubi vera sunt gáudia. Per Dóminum.

Ad Laudes matutinas

Anno A

Tu es Petrus, et super hanc petram ædificábo Ecclésiam meam.

Anno B

Nemo potest veníre ad me, nisi fúerit ei datum a Patre, dicit Dóminus.

21st Sunday

throughout the year

First Vespers

Year A

You are the Christ, the Son of the living God. And you are blessed, Simon Bar-Jona.

Year B

It is the spirit that gives life, the flesh is of no avail; the words that I have spoken to you are Spirit and life.

Year C

Strive to enter through the narrow door; for many, I tell you, will seek to enter and will not be able.

Oration

O God, Who make the minds of the faithful to be of one accord, grant to Your people to love what You command and to desire what You promise that, among the changes of this world, our hearts may there be fixed where true joys are.

Lauds

Year A

You are Peter, and upon this rock I will build My Church.

Year B

No one can come to me unless it is granted him by the Father, says the Lord.

Anno C

Multi ab oriénte et occidénte vénient et recúmbent cum Ábraham et Ísaac et Iacob in regno cælórum.

Ad II Vesperas

Anno A

Quodcúmque ligáveris super terram, erit ligátum et in cælis: et quodcúmque sólveris super terram, erit solútum et in cælis, dicit Dóminus Simóni Petro.

Anno B

Dómine, ad quem íbimus? Verba vitæ ætérnæ habes: et nos credídimus et cognóvimus quia tu es Fílius Dei.

Anno C

Ecce sunt novíssimi, qui erunt primi, et sunt primi, qui erunt novíssimi, dicit Dóminus.

Year C

Many will come from east and west and sit at table with Abraham and Isaac and Jacob in the kingdom of heaven.

Second Vespers

Year A

Whatever you bind on earth shall be bound in heaven, and whatever you loose on earth shall be loosed in heaven, says the Lord to Simon Peter.

Year B

Lord, to whom shall we go? You have the words of eternal life; and we have believed and come to know that You are the Son of God.

Year C

Behold, some are last who will be first, and some are first who will be last, says the Lord.

Dominica XXII

per annum

Ad I Vesperas

Anno A

Cœpit Iesus osténdere discípulis suis quia oportéret eum ire Ierosólymam, et multa pati, et occídi, et tértia die resúrgere.

Anno B

Custodíte mandáta Dómini Dei vestri. Hæc est enim vestra sapiéntia et intelléctus coram pópulis.

Anno C

Cum vocátus fúeris ad núptias, recúmbe in novíssimo loco ut dicat tibi, qui te invitávit: Amíce, ascénde supérius; tunc erit tibi glória coram ómnibus simul discumbéntibus.

Oratio

Deus virtútum, cuius est totum quod est óptimum, ínsere pectóribus nostris tui nóminis amórem, et præsta, ut in nobis, religiónis augménto, quæ sunt bona nútrias, ac, vigilánti stúdio, quæ sunt nutríta custódias. Per Dóminum.

Ad Laudes matutinas

Anno A

Quid prodest hómini, si mundum univérsum lucrétur, ánimæ vero suæ detriméntum patiátur?

22nd Sunday

throughout the year

First Vespers

Year A

Jesus began to show His disciples that He must go to Jerusalem and suffer many things, and be killed, and rise on the third day.

Year B

Keep the commandments of the Lord your God. For this is your wisdom and knowledge before men.

Year C

When you are called to a marriage feast, sit in the lowest place so that the one who invited you may say to you: Friend, come up higher; then you will be honored in the presence of all who sit at table with you.

Oration

O God of strength, to Whom belongs all that is best, fill our hearts with the love of Your name and grant that, by the increase of religion, You may nurture within us that which is good and, by watchful diligence, you may preserve what have nurtured.

Lauds

Year A

What does it profit a man if he gains the whole world, and suffers the loss of his very soul?

Anno B

In mansuetúdine suscípite ínsitum verbum, quod potest salváre ánimas vestras.

Anno C

Omnis qui se exáltat, humiliábitur, et qui se humíliat, exaltábitur.

AD II VESPERAS

Anno A

Fílius hóminis ventúrus est in glória Patris sui cum ángelis suis, et tunc reddet unicuíque secúndum opus eius.

Anno B

Audíte et intellégite traditiónes, quas Dóminus dedit vobis.

Anno C

Cum facis convívium, voca páuperes, débiles, claudos, cæcos; et beatus eris, quia non habent retribúere tibi. Retribuétur enim tibi in resurrectióne iustórum.

Year B

Take up in mildness the implanted word, which is able to save your souls.

Year C

Every one who exalts himself will be humbled, and he who humbles himself will be exalted.

Second Vespers

Year A

The Son of Man is to come with His angels in the glory of His Father, and then He will repay every man according to what he has done.

Year B

Hear and understand the traditions which the Lord has given to you.

Year C

When you give a feast, invite the poor, the maimed, the lame, the blind, and you will be blessed, because they cannot repay you. For you will be repaid in the resurrection of the righteous.

Dominica XXIII

per annum

Ad I Vesperas

Anno A

Si peccáverit in te frater tuus, vade, córripe eum inter te et ipsum solum. Si te audíerit, lucrátus es fratrem tuum.

Anno B

Dum transíret Dóminus per médios fines Tyri, addúcunt ei surdum et mutum, et deprecántur eum ut impónat illi manum.

Anno C

Si quis venit ad me et non odit adhuc et ánimam suam, non potest esse meus discípulus.

Oratio

Deus, per quem nobis et redémptio venit et præstátur adóptio, fílios dilectiónis tuæ benígnus inténde, ut in Christo credéntibus et vera tribuátur libértas et heréditas ætérna. Per Dóminum.

Ad Laudes matutinas

Anno A

Si duo ex vobis consénserint super terram de omni re quamcúmque petíerint, fiet illis a Patre meo qui in cælis est.

23rd Sunday

throughout the year

First Vespers

Year A

If your brother sins against you, go and tell him his fault between you and him alone. If he listens to you, you have gained your brother.

Year B

While the Lord passed through the region of Tyre, they brought to Him a man who was deaf and mute, and they besought Him to lay His hand upon him.

Year C

If anyone comes to Me and does not hate even his own life, he cannot be My disciple.

Oration

O God, through Whom redemption comes to us and adoption is granted, kindly look upon the sons of Your choosing, that to those who believe in Christ may be granted both true freedom and an everlasting inheritance.

Lauds

Year A

If two of you agree on earth about anything you ask, it will be done for them by My Father in heaven.

Anno B

Suspíciens Iesus in cælum ingémuit et ait surdo et muto: Éffetha, quod est: Adaperíre.

Anno C

Qui non báiulat crucem suam et venit post me non potest esse meus discípulus.

AD II VESPERAS

Anno A

Ubi sunt duo vel tres congregáti in nómine meo, ibi sum in médio eórum, dicit Dóminus.

Anno B

Bene ómnia fecit, et surdos facit audíre et mutos loqui.

Anno C

Qui non renúntiat ómnibus quæ póssidet, non potest meus esse discípulus.

Year B

Looking up to heaven, Jesus sighed, and said to the deaf mute: Ephphatha, that is: Be opened.

Year C

Whoever does not bear his own cross and come after Me cannot be My disciple.

Second Vespers

Year A

Where two or three are gathered in My name, there am I in the midst of them, says the Lord.

Year B

He has done all things well; He even makes the deaf hear and the dumb speak.

Year C

He who does not renounce all that he has cannot be My disciple.

Dominica XXIV

per annum

AD I VESPERAS

Anno A

Dixit Iesus Petro: Non dico tibi ut dimíttas usque sépties, sed usque septuágies sépties.

Anno B

Vos quem me esse dícitis? Respóndens Petrus ait Iesu: Tu es Christus, allelúia.

Anno C

Quis ex vobis homo, qui habet centum oves, et si perdíderit unam ex illis, nonne dimíttit nonagíntanovem in desérto, et vadit ad illam quæ períerat, donec invéniat eam?

Oratio

Réspice nos, rerum ómnium Deus creátor et rector, et, ut tuæ propitiatiónis sentiámus efféctum, toto nos tríbue tibi corde servíre. Per Dóminum.

AD LAUDES MATUTINAS

Anno A

Misértus dóminus servi illíus dimísit eum et débitum dimísit ei.

Anno B

Opórtet Fílium hóminis pati multa, et reprobári a senióribus, et occídi, et post tres dies resúrgere.

24th Sunday

throughout the year

First Vespers

Year A

Jesus said to Peter: I do not say to you that you forgive seven times, but seventy times seven.

Year B

Who do you say I am? Responding, Peter said to Jesus: You are the Christ, alleluia.

Year C

What man of you, having a hundred sheep, if he has lost one of them, does not leave the ninety-nine in the wilderness, and go after the one which is lost, until he finds it?

Oration

O God, Creator and Ruler of all things, look down upon us and, that we may know the effect of your mercy, grant us to serve you with all our heart.

Lauds

Year A

Out of pity the lord of that servant released him and forgave him the debt.

Year B

The Son of Man must suffer many things, and be rejected by the elders, and be killed, and after three days rise again.

Anno C

Dico vobis: Gáudium est ángelis Dei super uno peccatóre pæniténtiam agénte.

Ad II Vesperas

Anno A

Serve nequam, omne débitum dimísi tibi, quóniam rogásti me; nonne opórtuit et te miseréri consérvi tui sicut et ego tui misértus sum?

Anno B

Qui perdíderit ánimam suam propter me et evangélium, salvam fáciet eam, dicit Dóminus.

Anno C

Quæ múlier habens drachmas decem, et si perdíderit drachmam unam, nonne accéndit lucérnam, et quærit dilígiter donec invéniat?

Year C

I say to you: There is joy before the angels of God over one sinner who repents.

Second Vespers

Year A

You wicked servant, I forgave you all that debt because you besought me; and should not you have had mercy on your fellow servant, as I had mercy on you?

Year B

Whoever loses his life for My sake and the Gospel's will save it, says the Lord.

Year C

What woman, having ten silver coins, if she loses one coin, does not light a lamp and seek diligently until she finds it?

Dominica XXV

per annum

Ad I Vesperas

Anno A

Ite et vos in víneam meam; et quod iustum fúerit dabo vobis.

Anno B

Si quis vult primus esse, erit ómnium novíssimus et ómnium miníster.

Anno C

Fácite vobis amícos de mammóna iniquitátis, ut, cum defécerit, recípiant vos in ætérna tabernácula.

Oratio

Deus, qui sacræ legis ómnia constitúta in tua et próximi dilectióne posuísti, da nobis, ut, tua præcépta servántes, ad vitam mereámur perveníre perpétuam. Per Dóminum.

Ad Laudes matutinas

Anno A

Símile est regnum cælórum hómini patrifamílias, qui éxiit primo mane condúcere operários in víneam suam, dicit Dóminus.

Anno B

Quicúmque me suscéperit, non me súscipit, sed eum qui me misit.

25th Sunday

throughout the year

First Vespers

Year A

You go into the vineyard, too, and whatever is right I will give you.

Year B

If anyone would be first, he must be last of all and servant of all.

Year C

Make friends for yourselves by means of unrighteous mammon, so that when it fails they may receive you into the eternal habitations.

Oration

O God, Who have grounded every statute of sacred law in the love of You and our neighbor, grant us that keeping Your precepts, we may merit to attain eternal life.

Lauds

Year A

The kingdom of heaven is like a householder who went out early in the morning to hire laborers for his vineyard, says the Lord.

Year B

Whoever receives Me, receives not me but Him Who sent Me.

Anno C

Qui fidélis est in mínimo, et in maióri fidélis est, dicit Dóminus.

Ad II Vesperas

Anno A

Voca operários, et redde illis mercédem suam, dicit Dóminus.

Anno B

Quisquis unum ex huiúsmodi púeris recéperit in nómine meo, me récipit.

Anno C

Nemo servus potest duóbus dóminis servíre. Non potéstis Deo servíre et mammónæ, dicit Dminus.

Year C

He who is faithful in a very little is faithful also in much, says the Lord.

Second Vespers

Year A

Call the laborers and pay them their wages, says the Lord.

Year B

Whoever receives one such child in My name receives Me.

Year C

No servant can serve two masters. You cannot serve God and mammon, says the Lord.

Dominica XXVI

per annum

Ad I Vesperas

Anno A

Cum avérterit se ímpius ab impietáte sua, et fécerit iudícium et iustítiam, vita vivet, non moriétur, dicit Dóminus.

Anno B

Nemo est qui fáciat virtútem in nómine meo, et possit cito male loqui de me. Qui enim non est advérsum vos, pro vobis est.

Anno C

Factum est ut moterétur pauper et portarétur ab ángelis in sinum Ábrahæ.

Oratio

Deus, qui omnipoténtiam tuam parcéndo máxime et miserándo maniféstas, grátiam tuam super nos indesinénter infúnde, ut, ad tua promíssa curréntes, cæléstium bonórum fácias esse consórtes. Per Dóminum.

Ad Laudes matutinas

Anno A

Amen dico vobis, quia publicáni et meretríces præcédunt vos in regnum Dei, quia credidérunt.

26th Sunday

throughout the year

First Vespers

Year A

When a wicked man turns away from the wickedness he has committed and does what is lawful and right, he shall save his life, says the Lord.

Year B

No one who does a mighty work in My name will be able soon after to speak evil of Me. For he that is not against you is for you.

Year C

The poor man died and was carried by the angels to Abraham's bosom.

Oration

O God, Who show forth Your almighty power most especially in pardon and mercy, pour forth Your grace upon us unceasingly that, hastening to Your promises, You may make us partakers of heavenly goods.

Lauds

Year A

Amen I say to you, the tax collectors and the harlots go into the kingdom of God before you, because they believed.

Anno B

Quisquis potum déderit vobis cálicem aquæ in nómine meo, quia Christi estis, amen dico vobis: non perdet mercédem suam.

Anno C

Fili, recordáre quia recepísti bona tua in vita tua, et Lázarus simíliter mala; nunc autem tu vero cruciáris et ille consolátur.

Ad II Vesperas

Anno A

Non omnis, qui dicit mihi: Dómine, Dómine, intrábit in regnum cælórum, sed qui facit voluntátem Patris mei, qui in cælis est, ipse intrábit in regnum cælórum.

Anno B

Bonum est tibi débilem introíre in vitam, quam duas manus habéntem ire in gehénnam, dicit Dóminus.

Anno C

Beáti páuperes, quia vestrum est regnum Dei. Beáti, qui nunc esurítis, quia saturabímini. Beáti, qui nunc fletis, quia ridébitis.

Year B

Whoever gives you a cup of water to drink in My name, because you are Christ's, amen I say to you: He will not lose his reward.

Year C

Son, remember that you in your lifetime received your good things, and Lazarus in like manner evil things; but now he is comforted here, and you are in anguish.

Second Vespers

Year A

Not every one who says to Me: Lord, Lord, shall enter the kingdom of heaven, but he who does the will of My Father Who is in heaven, he shall enter the kingdom of heaven.

Year B

It is better for you to enter life maimed than with two hands to go to hell, says the Lord.

Year C

Blessed are you poor, for yours is the kingdom of God. Blessed are you that hunger now, for you shall be satisfied. Blessed are you that weep now, for you shall laugh.

Dominica XXVII

per annum

Ad I Vesperas

Anno A

Cum tempus frúctuum appropinquásset, dóminus víneæ misit servos suos ad agrícolas, ut accíperent fructus eius.

Anno B

Accedéntes pharisǽi interrogábant Iesum: Si licet viro uxórem dimíttere. Quibus respóndens ait: Quod Deus coniúnxit, homo non séparet

Anno C

Dixérunt apóstoli Dómino: Adáuge nobis fidem! allelúia.

Oratio

Omnípotens sempitérne Deus, qui abundántia pietátis tuæ et mérita súpplicum excédis et vota, effúnde super nos misericórdiam tuam, ut dimíttas quæ consciéntia métuit, et adícias quod orátio non præsúmit. Per Dominum.

Ad Laudes matutinas

Anno A

Dóminus víneæ malos male perdet, et víneam locábit áliis agrícolis, qui reddant ei fructum tempóribus suis.

27th Sunday

throughout the year

First Vespers

Year A

When the season of fruit drew near, the lord of the vineyard sent his servants to the farmers to get his fruit.

Year B

Pharisees came up and asked Jesus: Is it lawful for a man to divorce his wife? He answered them: What God has joined together, let not man put asunder.

Year C

The apostles said to the Lord: Increase our faith! alleluia.

Oration

Almighty and everlasting God, Who exceed the merits and prayers of those who implore you by the abundance of Your kindness, pour out Your mercy upon us that You may discharge what our conscience fears and supply what our prayer does not presume.

Lauds

Year A

The lord of the vineyard will put those wretches to a miserable death, and lease the vineyard to other farmers, who will give him the fruits in their seasons.

Anno B

Sínite párvulos veníre ad me. Ne prohibuéritis eos; tálium est enim regnum Dei.

Anno C

Si haberétis fidem sicut granum sinápis, dicerétis huic árbori moro: Eradicáre et transplantáre in mare, et obœdíret vobis, dicit Dóminus.

Ad II Vesperas

Anno A

Lápidem, quem reprobavérunt ædificántes, hic factus est in caput ánguli; a Dómino factum est istud et est mirábile in óculis nostris.

Anno B

Amen dico vobis: Quisquis non recéperit regnum Dei velut párvulus, non intrábit in illud.

Anno C

Cum fecéritis ómnia, quæ præcépta sunt vobis, dícite: Servi inútiles sumus: quod debúimus fácere, fécimus.

Year B

Let the children come to me, do not hinder them; for to such belongs the kingdom of God.

Year C

If you had faith as a grain of mustard seed, you could say to this sycamore tree: Be rooted up, and be planted in the sea, and it would obey you, says the Lord.

SECOND VESPERS

Year A

The stone which the builders rejected has become the head of the corner; this was the Lord's doing, and it is marvelous in our eyes.

Year B

Amen I say to you: Whoever does not receive the kingdom of God like a child shall not enter it.

Year C

When you have done all that is commanded you, say: We are unworthy servants; we have only done what was our duty.

Dominica XXVIII

per annum

Ad I Vesperas

Anno A

Símile est regnum cælórum hómini regi, qui fecit núptias fílio suo et misit servos suos vocáre invitátos ad núptias.

Anno B

Unum tibi deest: vade, quæcúmque habes vende et da paupéribus, et habébis thesáurum in cælo et veni, séquere me.

Anno C

Occurrérunt decem viri leprósi, qui stetérunt a longe, et levavérunt vocem dicéntes: Iesu præcéptor, miserére nostri.

Oratio

Tua nos, quæsumus, Dómine, grátia semper et prævéniat et sequátur, ac bonis opéribus iúgiter præstet esse inténtos. Per Dóminum.

Ad Laudes matutinas

Anno A

Dícite invitátis: Ecce prándium meum parávi: veníte ad núptias.

28th Sunday

throughout the year

First Vespers

Year A

The kingdom of heaven is like a king who gave a marriage feast for his son, and sent his servants to call those who were invited to the marriage feast.

Year B

You lack one thing; go, sell what you have, and give to the poor, and you will have treasure in heaven; and come, follow Me.

Year C

He was met by ten lepers, who stood at a distance and lifted up their voices and said: Jesus, Teacher, have mercy on us.

Oration

We beseech You, O Lord, that Your grace may always precede and follow us and make us continually intent on good works.

Lauds

Year A

Tell those who are invited: Behold, I have made ready my dinner; come to the marriage feast.

Anno B

Quam diffícile, qui pecúnias habent, in regnum Dei introíbunt!, dixit Iesus discípulis suis.

Anno C

Unus ex illis, ut vidit quia mundátus est, regréssus est cum magna voce magníficans Deum, allelúia.

Ad II Vesperas

Anno A

Núptiæ quidem parátæ sunt, sed qui invitáti erant non fuérunt digni; ite ergo ad éxitum viárum et quoscúmque invenéritis, vocáte ad núptias.

Anno B

Vos qui reliquístis ómnia, et secúti estis me, céntuplum accipiétis, et vitam ætérnam possidébitis.

Anno C

Non sunt invénti qui redírent et darent glóriam Deo, nisi hic alienígena? Et ait illi: Surge, vade: fides tua te salvum fecit.

Year B

How hard it will be for those who have riches to enter the kingdom of God!, said Jesus to His disciples.

Year C

One of them, when he saw that he was healed, turned back, praising God with a loud voice, alleluia.

SECOND VESPERS

Year A

The wedding is ready, but those invited were not worthy. Go therefore to the thoroughfares, and invite to the marriage feast as many as you find.

Year B

You who have left everything, and are My followers, will receive a hundredfold, and you will possess eternal life.

Year C

Was no one found to return and give praise to God except this foreigner? And He said to him: Rise and go your way; your faith has made you well.

Dominica XXIX

per annum

Ad I Vesperas

Anno A

Magíster, scimus quia verax es et viam Dei in veritáte doces.

Anno B

Cálicem, quem ego bibo, bibétis et baptísmum quo ego baptízor, baptizabímini, dicit Dóminus.

Anno C

Dicébat Iesus discípulis suis quóniam opórtet semper oráre et non defícere.

Oratio

Omnípotens sempitérne Deus, fac nos tibi semper et devótam gérere voluntátem, et maiestáti tuæ sincéro corde servíre. Per Dóminum.

Ad Laudes matutinas

Anno A

Sciant ab ortu solis et ab occidénte quóniam absque me nullus est. Ego Dóminus, et non est alter.

Anno B

Quicúmque volúerit fíeri maior inter vos, erit vester miníster, et quicúmque volúerit in vobis primus esse, erit ómnium servus.

29th Sunday

throughout the year

First Vespers

Year A

Teacher, we know that You are true, and teach the way of God truthfully.

Year B

The cup that I drink you will drink; and with the baptism with which I am baptized, you will be baptized, says the Lord.

Year C

Jesus said to His disciples that they ought always to pray and not lose heart.

Oration

Almighty and everlasting God, make us always both to have a will devoted to You and to serve Your majesty with a sincere heart.

Lauds

Year A

May they know, from the rising of the sun and from the setting, that there is none besides Me. I am the Lord, and there is no other.

Year B

Whoever would be great among you must be your servant, and whoever would be first among you must be the slave of all.

Anno C

Deus fáciet vindíctam electórum suórum clamántium ad se die ac nocte, et patiéntiam habébit in illis.

Ad II Vesperas

Anno A

Réddite, quæ sunt Cǽsaris, Cǽsari, et quæ sunt Dei, Deo.

Anno B

Fílius hóminis non venit, ut ministrarétur ei, sed ut ministráret et daret ánimam suam redemptiónem pro multis.

Anno C

Dum vénerit Fílius hóminis, putas invéniet fidem super terram?

Year C

God will vindicate His elect, who cry to Him day and night, and He will be patient with them.

SECOND VESPERS

Year A

Render to Caesar the things that are Caesar's, and to God the things that are God's.

Year B

The Son of Man came not to be served but to serve, and to give His life as a ransom for the many.

Year C

When the Son of Man comes, will He find faith on earth?

Dominica XXX

per annum

AD I VESPERAS

Anno A

Magíster, quod est mandátum magnum in Lege? Ait illi Iesus: Díliges Dóminum Deum tuum in toto corde tuo.

Anno B

Iter faciénte Iesu, dum appropinquáret Iéricho, cæcus clamábat ad eum, ut lumen recípere mererétur.

Anno C

Stans a longe publicánus nolébat nec óculos ad cælum leváre, sed percutiébat pectus suum dicens: Deus, propítius esto mihi peccatóri.

Oratio

Omnípotens sempitérne Deus, da nobis fídei, spei et caritátis augméntum, et, ut mereámur ássequi quod promíttis, fac nos amáre quod præcipis. Per Dóminum.

AD LAUDES MATUTINAS

Anno A

Díliges próximum tuum sicut teípsum, dixit Dóminus discípulis suis.

30th Sunday

throughout the year

First Vespers

Year A

Teacher, which is the great commandment in the Law? Jesus said to him: You shall love the Lord your God with all your heart.

Year B

When Jesus was making a journey, and while He approached Jericho, a blind man cried out to Him asking that he might receive his sight.

Year C

The tax collector, standing far off, would not even lift up his eyes to heaven, but beat his breast, saying: O God, be merciful to me a sinner.

Oration

Almighty and everlasting God, give to us an increase in faith, hope and charity and, that we may merit to attain what You promise, make us to love what you command.

Lauds

Year A

You shall love your neighbor as yourself, said the Lord to His disciples.

Anno B

Iesu fili David, miserére mei! Quid vis tibi fáciam? Dómine, ut vídeam.

Anno C

Descéndit publicánus iustificátus in domum suam, ab illo, qui in se confidébat.

Ad II Vesperas

Anno A

Díliges Dóminum Deum tuum; díliges próximum tuum sicut teípsum: in his duóbus mandátis univérsa Lex pendet et Prophétæ.

Anno B

Ait Iesus cæco: Vade, fides tua te salvum fecit. Et conféstim vidit, et sequebátur eum in via.

Anno C

Omnis qui se exáltat humiliábitur, et qui se humíliat exaltábitur.

Year B

Jesus, Son of David, have mercy on me! What do you want me to do for you? Lord, let me receive my sight.

Year C

The tax collector went down to his house justified, rather than the one who confided in himself.

Second Vespers

Year A

You shall love the Lord your God; you shall love your neighbor as yourself: On these two commandments depend all the Law and the Prophets.

Year B

Jesus said to the blind man: Go your way; your faith has made you well. And immediately he received his sight and followed Him on the way.

Year C

Every one who exalts himself will be humbled, but he who humbles himself will be exalted.

Dominica XXXI

per annum

Ad I Vesperas

Anno A

Omnes vos fratres estis: unus est Pater vester, qui in cælis est.

Anno B

Díliges Dóminum Deum tuum ex toto corde tuo. Díliges próximum tuum tamquam teípsum. Maius horum áliud mandátum non est.

Anno C

Zachǽe, festínans descénde, quia hódie in domo tua opórtet me manére; at ille festínans descéndit et excépit illum gaudens in domo sua.

Oratio

Omnípotens et místericors Deus, de cuius múnere venit, ut tibi a fidélibus tuis digne et laudabíliter serviátur, tríbue, quǽsumus, nobis, ut ad promissiónes tuas sine offensióne currámus. Per Dóminum.

Ad Laudes matutinas

Anno A

Unus est magíster vester, qui in cælis est, Christus Dóminus.

31st Sunday

throughout the year

First Vespers

Year A

You are all brothers: you have one Father Who is in heaven.

Year B

You shall love the Lord your God with all your heart. You shall love your neighbor as yourself. There is no other commandment greater than these.

Year C

Zachaeus, make hast and come down; for I must stay at your house today. So he made haste and came down, and received Him joyfully into his house.

Oration

Almighty and merciful God, of Whose gift it comes that Your faithful people do You worthy and laudable service, grant us, we beseech You, that we may hasten to Your promises without stumbling.

Lauds

Year A

You have one Master, Who is in heaven, Christ the Lord.

Anno B

Unus est Deus, et non est álius præter eum, et díliges Dóminum ex tota ánima tua.

Anno C

Hódie salus dómui huic facta est, eo quod et ipse fílius sit Ábrahæ.

Ad II Vesperas

Anno A

Qui maior est vestrum erit minister vester. Qui autem se exaltáverit humiliábitur, et qui se humiliáverit exaltábitur.

Anno B

Iesus videns quod scriba sapiénter respondísset, dixit illi: Non es longe a regno Dei.

Anno C

Venit Fílius hóminis quærere et salvum fácere quod períerat.

Year B

There is one God, and there is not any other except Him, and you shall love the Lord with your whole soul.

Year C

Today salvation has come to this house, since he also is a son of Abraham.

SECOND VESPERS

Year A

He who is greatest among you shall be your servant. Whoever exalts himself will be humbled, and whoever humbles himself will be exalted.

Year B

Jesus, seeing that the scribe answered wisely, said to him: You are not far from the kingdom of God.

Year C

The Son of Man came to seek and save the lost.

Dominica XXXII

per annum

Ad I Vesperas

Anno A

Prudéntes vírgines, aptáte vestras lámpades: Ecce sponsus venit, exíte óbviam ei.

Anno B

Sedens Iesus contra gazophylácium aspiciébat víduam unam páuperem, quæ misit duo minúta: ómnia quæ habébat Dómino.

Anno C

Illi qui digni habéntur resurrectióne ex mórtuis, æquáles ángelis sunt et fílii sunt Dei.

Oratio

Omnípotens et miséricors Deus, univérsa nobis adversántia propitiátus exclúde, ut, mente et córpore páriter expedíti, quæ tua sunt líberis méntibus exsequámur. Per Dóminum.

Ad Laudes matutinas

Anno A

Média nocte clamor factus est: Ecce sponsus venit, exíte óbviam ei.

Anno B

Amen dico vobis, vídua hæc pauper plus ómnibus misit, qui misérunt in gazophylácium.

32nd Sunday

throughout the year

First Vespers

Year A

Wise virgins, take up your lamps: Behold, the bridegroom comes, go out to meet him.

Year B

Jesus sat down opposite the treasury, and watched a poor widow who put in two copper coins, everything she had, for the Lord.

Year C

Those who are accounted worthy to attain to the resurrection from the dead are equal to the angels and are sons of God.

Oration

Almighty and merciful God, put aside from us all things which are harmful that, prepared in mind as in body, we may follow with free minds those things which are Yours.

Lauds

Year A

At midnight there was a cry: Behold, the bridegroom comes, go out to meet him.

Year B

Amen I say to you, this poor widow has put in more than all those who have contributed to the treasury.

Anno C

Móyses osténdit secus rubum, quia resúrgent mórtui, sicut dicit: Dóminum Deum Ábraham et Deum Ísaac et Deum Iacob. Deus autem non est mortuórum sed vivórum.

Ad II Vesperas

Anno A

Amen dico vobis, vigiláte, quia nescítis diem neque horam.

Anno B

Vídua illa pauper de penúria sua ómnia, quæ hábuit, misit, totum victum suum.

Anno C

Deus non est mortuórum, sed vivórum: omnes enim vivunt ei.

Year C

Moses showed, in the passage about the bush, that the dead shall rise, as it says: The Lord the God of Abraham, and the God of Isaac, and the God of Jacob. For He is not God of the dead, but of the living.

Second Vespers

Year A

Amen I say to you, watch, for you know neither the day nor the hour.

Year B

That widow out of her poverty has put in everything she had, her whole living.

Year C

He is not God of the dead, but of the living; for all live to Him.

Dominica XXXIII

per annum

Ad I Vesperas

Anno A

Dómine, quinque talénta tradidísti mihi: ecce ália quinque superlucrátus sum.

Anno B

Vidébunt Fílium hóminis veniéntem in núbibus cæli cum virtúte multa et glória, allelúia.

Anno C

Cum audiéritis prœlia et seditiónes, nolíte terréri; opórtet enim primum hæc fíeri, sed non statim finis, dicit Dóminus.

Oratio

Da nobis, quǽsumus, Dómine Deus noster, in tua semper devotióne gaudére, quia perpétua est et plena felícitas, si bonórum ómnium iúgiter serviámus auctóri. Per Dóminum.

Ad Laudes matutinas

Anno A

Serve bone et fidélis, quia super pauca fuísti fidélis, super multa te constítuam.

33rd Sunday

throughout the year

First Vespers

Year A

Master, you delivered to me five talents; here I have made five talents more.

Year B

They will see the Son of Man coming on the clouds of heaven with great power and glory, alleluia.

Year C

When you hear of wars and tumults, do not be terrified; for this must first take place, but the end will not be at once, says the Lord.

Oration

Grant us, we beseech you, O Lord our God, always to rejoice in Your devotion because happiness is everlasting and full if we perpetually serve the author of all good things.

Lauds

Year A

Well done, good and faithful servant; you have been faithful over a little, I will set you over much.

Anno B

Dóminus mittet ángelos et congregábit eléctos suos a quáttuor ventis, a summo terræ usque ad summum cæli.

Anno C

Ego dabo vobis os et sapiéntiam, cui non póterunt resístere vel contradícere omnes adversárii vestri.

Ad II Vesperas

Anno A

Euge, serve bone, in módico fidélis: intra in gáudium dómini tui.

Anno B

Amen dico vobis: cælum et terra transíbunt, verba autem mea non transíbunt.

Anno C

In patiéntia vestra possidébitis ánimas vestras.

Year B

The Lord will send out the angels and gather His elect from the four winds, from the ends of the earth to the ends of heaven.

Year C

I will give you a mouth and wisdom, which none of your adversaries will be able to withstand or contradict.

SECOND VESPERS

Year A

Well done, good servant, faithful in little things: Enter into the joy of your master.

Year B

Amen I say to you: heaven and earth will pass away, but my words will not pass away.

Year C

By your endurance you will gain your lives.